Dec. 1981

THESAURUS OF ENGLISH WORDS

A dictionary of synonyms

THESAURUS OF ENGLISH WORDS

Edited by M.H. Manser

HAMLYN

LONDON · NEW YORK · SYDNEY · TORONTO

First published in 1979 by
The Hamlyn Publishing Group Limited
London · New York · Sydney · Toronto
Astronaut House, Feltham, Middlesex, England

This edition published in 1981

ISBN 0 600 33213 6

Compiled by
Laurence Urdang Associates Ltd,
Aylesbury, Bucks.

7½ on 8½ point Intertype Fototronic
Times Roman

Printed in Great Britain by
Hazell Watson & Viney Ltd,
Aylesbury, Bucks.

INTRODUCTION

A thesaurus is a book of words arranged according to ideas. You use it when you can think of an idea but cannot find the exact word to express it or when you have a word in mind that isn't close enough to the one you really want. This is where a thesaurus comes in: it gives words in lists according to the ideas they stand for.

This thesaurus covers the central part of the vocabulary of English — the 'core' of the language we all use most of the time — and groups this under 990 categories, each representing a different idea. It does not include highly technical words but does reflect the fact that the English language used today is becoming more colloquial. By looking up a word in the index and referring to one of the categories in the book you will find a list of words with a similar meaning and you will then be able to choose the one you want.

The first thesaurus was written by Peter Mark Roget (1779 – 1869), and published in 1852. Its full original title was *The Thesaurus of English Words and Phrases Classified and Arranged so as to Facilitate the Expression of Ideas and Assist in Literary Composition*. It has since been published in many editions and the concept has been taken over and used for other languages. Many changes have been made in writing this thesaurus: categories have been re-ordered, many have been given more intelligible names, and there is a thorough coverage of new words that have entered the language. A large number of older words and phrases have been rejected as no longer used.

This thesaurus is written for those who use language — those who speak and write English and want to use a variety of words, for those who solve crosswords, and for those who just like browsing through its pages to pore over the richness of the language. After all, the word 'thesaurus' itself comes from the Greek word for 'treasure', and we hope that something of the deep resources of the language will be discovered in these pages.

Aylesbury, February 1979

M.H. Manser
John Daintith

HOW TO USE THIS THESAURUS

Imagine that you have a word in mind, let us say, 'beautiful'. You have used this word already and don't want to use it again, or you want something more expressive. The first thing to do is to look up this word – 'beautiful' – in the index. The index is arranged in alphabetical order. Every entry in the index consists of a word or words, a part of speech, and a number or numbers. Parts of speech have been abbreviated as follows: *n.* = noun; *adj.* = adjective; *vb.* = verb; *adv.* = adverb; *prep.* = preposition. The numbers refer to categories. The entry for 'beautiful' looks like this:

beautiful *adj.* 844

If you turn to category **844** in the main part of the book and look under the appropriate part of speech – here *adj.* – you will find a list of alternative words that you can use: beautiful, attractive, good-looking,... Some of the entries in the index have numbers printed in a darker, bold type. These show main references for particular words.

The words listed have slightly different meanings from each other. If you are not familiar with a word it would therefore be advisable to look up the word in a good modern dictionary before using it. Otherwise you may risk using the word in the wrong context. Two further abbreviations are used. Informal or colloquial words are marked as *(inf.)* and slang words *(sl.)*. At the end of many entries there are cross-references to other categories (e.g. see also **56, 112**). These can usefully be followed up to find further lists of related words. You should also consult the words given at the other parts of speech in an entry, as some words there may suggest others to you.

If you look at the adjacent categories, too, you will find further help or perhaps the possibility of using a word meaning something opposite, e.g. the categories **534 resolution, 535 perseverance, 536 irresolution**.

A list of the 990 categories is given after the index and you can check that the number of the category you are looking up is the one you want.

NOTE ON THE INDEX

The index does not list every word or phrase in the main part of the book. In particular, many words derived from other related words, e.g. adverbs ending in -*ly* derived from adjectives, have been excluded. If you want to look up a word that is not in the index, you should therefore look up the word closest to it, and refer to the categories in the main part of the book, looking at the part of speech of the word you originally wanted. Further, a reference to a particular entry does not necessarily mean that the word looked up will appear at that entry — but since you are interested in other words related to this one, the fact that it does not occur at the entry is of no consequence.

Numbers printed in darker, bold type show the main categories for the particular words. The titles of categories are also printed in the bolder typeface. For further help on finding the word you want, see the section 'How to use this thesaurus' at the front of the book.

PLAN OF CATEGORIES

I Abstract Relations

A Existence

1 existence

n. existence, being, essence, self-existence, reality, actuality, presence; subsistence, givenness, historicity, factuality; actualization, creating, becoming, potentiality, possibility; ontology, existentialism, metaphysics, realism.
fact, truth, *fait accompli*, real thing, entity, vital principle.

adj. existing, being, in being, in existence, afoot, given, uncreated; ontological, metaphysical; extant, living, current, present, standing, surviving; subsisting, subsistent, obtaining, prevailing, prevalent; real, actual, true, authentic, genuine, mere, objective; essential, substantial, substantive, self-existing, self-existent, intrinsic, factual.

vb. be, exist, have being, live, breathe, abide, remain, stay, prevail, be so, be the case; subsist, obtain; consist in, inhere in, reside in; stand, find itself, lie, be situated, be found; occur, take place, happen, continue, go on, endure, last.

adv. actually, really, in fact, in reality.

2 non-existence

n. non-existence, inexistence, non-being, nonentity, nothingness, nullity, nihility, neverness; vacuum, vacuity, emptiness, void, blank; extinction, destruction, abolition, obsolescence.

adj. non-existent, void, vacuous, blank; extinct, dead, obsolete, vanished; unreal, wrong, untrue, false, specious, imaginary, fictitious, hypothetical, groundless, unfounded.

vb. come to nothing, pass away, die, vanish, disappear, dematerialize, evaporate, dissolve; bring to nothing, nullify, destroy, abolish, kill.

3 material existence

n. materiality, substantiality, actuality, essentiality, reality, objectivity, substantivity, corporeity, corporality, concreteness, solidity, tangibility.
substance, thing, body, solid, stuff, matter, entity, flesh and blood (*inf.*).

adj. material, substantial, actual, solid, corporeal, objective, substantive, concrete, physical, real, natural; visible, tangible.
see also 327

4 non-material existence

n. immateriality, insubstantiality, inessentiality, intangibility.
shadow, token, dream, vision, apparition, spirit, illusion, optical illusion, mirage, breath, mist, vapour, wisp.

adj. immaterial, insubstantial, abstract, intangible, imponderable, airy, vaporous, ethereal, spiritual, ghostly, spectral, bodiless, disembodied, visionary, shadowy, vague.
see also 328

5 being according to internal form

n. intrinsicality, inherence, inwardness, internality, essentiality, immanence.
essence, substance, basis, being, soul, fundamental, principle, quintessence, essential, heart, core, character, nature, constitution, structure, make-up, bearing, framework, frame; attribute, element, aspect, quality, feature, manner, temper, temperament, mood, humour, disposition, personality, particularity, idiosyncrasy, endowment, heredity, gene.

adj. intrinsic, essential, inherent, inward, central, fundamental, immanent, implicit, internal, original, integral, innate, distinctive, specific, characteristic, particular, peculiar, unique; native, genetic, hereditary, inborn, congenital, ancestral.

vb. inhere, be intrinsic; internalize.
see also 223, 224

6 being according to external form

n. extrinsicality, externality, objectivity, outwardness, transcendence, projection, extrapolation; accessory, external.

adj. extrinsic, external, objective, transcendent, exterior, outward, extraneous, foreign, independent, additional, outside.

vb. be extrinsic, transcend, surpass; make extrinsic, objectify, project, extend, extrapolate.
see also 222, 825

7 absolute state

n. state, standing, condition, station, status, case, position, stand, rank, class, degree, estate, style, fashion, mode, aspect, facet, posture, attitude.

8 circumstance

n. circumstance, circumstances, situation, environment, surroundings, setting, background, backdrop, *milieu*, context, how the land lies, ambience, atmosphere, climate; conditions, factors, details, items, features, particulars, requirements, necessities; cause, reason, motives, grounds.

adj. circumstantial, modal, surrounding, environmental, contextual, incidental, background, contingent; detailed, itemized, particular.

adv. under the circumstances, this being the case, incidentally, under these conditions, in the event of.

B Relation

9 relation

n. relation, relatedness, association, relationship, arrangement, connection, link, dependence, involvement, implication, bearing; relativity, correspondence, analogy, correlation; relevance, suitability, appositeness.

adj. relative, related, connected, involved, arranged, linked, bearing upon, concerning, belonging, appertaining; reciprocal, mutual; analogous, comparable; relevant, suitable, apposite, appropriate, proper, applicable, pertinent.

vb. be related to, concern, refer to, touch upon, bear upon, deal with, treat, have to do with, apply, hold true for, be a factor in; relate, associate, link, refer; correspond to, be analogous to; belong, pertain.

adv., prep. concerning, regarding, as regards, on, about, with reference to, with respect to, on the subject of, in the matter of, à propos, re, in re.

10 absence of relation

n. irrelation, dissociation, unrelatedness, non-involvement, independence, arbitrariness; disproportion, difference, misfit, irreconcilability, irrelevance, unsuitability, inconsequence.

adj. unrelated, independent, unconcerned, uninvolved, unconnected, inappropriate, incongruent; isolated, arbitrary, free, unallied, unilateral; irrelevant, unsuitable, inapplicable, inapposite, inconsequential.

vb. be unrelated to, have no relation with, not concern, have no bearing upon, have nothing to do with, not be one's business.

adv. by the way, incidentally.

11 kindred relations

n. consanguinity, blood relationship, blood, ties of blood, kinship, kindred, relations, relatives, kith and kin; ancestry, parentage, antecedents, forbears, patrimony, heritage, lineage; descent, descendants; affiliation; children, offspring, issue, progeny;

sibling, brother, sister, twin, cousin, uncle, aunt, nephew, niece, parent, father, mother; kinsman, clansman, fellow, compatriot; family, matriarch, patriarch, fatherhood, paternity, motherhood, maternity, brotherhood, fraternity, sisterhood, sorority; in laws; household, one's folks (*inf.*), home, family circle; race, stock, generation, strain, breed, line, side, clan, tribe, stirps.

adj. related, akin, kindred, consanguineous; parental, maternal, paternal, brotherly, fraternal, sisterly, sororal, cousinly, avuncular; collateral, allied; ethnic, racial, minority, tribal.

vb. be related to, be akin, generate, adopt, affiliate.

12 correlation

n. correlation, relation, correspondence, mutuality, reciprocity, interchange, interrelation, interdependence, interaction, interplay, exchange, alternation, equivalence.

adj. correlative, reciprocal, reciprocating, mutual, relative, corresponding, equivalent, interchangeable.

vb. correlate, interrelate, interconnect, interplay, interact, reciprocate, correspond, alternate.

adv. correlatively, mutually, reciprocally, alternately.

13 identity

n. identity, identicalness, oneness, sameness, selfsameness, equality, unity, homogeneity, uniformity, invariability, interchangeability.

adj. same, identical, one, very, constant, invariable, unchangeable, unvarying, homogeneous; like, alike, indistinguishable; equivalent, duplicate, equal, twin.

vb. be identical, coincide, coalesce, equate; not distinguish, not know from Adam.

14 absolute difference

n. contrariety, inequality, inequity, contrariness, oppositeness, adverseness; incompatibility, irreconcilability; contradiction, inconsistency, polarity, antithesis.

adj. contrary, different, contrasting, inconsistent, contradictory, mutually exclusive, opposite, reverse, diametrical, adverse, opposing.

vb. be contrary, differ, contrast, contradict, oppose, go against the grain; clash.

adv. on the other hand, on the contrary, contrariwise, conversely, in the opposite way.

15 variance

n. variance, difference, variation, unlikeness, heterogeneity, diversity; disparity, deviation, divergence, deflection, discrepancy, disagreement; differentiation, discrimination.

variant, irregularity, special case.

adj. different, unlike, unidentical, dissimilar, variable, changeable, varying, variant; heterogeneous, diverse, indiscriminate; changed, modified; contrasting, incongruous, contrary, deviating, divergent, disparate, incompatible.

vb. differ, vary, change, modify; diverge, deviate; differentiate, discriminate, distinguish.

16 uniformity

n. uniformity, homogeneity, constancy, sameness, invariability, stability, regularity; symmetry, evenness, unity, congruity; conformity; monotony, routine, ritual, standardization, stereotype.

adj. uniform, homogeneous, same, consistent, invariable, steady, stable, regular, symmetrical, even, unchanging, unvarying; monotonous, routine, standardized, stereotyped.

vb. be uniform, accord, conform; make uniform, characterize, standardize, normalize, level, smooth.

17 non-uniformity

n. non-uniformity, heterogeneity, inconstancy, variability, diversity, instability, irregularity, asymmetry, unevenness, disunity, incongruity.

adj. non-uniform, heterogeneous, inconsistent, variable, diversified, motley, unsteady, irregular, asymmetrical, uneven, changing, varying, incongruous.

18 similarity

n. similarity, likeness, resemblance, affinity, analogy, similitude; disguise, camouflage; correlation, comparison, equivalent, correspondence; counterpart.

adj. similar, like, alike, resembling, twin, analogous, à la, equivalent, typical, representative; lifelike, realistic, faithful, true, exact, simulating, imitative; camouflaged, disguised, mock.

vb. be similar, look like, seem, pass for, take after, approximate; liken, assimilate to, imitate; answer to the description of.

19 dissimilarity

n. dissimilarity, difference, unlikeness, dissimulation, diversity, disparity; variety, variation.

adj. dissimilar, different, unlike, disparate, incongruent; atypical; unrealistic, inexact.

vb. be unlike, differ from, bear no resemblance, have nothing in common with.

20 imitation

n. imitation, imitativeness, copying, representation, portrayal, mimicry, impersonation, caricature, parody; simulation, patterning; likeness, replica, reflection, portrait, echo, copy, reprint, facsimile, counterpart; translation, paraphrase, interpretation; cribbing, plagiarism; counterfeit, forgery, fake, sham.

imitator, simulator, ape, copycat (*inf.*), parrot, conformist, sheep, mimic, impersonator; translator, paraphraser, interpreter; plagiarist; forger, counterfeiter, faker.

adj. imitative, apish, parrot-like, counterfeit, pseudo-, sham, fake, mock, phoney (*sl.*); modelled on, based on.

vb. imitate, emulate, portray, depict, represent, simulate, do likewise, take after, follow suit, take a leaf out of someone's book; parrot, take off (*inf.*), send up (*inf.*), mimic, parody, caricature; repeat, mirror; pretend, disguise; copy, quote, reproduce, paraphrase, translate; crib, plagiarize; counterfeit, fake.

21 non-imitation

n. originality, creation, creativeness, inventiveness, ingenuity, independence, newness, novelty, individuality, authenticity, genuineness; real thing.

adj. unimitative, uncopied, underived, authentic, primary, genuine, creative, inventive, original, independent, first hand, incomparable, unique, rare, exceptional.

22 copy

n. copy, reprint, facsimile, reproduction, transcript, translation, paraphrase, interpretation, crib, forgery; semblance; study, representation, portrait, echo; parody, caricature, travesty; counterpart, duplicate, replica, reflection, likeness, impression, dummy, cast, tracing, model, transfer; analogue, correlate.

23 prototype

n. prototype, archetype, type, primitive form, original; precedent, first occurrence; principle, basis, standard, pattern, frame of reference, criterion; blueprint, design, plan, example, instance, illustration; dummy, mock-up; model, poser, sitter, mannequin;

die, stamp, mould, shell, negative, plate, mint.

vb. be an example, set an example; act as a mould; model for, sit, pose; typify, exemplify.

24 agreement

n. agreement, understanding, harmony, unity, integration, uniformity, unanimity, consensus, unison, accord, concord, correspondence, concurrence, consonance; coincidence, congruity; reconciliation, sympathy; treaty, contract.

adj. agreeing, like-minded, unanimous, agreed, corresponding, conforming, concurrent, coinciding, concerted, harmonious, unifying, consonant, concurring, united, collective, undisputed, in step, in concert, of one accord, with one voice, sympathetic, reconcilable, compatible, consistent.

vb. agree, concur, assent, accord, tally, harmonize, match, reconcile, coincide, correspond, fit in with, dovetail, square with, synchronize, adapt, adjust, go hand in hand with, say yes to, see eye to eye, get along with, get on with, click (*inf.*), hit it off (*inf.*); keep in with (*inf.*), keep on the right side of (*inf.*).

see also **643, 699**

25 disagreement

n. disagreement, discord, misunderstanding, division, tension, dissidence, argument, dispute, contention, quarrel, disunion, dissension, strife; discrepancy, dissonance, dissimilarity, disparity, incongruence.

adj. disagreeing, differing, disputing, contradictory, inconsistent, incongruous, out of character, disproportionate, at odds, at variance, at loggerheads, out of step; hostile, inimical, factious, dissenting, non-conformist.

vb. disagree, object, not accept, say no to, speak against, contradict, defy, reject; oppose, fight, quarrel, dispute, come into conflict with, come up against; not conform, be contrary to.

see also **642**

C Quantity

26 quantity

n. quantity, amount, number, sum, extent, scope, expanse, size, dimensions, measure; length, breadth, width, height, depth, volume, capacity, area; mass, bulk, weight; mouthful, handful, spoonful, dose, portion, lot, batch, deal, whole, heaps (*inf.*), masses (*inf.*), load

(*inf.*), abundance, profusion, greatness, magnitude, largeness.

adj. quantitative, quantified, measured, some, any.

vb. quantify, measure.

see also **32**

27 relative quantity

n. degree, level, grade, point, stage, rate, proportion, ratio, scale, measure, standard, comparison, criterion; extent, scope, range, intensity, frequency, size, speed, shade, nuance, tint; gradation, graduation, calibration, measurement.

adj. graded, graduated, calibrated, measured, scaled, comparative, proportional, relative; gradual, tapering, shading off, fading.

vb. graduate, grade, measure, calibrate; compare, rank, classify; taper off, shade off, fade, narrow, reduce, lessen, thin out.

adv. gradually, in stages, little by little, step by step.

28 equality

n. equality, parity, uniformity, sameness, equivalence, equalization, equation, adjustment, equilibrium, balance, symmetry, steadiness, synonymity, six of one and half a dozen of the other (*inf.*), six and two threes (*inf.*).

equivalent, draw, tie, dead heat, stalemate, no decision; counterpart, opposite number, equal, complement, twin, double, peer; synonym.

adj. equal, equivalent, equilateral, regular, symmetrical, fifty-fifty, on equal terms, even, level, flush, parallel, reciprocal, uniform, comparable, commensurate, proportionate, coextensive, tantamount, synonymous.

vb. be equal, agree with, coincide, suffice, rank with, match, rival, meet, touch, live up to, measure up to, come up to, be the equivalent of. keep pace with, come to the same thing, go halves; tie, draw, balance.

equalize, make equal, adjust, square.

29 inequality

n. inequality, disparity, non-uniformity, unlikeness, disproportion, dissimilarity, deviation, divergence, dissemblance, inferiority, shortcoming, deficiency; unevenness, imbalance, lopsidedness, unsteadiness.

adj. unequal, disparate, non-uniform, uneven, odd, inferior, deficient, insufficient, inadequate; disproportionate, lopsided, top-heavy, crooked, overbalanced.

vb. be unequal, outclass, outstrip, have the

advantage, fall short of, not come up to, not hold a candle to (*inf.*).

30 mean

n. average, mean, golden mean, medium, happy medium, median, balance, norm, par, middle term, middle point, midpoint, centre, halfway, middle, compromise.

adj. mean, average, median, middle, grey, intermediate, halfway, lukewarm, middling, fair to middling, medium; typical; mediocre, run of the mill.

vb. average out, take the average, split the difference, strike a balance, go halfway.

31 compensation

n. compensation, weighting, equalization, balance, counterbalance, ballast, allowance, amends, costs, damages, remuneration, reimbursement, indemnification, indemnity, reparation, restitution, recompense, repayment, refund, offset, satisfaction, atonement, requital.

adj. compensatory, indemnificatory, restitutory, balancing.

vb. compensate, make amends, balance, neutralize, equalize, counterbalance, counteract, overcompensate, pay costs, indemnify, remunerate, recompense, reimburse, redeem, refund, recoup, satisfy, make up for, make reparation, allow for, set off, offset, take back.

32 greatness

n. greatness, largeness, bigness, vastness, enormity, immenseness, magnitude, size, bulk; spaciousness; might, mightiness, power, strength, intensity; amplitude, fullness, plenitude.

great quantity, profusion, abundance, masses, lots, quantities, oodles (*inf.*), stacks (*inf.*); excess, redundance, superfluity, superabundance.

adj. big, large, great, considerable, numerous, massive, enormous, vast, colossal, huge, sizeable; tall, lofty, high, towering; strong, mighty, powerful, energetic; ample, plentiful, abundant, profuse, plenteous, copious; noble, sublime, stately, exalted; remarkable, notable, unspeakable; extensive, far-reaching, widespread, prevalent, sweeping, universal, worldwide; marvellous, exceptional, surpassing, wonderful, overwhelming, unbelievable, stupendous, astounding.

vb. be great, be big, be large; mount, soar, tower, exceed, rise above, transcend.

adv. enormously, vastly, highly, on a big scale, in a big way; heavily, strongly, mightily, powerfully, actively; greatly, very, much, in a great measure, extremely, exceedingly, considerably; plenteously, plentifully, abundantly, immeasurably, unspeakably, ineffably, awfully (*inf.*), tremendously; excessively, inordinately, immoderately; unbelievably, exceptionally.

see also 75

33 smallness

n. smallness, littleness, tininess, diminutiveness, minuteness; shortness, slightness, slenderness; meagreness, scantiness, paucity, scarcity, fewness, sparseness, rareness.

small quantity, dash, trace, *soupçon*, shade, morsel, crumb, iota, jot, tittle; point, dot, spot, fleck, speck, grain, atom, particle, modicum, chip, flake, shred, bit, rag, fragment, trifle.

adj. small, little, diminutive, minimal, infinitesimal, imperceptible, tiny, minute, miniature; slim, slender, thin, slight, scanty, meagre, insufficient, few, sparse, rare, inconsiderable, minor, trifling; modest, poor, pitiful.

adv. slightly, little, to a small extent, faintly, on a small scale, in a small way; humbly, modestly; scarcely, hardly, barely, pitifully.

see also 76

34 superiority

n. superiority, supremacy, dominance, transcendence, excellence, perfection, nobility, sublimity, eminence, pre-eminence; advantage, privilege, prerogative, favour, upper hand, head start, start.

superior, better, elder, master, overlord, chief, boss, management, senior, top dog (*inf.*).

adj. superior, eminent, upper, higher, greater, major; better, preferred, surpassing, exceeding; supreme, pre-eminent, greatest; first, chief, principal, main, capital, leading, mainline, cardinal, paramount; best, excellent, superlative, first-class, matchless, unrivalled, unsurpassed, beyond compare.

vb. be superior, rise above, tower, transcend, exceed, excel, surpass, eclipse, top, cap, overshadow, outmatch, get the better of, lord it over; prevail, predominate; have the advantage, have the edge on (*inf.*).

adv. eminently, superlatively, prominently, above all, *par excellence*, principally, especially, particularly.

35 inferiority

n. inferiority, deficiency, imperfection, shortcoming; mediocrity, poorness; lowliness, subordination, subjection, back seat (*inf.*).

inferior, subordinate, servant, slave, junior, auxiliary, accessory, workers, poor relation, underdog (*inf.*).

adj. inferior, low, lower, junior, minor, lesser, subordinate, secondary, accessory, auxiliary, ancillary, unclassified; lowly, humble, menial, subject, obedient; deficient, mediocre, substandard, imperfect, worse, worst, common, below par, not a patch on (*inf.*).

vb. be inferior, fall short of, not come up to, not compare with, not come near, want, lack, not hold a candle to (*inf.*); take a back seat (*inf.*).

see also 571

36 increase

n. increase, rise, augmentation, growth, progression, development, spread, proliferation, build-up, prolongation, extension, expansion, enlargement, escalation, magnification, heightening, swelling, incorporation, merger, cumulative effect, snowball (*inf.*).

adj. increasing, rising, growing, progressing, developing, proliferating, expanding, escalating, enlarging, intensifying, cumulative, crescent.

vb. increase, grow, rise, gain; thrive, flourish; multiply, enlarge, magnify, amplify, aggrandize; develop, escalate, boost, build, build up, expand, swell, add, compound, upsurge, strengthen, intensify, accumulate, accrue, snowball (*inf.*); prolong, lengthen, broaden, widen, thicken, deepen, heighten; enhance; exacerbate, aggravate.

37 decrease

n. decrease, decline, fall, drop, reduction, wane, restriction, restraint, curtailment, paring, pruning, squeeze; fade-out, regression, depression, depreciation, shortening.

adj. decreasing, falling, declining, reducing, dwindling, fading, on the wane.

vb. decrease, lessen, fall, drop, diminish, moderate, subside, decline, abate, recede, dwindle, wane, shrink, ebb, drain away, tail off; peter out, taper off; deteriorate; reduce, restrain, limit, check, curb, curtail, cut back, economize, consume, use up, shorten, trim, squeeze, compress, erode, dilute, quell.

38 numeration

n. numeration, numbering, enumeration, counting, count, census, figuring, reckoning, calculation, computation; mathematics, arithmetic, algebra, geometry, trigonometry, calculus, analysis; addition, subtraction,

multiplication, division; statistics, figures, data, tables, measurements; abacus, ready reckoner, computer, electronic brain, microprocessor, calculator; addent, subtrahend, product, quotient.

adj. numerable, countable, calculable, computable, statistical, numbered, mathematical, arithmetical, algebraical, geometrical, analytical.

vb. number, count, tell, score, tally, cast, enumerate, poll; calculate, add, total, subtract, multiply, divide, compute, figure, work out, reckon, estimate; inventorize, list; classify; measure.

39 number

n. number, numeral, figure, digit, cipher, integer, whole number, prime number, symbol, character, sign, notation; function, variable, expression, formula; fraction, denominator, numerator, decimal, power, root.

adj. numerical, arithmetical, even, odd, prime, whole, positive, negative, rational, irrational, transcendental, exponential, integral, digital, decimal, binary; multiple, reciprocal, fractional.

40 addition

n. addition, summation, total; increase, enlargement, annexation, accession, accretion, accruing, supplement; prefixion, suffixion, affixation.

adj. additional, additive, adopted, extra, new, further, added, fresh, other, extraneous, accessory, auxiliary, supplementary.

vb. add, add up, sum, total; append, annex, attach, tack on, clap on (*inf.*), slap on (*inf.*), join, insert, contribute, supplement, increase, accumulate; accrue; affix, suffix, prefix, infix.

adv. in addition, moreover, furthermore, further, besides, as well, also, additionally, extra, and, too, over and above, in conjunction with.

41 thing added

n. adjunct, addition, attachment, fixture, extension, accretion, accession, accessory, appurtenance, increment, rise, interest, bonus, contribution, supplement; qualification, rider; annexe, wing; *addendum*, appendix, appendage, postscript, note; prefix, suffix, infix.

42 subtraction

n. subtraction, deduction, removal, withdrawal, curtailment, reduction, decrease, cutback, deletion, discount; amputation; abbreviation.

vb. subtract, deduct, take away, detract

from, remove, exclude, withdraw, withhold, cut back; unload, unpack; shorten, abbreviate, delete; sever, amputate.

adv., prep. minus, without, with the exception of, bar, excepting, save.

43 thing subtracted

n. deduction, decrement, cut, decrease, reduction, rebate, discount, allowance, credit, depreciation, remission, forfeit, loss, write-off; shortcoming, defect.

44 remainder

n. remainder, rest, remnant, vestige, remains, residue, relic, hangover; result; balance, surplus, excess, margin; left-overs, waste, garbage, rejects, salvage, debris, sediment, dregs, slag, scum, leavings, clippings, crumbs, pairings, trimmings, castoffs.

adj. remaining, left, left over, over, residual, surviving; outstanding, carried over; surplus, unused, spare, to spare, superfluous; outcast.

45 mixture

n. mixture, mingling, combination, fusion, infusion, amalgamation, merger, integration; adulteration, transfusion.

blend, compound, composite, composition, conglomeration, amalgam, alloy, tincture, admixture; medley, miscellany, patchwork, pastiche, jumble, tangle, potpourri, *mélange*, mishmash, gallimaufry; hybrid, mongrel.

adj. mixed, composite, fused, merged, combined, united, amalgamated, half-and-half; stirred, blended, heterogeneous, adulterated, hybrid, mongrel; miscellaneous, assorted, motley, varied, jumbled, hotchpotch.

vb. mix, mix up, join, fuse, alloy, merge, combine, unite, amalgamate, conjoin, mingle, intermingle, stir, transfuse, shake, scramble; adulterate, water down; jumble; be mixed, permeate, infect, infiltrate; interbreed, cross with.

46 freedom from mixture

n. simpleness, purity, homogeneity, simplicity, plainness, purification, sifting, elimination.

adj. simple, pure, clean, clear, plain, uniform, absolute, homogeneous, uncomplicated, unadulterated, unqualified; mere, only, sheer.

vb. simplify, purify, unmix, unscramble, disentangle, eliminate, sift, winnow.

47 junction

n. junction, joining, connection, union, reunion, contact, tying, fastening, coupling, merging, fusion, bonding, marriage, concatenation; assemblage, structure, tie-up.

adj. joined, connected, linked, coupled, allied, married, wed, attached, fixed, secure, tied, hooked, stuck, firm, fast, close, rooted; tight, inextricable, inseparable; united, together, whole.

vb. join, attach, fix, stick on, affix, bolt, nail, screw; connect, link, make contact, span, bridge; put together, merge, fuse, combine, marry, juxtapose, cement; secure, tie, hook, couple, fasten, bind, splice, yoke, harness, knit, string, tether, clamp, clinch, twist; assemble, confederate, band together; dovetail, fit, set; unite, become one, meet, converge; unify, associate, ally with.

48 separation

n. separation, disconnection, dissociation, disjoining, detachment, segregation, disunion, disengagement, removal, withdrawal, dislocation, dismemberment, severance, division, cut, parting, divorce; dissolution, disintegration, break-up, dissection, breakdown, analysis; rupture, fracture, cleavage; burst, puncture, blowout.

adj. disjoined, discontinuous, unattached, unconnected; separable, detachable, divisible; apart, distinct, discrete, detached, divorced, isolated, alone, broken, fractured, in pieces, interrupted, torn, rent, cut, split, dismembered.

vb. separate, part, disunite, detach, disengage, break away, set apart, keep apart, disconnect, partition, demarcate, hive off, divide, subdivide, dissociate, divorce, isolate; disintegrate, decompose; fracture, rupture, break, fragment; unravel, disentangle; uncouple, unhitch, dislocate, unbind, loose, free, set free, release; tear, undo, rend; cut, dissect, hew, fell, reap, dice, chop, snip, slit, split, burst, puncture, sever, saw, chip, behead, carve; distribute, disperse; diverge; decollate.

49 bond

n. bond, link, connection, channel, passage, bridge; line, cable, string, rope, cord, chain, thread, ribbon, band, bandage, ligature, strip, girdle, belt, harness, lace, braid, tie, plait; knot, fastening, zip, hook, hook and eye, nut, bolt, screw, clasp, coupling; joint, junction, nexus, node, weld, seam, splice, swivel, hinge; adhesive, fixative, glue, paste, cement, epoxy, sticky tape.

50 coherence

n. coherence, cohesion, cohesiveness, consistency, adhesiveness; continuity, attachment, solidarity, inseparability, indivisibility.

adj. cohesive, adhesive, sticky, clinging, tenacious; inseparable, indivisible, inextricable, close, compact, solid.

vb. cohere, hold, hold fast, hold together; congregate; fit tight; adhere, stick, cleave, cling, fasten, unite, glue, gum, paste, weld, solder; hug, embrace, grasp, clasp, grip, clinch.

see also 332

51 incoherence

n. incoherence, non-coherence, non-adhesion, separability, divisibility, looseness, laxity.

adj. non-adhesive, slippery, loose, disconnected, lax, runny, inconsistent.

vb. unstick, unglue, detach, disjoin, disunite, peel off; come unstuck, fall apart, shake.

52 combination

n. combination, coalescence, fusion, mixture, synthesis, amalgamation, merger, integration, union, incorporation, embodiment, association, affiliation.

adj. combined, linked, integrated, connected, synchronized, harmonious, unified.

vb. combine, join, link, integrate, fuse, put together, merge, consolidate, unify, compound, group, incorporate, embody, coalesce, amalgamate; mix, blend, absorb; harmonize, synchronize; affiliate, cooperate, work together; kill two birds with one stone; make the best of both worlds, have one's cake and eat it.

see also 639

53 decomposition

n. decomposition, resolution, dissolution, analysis, breakdown, disintegration; decentralization; destruction; decay, putrefaction, corrosion, rottenness, putrescence, mould, rot, blight, mildew.

adj. decomposed, rotten, off, bad, rancid.

vb. decompose, resolve, break down, analyse, reduce, simplify, dissolve, dissect, atomize; decentralize, disband; disintegrate, break up; degenerate, waste away, decay, erode, corrode, rust, rot.

see also 588

54 whole

n. wholeness, completeness, entirety, totality, unity, comprehensivity, inclusiveness, panorama, catch-all; all, everyone, everybody, everything, total, whole, aggregate, sum, ensemble.

adj. whole, all, every, entire, full, complete, single, integral, total, universal, aggregate, gross, outright, inclusive, undivided, indivisible, inseparable, indissoluble; comprehensive, all-inclusive, all-embracing, sweeping, extensive, widespread, far-reaching, omnibus, wholesale, indiscriminate, blanket, catch-all, compendious, encyclopedic; intact, solid, perfect, safe, good, unbroken, undamaged, unblemished, unimpaired, flawless.

adv. wholly, entirely, completely, altogether, a hundred per cent, all in all.

55 part

n. part, portion, share, cut, division, section, sector, segment, compartment, department, class, group, family, branch; genus, phylum; piece, fragment, bit, scrap; detail; splinter, sliver, chip, chunk, lump, wedge, slice; instalment, part payment, foretaste, down-payment, deposit; excerpt, extract; constituent, component, factor, element, member, ingredient, integral part; aspect, facet, feature.

adj. in parts, fragmentary, broken, in bits and pieces, defective; partial, incomplete, half-finished; constituent, integral, inherent, built-in, inclusive.

vb. part, divide, separate, allot, share.

adv. partly, piecemeal, in part, bit by bit.

see also 73, 717

56 completeness

n. completeness, wholeness, fullness, plenitude, saturation, one's fill, replenishment, refill; entirety, universality, comprehensivity, nothing lacking, nothing to add, integration; perfection, integrity, soundness; last touch, finish.

adj. complete, full, utter, entire, whole, plenary, all, gross, replete; comprehensive, exhaustive; absolute, extreme, thorough, thoroughgoing, radical, sweeping, wholesale, unqualified, unconditional; integral, perfect; abounding, profuse, brimful, saturated, swamped, drowned, sated, laden.

vb. be complete, come to maturity, culminate; overflow, bulge; make complete, consummate, add, perfect; conclude, fulfil; fill, replenish, top up, soak, overwhelm, saturate, swamp, drown; cloy, glut, gorge, sate, cram, pack, stuff.

adv. completely, wholly, entirely, fully, utterly, perfectly, altogether, quite, undividedly, exclusively, absolutely, out and out;

hook, line, and sinker; with a vengeance, from beginning to end.

see also **659**

57 incompleteness

n. incompleteness, defectiveness, deficiency, shortcoming, deficit, shortage, shortfall, omission, defect, want, need, lack, break, decrease.

adj. incomplete, defective, imperfect, deficient, short, lacking, not enough, sparing, depleted; superficial, unfinished, half-done, under construction, in preparation, in progress; sketchy, meagre, skimpy, scrappy, rough.

vb. be incomplete, lack, want.

adv. incompletely, partially, imperfectly, inadequately.

see also **660**

58 composition

n. composition, constitution, organization, make-up; nature, character, condition, quality, personality; design, pattern; compilation.

vb. constitute, compose, form, make up, comprise, consist, comprehend, include, incorporate, belong to, be a component of; arrange, mix, organize, systematize, construct, compile, assemble, devise, design, plan, write.

59 unity

n. unity, oneness, wholeness, homogeneity, unification, integration, uniqueness, singularity, individuality, singleness, isolation, solitude, indivisibility.

unit, item, bit, piece, one, point, entity, whole, entirety; assembly, system.

adj. one, singular, individual, peculiar, specific, special; sole, single, only, unique, unprecedented, unequalled, *sui generis*, indivisible; lone, alone, lonely, lonesome, homeless, rootless, on one's own, singlehanded, unaccompanied.

60 accompaniment

n. accompaniment, togetherness, concomitance, coexistence, society, association, partnership, cooperation, fellowship.

concomitant, accessory, adjunct, attachment, appendage, belongings, appurtenance, attendant, complement; satellite; *sine qua non;* coincidence; consequence.

adj. accompanying, concomitant, coexistent, attendant, accessory, connected, related, associated, belonging, attending, coincidental, incidental, ancillary; contem-

porary, concurrent, synchronous, simultaneous; symptomatic; united.

vb. accompany, be found with, exist with, happen with, coexist, belong, characterize, coincide, be connected with, go hand in hand, go together, be related, follow.

adv. together, hand in hand, collectively.

61 duality

n. duality, dualism, doubleness, doublesidedness; two, deuce, pair, couple, couplet, twosome, tandem.

adj. dual, duple, dualistic, binary, both, twin, paired, duplex, bilateral, bipartite, bipartisan, bi-.

vb. pair, couple, match, mate, dualize; combine.

62 duplication

n. duplication, doubling, reduplication, repetition, iteration, encore, copy.

adj. double, duplicate, twofold, twin, second.

vb. double, repeat, twin, duplicate, reduplicate, copy.

adv. twice, again, once more.

63 bisection

n. bisection, halving, forking, bifurcation; half, hemisphere, dichotomy; dividing line, equator.

adj. bisected, half, bifurcated, semi-, demi-, hemi-.

vb. bisect, halve, cut in two, divide, split, sunder, bifurcate; go halves; diverge, fork.

64 triality

n. triality, trinity; three, triad, threesome, trio, triplet, trilogy, triangle.

adj. three, tertiary, tripartite, trilateral, triangular, triplex, triform, tri-; triune.

65 triplication

n. triplication, triplicity, hat trick.

adj. treble, threefold, triplicate, third.

vb. treble, triple, triplicate.

66 trisection

n. trisection, tripartition, third, trichotomy.

vb. trisect, cut in three.

67 quaternity

n. quaternity; four, tetrad; square, quadrilateral, quadrangle; quartet, foursome, quadruplet, tetragon.

adj. four, quaternary, quaternal; quadratic, biquadratic, square, quadrilateral, quadri-, tetra-.

68 quadruplication

n. quadruplication, quadruplicity.
adj. fourfold, quadruplicate, fourth, quadruple.
vb. quadruple, quadruplicate.

69 quadrisection

n. quadrisection, quadripartition; fourth, quarter, quart.
vb. quadrisect, quarter, cut in four.

70 five and over

n. five, fiver, pentad, quintuplet, pentagon, quintet, quincunx, Pentateuch; six, half a dozen, hexad, sextuplet, hexagon, sextet; seven, heptad, septuplet, heptagon, septet; eight, octad, octagon, octet, octave; nine, ennead, nonagon, enneagon, nonet; ten, decade, decagon; double figures; eleven, endecagon; twelve, dozen, dodecagon; thirteen, baker's dozen; teens; twenty, score; hundred, century, centenary; three figures, treble figures; gross; thousand, grand, millenium; ten thousand, myriad; million; billion; trillion.
adj. five, quintuple; six, sextuple; seven, septuple; eight, octuple; ten, decimal; twelve, duodecimal; -fold.

71 multisection

n. multisection, quinquesection.
vb. multisect, quinquesect.

72 plurality

n. plurality, plural, number, multiplicity, variety, abundance, some; majority.
adj. plural, pluralistic, pluralistical, multiple, many, some, numerous; more.

73 fraction

n. fraction, fragment, part, section, portion, segment.
adj. fractional, partial, fragmentary, constituent, sectional.
see also 55, 717

74 zero

n. zero, nil, nought; nothingness, nullity, void; nothing, none, no one, nobody; no score, duck, love.
adj. zero, null, not one.

75 multitude

n. multitude, numerosity, multiplicity; great amount, quantity, lot; great number, hundreds, thousands, myriads, millions; crowd, mob, army, throng, flock, legion, host, posse; plenty, a great deal, abundance, profusion, bonanza (*inf.*); majority, main part, mass, bulk, main emphasis, weight.
adj. many, not a few, several, considerable, numerous, manifold, countless, legion; much, sufficient, enough, ample, galore (*inf.*); profuse, abundant, overflowing, prevalent, plentiful; crowded, populous, peopled; dense, teeming with, alive with, thick.
vb. be many, crowd with, throng with, flock, mass, swarm with, teem with, crawl with; overflow with; pack, stuff; outnumber.

76 fewness

n. fewness, paucity, scarcity, sparseness, thinness, rarity; a few, handful, smattering, sprinkling; remnant, minority, insufficiency, absence, lack.
adj. few, not many, sparse, scant, thin, inconsiderable, negligible, infrequent, few and far between.
vb. diminish, reduce, lessen; lack, need.

77 repetition

n. repetition, recurrence, repetitiveness, reappearance; reproduction, copy, duplication; renewal, resumption; reiteration, rehearsal, recapitulation.
repeat, encore, replay; reprint, reissue, rehash.
adj. repeated, reiterated, restated, reworded, retold; reproduced, remade, redone, copied; repetitious, repetitive, boring.
vb. repeat, reiterate, restate, reword, retell, iterate; recite, say after, echo; rehearse, go over, take it from the top (*inf.*); recapitulate; redo, remake, renew, rework, remodel; rehash, revive; reissue, republish, copy; reoccur, reappear.
adv. again, over again, anew; ditto, encore; repeatedly.

78 infinity

n. infinity, endlessness, limitlessness; eternity; infinitude, perpetuity.
adj. infinite, immense, vast, untold, boundless, endless, immeasurable, unexhaustible, interminable; countless, numberless, unnumbered; eternal, perpetual.
vb. go on and on, know no bounds.
adv. infinitely, ad *infinitum*, without end.

D Order

79 order

n. order, organization, arrangement, array, state of order; tidiness, orderliness, neatness; method, pattern, regularity, system; uniformity, routine, habit; discipline.

adj. orderly, organized, methodical, systematic, regular, harmonious; under control, businesslike; neat, tidy, shipshape, well-ordered.

vb. order, organize, harmonize; take shape, fall into place.

adv. in order, all right, all correct, O.K., orderly, systematically, methodically.

80 disorder

n. disorder, disarrangement, muddle, clutter, mess, disarray, disharmony, disorderliness, untidiness; chaos, crisis; confusion, disturbance, shambles, Bedlam, mix-up.

turmoil, tumult, turbulence, agitation, to-do, ferment, storm, upheaval, *mêlée, fracas,* uproar, hullabaloo, frenzy, row, riot; anarchy, unruliness.

adj. orderless, out of order, unorganized, disorganized, in disarray, out of order, untidy; unsystematic, unmethodical, irregular, non-uniform; incoherent, muddled, confused, mixed up (*inf.*), disconnected; chaotic; tumultuous, turbulent; anarchical, lawless.

adv. confusedly, anyhow, irregularly, in disorder, higgledy-piggledy, upside down.

81 arrangement

n. arrangement, ordering, reduction to order, composition, preparation, organization, reorganization, regulation, marshalling, disposal, distribution; plan, method, system.

adj. arranged, well-arranged, ordered, organized, well-organized, methodical, regular, systematic, well-regulated, classified, sorted; coordinated, connected, disposed; disciplined; disentangled, unravelled, straightened out.

vb. arrange, plan, prepare, compose, put in order, set in order, reduce to order, array, dispose; assign, set, establish, formulate, coordinate, line up, regulate, marshal, range; organize, systematize, standardize, formalize, coordinate, connect; collocate; classify, pattern; disentangle, unravel, untwist, uncoil, straighten out; put one's own house in order.

82 disarrangement

n. disarrangement, derangement, disorganization, dishevelment, discomposure; irregularity, tangle, entanglement.

adj. disarranged, discomposed, disorganized, disorderly.

vb. disturb, disorganize, disorder, jumble, shuffle, mix up, muddle, derange, upset, unsettle; agitate, disconcert, discompose; ruffle, dishevel; confuse, perturb, confound, trouble; disperse, scatter; destroy, disrupt,

dislocate; disband; overturn, overthrow; stir up, put the cat among the pigeons (*inf.*).

83 list

n. list, enumeration, classification, record, register, catalogue, directory, file; statement, schedule, agenda, table; roll, roll-call; roster, rota; enrolment; inventory, stock list, checklist; programme, prospectus, syllabus, synopsis; index, table of contents, bibliography, thesaurus, dictionary, glossary, lexicon.

vb. list, enumerate, catalogue, itemize, classify; enter, register, book, inscribe, record, file, log; enrol, enlist, matriculate; schedule.

84 precedence

n. precedence, antecedence, priority, precedency, previousness; coming before, anteriority; pre-eminence, precedent, preference, superiority.

adj. preceding, precedent, antecedent, anterior; previous, earlier, former, foregoing, prior, aforementioned.

vb. come before, go before, go ahead, precede, have precedence, take precedence; lead, be in front, head, place before; herald, pioneer, forerun, blaze the trail (*inf.*), clear the way, show the way, set the fashion; preface, introduce, prelude, preamble, usher in.

adv. before, in advance, above.

85 sequence

n. sequence, going after, following, placement, succession; successiveness, consequence; order, series, progression, set, string, row, chain, train, flow, concatenation.

adj. following, succeeding, ensuing, resulting, subsequent, successive, consequent; next, later, posterior; sequential, consecutive, serial; connected.

vb. come after, go after, go behind; ensue, follow, result; place after, append; succeed, come next, supersede, displace, supplant, become heir to.

adv. after, afterwards, behind, subsequently.

86 precursor

n. precursor, predecessor; pioneer, herald, vanguard, scout, pathfinder, forerunner, harbinger; parent, ancestor, forbear.

precedent, antecedent; prelude, preliminary, introduction, prologue, foreword, preface, exordium, prolegomena, preamble; prefix; authoritative example; preparation.

adj. precursory, preliminary, prefatory, introductory; exploratory, preparatory.

87 sequel

n. sequel, consequence, effect, result, end, issue, outcome, upshot, aftermath; after-effect, by-product, spin-off; inference, deduction, conclusion; afterthought, second thoughts; follow-up; continuation, tail, tailpiece, supplement, postscript, epilogue, appendage; suffix.

88 beginning

n. beginning, start, commencement, outset, onset, outbreak; foundation, establishment, origination, invention, birth, origin, genesis, cause, source, root, spring; infancy, primitiveness, youth; starting-point, square one.

inauguration, initiation, début, coming out, unveiling, *première*, opening, inception.

preliminaries, introduction, prelude, foreword, preface; rudiments, first principles, ABC, primer, basics.

adj. beginning, first, starting, initial, maiden; introductory, precursory, opening, inaugural; foundational, elementary, fundamental, basic, rudimentary; original, embryonic, primitive.

vb. begin, start, commence, go ahead, make a beginning, make a start, kick off (*inf.*); come into existence, arise, break out, burst forth, rise, be born, see the light of day; make one's début, come out; undertake, do, set about, tackle, enter upon, set in motion, start up, get under way, start the ball rolling, activate; take the first step, break the ice; begin again, go back to square one (*inf.*).

initiate, conceive, introduce, found, establish, institute, inaugurate, open, originate, invent.

adv. initially, in the first place, first, *ab initio*, at the outset, to begin with, for a kickoff (*inf.*).

see also **605**

89 end

n. end, conclusion, close, termination, ending, finish, stop, cessation, completion, closure, adjournment, dissolution; expiration, death, decease, demise; retirement; finale, swan song, last word, death blow, curtains (*inf.*), *finis*, end of the line (*inf.*).

extreme, extremity, terminus, terminal, furthest point, achievement; consummation, perfection, culmination, climax, *dénouement*; goal, limit, point, boundary, top, peak, summit, head, bottom, base, tail; postscript, epilogue, appendage.

adj. ending, final, last, ultimate, terminal, concluding, consummate, ended, settled, concluded; extreme.

vb. end, finish, stop, conclude, terminate, cease, discontinue, desist, refrain, come to an end; expire, breathe one's last, die; run out, run its course, come to a close, draw to a close, break off; settle, determine, bring to an end, put an end to, dispose of, suspend, postpone, cancel, bring to a standstill, arrest, quell; switch off, wind up; end up.

adv. finally, lastly, at last, in conclusion, ultimately.

see also **144**

90 middle

n. middle, midpoint, centre, middle distance, equidistance, halfway house; pivot, heart, kernel, core; focus, focal point; average, mean, median; midst, thick of things.

adj. middle, centre, central, mid, equidistant, halfway, medial, intermediate; focal; mean, average; moderate, neutral, compromising.

adv. in the middle, midway, halfway, in between.

91 continuity

n. continuity, continuousness, consecutiveness, progression, continuance, one thing after another, constancy, flow, succession, endlessness, perpetuation, perpetuity; routine, daily round, monotony; sequence, queue, crocodile, procession, march, cortège, column, train, suite, retinue, single file, tail, tailback.

adj. continuous, consecutive, running, serial, successive, progressive, constant, endless, perpetual, sustained, persisting, unbroken, uninterrupted; regular.

vb. continue, carry on, maintain, sustain, remain, succeed, follow in a line; file, march, parade, queue; endure.

adv. continuously, in succession, successively, in file, in train.

92 discontinuity

n. discontinuity, disconnectedness, disjunction; interruption, intervention, break, interval, intermission, pause, breather, rest, stop-over; gap, missing link.

adj. discontinuous, disconnected, unconnected, interrupted, broken; intermittent, irregular, infrequent, few and far between; spasmodic, jerky, uneven, desultory.

vb. discontinue, break, interrupt, pause, stop over; disconnect.

adv. at intervals, irregularly, in fits and starts, discontinuously.

see also **200**

93 position in a series

n. term, serial position, order, rank, grade, station, position, situation, status, standing, footing, level, tier, rung, degree.

94 assemblage

n. assemblage, bringing together, juxtaposition, mobilization.

gathering, assembly, association, collection, company, society; circle, clique; meeting, reception, party; council, committee, conference, congress, commission, convention, congregation, convocation, symposium.

group, body, mass, crowd, throng, mob, crush, huddle, band, gang, troop, horde; team, cast, crew, squad; swarm, colony, herd, flock, pack, brood, shoal, school; set, cluster, bunch, lot, batch, bundle.

adj. gathered, assembled, met, convened; crowded, dense, swarming.

vb. gather, assemble, meet, come together, associate, congregate, converge, rendezvous; group, crowd, throng, rally, flock in, pour in; swarm, huddle, bunch; accumulate, pile up, amass; collect, bring together, call up, summon, convene, muster, round up.

95 dispersion

n. dispersion, dispersal, scattering, dissemination, broadcasting, dissipation, diffusion, divergence, decentralization.

adj. dispersed, scattered.

vb. disperse, scatter; disseminate, broadcast, sow, seed; sprinkle, strew, spread, dissipate; separate, divide; shed, distribute, propagate, dispense, dole out, dispel, diffuse, decentralize, disband; evaporate; sprawl, diverge.

96 focus

n. focus, focal point, centre; meeting place, forum, market, club, rendezvous; heart, hub, centre of interest, headquarters, nerve centre; Mecca, promised land.

vb. focus, converge, concentrate, centre, attract, draw attention.

see also 224

97 class

n. class, sort, kind, type, category, section, division, group, grouping, department, branch; mark, brand, make; strain, breed, line, family, genus, species, phylum, caste; hierarchy, rank.

classification, categorization, specification, taxonomy, systematization, list.

adj. classificatory, taxonomic.

vb. class, sort, classify, categorize, hierarchize, rank, grade, group, divide.

98 inclusion

n. inclusion, admission, reception, incorporation, embodiment, composition.

adj. inclusive, comprehensive, all-inclusive, all-embracing, overall, wholesale, sweeping.

vb. include, admit, incorporate, embody, comprehend, comprise, consist of, constitute, contain, involve, take in, entail, embrace, enclose, subsume.

99 exclusion

n. exclusion, exclusiveness; omission, rejection, ejection; prohibition, boycott, embargo, blockade; eviction, dismissal, suspension, expulsion, excommunication, ostracism, segregation, apartheid; bar, ban, closed shop, lock-out.

adj. exclusive, restrictive, segregated, prohibitive.

vb. exclude, omit, leave out, remove, eliminate, except, disregard; disqualify, reject, dismiss, suspend, deport, banish, expel, excommunicate, send to Coventry, ostracize; feel left out, feel out of things; restrict, forbid, prohibit, bar, segregate, ban, black, blacklist, boycott; prevent, preclude, obviate.

prep. except, excluding, apart from, save, bar.

100 extraneousness

n. extraneousness, foreignness; outsider, foreigner, alien, stranger, immigrant, expatriot, migrant, emigrant, refugee; newcomer, guest, visitor; squatter, interloper, invader.

adj. extraneous, extrinsic, external, outward, outside; foreign, alien, strange, immigrant; exotic, imported, borrowed, adopted, introduced, naturalized; alienated, estranged.

101 generality

n. generality, universality; ubiquity; broadness; generalization, abstraction, observation, simplification, overview; average man, man in the street, everybody, every mother's son (*inf.*), all the world and his wife (*inf.*).

adj. general, overall, universal, global, catholic; worldwide, international, cosmopolitan; typical, representative, generic; broad, wide; comprehensive, widespread, ubiquitous, blanket, average.

vb. be general, prevail, predominate; generalize, expand, broaden; conclude, infer.

see also 54

102 speciality

n. speciality, particularity, originality, individuality, distinctiveness, peculiarity, uniqueness, idiosyncrasy, characteristic; particulars, specifications, details, minutiae.

adj. special, particular, peculiar, especial, distinct, unique, original, *sui generis*, individual, individualistic, characteristic, idiosyncratic; specific, precise.

vb. specify, define, particularize, itemize, designate, enumerate, go into detail; single out, isolate, put one's finger on (*inf.*).

103 rule

n. rule, regulation, law, direction, instruction, ordinance, code, order, precept, norm, principle, maxim, proposition, formula, guide, criterion, model, standard, procedure, system, convention.

adj. regulated, normative, prescriptive; legislative; formulaic, conventional.

see also **626, 954**

104 diversity

n. diversity, variation, variousness, heterogeneity, multiformity, variability, difference; medley, mixture, variety, miscellany.

adj. diverse, diversified, various, manifold, heterogeneous, multifarious, motley, irregular; different, disparate, variable, changeable.

see also **45**

105 conformity

n. conformity, correspondence, congruity, consistency, coincidence, compatibility, agreement, affinity, resemblance, similarity, adjustment, acclimatization.
conformist, conventionalist, traditionalist, loyalist, conservative.

adj. conforming, agreeing, harmonious, corresponding, appropriate, applicable, consonant; similar, resembling, well-matched, conformable, adaptable, adjustable, compatible, consistent.

vb. conform, comply, agree, accord; accommodate, adapt, adjust, fit, suit, integrate, bend, square, accustom, acclimatize, harmonize, reconcile; follow, obey, observe, fall into line, toe the line, adhere to.

106 unconformity

n. unconformity, difference, contrast, dissimilarity, disagreement, inconsistency, incongruity, incompatibility; nonconformity, unorthodoxy, heresy, schism; eccentricity, peculiarity, unconventionality, abnormality, irregularity.
nonconformist, dissenter, rebel, angry young man, separatist, demonstrator, maverick; eccentric, crank; homosexual, queer (*sl.*), gay (*sl.*), lesbian.

adj. unconformable, different, dissimilar, inconsistent, incongruous, incompatible, inappropriate, inapplicable; nonconformist, unorthodox; heretical, dissident, unconventional, eccentric, peculiar, abnormal, irregular, unusual, unfamiliar.

E Time

107 time

n. time, duration, continuance, extent, life, span, season, date.

adj. temporal; dated.

vb. elapse, pass; continue, last; spend time, employ, fill, occupy oneself, use, what do with oneself, while away, idle, fritter, squander; happen, occur, transpire.

adv., prep. during, when, while, whilst, in the course of, throughout, in the process of; meanwhile, in the meantime, in the interim.

see also **109**

108 absence of time

n. timelessness, neverness, nothingness, eternity.

adv. never, at no time, never again, nevermore.

109 period

n. period, era, epoch, time, season, interval, phase, age, generation; term, span, spell, stint, stretch; cycle; second, minute, hour, day, week, fortnight, month, year, leap year, decade, decennium, jubilee, centenary, millenium, aeon.

adj. periodic, seasonal, recurring, recurrent, cyclic, regular.

110 course of time

n. course of time, lapse of time.

vb. elapse, pass, lapse; flow, proceed, run, fly.

see also **109**

111 contingent duration

adv., prep. as long as, provisionally, for the present, for the time being.

112 long duration

n. lifetime, ages, eternity, month of Sundays (*inf.*), prolongation, permanence; endurance.

adj. long-term, long-standing, long-lasting, abiding, lasting, durable, permanent; enduring, steadfast, unyielding, persistent, surviving.

vb. last, endure, continue, stay, persist, remain, abide, never end, prevail, persevere; survive, outlive, outlast, outstay, live on, linger.

113 short duration

n. transience, ephemerality, evanescence, impermanence; brief period, flash in the pan (*inf.*), nine days' wonder (*inf.*).

adj. transient, transitory, brief, temporary, quick, short, short-term, momentary, short-lived; fading, passing, fleeting, cursory, ephemeral, evanescent, impermanent, perishable, before one can say Jack Robinson (*inf.*).

vb. be transient, pass, pass away, fly, fleet, flit, fade, vanish, disappear.

114 endless duration

n. perpetuity, endlessness, eternity, infinity, everlastingness, timelessness, immortality, constancy, endurance.

adj. perpetual, eternal, endless, interminable, continual, unceasing, incessant, unremitting, infinite, everlasting, enduring, around-the-clock, timeless, ageless, immortal, incorruptible, imperishable; perennial.

vb. perpetuate, immortalize, eternalize, preserve, keep alive; never end, go on forever.

adv. always, forever, on and on, perpetually.

115 point of time

n. instantaneousness, suddenness, abruptness; instant, second, moment, flash, jiffy (*inf.*), twinkling, point of time.

adj. instantaneous, immediate, spontaneous, sudden, abrupt, prompt, punctual.

adv. instantaneously, instantly, immediately, at once, directly, forthwith, without delay, promptly, suddenly, abruptly, at the drop of a hat, on the spur of the moment.

116 chronometry

n. chronometry, horology, chronology, timing, timekeeping, dendrochronology; date, day, time; local time, summer time, daylight saving.

timepiece, timekeeper, chronometer, clock, alarm clock, digital clock, watch, wristwatch, digital watch, stopwatch, hourglass, sun-dial, egg-timer; time-signal, pips, siren, hooter; calendar, schedule, timetable, diary, journal, register, almanac, chronicle, annals, log, memoirs.

adj. chronological, horological, temporal, horometrical, chronometrical.

vb. time, date; put the clocks back, put the clocks forward, set the alarm, wind up, keep time, gain, lose; clock in, clock out.

117 anachronism

n. anachronism, wrong date, misdating, mistiming, parachronism, prochronism.

adj. anachronistic, misdated, undated; early, beforehand; late, overdue.

vb. misdate, antedate, predate, postdate.

118 priority

n. priority, antecedence, anteriority, previousness; pre-existence, pre-occurrence; precedent, antecedent, foretaste, preview.

adj. prior, earlier, before, preceding, previous, anterior, past, antecedent, ahead of; pre-existing; one-time, ex-, retired, former; foregoing, above-mentioned, above, aforesaid.

vb. go before, come before, precede, forerun, antecede, herald.

see also **84, 124**

119 posteriority

n. posteriority, succession, subsequence; sequel, follower, successor.

adj. following, subsequent, later, after, coming after, next, posterior; designate, elect, to-be; consequential, resulting.

vb. come after, go after, succeed, ensue, follow, result.

see also **85, 123**

120 present time

n. contemporaneity; present time, present moment, present, the time being, this day and age, modern times, today.

adj. present, contemporary, modern, current, present-day, latest, newest, actual, contemporaneous, existent.

adv. now, at present, at the moment, today, nowadays, right now, at this moment in time.

121 different time

n. different time, not now, other time.

adv. not now, yesterday, earlier, tomorrow, later, sometime, sooner or later, at one time or other, at a different time.

122 synchronism

n. synchronism, simultaneousness, coexistence, concurrence, coincidence, contemporaneity; same age; contemporary, own generation, peers, fellows, year, class, set.

adj. synchronous, contemporary, concurrent, coincident, coexistent, simultaneous, contemporaneous; accompanying.

vb. synchronize, coexist, exist together, coincide; accompany.

adv. at the same time, simultaneously, concurrently, in phrase, in step.

123 future

n. futurity, future, tomorrow, time to come; prospect, fate; the shape of things to come; afterlife, world to come, next world, hereafter.

adj. future, later, coming, to come, approaching, unfolding, at hand; prospective, designate; imminent, impending; likely, expected, inevitable.

vb. lie in the future, be near, draw near, approach; impend, threaten.

adv. tomorrow, in the future, in the course of time, hereafter.

124 past

n. past, history, antiquity, prehistory, archaism; retrospection, memory; olden times, yesterday, good old days (*inf.*).

adj. past, historical, ancient, prehistoric, primitive, proto-; gone, bygone, lost, forgotten, no more; former, late, old, once, one-time, ex-, retired, sometime, erstwhile.

vb. be past, have run its course, have had its day (*inf.*), be a thing of the past.

adv. yesterday, formerly, in the past, ago, of old.

125 newness

n. newness, modernity, renovation, modernization, novelty, innovation.

fad, craze, passing fancy, vogue, fashion, the latest thing (*inf.*), all the rage (*inf.*), the last word (*inf.*), the in-thing (*inf.*); innovator, pioneer, leader, futurist, trendsetter, pacesetter, *avant-garde*, upstart, fledgling.

adj. modern, new, novel, current, topical, recent, original; contemporary, present-day, up-to-the-minute, up-to-date, brand-new, just out, hot off the press (*inf.*); newfangled (*inf.*); untraditional, in fashion, in vogue, stylish, chic, smart, modish, trendy (*inf.*), in (*inf.*), *à la mode*, *avant-garde;* advanced, forward-looking, progressive, ultra-modern, streamlined, futuristic, space-age; convenient, automatic, electronic; fresh, virgin, budding, inexperienced.

vb. modernize, bring up to date, adapt, renew, reissue, republish, refurbish, renovate, streamline, update; innovate.

adv. recently, newly, lately, afresh, anew, of late.

126 oldness

n. oldness, antiquity; obsolescence, extinc-

tion, decay, deterioration, decline; maturity, ripeness; tradition, footsteps; old age, senility, infirmity.

adj. old, archaic, prehistoric, antique, ancient, primitive, primeval, aboriginal, extinct; time-worn, time-honoured, venerable, forgotten, antediluvian, distant, former, unrecorded, of earliest time; old-fashioned, antiquated, obsolete, obsolescent, outmoded, discarded, disused, unstylish, *passé*, out of date, old hat (*inf.*), out of fashion, behind the times, anachronistic, dated, outdated; traditional, handed down, established, customary, Victorian; dilapidated, secondhand, used, decrepit, decayed, faded; patched, mended, in holes, rusty, moth-eaten.

see also 30

127 morning; spring; summer

n. morning, morn, a.m., sunrise, dawn, daybreak, break of day, cockcrow, the small hours, forenoon, matin, matins, aurora; noon, midday, meridian; spring, springtime, springtide, flowering, budding; summer, summertime, summertide, midsummer, Indian summer, St. Luke's summer, St. Martin's summer.

adj. morning; spring, springlike, vernal; summer, summery, aestival.

128 evening; autumn; winter

n. p.m., afternoon, evening, eventide, eve, evensong, vesper, vespers; sunset, sundown, twilight, dusk, dimness, half-light, gloaming, curfew, night, nightfall, nighttime; midnight, witching time of night, dead of night; autumn, fall, harvest; winter, wintertime, wintertide, midwinter.

adj. afternoon, vespertine, evening; crepuscular; night, nocturnal; autumn, autumnal; wintry, winter, brumous.

129 youth

n. youth, youthfulness, young blood, juniority, juvenility; infancy, tender age, childhood, adolescence, puberty, pubescence, boyhood, girlhood, school-going age, teens, boyishness, girlishness, next generation; freshness, salad days, awkward age, growing pains, younger generation, immaturity, inexperience, callowness, greenness, prime, spring, springtime; minority, wardship, nonage, pupilage.

adj. young, youthful, boyish, girlish, childlike, teenage, adolescent, pubescent, in one's teens; formative, budding, flowering, unwrinkled, ageless, tender, developing; childish, unripe, green, callow, awkward, raw, unfledged, immature, inexperienced, puerile,

juvenile; minor, under-age, infant, younger, junior, youngest.
see also 131

130 age

n. age, oldness, old age, senility, second childhood, senescence, seniority, dotage, infirmity; middle age, middle years, older generation; responsibility, experience, wisdom, maturity, caution.

adj. old, aged, elderly, advanced in years, senile, senescent, matured, seasoned, grey, balding, wrinkled, toothless; superannuated; inactive, infirm, debilitated, feeble, enfeebled, doddery, decrepit, moribund, dying, with one foot in the grave; experienced, qualified, expert, respected, venerable; major, senior, older, elder, oldest, eldest, first-born.

vb. age, grow old, decline, progress, advance in years, have seen better days, show one's age; superannuate; mellow, develop, mature.
see also 132

131 infant

n. baby, babe, infant, suckling, mite, toddler, tot, bairn; child, youngster, kid, brat (*sl.*); young person, juvenile, pupil, schoolchild, minor, teenager, adolescent, student; boy, schoolboy, lad, junior, master; young man, youth, stripling, fellow; girl, schoolgirl, young lady, lass, miss.

adj. baby, newborn, childlike; infantile, babyish, childish, puerile, juvenile; boyish, girlish; adolescent, youthful, teenage, pubescent; immature, naive, innocent, spontaneous.

132 veteran

n. old person, elder, senior, retired person, old age pensioner, senior citizen, dependant; veteran, patriarch, old hand (*inf.*), old timer (*inf.*), grand old man, elder statesman; old woman, matriarch.

133 adulthood

n. adulthood, years of discretion, manhood, womanhood, maturity, age of majority, majority.
adult, grown-up, man, woman.

adj. adult, grown-up, manly, womanly, mature, responsible; marriageable.

vb. come of age, grow up, attain majority; mature.
see also 380, 381

134 earliness

n. earliness, primitiveness, anticipation, presentiment, recency, immediacy, punctual-ity, promptness, promptitude, prematurity; foresight, hunch; early riser, early bird (*inf.*).

adj. early, prior, previous, recent, primitive; new, fresh, budding; premature, in advance, precocious, preceding, anticipatory, preparatory, advanced, prevenient; immediate, precipitant, speedy; imminent; punctual, prompt, timely, on time, sharp.

vb. be early, anticipate, foresee, forestall, prepare for; precede, take precedence, get a head start, pre-empt, jump the queue.

135 lateness

n. lateness, belatedness, tardiness, retardation, slowness, dilatoriness, backwardness; late hour, high time, last minute; delay, deferment, postponement, adjournment, discontinuation, suspension, procrastination, cooling-off period, moratorium, respite, days of grace, stay, reprieve, remission, wait and see, filibuster; slow starter, late riser.

adj. late, advanced, tardy, dilatory; too late, overdue, belated, delayed, behind, behindhand; last-minute; unready, unpunctual.

vb. be late, stay up, burn the midnight oil; tarry, be slow, linger, saunter, dawdle, dally, shilly-shally; delay, defer, postpone, procrastinate, retard, stay, adjourn, put off, suspend, withhold, hold back, wait and see, play for time, filibuster; put in cold storage, mothball (*inf.*), put in mothballs (*inf.*), put on ice (*inf.*), shelve.

136 timeliness

n. timeliness, opportuneness, opportunism, expediency, fortuity.
opportunity, chance, occasion, right time; crisis, emergency, turning point, dilemma, eleventh hour, nick of time, moment of truth, hour of decision.

adj. opportune, fortuitous, timely, well-timed, punctual, on time, propitious, auspicious, providential, suitable, expedient, advantageous, convenient; critical, crucial, decisive, momentous, significant, key, urgent.

vb. grasp the opportunity, use to the full, take advantage of, cash in on, exploit, capitalize, make capital out of, opportunize, play on, profit by; hang in the balance.
see also 577, 915

137 untimeliness

n. untimeliness, inopportuness, inexpediency, mistiming; disturbance, interruption, intrusion.

adj. mistimed, ill-timed, untimely, unpunctual, too early, premature, too late; wrong, ill-chosen, improper, untoward, unseemly, intrusive, interrupting, disturbing, inconvenient, disadvantageous, unsuitable, inappropriate, unseasonable, unfavourable, inopportune, inauspicious.

vb. mistime; interrupt, disturb, intrude, break in on (*inf.*); miss an opportunity, let an opportunity slip, miss the boat, fail to exploit.

see also **578, 916**

138 frequency

n. frequency, recurrence, reoccurrence, regularity, constancy, oftenness.

adj. frequent, regular, recurrent, successive, reiterated, rhythmic; common, commonplace, customary, not rare, familiar, habitual, general, expected, usual, periodic; incessant, non-stop, perennial, constant, monotonous, continual, steady.

vb. recur, repeat; go on, continue, occur regularly.

adv. often, frequently, usually, generally, as a rule, commonly, regularly, repeatedly; sometimes, now and again, occasionally, at times, from time to time.

see also **140**

139 infrequency

n. infrequency, rarity, uncommonness, scarcity, intermittence, unpredictability, irregularity.

adj. infrequent, occasional, rare, sparse, scarce, few, few and far between, scanty, sporadic, meagre, precious; unique, single, individual; uncommon, unusual, bizarre; intermittent; casual, chance, incidental.

adv. infrequently, scarcely, hardly, hardly ever, occasionally, uncommonly, now and then, rarely, seldom.

see also **141**

140 regularity

n. regularity, recurrence, periodicity, repetition, frequency; stabilization, evenness, steadiness, constancy; timing, phasing, alternation, oscillation; current, wave, rota, cycle, rotation, swing, circuit, pulsation, beat, rhythm, pulse; routine, daily round; anniversary, birthday, commemoration.

adj. periodical, regular, routine, periodic, systematic, methodical, organized, steady, constant, uniform, serial, cyclic, rotational, pulsating, rhythmic, alternating.

vb. recur, repeat, reiterate, come round again, alternate, undulate, regulate, revolve, throb, beat, pulsate, swing.

adv. periodically, systematically, regularly,

at regular intervals, like clockwork; hourly, daily, weekly, monthly, annually.

see also **138**

141 irregularity

n. irregularity, fitfulness, jerkiness, unsteadiness, inconstancy, unevenness, variability; jerk, fits and starts, spasm, stop, break, bump.

adj. irregular, sporadic, off and on, fitful, jerky, spasmodic, uneven; unsteady, shaky; inconstant, random, fluctuating, faltering, wavering, flickering; capricious, changeable, casual.

vb. fluctuate, come and go.

see also **139**

F Change

142 change

n. change, variation, alteration, modification, adjustment, qualification, transformation, refinement, evolution, alternation; fluctuation, wavering, modulation; exchange, transference, substitution, mutation, permutation, conversion; transition, diversion, deviation; renewal, innovation, novelty, reconstruction, improvisation, reformation, revision, rearrangement, reorganization, readjustment, metamorphosis, vicissitude, transmutation; deterioration, withdrawal, removal.

modifier, changer, converter, transformer, catalyst, agitator, leaven, adapter.

adj. variable, varying, changeable, modifiable, qualifiable, alternating, inconstant, mutable, plastic, transformable, movable, mobile.

vb. change, alter, vary, modify, qualify, transform, adapt, adjust, improvise; exchange, transfer, substitute; turn, shift, veer; convert, commute; renew, revise, rearrange, reorganize, reform, translate, reconstruct, renovate; refine, moderate, temper; evolve; alternate, fluctuate, waver, modulate.

143 permanence

n. permanence, constancy, invariability, continuity, steadiness, stability; immobility, solidness, consistency; durability, endurance; conservatism, *status quo*, traditionalist, conservative, reactionary, die-hard, stick-in-the-mud.

adj. permanent, immovable, unchangeable, changeless, certain, fixed, uninterrupted, unchanging, continual, constant, lasting; enduring, unwavering, abiding; stable, unremitting; strong, robust, firm, steady, steadfast; conservative, traditional, unprogressive, reactionary, conventional; obstinate, stubborn.

vb. stay, remain, abide, persist; stabilize, maintain, preserve, uphold, sustain, support.

144 cessation

n. cessation, discontinuation, discontinuance, expiration, termination, conclusion.

stop, halt, standstill, closure, interruption, suspense, lapse; industrial action, stoppage, shut-down, strike, go-slow, work-to-rule, sit-in, walkout, unofficial strike, wildcat strike, general strike, lock-out; deadlock, confrontation; ceasefire, armistice, truce; rest, pause, holiday, vacation, respite, lull, breathing space, remission, recess; intermission, interlude, interval, interim, interregnum.

vb. cease, terminate, stop, discontinue, desist, refrain, finish, knock off (*inf.*), break up, quit, shut down, close down, shut up shop, call it a day (*inf.*); pack it in (*inf.*), knock it off (*sl.*); halt, check, restrain, put a stop to, arrest, stall, interrupt; strike, down tools, come out, go out, walk out, lock out, picket, boycott; pause, break, take five (*inf.*), rest, relax, let up (*inf.*); fizzle out (*inf*).

see also **89**

145 continuance

n. continuance, continuation, perpetuation, maintenance, persistence, duration, prolongation.

adj. continual, uninterrupted, unbroken, connected, steady, constant, unceasing, incessant, ceaseless, sustained, inexhaustible.

vb. continue, carry on, keep on, go on, maintain, sustain, uphold, keep at it; stay, remain, last, survive, abide; endure, progress, persist, persevere, stay the course.

see also **535**

146 conversion

n. conversion, convertibility, processing, development, change-over, transformation, alteration; regeneration, new birth, rebirth, evangelization; convert, disciple, follower, believer, proselyte, catechumen.

adj. converted, altered, changed, transformed; regenerate, born again.

vb. convert, turn into, alter, transform, transmute; evangelize, proselytize, save, redeem; camouflage, disguise, mask, hide, conceal, obscure; remodel, improve, mend, reconstruct, reshape, reform, mould, metamorphose.

see also **142**

147 reversion

n. reversion, return, regress, regression, reaction, rebound, flashback, boomerang, recoil, backfire, backlash; restoration, restitution, re-establishment, reconditioning, refreshment, rejuvenation, recovery, reopening; atavism, throwback; resurrection, renewal, revival, comeback; reversal, *volte-face*, about-turn, backsliding, apostasy, lapse, relapse.

adj. reverted; atavistic; apostate, degenerate.

vb. revert, go back, return, turn back, reverse; recur, reappear, restore, restitute, reinstate, replace; recoil, rebound; regress, retrogress, throw back; backslide, fall away, lapse, relapse, degenerate.

148 revolution

n. revolution, disaster, *débâcle*, explosion, eruption; *coup*, shake-up, overthrow, upheaval, revolt, rebellion, insurrection, anarchy, plot, subversion.

radical, revolutionary, extremist, fanatic, demonstrator, agitator, rebel, anarchist, guerrilla, freedom fighter, insurrectionist, traitor.

adj. revolutionary, radical, progressive, extreme, thorough, deep, complete, rabid; earth-shaking, catastrophic, cataclysmic, shattering; militant, rebellious, revolting, anarchistic, insurgent, underground, subversive, seditious.

vb. revolutionize, subvert, overthrow, upset, shake up; rise up, revolt.

149 substitution

n. substitution, exchange, transference, alternation, commutation, shift, shuffle, switch, rearrangement, transposition, vicariousness.

substitute, transfer, alternative, replacement, understudy, proxy, ghost-writer, locum, reserve, stand-in, stand-by, relief; deputy, agent, delegate; double, dummy, stopgap, makeshift; scapegoat, whipping boy.

adj. substitutional, alternative, vicarious, reserve, provisional, temporary, makeshift; dummy, mock, imitation.

vb. substitute, exchange, transfer, replace, commute, transpose, shuffle, shift, switch, act for, stand in for, cover for, fill in, relieve, fill in for, put in the place of, ghost, double for, serve in one's stead; take it out on (*inf.*), work off.

adv. instead, in the place of, in lieu.

150 interchange

n. interchange, exchange, transfer, reciprocation, swap, mutuality, interrelation, interchangeability, tit for tat; barter, trade, commerce, correspondence, give and take (*inf.*).

adj. in exchange, mutual, reciprocal, reciprocating, interchangeable, commutable.

vb. interchange, exchange, swap, commute, interact, trade, barter, correspond; give and take (*inf.*).

151 changeableness

n. changeableness, changeability, variability, mutability, irregularity, instability, inconstancy, mobility, fluctuation, vacillation, wavering; fickleness, indecision, unreliability, erraticness, waywardness.

adj. changeable, variable, irregular, inconstant, mobile, vacillating, wavering, fluctuating, volatile, many-sided, versatile, flexible, malleable, adaptable, plastic, unstable, unsteady, protean; fickle, flighty, indecisive, fidgety, capricious, unreliable, erratic, wayward.

vb. vary, range, mutate, chop and change, waver, shift, vacillate, fluctuate, variegate, differ, depart, diverge, dissent.

152 stability

n. stability, immutability, invariability, firmness, permanence, constancy, irreversibility, immobility, immovableness, solidity; regularity; reliability, resoluteness, endurance; stabilization, equilibrium, balance, homeostasis.

fixture, establishment, constant, invariant; rock, pillar; stabilizer, ballast, counterbalance, counterweight, sandbags.

adj. unchangeable, invariable, changeless, stable, constant, steady, immovable, immobile, stationary; unwavering, inflexible, unadaptable; resolute, reliable, steadfast; stereotyped, uniform; fixed, fast, set, sure, established, entrenched, inveterate.

vb. stabilize, fix, set, steady, secure, sustain, support, fasten; balance; establish, entrench, anchor, transfix.

see also 535

153 present events

n. eventuality, incidence; event, occurrence, incident, episode, happening, situation, circumstance, development, chance, proceeding, transaction, phenomenon, adventure, experience, triumph, celebration; affair, matter, concern; predicament, accident, misadventure, misfortune, mishap, calamity, emergency, catastrophe.

adj. happening, current, present, afloat, in the air, in the wind, about, prevailing.

vb. happen, take place, occur, come about, follow, ensue, arrive, transpire, fall on, befall, arise, come up, turn up, crop up; be realized, come off, turn out, feel, undergo, experience, meet.

154 future events

n. prospect, outlook, forecast, prediction, approach, promise; fate, destiny; imminence, threat, menace.

adj. impending, approaching, coming, near, close, forthcoming, imminent; threatening, brewing, ominous, certain, inevitable, inescapable, unavoidable, fateful, destined, fated; in prospect, in store, to come, in the offing, on the horizon.

vb. impend, approach, draw on, near, advance, hover, be in store; loom, threaten, hang over, overshadow, menace; forecast, prognosticate; anticipate, expect.

see also 902

G Causation

155 cause

n. causation, causality, origination, motivation, authorship.

cause, origin, source, root, spring, foundation, seed; beginning, birth, derivation, nativity, genesis; means, basis, grounds, ground, agent, occasion, influence, mainspring, determinant, antecedent; first cause, prime mover, producer, creator, author, originator, inventor, discoverer, founder; motive, inducement, activation; factor, element, rudiment, principle; reason, explanation.

adj. causal, original, determinant; basic, fundamental, primary, radical, initial.

vb. cause, make, create, produce, originate, effect, determine, bring about, provoke, generate, evoke, elicit, induce, call forth, give rise to, arouse, occasion, motivate, suggest, influence, lead to; conduce, contribute to, involve.

156 effect

n. effect, result, consequence, end, outcome, upshot, issue, product; consummation, after-effect, aftermath, repercussion, wake, reaction, backlash, sequel, fruit, harvest, emanation; by-product, spin-off.

adj. caused, consequent, consequential,

resultant, resulting, following, ensuing, subsequent, derivative.

vb. result, follow, ensue, spring from, proceed from, derive from, emanate from, originate in; become of, come of.

157 assignment of cause

n. assignment, attribution, imputation, reference, ascription; association; explanation, theory, hypothesis, rationale.

adj. attributable, assignable, referable, imputable, derivable, culpable; linked, associated; explanatory.

vb. attribute, assign, ascribe, impute, refer, charge, blame, trace, credit with, derive from, lay at; connect, associate, link; explain, account for, solve.

158 chance

n. chance, fortuity, randomness, unpredictability; odds, risk-taking, probability; fate, lot, fortune, luck, good luck, bad luck, pot luck; fluke (*inf.*), gamble.

adj. casual, chance, accidental, coincidental, fortuitous, random, haphazard, unthinking, hit-or-miss, aimless, fluky (*inf.*); unmotivated, inexplicable, unintentional.

vb. chance, fall to one's lot; chance upon, stumble on, venture, happen on, gamble, risk; stand a chance.

adv. by chance, by accident, unexpectedly, unintentionally, fortuitously, randomly, casually, perchance.

see also 553

159 power

n. power, potency, might, strength, energy, vigour, life, liveliness, dynamism; dominance, domination, omnipotence; sway, control, teeth, muscle, influence; ability, capability, skill, potentiality, competence, efficiency, capacity, faculty, efficacy; force, potential, thrust, pressure, horse-power, steam, electricity, juice (*sl.*), gas, nuclear power, solar energy, hydro-electricity; power station, grid, pylon.

adj. powerful, mighty, energetic, vigorous, strong, lively, dynamic, empowered, forceful, dominant, potent; omnipotent, almighty; able, capable, up to (*inf.*), equal to, potential, competent, efficient, effective.

vb. be able, be up to (*inf.*), be capable of, lie in one's power; be powerful, perform, operate, accomplish; empower, confer, enable, power, charge, invest, arm, strengthen, electrify.

see also 161

160 impotence

n. impotence, lifelessness, powerlessness, ineffectuality, ineffectivity, helplessness; inability, incapability, incompetence; unproductiveness, infertility, barrenness; eunuch, gelding.

adj. powerless, unenergetic, unable, incapable, incompetent, inefficient, ineffective, inadequate, disabled, incapacitated, inept; infirm, helpless, unprotected, defenceless; spineless, nerveless, feeble; impotent, sterilized, sterile, barren, infertile, frigid.

vb. not be able, cannot, not find it in oneself to; disable, impair, exhaust, wear down, run down, incapacitate, disarm, unman, paralyze, put out of action, throw a spanner in the works; disqualify, invalidate; castrate, emasculate, spay, geld.

161 strength

n. strength, might, energy, vigour, force, vitality, toughness, stamina, hardness, brawn, muscle; invincibility.

adj. strong, mighty, powerful, forceful, energetic, firm; unyielding, unresisting, persistent; brawny, muscular, stout, hardy, tough, robust, stalwart, strapping, burly, beefy, big, solid, hefty, virile, athletic; secure, durable.

vb. strengthen, fortify, confirm, reinforce, establish, substantiate, empower, energize, stimulate, build up, brace, refresh, invigorate.

see also 535, 537

162 weakness

n. weakness, feebleness, frailty, faintness, fragility, flimsiness, delicacy, tenderness; infirmity, debility; effeminacy, femininity.

weakling, coward, cry-baby, sissy (*sl.*), pansy (*sl.*).

adj. weak, powerless, feeble, helpless, delicate, puny, frail; fragile, flimsy, brittle, insubstantial, makeshift, unsteady; effeminate, womanly; weak-minded, spineless, anaemic (*inf.*), faint-hearted, insipid, diluted, wishy-washy (*inf.*); worn, rotten, decrepit.

vb. faint, sicken, languish, crumble, decline; weaken, exhaust, enfeeble, impoverish, debilitate, enervate, disable, handicap; dilute, water down, blunt, sap; fade, give way, fizzle out (*inf.*).

163 production

n. production, productivity, output, performance, through-put; foundation, manufacture, establishment, construction, fabrication, processing; propagation, generation, procreation, fertility, reproduction, breeding, copulation.

product, creation, work, article, piece, goods, merchandise, handiwork, fruit, harvest, produce, yield, result, opus; edifice, building, structure, erection, invention, concoction, brain-child (*inf.*), baby (*sl.*), thing (*sl.*).

adj. productive, generative, creative, manufacturing; fruitful, rich, prolific, fertile; pregnant, expecting, with child, with young, in the family way (*inf.*), in the club (*sl.*).

vb. produce, create, make, manufacture, put together, make up, fabricate, construct, build; devise, compose; furnish, effect, perform, return, render, provide; invent, concoct, cook up; carve, chisel; yield, blossom, flower; reproduce, generate, procreate, propagate, multiply, conceive, beget, breed.

164 destruction

n. destruction, annihilation, elimination, liquidation, extirpation, disintegration, demolition, eradication, obliteration, nullification, abolition, dissolution, suppression; slaughter; waste, overthrow, subversion, desolation, havoc, wreckage, sabotage, ruin, ravage, downfall, collapse, ruination.

adj. destructive, hurtful, troublesome, harmful, detrimental, ruinous, deadly, fatal, lethal, poisonous, venomous, toxic, internecine, shattering, annihilative.

vb. destroy, terminate, nullify, abolish, suppress, eradicate, wipe out, blot out, obliterate, wipe off the face of the earth, dissolve; annihilate, eliminate, liquidize, extirpate, exterminate, atomize, pulverize, decimate, decapitate; demolish, break, dismantle, knock down, pull down; crush, overthrow, overturn; blitz, bombard, smash, shatter, mutilate, undo; damage, lay waste, devastate, raze, plunder, ruin, pillage, ravage, despoil, sack.

be destroyed, perish, disintegrate, deteriorate, decay, crumble, go to rack and ruin.

see also 370

165 reproduction

n. reproduction, reconstruction, remaking, renovation, reforming; regeneration, resurrection; rediscovery, revival, renaissance; duplication, reduplication, reprinting.

adj. reproductive, regenerative, renascent.

vb. reproduce, reconstruct, rebuild, remake, redo, refashion, remould, reform, renovate, renew, revive, rediscover, regenerate, repeat; propagate, multiply, proliferate, duplicate, reprint, copy.

166 producer

n. producer, creator, maker, instigator, mover, manufacturer, constructor, builder, architect, composer, author, writer, originator, inventor, discoverer.

167 destroyer

n. destroyer, breaker; anarchist, terrorist, desperado, gunman, murderer; disrupter, ravager, vandal, defacer, wrecker, iconoclast, nihilist, abolitionist.

plague, pestilence, moth, locust, erosion, rust, cancer, poison, virus, fungus, mildew, blight; demolition expert, demolisher.

see also 370

168 productiveness

n. productiveness, productivity, generative capacity; prolificness, fruitfulness, fertility, proliferation, fecundity; lushness, luxuriance, exuberance, profusion, richness, abundance, wealth, plenty, horn of plenty, cornucopia, bounty, plethora, hotbed, warren; prosperity, boom.

adj. productive, fruitful, prolific, profuse, fertile, rich, fecund; bounteous, spawning, abundant, plenty, copious, lush, luxurious, fulsome, exuberant, booming; prosperous, wealthy.

vb. be fruitful, blossom, prosper, thrive, flourish, proliferate, grow, swarm.

see also 163

169 unproductiveness

n. unproductiveness, stagnation, unprofitability, incapacity, barrenness, desolateness, infertility; sterilization, contraception; slump, recession, depression, austerity.

adj. unproductive, unprofitable, fruitless, profitless; desolate, barren, poor, unfruitful; ineffectual, ineffective; infertile, unbearing, sterilized, sterile, impotent, frigid, childless, celibate.

vb. stagnate, vegetate, fail; exhaust; castrate, emasculate, spay, geld.

170 parenthood

n. parenthood, ancestry, origin, genealogy, parentage, line, lineage; fatherhood, paternity; parent, progenitor, procreator, begetter; father, dad, daddy, pop (*sl.*); motherhood, maternity; mother, mum, mummy.

adj. generative, procreative, life-giving; ancestral, genealogical; family, familial; parental, paternal, fatherly, maternal, motherly.

171 offspring

n. offspring, issue, progeny, posterity; lineage, generation, next generation; adoption; descent, sonship, filiation; family, child, son, daughter; heir, descendant; bastard.

adj. descended, familiar, lineal; filial, daughterly; bastard, illegitimate; adopted.

172 operation

n. operation, agency, action, execution, application, performance, running, management, conduct, function, process, instrumentality, means.

adj. operative, active, functioning, in operation, in action, in force; live, running, working, effective; executive, operational, functional, agential.

vb. operate, function, work, go, move, run; act, behave, perform, handle; produce, bring about.

see also **564, 565**

173 vigour

n. vigour, energy, power, dynamism, vehemence, strength, lustiness, élan, dash, verve, vitality, get-up-and-go (*inf.*), go (*inf.*), zest, pep, bounce, zip; drive, push, thrust, enterprise, initiative, aggression.

stimulant, invigorator, activator, incentive, stimulus, fillip, pick-me-up, catalyst, booster, drug, shot.

adj. vigorous, powerful, potent, dynamic, strong, vehement, intense, lively, brisk, energetic; enterprising; aggressive, pushy (*inf.*), self-assertive; stimulating, invigorating, activating.

vb. invigorate, energize, activate, strengthen, fortify, reinforce, stimulate, animate, enliven, vitalize, drive, push, intensify.

see also **159, 161**

174 inertness

n. inertness, inertia, inactivity, motionlessness, lifelessness, immobility, dullness, passivity, indolence, idleness, lethargy, listlessness.

adj. inert, lifeless, immobile, motionless, dead, inactive, idle, languid, torpid, lethargic, listless, indolent, passive, slow, still, pacific, dull, sluggish, dormant.

vb. slumber, languish, idle, stagnate, vegetate.

see also **267**

175 violence

n. violence, force, boisterousness, turbulence, destructiveness; outburst, outbreak, uproar, explosion, eruption, disruption, clash, clammer, assault, onslaught; disorder, disturbance, turmoil, ferment, fury, frenzy, tumult; storm, blizzard, gale, hurricane, tornado, thunderstorm, hailstorm, cloudburst, tempest.

savage, barbarian, brute, beast, monster, animal, maniac, fiend, terrorist, bully, ruffian.

adj. violent, extreme, severe; vehement, forceful, boisterous, turbulent; rough, raging, wild, stormy, furious, outrageous, rampageous, destructive; aggressive; brutal, brutish, savage, fierce, barbarous.

vb. run wild, rush, mob; erupt, explode, blast, break out; roar, fume, boil, seethe; incite, stir up, whip up, lash; force, coerce; provoke.

176 moderation

n. moderation, assuagement, alleviation, pacification, placating, soothing; reduction; gentleness, calmness, mildness; control.

moderator, balm, consolation, relief, cure, tranquillizer, restraint.

adj. moderate, modest, reasonable; calm, gentle, tranquil; restrained, temperate.

vb. be moderate, be at peace, keep a low profile; keep a happy medium; moderate, restrain, temper, alleviate, reduce, decrease, abate, tone down, cushion, soften the blow, mitigate, mollify, soothe, relieve, console, assuage, pacify, placate, still, quieten; relax, let up.

see also **834**

177 influence

n. influence, weight, dominance, power, control, force, pressure, sway, authority, pull (*inf.*); significance; prestige, reputation.

adj. influential, weighty, dominant, powerful, forceful, controlling, prevailing, authoritative, important, significant, momentous; prominent, reputable.

vb. influence, determine, affect, convince, persuade, sway, compel, turn, dominate, govern, control, lobby, bring pressure to bear, put pressure on, carry weight with, pull strings (*inf.*), get in with (*inf.*).

see also **420**

178 tendency

n. tendency, trend, direction, bent, drift, aim; tenor, thrust, spirit; inclination, bias, leaning, propensity, proneness, predisposition, predilection, penchant, fondness, liking, preference, weakness, proclivity.

adj. tending, conducive, predisposed.

vb. tend, lean, incline, drift, predispose, point to, aim, gravitate towards.

179 liability

n. liability, liableness, susceptibility, amenability; subjection, responsibility.

adj. liable, apt, inclined, disposed, prone, likely to, subject to; answerable, responsible, amenable.

vb. be liable, run the risk of, incur, fall on, be subject to, succumb to, fall prey to, expose oneself to, lay oneself open to.

180 concurrence

n. concurrence, collaboration, cooperation, partnership, working together, joint action; union, concert.

adj. concurrent, combined, allied, united, joint, cooperative; mutual.

vb. concur, cooperate, collaborate, work together, unite, combine; agree, harmonize, accord.

see also **639**

181 counteraction

n. counteraction, opposition, polarity, antagonism, contradiction; retroaction, offsetting, neutralization; friction, resistance, drag, counterweight, cross-current, countermeasure; antidote, cure, medicine, relief, preventive, antibiotic, injection.

adj. counter, counteractive, neutralizing, retarding.

vb. counteract, work against, militate against, run counter to; neutralize, cancel out, invalidate, hinder, prevent, frustrate; interfere, oppose, contradict; drag; counterbalance, countervail.

II Space

A Space in general

182 indefinite space

n. space, expanse, extent, expansion, span, area, surface; range, scope, compass, reach, sweep, stretch, gamut, spread; room, open space, clearance, elbow-room, breathing space, latitude, margin, leeway.

adj. spatial; spacious, ample, extensive, roomy, capacious, vast, expansive, deep, broad, wide, long, far-reaching, widespread.

vb. reach, extend, spread, stretch, sweep, flow, range, encompass, span; open, expand, widen.

183 definite space

n. region, area, district, zone; patch, section, sector, quarter, square.

territory, country, state, kingdom, realm, principality, duchy, province, county, shire, community, city, capital, centre, borough, town, village, hamlet; constituency, ward; diocese, parish; conurbation, metropolitan county, metropolitan district, metropolis, suburb, suburbia; locality, surroundings, environment, neighbourhood, environs, locale, milieu.

adj. territorial, regional; provincial, local, municipal, urban, suburban, rural; parochial, insular.

184 limited space

n. place, spot, position, point, stand, locus, corner; enclosure, field, compound, pen, close, sty, pound, paddock, plot, zone, square, quadrangle, yard, patio, precinct; niche, groove, socket.

185 situation

n. situation, position, location, station, setting, site, place, scene, scenery; whereabouts, bearings.

adj. situated, located, placed, positioned, sited, set, situate.

vb. be situated, be, be found, lie, be there, stand, sit, be located.

186 location

n. location, position, site, place, seat, station, locus, stand, scene, placing, placement, emplacement; encampment, mooring, lodging.

adj. located, positioned, entrenched, installed, settled, encamped.

vb. locate, position, establish, determine, set, place, unearth, discover, search out, come across, find; park, encamp, set up, install, settle, entrench, camp, moor, lodge.

187 displacement

n. displacement, dislocation, derangement, misplacement, shift, unloading, unpacking; loss, mislaying.

adj. displaced, disturbed; dislocated, uprooted, homeless, rootless; out of place, uncomfortable.

vb. displace, disarrange, disturb, confuse; dislodge, dislocate, disestablish, unseat, uproot, unsettle, derail; shift, move, remove, replace, transpose, transport; discharge, unload, unpack, extract, withdraw, evacuate, vacate; misplace, lose, mislay; feel out of place.

188 presence

n. presence, attendance, participation; occupancy, residence, inhabitance, habitation; ubiquity, omnipresence.

adj. present, in attendance, attendant, resident; available, at one's disposal, at hand, ready, on call, on tap.

vb. be present, be there, be, be around, kick around (*inf.*); attend, visit; haunt, hang around (*inf.*), frequent; live, inhabit, occupy, reside; appear, make an appearance, turn up, show up (*inf.*), present oneself.

189 absence

n. absence, disappearance, non-appearance; absenteeism, non-attendance, truancy, defection, desertion; non-residence, inexistence; emptiness, vacuity, vacuum, bareness, void, loss, vacancy; lack, need, deficiency.

adj. absent, not here, away, missing, lost, out, not in, elsewhere, not at home, moved, removed, vanished, disappeared; wanting, lacking, minus, unavailable, omitted; empty, vacant, bare, vacuous, unoccupied, uninhabited.

vb. be absent, stay away, be missing, lack, want; absent oneself, take no part in, play truant, play hooky (*sl.*), take French leave.

190 inhabitant

n. inhabitant, native, national; citizen, resident, house-dweller, householder; tenant, lodger, paying guest, incumbent, boarder, occupier, squatter; tax-payer, commuter, voter; city-dweller, townsman, town-dweller, suburbanite; denizen; population, populace.

settler, colonist, pioneer; immigrant, foreigner, guest worker; aborigine, autochthon, primitive, ancient.

adj. native, vernacular, common, popular, national, indigenous, domestic, home, local, domesticated, naturalized, aboriginal.

191 habitation

n. habitation, abode, habitat, accommodation, dwelling, residence, residency, domicile, establishment.

house, address; mansion, country house, hall, lodge, grange, manor, castle, villa, chalet, cottage, bungalow; flat, apartment, suite, maisonette, pad (*sl.*), penthouse, bedsitter, block of flats, tenement, mews, skyscraper, high-rise flats; shelter, hut, shanty; home, fireside, hearth, homestead; lodgings, rooms, quarters, billet, berth, barrack, camp, digs (*inf.*), diggings (*inf.*).

inn, hotel, guest house, boarding house, bed and breakfast, hostel, motel, pension; public house, pub (*inf.*), local (*inf.*), tavern, hostelry, club; bar.

restaurant, café, cafeteria, snack bar, buffet, canteen, refreshment room, tea-room, teashop, coffee-bar, ice-cream parlour, takeaway; pull-up.

vb. live, dwell, inhabit, people, populate; settle, colonize; reside, abide, stay, visit, sojourn, stop (*inf.*); settle down, take up residence, put down roots; occupy, rent, lodge, keep, squat.

192 contents

n. contents, items, pieces, ingredients, parts, elements, constituents, components; equipment, material, implements, accessories, articles; load, cargo, freight, stuffing.

vb. load, charge, store, freight, ship, weight, pile, mass, take on, pack.

193 container

n. container, receptacle, holder, cover, envelope; depository, reservoir; packet, package, parcel; bag, sack, purse, wallet, pouch, case, suitcase, trunk, briefcase, grip; box, carton, tin, can, chest, coffer, locker, capsule, canister, crate, bin, hopper, bunker, granary, basket, hamper, pannier; pot, jug, glass, beaker, cup, bucket, pail, bowl, plate, vessel, jar, pitcher, urn, basin, boat, crock, vase; bottle, flask, flagon; cauldron, vat; cistern.

B Dimensions

194 size

n. size, proportions, dimension, measurement, distance, area, extent, mass, weight, volume, capacity; largeness, greatness, hugeness, bigness, enormity, vastness, amplitude, immensity, capaciousness, solidness, bulkiness, corpulence, plumpness, obesity, fleshiness, stoutness.

giant, monster, colossus, leviathan, whale.

adj. big, large, great, huge, enormous, vast, jumbo; fat, obese, stout, plump, podgy, corpulent, fleshy, beefy, pot-bellied; overgrown, larger-than-life; bulky, heavy, solid.

see also 32

195 littleness

n. littleness, shortness, smallness, minuteness, tininess, slightness, scantiness, exiguity, diminutiveness, brevity.

dwarf, pigmy, midge, midget; atom, particle; reduction, miniature.

adj. little, small, tiny, slight, miniature, limited, puny; dwarfed, stunted, squat, dumpy; minute, microscopic, diminutive, atomic, infinitesimal, wee.

see also 33

196 expansion

n. expansion, increase, growth, spread, enlargement, augmentation, extension, supplementation, reinforcement, development, escalation, elaboration, amplification, intensification; dilation; inflation.

adj. expanded, expansive, dilated, stretched, swollen, tumescent.

vb. expand, grow, spread, increase, develop, boost, enlarge, blow up, extend, augment, supplement, reinforce, escalate, elaborate, amplify, intensify, magnify; dilate, distend, let out, gather, swell, bloat, stretch, protract, inflate.

197 contraction

n. contraction, reduction, lessening, decrease, shortening, abridgment, curtailment, compression, confinement, narrowing; shrinkage, constriction, recession, deflation; compressor, roller, constrictor.

adj. contracted, shrunken, shrivelled, astringent, wizened.

vb. contract, weaken, lessen, reduce, decrease, decline, abate, subside, dwindle; curtail, abridge, shorten; shrink, shrivel, wrinkle; constrict, confine, compress, squeeze, pinch, nip.

198 distance

n. distance, length, reach, extent, range, space, way, mileage; horizon, skyline, background; farness, remoteness, back of beyond, world's end, outpost, foreign parts, outskirts, limit; aloofness, reserve.

adj. distant, far, far-away, far-flung, far-off, furthest, farthest, furthermost, long-distance, long-range, out of range, out of sight, ultimate, hindmost; remote, inaccessible, out-of-the-way, God-forsaken; unapproachable, aloof.

vb. distance, outstrip, outpace, outrun, outspeed; keep one's distance, keep out of the way of, keep away from.

adv. far, away, at a distance, to the ends of the earth, to the back of beyond; out of reach, out of range, out of bounds.

199 nearness

n. closeness, proximity, vicinity; adjacency, juxtaposition, contiguity.

near place, foreground, neighbourhood, locality; close quarters, close range, short step, stone's throw, earshot, spitting distance, hair's breadth.

adj. near, close, nearest, nearby; local, neighbouring; adjacent, adjoining, next; short-distance, short-range; intimate.

vb. be near, approach, approximate; adjoin, abut, connect, border, neighbour; juxtapose.

adv. nearby, in the neighbourhood, locally; at close quarters, at hand, close at hand; within hearing, within range, within earshot.

nearly, almost, approximately, virtually, practically, nigh; tantamount to, to all intents and purposes, substantially, in effect, all but.

200 interval

n. interval, space, separation, clearance, margin, leeway, gap, hole, ditch, cleft, break, crack, chink, rift, fault, passage, pass, gorge, ravine, gulf, chasm, valley, leap, interstice, interspace.

vb. space, keep apart, separate, split, intervene, interspace.

201 contact

n. contact, juxtaposition, contiguity, tangency, junction, connection, meeting, touching.

adj. contiguous, in contact, tangential.

vb. contact, touch, meet, brush, graze, kiss; adjoin, abut, border; juxtapose, bring together; unify.

202 length

n. length, space, measure, span, reach, extent; line, mark, stroke, strip, row, file, string, channel; longness, linearity, longimetry, linear measure; lengthening, extension, prolongation, elongation.

adj. long, lengthy, extensive; high, tall, lofty; lengthened, extended, outstretched, elongated, stretching, drawn out, long drawn out, protracted, enlarged; interminable, limitless, boundless, unending.

vb. be long, stretch out; lengthen, extend, stretch, elongate, draw out, prolong, spin out, protract, enlarge, expand.

203 shortness

n. shortness, briefness, brevity, abridgment, curtailment, reduction, shortening.

adj. short, small, low, slight, tiny, little, stunted, dwarf, compact, square, dumpy, stubby, chunky, thickset; curt, concise, succinct, terse.

vb. shorten, abbreviate, abridge, condense, abstract, summarize, telescope, epitomize, concentrate, boil down; curtail, cut back, truncate, slash; contract, reduce; cut down, shave, prune, shear, trim, strip, clip, nip, pare, whittle, crop, stunt.

204 breadth; thickness

n. breadth, broadness, width, wideness,

expanse, latitude, amplitude; bore, calibre, diameter, girth; thickness, plumpness, density, solidity, crassitude; bulk, mess, body.

adj. broad, wide, extended, large, spacious, extensive, roomy, bulky, massive, full, thick, thickset, stout, compact, squat, dumpy, chunky, stubby.

vb. broaden, widen, thicken, fatten.

205 narrowness; thinness

n. narrowness, confinement, restriction, contraction, thinness, slimness, emaciation, leanness, tenuity, shallowness, delicacy; neck, strait, narrows, bottleneck.

adj. narrow, confined, limited, restrained, close; thin, slender, slim, meagre, lanky, lean, threadlike, fine, delicate, skinny, scraggy, weedy, emaciated, bony, spindly, flimsy; wasted, withered, haggard, shrivelled, wizened.

vb. make narrow, taper, confine, straiten; make thin, attenuate, compress; slim, reduce weight, lose weight, take off weight, diet, go on a diet, bant, watch one's weight, starve; shrink, contract.

206 layer

n. layer, stratum, thickness, bed, course, band, substratum, fold, overlap, overlay; row, tier, level, class, zone, storey, floor; coat, coating, ply, seam, laminate, lamina, sheet, slab, foil, panel, slate, plate, scale, flake, squama; lamination, stratification.

adj. layered, laminated, laminate, flaky, scaly, squamous, laminar, lamellar, lamellate, lamelliform, lamellose, laminose.

vb. laminate, layer, overlay, overlap, cover, stratify, scale, flake; veneer.

207 filament

n. filament, wire, thread, cord, strand, string, rope, cable, twine, twist, wisp, lock, shred, hair, whisker, fibre, tendril, eyelash, gossamer; sinew, tendon; strip, tape, band, ribbon, belt, sash, bandage, scarf, strap.

adj. fibrous, threadlike, wiry, stringy, hairy, capillary, sinewy, tendinous.

208 height

n. height, elevation, altitude; loftiness, highness, tallness, stature; uplands, hill, mountain, rise, slope, escarpment, fell, moor; tower, spire, steeple, mast, skyscraper, pillar, column; summit, top.

adj. high, giant, towering, soaring, elevated, sky-high; multi-storey, high-rise; tall, lanky; eminent, distinguished, sublime, exalted, lofty.

vb. tower, soar, extend above, mount, look over, look out on, overlook, command, dominate, overshadow.

adv. high, up, aloft.

209 lowness

n. lowness, depression, netherness, debasement; lowlands, valley, hollow; depths, floor.

adj. low, low-lying, depressed, sunken, nether; squat, crouched; underlying; lesser, inferior.

vb. be low, lie low, crouch, squat, grovel; lower, depress, debase, sink.

adv. under, underneath, beneath, below, down; underfoot, underground.

210 depth

n. depth, lowness, profundity; drop, depression, bottom, abyss, gorge, pit, space, charm, hollow, trench, mine, chamber, ravine; deeps.

adj. deep, low, profound; deep-seated, deep-rooted; bottomless, fathomless; sunken, buried, immersed; submerged, underwater, deep-sea; subterranean, underground; yawning, gaping.

vb. deepen, hollow, dig, excavate, scrape out, sink, plunge.

adv. deeply, out of one's depth.

211 shallowness

n. shallowness, superficiality; shallow, shoal; covering, veneer, gloss, façade, surface.

adj. shallow, superficial, surface, skin-deep; cosmetic; light, inconsiderable, cursory, slight.

vb. skim, brush, touch on, scratch the surface.

212 summit

n. summit, top, peak, apex, zenith, pinnacle, tip, vertex, acme; consummation, maximum, limit, climax; crown, head, crest, brow, cap, spire.

adj. top, topmost, uppermost, highest, maximal, tip-top; apical, acmic, zenithal; head, capital.

vb. crown, top, tip, head, cap; culminate.

213 base

n. base, root, foundation, support, prop, stand, stay, pier, rest, bottom, basement, floor, basin, substratum, bed, channel, ground, understructure, shaft, groundwork; foot, toe, pedestal.

adj. bottom, undermost, fundamental, basic, underlying.

214 being vertical

n. verticality, uprightness, perpendicularity, erectness, plumbness, straightness, sheerness; steep, cliff, precipice.

adj. vertical, perpendicular, upright, erect, upstanding, plumb, on end, straight up; steep.

vb. be vertical, stick up, rise; make vertical, erect, raise, elevate.

215 being horizontal

n. horizontality, planeness, flatness, evenness; level, plane.

adj. horizontal, plane, level, even, flush; prostrate, prone, supine, recumbent.

vb. be horizontal, lie down, recline, repose; flatten, level, even out, smooth, plane, squash, prostrate, roll out, straighten.

216 hanging

n. pendency, suspension, hanging; pendant, locket, earring; curtain, hangings; pendulum, stalactite.

adj. hanging, suspended, pendent, dangling, drooping, swaying, pendulous, stalactitic, overhanging.

vb. hang, suspend, fall, hover, float, poise, dangle, drape; droop, sag, swing, sway, oscillate, flap.

217 support

n. support, sustenance, maintenance, reinforcement, back-up; supporter, guide, backing, stiffener, strengthener, sustainer; foundation, base, carriage, bearing, undercarriage, underframe, chassis, bogie, truck; stilt, stay, mainstay, buttress, pole, post, prop, stake, boom, column, pillar, corner-stone, pile, timber, brace, beam, rafter, girder, strut, joist; breakwater, pier, wall; splint, crutch, truss; back, rest, headrest, backrest, backbone; wedge, chock; pivot, lever, hinge, axis, fulcrum; stand, board, table, seat, saddle, cushion, pillow; shelf, ledge, rack; backer, provider, patron.

adj. supporting, sustaining.

vb. support, hold up, prop, sustain, maintain, carry, bear, keep up; bolster, shore, brace, stay, truss, underpin, undergird, back, buoy up, shoulder; uphold, establish, promote, advance, further, encourage, confirm, strengthen, corroborate, back up, stand by, stick by (*inf.*), stand up for, stand behind, stick up for (*inf.*).

see also **636**

218 parallelism

n. parallelism, equidistance, coextension; likeness, correspondence, similarity, affinity; parallelogram; parallelepiped.

adj. parallel, equidistant, not meeting, not converging, coextensive; corresponding, similar, uniform.

vb. parallel, correspond, be equal; match, equate, compare.

219 being oblique

n. obliqueness, obliquity, skewness, curvature, asymmetry; curve, bend, twist, squint, divergence, diagonal; slope, inclination, slide, acclivity, decline, declivity.

adj. oblique, inclined, leaning, angled, skew, askew, skew-whiff (*inf.*), asymmetrical, awry, crooked, askance; sloping, upward, acclivitous, downward, declivitous; divergent, sideways, slanted, bent, curved, twisted, contorted; cross-wise, diagonal, transverse.

vb. incline, lean, slope, tilt, angle, bend, curve, twist, warp; diverge, deviate, slant.

220 inversion

n. inversion, transposition, reversion, reversal; palindrome, about-turn, *volte-face*; upset, capsizal, somersault.

adj. inverted, inverse, opposite, upside-down, back-to-front, topsy-turvy.

vb. invert, transpose, rearrange, exchange, reverse, revert, put the cart before the horse (*inf.*); turn over, overturn, overthrow, turn upside down, stand on its head, tip, topple, tilt, capsize, keel over, somersault; turn inside out.

221 crossing

n. crossing, junction, intersection, confluence, crossroads, crossover; cross, crux, crucifix, cruciform, swastika; network, system, intercommunication; wickerwork, lattice, grid, grill, web, net, netting, mesh, textile, fabric, weave, loom, plait.

vb. cross, intersect, interlink, cut, pass across, mesh, weave, loom, knit, sew, plait, twist, interlace, spin, twine, intertwine, interlock, tangle, entangle.

222 being exterior

n. exteriority, extraneousness, externality, outwardness; outside, exterior, surface, top, front, face, appearance, façade, covering.

adj. exterior, outside, external, outward, outer, outermost, outlying; extrinsic, foreign.

vb. be outside; externalize, extrapolate, project, objectify, embody.

see also **825**

223 being interior

n. interiority, internality, inwardness; inside, interior; substance, contents, heart, centre, soul.

adj. interior, inside, internal, inward, inner,

innermost; intrinsic, inborn, innate; central, integral; inland.

vb. be inside; internalize.

see also 5, 224

224 centrality

n. centrality, centralization; centre, middle, bull's eye; focus, concentration, convergence; nucleus, core, heart, hub, nub, gist, kernel, marrow, pith.

adj. central, centre, middle, inner, focal, pivotal.

vb. centre, centralize, concentrate, focus, converge, draw, attract.

see also 96

225 covering

n. covering, superimposition, cover, lid, flap, box, wrapping; ceiling, roof, shelter, dome, awning, tent, marquee, tarpaulin, canopy, mask, hood, shade, film, blind, umbrella, parasol, sunshade, sheath; sheet, blanket, robe, carpet, rug, mat; coating, varnish, paint, veneer, lacquer, glaze, enamel, wash, polish, stain, distemper, gloss; skin, peel, shell, rind, coat, husk, hull, pod, jacket, integument, tegument.

adj. covered, sheltered, hooded, wrapped, enveloped, veiled, varnished, painted, surfaced.

vb. cover, put on, lay over, protect, shield, shelter, wrap, envelop, enshroud, enclose, veil, superimpose, superpose; roof, carpet, pave, paper; coat, surface, varnish, paint, plate, gloss, glaze, spray, veneer, wax; mask, hide, conceal.

226 lining

n. lining, insulation, interlining; inner surface, inside; filling, stuffing, wadding, padding, quilting, inlay.

vb. line, insulate, interline, inlay, stuff, wad, pad, fill, quilt, reinforce, overlay, face, encrust.

227 dressing

n. dressing, toilet; dress, clothing, wardrobe, outfit, vesture, garb, gear, guise, raiment, apparel, attire; clothes, garment, vestment, costume, suit; uniform, livery.

adj. dressed, well-dressed, dressed-up, clad.

vb. dress, clothe, turn out, deck out (*inf.*), equip, fit out; wear, have on, be dressed in; put on, get dressed, don, slip on, throw on, assume; dress up, get dressed up, smarten oneself up; change into; wrap up.

228 undressing

n. undressing, divestment; bareness, undress, nakedness, nudism, nudity, naturism, *déshabillé*, stripping, striptease; nude, nudist, naturist; baldness, alopecia, shaving, tonsure.

adj. bare, exposed, unveiled, uncovered, unprotected; revealing, *décolleté*; undressed, naked, nude, stark naked, stripped, in one's birthday suit (*inf.*), in the altogether (*inf.*), starkers (*sl.*); bald, hairless, bald-headed, balding, shaven, tonsured, shining, smooth; threadbare, denuded.

vb. uncover, expose, unveil, reveal; remove, take off, cast off; undress, unclothe, strip, disrobe, divest; pluck, peel, pare, shed, bare, skin, flay, scalp, shell, stone, excoriate, decorticate; denude, ravage.

229 being around

n. environment, ambience, circumstances, surroundings; circumjacence; scene, *milieu*, background, setting, habitat, situation; atmosphere, climate; environs, suburbs, vicinity.

adj. environmental, ambient, surrounding, background, situational.

vb. surround, circle, enclose, close in, envelop, girdle, encompass.

adv., prep. around, about.

see also 8

230 being between

n. interposition, intermediacy, intercurrence, intervention, interruption, interjection, interpolation; mediation, intercession; partition, wall, watershed, fence, hurdle; insert, inset, wedge.

adj. intermediary, intermediate, intervening.

vb. place between, mediate, interpose; insert, intersperse; interrupt, interject, intervene.

prep. between, among.

see also 653

231 circumscription

n. circumscription, encircling, circumnavigation; limitation, demarcation, boundary, restriction.

vb. circumscribe, encircle, ring, encompass, surround, circumambulate, circumnavigate, circumvent; surround; limit, restrict, bound, mark off, confine.

232 outline

n. outline, perimeter, periphery, outside, circumference, circuit, border, boundary, contour; sketch, skeleton, silhouette, profile, framework, tracing, delineation.

vb. outline, sketch, trace, delineate.

233 edge

n. edge, extremity, end, limit, verge; border, frontier, boundary; threshold, brink, brim, rim, side, corner, point, tip, margin, skirt; edging, skirting, fringe, hem.

vb. border, verge, edge, skirt; rim, hem, margin, fringe.

234 enclosure

n. enclosure, confinement; envelope, wrapping; area, ground, pitch, arena; plot, court, yard, garden, park; cell, prison, dungeon, den; pen, cage, pound, aviary, coop, warren.

fence, wire, wall, hedge, fencing, paling, rail, railing, balustrade, barrier, ditch, moat, trench, ha-ha.

vb. enclose, envelop, wrap, enfold, confine, contain, blockade, shut in, shut up, lock up, fence, impound, hedge in, hem in; package, parcel; bottle; jail, imprison.

235 limit

n. limit, end, utmost, extremity, destination, terminus, conclusion; limitation, delimitation, restriction, definition, control; hurdle, barrier, frontier, boundary, border, borderline; threshold, upper limit, ceiling; demarcation line, mark, fringe, edge.

adj. limited, set, defined.

vb. limit, set, settle, define, delimit, demarcate, bound, confine, restrict, draw the line at, curb.

236 front

n. front, frontage, exterior, façade, anterior, foreground, face, head, forehead, vanguard, front line; visage, countenance, physiognomy; semblance.

adj. front, forward, fore, foremost, frontal, frontmost, head, obverse, anterior, leading, advance.

vb. face, front, look out on, border; head, lead; meet, confront, encounter, come face to face with.

adv. in advance, ahead; in the foreground.

237 rear

n. rear, back, tail, end, reverse, posterior, backside, bottom, dorsum; wake, rearguard; background, hinterland, backstage.

adj. rear, back, hind, tail, posterior, after, terminal, final, bottom, dorsal, backmost, hindmost, rearmost, background, backstage.

vb. be behind, follow, back on to; bring up the rear.

adv. at the rear, behind, in the background.

238 sidedness

n. sidedness, laterality; juxtaposition, adjacency; side, hand, flank, shoulder.

adj. side, lateral, sidelong, sidewise, sideways, flanking; adjacent.

vb. be side by side, flank, skirt; juxtapose.

adv. laterally, sideways, abreast, alongside, side by side.

239 being opposite

n. opposition, contraposition, polarity; opposite, converse, reverse, contrary, contrast, contradiction, antipode, antipole.

adj. opposite, contrary, opposing, contradictory.

vb. be opposite, oppose, confront, face.

adv., prep. opposite, over against, facing, *vis à vis.*

240 right side

n. right-handedness, dexterity, dextrality; right, right hand; right-hander, dextral; starboard.

adj. right, right-hand, right-handed, off, offside, dextral, dextrorse.

241 left side

n. left-handedness, sinistrality; left, left hand; left-hander, sinistral; port.

adj. left, left-hand, left-handed, nearside, sinistrorse.

C Form

242 form

n. form, shape, style, look, appearance, fashion, design, outline, profile, contour; structure, construction, formation; morphology.

adj. formed, shaped, developed; formative, impressionable, plastic, mouldable.

vb. form, make, create, fashion, pattern, model, mould; cast, stamp, impress, carve, cut; arrange, construct, build, assemble; take shape, develop, express, grow, materialize.

243 absence of form

n. formlessness, shapelessness, amorphism, fuzziness; chaos, liquid; fluid.

adj. formless, shapeless, amorphous; vague, unclear, indistinct, blurred, fuzzy; indeterminate, indefinite; chaotic, misshapen, unshapely, deformed.

244 symmetry

n. symmetry, regularity, conformity, proportion, equality, evenness, balance, harmony, arrangement, order; shapeliness.

adj. symmetrical, balanced, even, proportioned, well-proportioned, regular, harmonious, shapely.

245 asymmetry

n. asymmetry, disproportion, lopsidedness, irregularity, distortion, contortion, twist, deformity, malformation.

adj. asymmetrical, disproportionate, irregular, misproportioned, uneven, unshapely, grotesque, ugly, hideous, distorted, deformed, malformed, disfigured, crippled, mangled, hunchbacked, crooked, awry, askew.

vb. distort, contort, twist, pervert, deform, misshape, disfigure, buckle, cripple; writhe, scowl, grimace.

see also **845**

246 angular form

n. angularity, pointedness, serration; angle, crotch, elbow, fork, corner, point, zigzag; right angle, acute angle, obtuse angle, reflex angle; triangle: quadrilateral, parallelogram, rhomboid, rectangle, oblong, square, diamond, lozenge, rhombus, rhomb, polygon, pentagon, hexagon, heptagon, octagon, nonagon, enneagon, decagon, endecagon, dodecagon; polyhedron, cube, tetrahedron, pyramid, prism, wedge.

adj. angular, pointed, sharp-cornered, scraggy, jagged, serrated, zigzag, wedge-shaped, cuneiform, cuneate; triangular, rectangular, multilateral.

vb. angle, bend, intersect, serrate, zigzag.
see also **259**

247 curved form

n. curvature, bending, flexion, flexure, arcuation; curve, bend, sweep, bow, curl, camber, arc, chord, arcade, rainbow, arch, crook, trajectory; catenary, parabola, hyperbola, circle, ellipse, epicycle; crescent, half-moon, lune, lunula, meniscus, lens, lunate.

adj. curved, bent, rounded, arched, vaulted, crescent, lunate.

vb. curve, turn, arch, bow, curl, crook, buckle, twist, warp, flex; waver, meander, swerve, deviate, veer.

248 straight form

n. straightness, rectilinearity; verticality, perpendicularity; horizontality; bee-line.

adj. straight, even, level, direct; upright, vertical, perpendicular, erect; horizontal; unbroken, uninterrupted.

vb. straighten, order, make straight; untwist, unbend, uncoil, disentangle, unravel, uncurl, unfold.

adv. in a straight line, as the crow flies.

249 round form

n. rotundity, roundness; round, globe, sphere, orb, ball, marble, balloon, bubble, drop, droplet, globule; cylinder, barrel, roll, drum.

adj. round, rotund, rounded, spherical, globular, orbicular, globe-shaped, globoid, globose, cylindrical.

vb. round, ball, roll, coil up.

250 simple circularity

n. circularity, roundness; circle, orbit, circuit, ring, loop, halo, crown, corona, aureola, circus, bowl, hoop, quoit, wheel, disc, equator; ellipse, oval, egg; band, belt, wreath, garland; circumference, perimeter, rim, periphery.

adj. round, circular, cyclic, orbicular; oval, elliptical.

vb. encircle, go round; make round.
see also **322**

251 complex circularity

n. convolution, intricacy, twisting, sinuosity, torsion; coil, turn, twine, twist, plait, kink, loop, spiral, helix, screw, curl, tendril, scroll.

adj. convoluted, intricate, involved; winding, spiral, coiled, helical, flexuous, sinuous, tortuous; serpentine, snake-like; meandering, undulating, wavy.

vb. turn, wind, curl, loop, twist, twirl, fold, twine, plait, intertwine, entwine, sinuate, wrinkle, contort, wreathe; crimp, ripple; meander, undulate; wriggle, squirm, wiggle.

252 convexity

n. convexity, protuberance, bulginess, outgrowth.

swelling, growth, bump, hump, lump, ridge, rising, bulge; tumour, cancer, corn, boil, inflammation, carbuncle, bunion, wart, pimple, bulb; dome, cupola, vault.

adj. convex, arched, raised, curved, bent; bulbous, swollen, bloated; bulging, swelling, excrescent, tumescent, tumid.

vb. swell, bulge, rise, project, protrude, jut.

253 prominence

n. prominence, salience; projection, protuberance, protrusion, extension, spur, spit, promontory, tongue, headland, relief; leader, figure-head, model, example.

adj. prominent, conspicuous, protuberant, extended, jutting, protruding, projecting, salient, obtrusive.

vb. protrude, extend, jut, project, stand out, stick out.

254 concavity

n. concavity, hollowness; hollow, hole, aperture, opening, depression; pit, abyss, mine, shaft, well, trench; corner, niche, recess, alcove, indentation, pocket; valley, dale, bowl, drop, gulf, basin, glen, ravine, crevasse, fissure, crater, gorge, canyon, gully, chasm; dip, dent, dimple; cave, burrow, cavern, grotto, furrow, covert, warren, pothole; excavation, tunnel, passage, retreat, dug-out, dig (*inf.*).

adj. concave, hollow, depressed, excavated, sunken, carved out, indented.

vb. hollow out, excavate, dig, spade, gouge, delve, mine, tunnel, bore; indent, depress; cave in, fall in, collapse.

255 sharpness

n. sharpness, acuteness; point, tip, prick, thorn, sting, spike, nail, pin, needle, fork, prong; barb, thorn, bramble, prickle, brier, spine; tooth, edge, scissors, shears, knife.

adj. sharp, acute, pointed, fine, keen, cutting, biting, piercing, incisive, trenchant; spiked, spiky, spiny, prickly, thorny, needle-pointed, barbed; pronged, tapered, tapering, acuminate.

vb. be sharp, prick, sting, taper; sharpen, grind, edge, file, hone, whet, strop; barb, point; puncture.

256 bluntness

n. bluntness, obtuseness, flatness.

adj. blunt, unsharpened, unpointed, dull, unsharp, obtuse; toothless.

vb. blunt, dull, take the edge off, round, turn, obtund; be blunt, not cut.

257 smoothness

n. smoothness, flatness, levelness, regularity; stillness, glossiness, silkiness; glass, ice, marble; gloss, varnish, polish, finish.

adj. smooth, flat, plane, level, even, uniform, steady, stable, continuous; quiet, still, sleek, polished, glossy, glassy, lustrous, silky, soft, slippery, oily.

vb. smooth, even, level, plane, scrape, shave, flatten, iron, sand, file, press; polish, shine, burnish, glaze, gloss, varnish; glide, slide, float, skim, drift, stream.

258 roughness

n. roughness, asperity, unevenness, coarseness, harshness, bumpiness, brokenness, irregularity, jaggedness, corrugation.

adj. rough, uneven, coarse, harsh, bumpy,

broken, jagged, rugged, choppy, ruffled; bristly, prickly, hairy, hirsute.

vb. roughen, coarsen, break, notch, serrate, crumple, ruffle.

259 notch

n. notch, indentation, cut, zigzag, cleft, trench, trough, gouge, saw, nick, incision, depression, serration.

adj. notched, jagged, saw-toothed, serrated.

vb. notch, serrate, cut, tooth, cog, indent, nick.

260 fold

n. fold, gather, pleat, lapel, overlap, tuck; crease, crimp, wrinkle, corrugation, turn.

adj. folded, gathered, creased, wrinkled, corrugated, pleated, puckered, overlapping.

vb. fold, double, crease, lap, overlap, plicate, pleat, curl, crimp, wrinkle, ruffle, pucker, gather, corrugate.

261 furrow

n. furrow, groove, slit, slot, trench, rut, gouge, moat, channel, canal, ditch, gutter; corrugation.

adj. furrowed, grooved, ribbed, fluted, corrugated, ridged.

vb. furrow, groove, slot, flute, corrugate, channel, plough.

262 opening

n. opening, aperture, orifice, hole, gap, hollow, slit, perforation, slot, break; mouth, throat, gullet; outlet, vent; window, porthole; door, doorway, gate, exit, entrance, hatch, hatchway, channel, passage.

adj. open, unlocked, unfastened, unsealed; clear, accessible; ajar, gaping, wide, yawning; torn, rent.

vb. open, unlock, unbolt, unbar, unfasten, undo; clear, admit, free, loosen; expose, reveal, unfold; gape, yawn.
see also **264, 462**

263 closure

n. closure, occlusion, stoppage, blockage, obstruction.

adj. closed, unopened, shut, fastened, bolted, blocked, sealed.

vb. close, shut, lock, fasten, bar, bolt.
see also **265**

264 perforator

n. perforator, sponge, sieve, strainer, colander; borer, awl, gimlet, drill, lancet, needle, pin, punch; perforation, porosity.

adj. perforated, porous, pervious, permeable, penetrable, spongy, absorbent, holey.

vb. cut, perforate, pierce, prick, slit, puncture, crack, stick, inject, drill, stab, lance, spear, spike, skewer, impale, bore, mine, tunnel; hole, riddle.

265 stopper

n. stopper, plug, cork, bung, tap, valve, stopcock, wedge, rammer, stuffing, filling, stopping.

adj. stopped up, blocked, obstructed, sealed, impenetrable, impervious, watertight.

vb. block, obstruct, blockade, stop, choke, clog, stuff, ram, fill, dam, seal, cork, plug, bung, occlude, obturate.

D Motion

266 motion

n. motion, mobility, movableness, movement, action, activity, unrest, restlessness, move, passage, progress, advance, ascension, descension; velocity, speed.

adj. moving, in motion, transitional, movable, mobile, restless, nomadic.

vb. move, go, run, progress, proceed; push, impel, stir, set in motion, activate, propel.

267 rest

n. rest, immobility, motionlessness, cessation, stillness, standstill, stop; discontinuance, interval, pause; silence, calm; quiet, calmness, peace, tranquillity.

adj. quiet, still, quiescent, asleep; immovable, immobile, motionless, unruffled, peaceful, placid, serene.

vb. rest, stand still, pause, halt, stop, cease; not stir, keep quiet; still, soften, quiesce, relax, lull, becalm, hush.

see also **174**

268 transference

n. transference, transferal, conveyance, movement, removal, shift, relay, conduct, remittance, dispatch, delivery, hand-over; transport, transportation, transit, carriage, shipment, trans-shipment, haulage, freight, consignment.

adj. transferable, transmittable, transmissible, conveyable, movable, portable.

vb. transfer, move, remove, conduct, carry, take, convey, shift; send, direct, remit, relay, dispatch, forward, deliver, hand over, consign; ship, cart, truck, haul, load, post, mail; convoy, escort; import, export; transmit, communicate; relocate, transplant; ply, shuttle.

see also **714**

269 land travel

n. travel, tourism, touring, sightseeing, globe-trotting, roaming; journey, tour, trip, outing, expedition, excursion, day out, picnic; pilgrimage; venture, adventure; visit, sojourn; exploration, quest, safari.

walk, step, pace, stride, gait, march; stroll, hike, jaunt, saunter, amble, ramble, wayfaring, tramp; promenade, constitutional, perambulation; peregrinations, wanderings.

riding, horse-riding, horsemanship, horse-racing, equestrianism, show-jumping, dressage; cycling, spin, ride; drive; driving, motoring; itinerary, route, course, circuit, direction, map.

adj. journeying, travelling, visiting; peripatetic.

vb. travel, journey, tour, rove, visit, cruise, explore, traverse; walk, step, pace, march, tread, amble, ramble, wander, hike, trek, stroll, ambulate, perambulate, promenade; gad about (*inf.*), gallivant about (*inf.*); ride, cycle, bike (*inf.*); drive, motor.

270 traveller

n. traveller, tourist, sightseer, globe-trotter, holiday-maker, daytripper, visitor, voyager, explorer, adventurer; itinerant, wanderer, roamer, pedlar, vagabond, vagrant, tramp, hobo; migrant, emigrant, immigrant, refugee, gypsy, nomad, bedouin.

pedestrian, walker, foot-passenger, hiker, trekker, rambler, pilgrim, wayfarer, runner, athlete; rider, horse-rider, jockey, show-jumper, hitch-hiker; passenger, commuter, season-ticket holder; motorist, driver.

271 water travel

n. navigation, cruising, circumnavigation; seamanship, seafaring, exploration; voyage, cruise; water sports, aquatics, sailing, yachting, boating, rowing, canoeing, swimming, diving, surfing.

adj. navigational, sailing, nautical, naval, marine, maritime.

vb. sail, cruise, voyage, ply, run, ferry; set sail; launch, cast off; navigate, steer, pilot, make for, head for, set a course; drop anchor, moor; swim, bathe, dive, dip, paddle, wade, surf, water-ski.

272 mariner

n. mariner, sailor, seaman, seafarer, pilot, boatman, marine, crew, captain, boatswain, navigator, helmsman.

273 air travel

n. air travel, aeronautics, aviation, flying, gliding, flight.

pilot, airman, aviator, flier, aeronaut.

adj. flying; aerial, aeronautical, aerodynamic.

vb. fly, pilot, taxi, take off, climb, rise, soar, zoom; spin, loop, roll; glide, dive, dart, shoot; plunge, plummet; parachute, bail out; touch down, land, come down, crash-land; talk down.

274 space travel

n. space travel, astronautics, cosmonautics; countdown, space flight, space walk; grand tour; re-entry, splashdown.

astronaut, spaceman, cosmonaut, space traveller.

adj. astronautical, cosmonautic, cosmonautical.

vb. take off, orbit, splash down.

275 carrier

n. carrier, bearer, porter, messenger, runner; basket, bag, container; horse, packhorse, llama, beast of burden.

vb. carry, transport, move, convey, transfer, bear.

276 vehicle

n. vehicle, conveyance; cycle, bike, bicycle, pushbike (*sl.*), velocipede, tandem, tricycle; moped, scooter, motor scooter, motorcycle, motorbike; car, automobile, motor, saloon, sports car, G. T., coupé, hard-top, convertible, hatchback, estate car, station wagon, shooting-brake, minibus; taxi, taxicab, minicab, cab, hackney carriage, rickshaw; bus, coach, motor bus, tram, trolley-bus; van, lorry, pick-up, dump truck; train, underground, rapid transit; engine, locomotive, diesel locomotive, electric locomotive, steam engine.

cart, trolley, pram, barrow, trailer; carriage, wagon, buggy, trap, gig, hansom.

adj. vehicular, locomotive, wheeled.

277 ship

n. ship, boat, vessel, craft; motorboat, steamer, steamboat, steamship, freighter, barge, lighter, packet, ferry, mail-ship, tanker, supertanker, liner; pilot, tug, launch; destroyer, warship, frigate, battleship, aircraft carrier, submarine; sailing ship, clipper, yacht, rowing boat, paddle boat, canoe, kayak, gondola, junk, galleon.

adj. nautical, marine, maritime, naval, seagoing, seaworthy.

278 aircraft

n. aircraft, aeroplane, plane, airliner, jet, jumbo jet, turbo-prop, shuttle, glider, bomber, seaplane; hovercraft, hydrofoil, helicopter; airship, balloon, Zeppelin.

adj. aviational, aeronautical.

279 spaceship

n. spaceship, spacecraft, capsule, module, space shuttle, space probe; space station, satellite, sputnik; flying saucer, UFO; rocket.

280 velocity

n. velocity, speed, quickness, rapidity, hurry, haste, rush, expedition, celerity; acceleration, hastening, quickening, speeding up, spurt, burst, charge.

adj. quick, fast, speedy, brisk, swift; nimble, agile, deft, spirited; light-footed, prompt, expeditious.

vb. go fast, speed, hurry, hasten, quicken, race, tear, fly, dash, rush, run, sprint, dart, whiz, zip, pelt, bomb, run like mad, go all out, do a ton (*sl.*), go full pelt (*inf.*); accelerate, go faster, speed up, spurt, put on speed, step on it (*inf.*), put one's foot down (*inf.*), get a move on (*inf.*), get one's skates on (*inf.*), make it snappy (*inf.*); overtake, gain on, catch up, reach, pass, overhaul, go after, outstrip, outpace, outdistance, capture, beat; run for dear life.

adv. fast, quickly, speedily, swiftly, at full speed, flat out, at full pelt.

see also **613**

281 slowness

n. slowness, sluggishness, lethargy, apathy, hesitation, reluctance; deceleration, retardation, slackening, delay, go-slow, brake, curb, restraint.

slowcoach, tortoise, snail, dawdler, lingerer, loiterer, loafer, idler.

adj. slow, slow-moving, dawdling, lingering; sluggish, listless, lethargic, apathetic, inactive, leisurely, hesitant, reluctant.

vb. go slowly, idle, stroll, saunter, dawdle, linger, tarry, take one's time, loiter, loaf, crawl, inch, falter, limp, hobble, shuffle, plod; decelerate, slow down, reduce speed, slacken, relax, let up, ease off, delay, retard, brake, put on the brakes; curb.

282 impulse

n. impulse, thrust, impetus, charge, rush, drive, pressure, momentum, impulsion; bump, shove, shock, jolt, impact, brunt, clash, crash, collision, pile-up, smash-up; hit, knock, rap, blow, smack.

vb. impel, push, drive, press, propel, move, set in motion, activate, get going, start; collide, crash, run into, bump into, smash, dash, meet, encounter, touch, impinge, clash, butt, bump, jog, shove, jolt, force, scrape, jar.

hit, strike, beat, smite; tap, rap, jab; slap, thump, clout, smack, pummel, thrash, whip, whack, wallop (*sl.*), sock, clap, box, punch, club, cudgel; hammer, pound, bash, slosh (*sl.*), flail; bang, knock, bruise; kick, knee.

283 recoil

n. recoil, reaction, rebound, spring, bounce, repercussion, echo, reverberation, boomerang, backlash, rebuff, answer, reply.

vb. recoil, react, respond, rebound, bounce, spring, kick back, backfire, echo, reverberate; shrink from, draw back, pull back, wince, flinch.

284 direction

n. direction, bearing, orientation, point of the compass, cardinal point, north, south, east, west; destination, aim, object, intention; tendency, thrust, tenor; outlook, standpoint, point of view.

vb. orientate oneself, take one's bearings, locate; direct, signpost, lead, aim for, go for, head for, make for, point to, steer; tend.

adv. towards, in the direction of, via, heading for, on the way to.

285 deviation

n. deviation, misdirection, disorientation, deflection, divergence, turning, departure, diversion, detour; digression, tangent; irregularity, deterioration.

adj. deviating, aberrant, deviant, divergent, misguided, mistaken, lost; tangential, off-beam.

vb. deviate, deflect, swerve, bend, wander, stray, err, depart from, veer, shift, lose one's bearings, get lost, turn aside; disorientate, misdirect; digress, get sidetracked, go off the point, go off at a tangent.

286 precedence

n. precedence, priority, leading, heading, vanguard.

vb. precede, go before, come first, take precedence, herald, go in advance, lead, lead the way, head, take the lead.

adv. in advance, ahead, before.

see also **84, 118**

287 following

n. following, succession; follower, disciple, hanger-on, attendant, dependant, adherent, supporter, recruit.

vb. follow, go after, come after, ensue, succeed, attend, wait on; shadow, chase, pursue, track, tail (*sl.*), dog; lag behind, trail.

see also **85, 119**

288 progression

n. progression, progress, advance, headway, gain; development, growth, furtherance, advancement, improvement.

adj. forward, progressive, tolerant, broadminded, forward-looking, enterprising; ongoing.

vb. progress, advance, proceed, move on, forge ahead, press on, strive forward, push ahead, make progress, make headway, gain ground, never look back (*inf.*); further, promote, develop, grow, evolve, become, mature, improve, move with the times.

adv. forward, onward, on, in progress.

289 regression

n. regression, retreat, withdrawal, retirement, return; regress, retrogression, reversal; departure, escape; about-turn, *volte-face*, about-face, U-turn.

adj. backward, backward-looking, reactionary, narrow-minded, reverse, retrograde, retrogressive.

vb. go backwards, regress, recede, retire, back out, withdraw, retreat, draw back, secede, fall back, lose ground; retrogress; go back on one's word, turn around.

290 propulsion

n. propulsion, impulsion, impetus, drive, push, thrust, pressure; missile, projectile, bullet, shell, torpedo, arrow, dart, propellant, shot.

vb. propel, push, move, impel, drive, direct, thrust, press, shove; launch, throw, cast, pitch, toss, chuck (*inf.*); shoot, discharge.

291 pulling

n. pulling, traction, drawing, tow, haul; tug, tractor, traction engine, draught animal; trailer, caravan, train.

vb. pull, draw, haul, drag, heave, tow, tug, take in tow; attract, magnetize; trail.

292 approach

n. approach, advance, arrival, coming; nearness, approximation.

adj. approaching, nearing, forthcoming, coming, looming, drawing near; accessible, get-at-able, approachable, obtainable, available, attainable, convenient, at one's disposal.

vb. approach, draw near, come near, advance, come forward, come into sight, close in on, sidle up to, loom up; approximate, verge on, near.

293 retreat

n. retreat, recession, withdrawal, departure, escape, retirement, removal, evacuation, flight.

vb. retreat, recede, withdraw, back out, depart, run away, fall back, evacuate, escape, retire, remove; fade, die away, sink.

294 attraction

n. attraction, drawing power, gravitation, affinity, pull, draw, influence; magnet, gravity, bait, lure, decoy.

adj. attracting, appealing, magnetic, charismatic.

vb. attract, pull, drag, draw, bring; interest, fascinate.

see also **547**

295 repulsion

n. repulsion, rebuff, snub, beating off, dismissal.

adj. repulsive, offensive, repelling.

vb. repel, repulse, drive back, put to flight, beat off, hold off, push back, throw off, turn away, drive away; dismiss, send packing; rebuff, snub; resist.

see also **892**

296 convergence

n. convergence, concurrence, confluence, concentration, confrontation, collision course, focalization; union, meeting, encounter.

adj. convergent, concurrent, converging.

vb. converge, come together, focalize, unite, gather, concentrate, meet, tend, narrow the gap, come to a point.

297 divergence

n. divergence, radiation, ramification; fork, bifurcation; fan, spoke, ray.

adj. divergent, deviating, radiating; centrifugal.

vb. diverge, radiate, branch, fork, bifurcate, diffuse, spread, fan out, disperse, scatter, ramify, divaricate.

298 arrival

n. arrival, coming, approach, entrance, entry, appearance, emergence; start, onset; reaching, attainment; return, homecoming; landing, touchdown, disembarkation, alighting, dismounting, docking, mooring.

destination, goal, terminus, journey's end, objective, resting place, harbour, port, dock, berth, landing place, airport.

vb. arrive, come, reach, get to, enter,

approach, appear, show up (*inf.*), turn up, return, come home; land, touch down, disembark, alight, dismount, get down, set foot on, dock, moor, drop anchor.

299 departure

n. departure, going, leaving, setting out, exit, withdrawing, abandonment, removal, retreat, flight, take-off, embarkation, sailing; leave-taking, parting, separating, farewell, send-off, dismissal, valediction, parting shot, *congé*; exodus; emigration.

vb. depart, go, leave, move, quit, retire, withdraw, evacuate, go away, take one's leave, make tracks, set out, start out, be off, push off (*inf.*), push along (*inf.*), shove off (*sl.*); rush off, run away, beat it (*sl.*), scram (*sl.*).

300 entrance

n. entrance, entry, ingress, incoming, induction, initiation, immigration; admittance, admission; introduction, influx, intrusion, infiltration, incursion, penetration, invasion, raid.

vb. enter, come in, step in, go in, set foot in, make one's way into, visit, drop in; intrude, invade, trespass, gatecrash; force into, break in; wriggle in, worm in; insert, put in, admit, introduce, implant, penetrate, infiltrate, percolate.

301 emergence

n. emergence, egress, outflow, emanation, issue, discharge, outflow, effluence, flow; escape, gush, spout, welling, oozing, outpour, leakage, seepage, eruption, secretion.

vb. emerge, go out, come out, come out into the open; emit, eject, discharge, expel, flow out, run out, effuse, give out, exhale, send forth, pour out, gush, spurt, shoot, secrete, seep, erupt, squirt; bleed, leak, empty, weep; exude, ooze.

see also **312**

302 reception

n. reception, admission, admittance, acceptance, receptivity; access, welcome, open arms, hospitality, registration, enlistment, enrolment; initiation, baptism, barmitzvah; incorporation, assimilation, absorption, digestion.

adj. admissible, acceptable, receivable; suitable; receptive, sympathetic.

vb. admit, receive, accept, take in; allow in, accommodate, welcome, make welcome; initiate, baptize, introduce, induct, install;

assimilate, incorporate, swallow, absorb, digest.

see also 716

303 ejection

n. ejection, expulsion, eviction, removal, elimination; dismissal, discharge, sack (*inf.*), push (*sl.*), deportation, exile, banishment, extradition; ejector, bouncer (*sl.*), chucker-out; nausea, sickness, vomiting.

vb. eject, emit, expel, remove, exclude, eliminate, eradicate, wipe out, evict; dismiss, get rid of, dispose of, discharge, sack (*inf.*); depart, exile, banish, extradite, relegate; urinate, excrete; be sick, vomit, bring up (*inf.*), throw up (*inf.*), spew, retch, heave.

304 eating; drinking

n. eating, ingestion, nourishment, feeding, nutrition, consuming, partaking; feasting, devouring, banqueting; digestion, chewing, mastication; drinking, imbibation, potation; gastronomy, epicurism, gourmandise, gluttony.

eater, partaker, consumer, nibbler, chewer, glutton; drinker, sipper, drunkard; connoisseur, gourmet, gourmand, epicure.

vb. eat, consume, feed on, partake; chew, masticate, champ; bite, digest, swallow; gorge, gobble, bolt, put away (*inf.*), eat up, tuck into (*inf.*), polish off (*inf.*), devour, dispose of; breakfast, lunch, sup; eat out, dine out, wine and dine, feast, banquet, gourmandize; stuff, eat one's fill.

nourish, feed, satisfy, provide, maintain, nurture, strengthen, sustain, tend, gratify; suckle, breast-feed, give suck, nurse.

drink, gulp, take in, imbibe, wash down (*inf.*); tipple, guzzle.

305 provisions

n. provisions, food, stores, sustenance, stock, foodstuffs, groceries, subsistence, rations, board; fodder, feed, pasture, pasturage, roughage, provender; portion, helping, share, slice, quota, division, ration; larder, pantry, refrigerator, freezer.

306 food

n. food, meat and drink, foodstuffs, edibles, comestibles, provisions, nutrition, aliment, nutriment, cooking, grub (*sl.*), tuck (*sl.*); victuals, pabulum, viands; delicacy, delicatessen, luxury, delight.

portion, mouthful, piece, bite, morsel, spoonful.

meal, refreshment, fare; repast, refection; breakfast, brunch, elevenses, lunch, luncheon, packed lunch, tea, afternoon tea, high tea, dinner, supper; snack, sandwich, bite, nibble, buffet, tiffin; feast, banquet, orgy, blow-out (*inf.*), beanfeast, beano (*sl.*); picnic, barbecue; menu, bill of fare, table, cover, spread; dish, course, hors-d'oeuvre, appetizer, soup, broth, pottage, aperitif, entrée, main course, sweet, dessert, afters (*inf.*), pudding, savoury.

meat, flesh, game, poultry, fowl; egg; flour, starch; fish, sea-food; milk product, butter, cream, cheese; oil, fat, grease, blubber, margarine, vegetable fat, vegetable oil; bread, staff of life, loaf, roll; pastry, patisserie, biscuit, wafer, cracker, cake; fruit, soft fruit, berry, jam, conserve, spread, extract, jelly, gelatin; vegetable, herb, edible root, greens, tuber, root; cereal, grain; nut, dried fruit, seed, stone, kernel, pip; sweet, confectionery, sweetmeat, confections; cookery, cuisine, catering, domestic science, home economics.

adj. edible, eatable, comestible, digestible, nutritious, delicious, succulent, palatable, appetizing, satisfying, tempting, scrumptious (*inf.*); culinary; prandial, pre-prandial, post-prandial.

vb. cook, prepare, fix, heat up, warm up; simmer, steam, boil, coddle; stew, casserole, braise; bake, roast, spit; grill, barbecue, broil; fry, sauté, sizzle; poach, scramble; toast, crisp, dry; curry, fricassee; dice, mince; lard, baste.

307 condiment

n. condiment, flavouring, seasoning, additive, sauce, relish, herb, plant, pickle, salt, pepper, mustard.

vb. season, flavour, spice, salt, pepper, bring out the flavour.

308 tobacco

n. tobacco, nicotine, snuff, cigarette, cigar, pipe.

vb. smoke, smoke a pipe, inhale, puff, draw, suck; take snuff.

309 drink

n. drink, beverage, potion, liquid, fluid, juice, sap, whey; infusion, decoction; soft drink, water, milk, tea, coffee, thirst-quencher, nightcap; alcoholic drink, beer, wine, champagne, toast, cocktail; sip, gulp, drop; draught, dram.

310 excretion

n. excretion, urination, evacuation, voiding, discharge, secretion, defecation, expulsion, ejection, excrement, exudation; faeces, excreta; waterworks (*sl.*); urine; bowel movement, diarrhoea, dysentry; offal, dung, droppings, manure; ordure, stool; smegma; perspiration, sweat.

adj. excretive, excretory, secretory; faecal.

vb. excrete, expel, defecate, discharge, evacuate, urinate, secrete, pass, spend a penny, go to the lavatory, be excused.

311 insertion

n. insertion, injection, infusion, introduction, insinuation.

vb. insert, put in, inject, infuse, introduce, interpolate, include, insinuate, pour in, impregnate, stick in, throw in; force in, drag in (*inf.*), embed, install, fix, implant, bury, sink, immerse.

312 extraction

n. extraction, removal, withdrawal, expulsion, discharge, ejection, extrication, pulling; quarrying, mining; scoop, digger, chisel, extractor, gouge, excavator, dredger.

vb. extract, remove, withdraw, pull out, draw out, pluck, wrench, extricate, cut out, extort, dislodge, uproot, displace, lever out; quarry, mine, excavate, dredge, gouge, chisel; get money out of a stone (*inf.*).

313 passage

n. passage, crossing, journey, trek, voyage; way, thoroughfare, traffic, flow; traffic control, traffic regulation, rule of the road, highway code.

vb. pass, cross, traverse, go through, penetrate, emerge, proceed, drive, weave, thread, ford, span.

314 overstepping

n. overstepping, overrunning, infestation, invasion; transcendence; encroachment, violation, transgression.

vb. go beyond, overstep, encroach, go too far, exceed the limit, overrun, overshoot; invade, infest, plague, swarm, ravage; excel, surpass, outdo, transcend, rise above, eclipse; outdistance, outstrip; trespass, violate, infringe, transgress.

315 shortcoming

n. shortcoming, inadequacy, imperfection, falling short; loss, deficit, shortfall, shortage, dearth, default; need, lack, requirement, deficiency, fault, weakness, lapse, weak point; privation, destitution.

adj. short, deficient, missing, lacking, inadequate, not up to scratch; imperfect, incomplete.

vb. fall short, come short, be deficient,

fail, need, miss, lack; lag behind, lose ground; collapse, come to nothing.

316 ascent

n. ascent, ascension, climbing, rise, mount, lift, jump, surge, towering, soaring; ladder, step-ladder, steps, stairs, staircase, escalator, moving staircase, travelator, elevator; hill, mountain, acclivity.

adj. ascending, rising, upward.

vb. ascend, go up, rise, tower, soar, rocket, surge, grow, sprout; take off; climb, mount, surmount, progress, top, scale, conquer, scramble, clamber, creep, work one's way up.

317 descent

n. descent, drop, fall, lapse, swoop, sinking, plunge, downfall, tumble; slump, recession, reduction, declination; subsidence, landslide, hole, cave, chasm.

adj. descending, downward.

vb. descend, go down, fall, drop, subside, decline, swoop, plunge, slump, sink, droop, land, come down, touch down; parachute; crash-land; splash down; topple, push over; tumble, overbalance, lose one's balance, stumble, capsize, turn over, tilt, lurch.

318 elevation

n. elevation, lift, raising, erection; exaltation, ennoblement, sublimation.

adj. raised, lifted, elevated, high, aerial, tall, erect, upstanding, upraised; exalted, noble, sublime, lofty.

vb. lift, elevate, raise, pick up, pull up, help up, uplift, hoist, heave, erect; support, prop; leaven; boost; glorify, heighten, enhance, exalt.

get up, stand up, get to one's feet, arise; jump up, spring to one's feet.

319 depression

n. depression, lowering, dip; hole, cavity; curtsy, bow, genuflexion; debasement.

adj. depressed; smoothed, even; sitting, sedentary, settled, inactive; prostrate.

vb. depress, lower, press, squash; settle, sink, dip, sag, droop, decline; push down, bring low, ground; fell, cut down, chop down, topple, pull down, demolish, raze to the ground.

drop, let fall, shed, loosen, release, let go, spill; fall, drip, dribble, leak, ooze, seep, drain, permeate, percolate, filter.

sit down, be seated, squat, crouch, kneel, genuflect; perch, roost; bend over, stoop, incline, hunch, bow, curtsy.

320 leap

n. leap, jump, dance, spring, vault, bound, hop, rise, pounce, hurdle, leapfrog, saltation.

adj. lively, frisky, saltatory.

vb. leap, jump, spring, vault, dance, hop, bounce, skip, leapfrog, surge, rise.

321 plunge

n. plunge, jump, rush, dive, drop, fall, plummet, leap, pitch, dip, swoop; ducking, immersion, submergence.

vb. plunge, dive, dip, jump, fall, pounce, cast down; duck, submerge, immerse, drown, souse, dunk; go down, sink, go under; splash down; crash-land; go to the bottom.

322 circulation

n. circulation, circumnavigation; spiral; compass, lap, course, circuit, loop, round trip, orbit, ambit, full circle; by-pass, ring road, detour, diversion.

vb. circle, circulate, go around, revolve around, circumnavigate, circumscribe, circumambulate, lap, tour, ring, gird, wind; by-pass.

see also 250

323 rotation

n. rotation, revolution, turn, circle, spin, cycle, roll, circuit, whirl, twirl, gyration, pirouette; spiral, orbit; whirlpool, eddy, whirlwind, cyclone, tornado, vortex.

adj. rotary, gyratory, rotating, revolving.

vb. rotate, revolve, twist, circle, circulate, spin, cycle, roll, whirl, twirl, loop, swing, spiral; swivel, pivot; swirl, eddy; pirouette.

324 evolution

n. evolution, development, growth, unfolding, unfurling; disentanglement; evolutionism, Darwinism; missing link.

adj. evolving, evolutionary.

vb. evolve, develop, grow, emerge; advance, progress, mature; unfold, open out, unfurl, unroll, unwind, uncurl, uncover, unwrap; unravel, disentangle, free, release, straighten.

325 oscillation

n. oscillation, fluctuation, vacillation, wavering, undulation, quiver, shake, swing, lurch, roll; vibration, tremor, thunder; faltering, hesitancy, uncertainty.

pulse, pulsation, throb, beat, drumming, pound, surge, palpitation, flutter, ripple, wave; earthquake, seismology.

pendulum, oscillator, vibrator, shuttle, see-saw, cradle, rocking-chair, rocking-horse.

adj. oscillating, fluctuating, throbbing, pulsatory; seismic; vacillating, hesitant, undecided, irresolute.

vb. oscillate, alternate, fluctuate, vacillate, vibrate, pulse, throb, beat, pound, surge, flutter, wave, waver, undulate, librate; nod, swing, sway, see-saw, wobble, totter, lurch, roll, rock, quake, quiver, teeter, zigzag; ebb and flow, back and fill; hesitate, falter.

adv. back and forth, to and fro, up and down, from side to side.

326 agitation

n. agitation, disturbance, vibration; jar, jolt, jog, bump, bounce; shudder, quake, tremble, wobble, tremor, jerk; shakes, jitters (*inf.*), shivers, heebie-jeebies (*sl.*), butterflies (*inf.*), apprehension; fit, convulsion, spasm, palsy, seizure, fever, attack, stroke; itch, twitch.

confusion, tumult, turmoil, turbulence; excitation, melodrama, emotion, commotion, fuss, bother, flap (*inf.*), dither (*inf.*), tizzy (*sl.*).

adj. agitated, shaking, unsteady, wavering, shaky, tremulous; jelly-like, itchy, twitching, nervous, apprehensive, jittery (*inf.*).

vb. shake, tremble, vibrate, quiver, quake, shiver, chatter, shudder, palpitate, flap, toss, flutter, totter, wobble, stagger; itch, twitch; twinkle, flicker, glimmer, sparkle.

agitate, sway, rock, swing, beat, disturb, jolt, jar, jerk, bounce; convulse, seize, throw a fit; go out of control.

III Matter

A Matter in general

327 materiality

n. materiality, substantiality, concreteness, corporeality, corporality, tangibility; materialism, Marxism, dialectical materialism; worldliness, unspirituality.

matter, body, material, stuff, mass, flesh and blood, flesh; thing, object, something, article, commodity, item, being; element, atom, molecule; component, part, ingredient, factor.

adj. material, substantial; corporeal, bodily; physical, concrete, tangible, real, objective, somatic; materialistic, unspiritual, worldly, mundane.

vb. materialize, realize, become real, take form, become flesh, take flesh, objectify, substantialize.

328 immateriality

n. immateriality, insubstantiality, dematerialization, intangibility, disembodiment; spirituality, otherworldliness; shadow, ghost.

adj. immaterial, incorporeal, insubstantial, bodiless, disembodied, intangible, ethereal, shadowy, ghostly, unreal; otherworldly, spiritual, psychic.

vb. dematerialize, disintegrate, disembody; spiritualize.

329 universe

n. universe, creation, space, outer space, cosmos, galaxy; world, earth, sphere, globe, orb, nature; heavenly body, celestial body, planet, planetoid, asteroid, moon, satellite, falling star, shooting star, meteor, meteorite, star, sun, constellation, nebula, quasar, pulsar, black hole; heavens, firmament, vault; atmosphere, air, ether, sky, night sky; astronomy, astrophysics, star-gazing; observatory, planetarium, telescope; astrology, horoscope, signs of the Zodiac; cosmology, cosmogony, cosmography, geography; map, atlas.

adj. universal, cosmic, galactic; terrestrial, earthly, worldly, mundane; heavenly, celestial, empyrean; extraterrestrial, planetary, solar, astral, lunar; astronomical; geographical.

330 weight

n. gravity, gravitation, attraction; weight, heaviness, pressure, force, mass, bulk; ballast, load, freight, sinker, counterweight, paperweight, stone, rock, sandbags, anchor, plumb; burden.
balance, scales, weighing machine, weighbridge.

adj. heavy, weighty, ponderous, bulky, cumbersome, top-heavy; burdensome, oppressive, troublesome.

vb. weigh, balance, poise, measure, put on the scales, counterpoise, counterbalance; weigh down, weight, load, overload; burden, overwhelm, saddle.

331 lightness

n. lightness, levity, weightlessness, imponderability; buoy, cork; leaven, lightener, ferment, yeast.

adj. light, insubstantial; underweight; weightless; feathery, dainty, airy, fluffy; gentle, delicate, soft; floatable, buoyant, unsinkable; lightweight, summerweight; small, portable.

vb. be light, float, surface, swim; levitate, defy gravity; lighten, raise, ferment; unburden, take off, remove, unload, disencumber, jettison.

B Inorganic matter

332 density

n. density, solidity, thickness, compactness, concreteness, heaviness, concentration, congestion, substantiality; incompressibility, impenetrability, impermeability; consolidation, crystallization, coagulation, solidification, thickening, stiffening; mass, solid, body, substance, lump, conglomerate.

adj. dense, solid, thick, compact, close, heavy, impenetrable, impermeable, condensed, compressed; clotted, curdled; frozen; indivisible, insoluble.

vb. solidify, thicken, coagulate, freeze, clot, fix, crystallize, harden, stiffen, set, congeal, jell (*inf.*), curdle; petrify, ossify; compress, condense, compact.
see also 50

333 rarity

n. rarity, thinness, fineness; low pressure, vacuum, emptiness; rarefaction, attenuation.

adj. rare, thin, light, rarefied, fine, attenuated, airy, ethereal; weak, tenuous, sparse, shrill, flimsy, fragile, insubstantial, subtle; empty, void.

vb. rarefy, lessen, reduce pressure, purify, refine, thin, attenuate.

334 hardness

n. hardness, stiffness, firmness, toughness, rigidity, solidity, impenetrability, inflexibility; hardening, stiffening.

adj. hard, solid, thick, dense, compact; rigid, firm, stiff, taut, tight; tough, unyielding, unbreakable, impenetrable, unbending, inflexible, inelastic, unmalleable, impermeable.

vb. harden, toughen, strengthen, set, stiffen, temper; concentrate, consolidate, solidify, crystallize, freeze, coagulate, congeal, fossilize, ossify, petrify, starch.
see also 537

335 softness

n. softness, penetrability, flexibility, plasticity, tractability, suppleness, pliancy, litheness; looseness, laxity.

adj. soft, smooth, fluffy, spongy, mellow; gentle, delicate; flimsy, limp; tender, pliant, flexible, plastic, elastic, supple, pliable, lithe, limber, mouldable.

vb. soften, ease, modify, temper, tenderize; subdue, assuage, mollify, appease; knead, mash; give, yield, relax, relent.

336 elasticity

n. elasticity, flexibility, pliability, springiness, spring, bounce, resilience, buoyancy; stretch, extensibility, tensility.

adj. elastic, flexible, pliant, resilient, buoyant; stretching, extensile, tensile.

vb. stretch; spring, bounce.

337 toughness

n. toughness, durability, strength, tenacity, cohesion; bone, gristle, cartilage.

adj. tough, durable, hard, firm, solid, robust, strong, stiff, enduring, unbreakable, tenacious; impervious, unyielding, resistant; fibrous, gristly, sinewy.

vb. toughen, strengthen, stiffen, harden.

338 brittleness

n. brittleness, frailty, fragility, delicacy.

adj. brittle, delicate, frail; breakable, fragile; crispy, crumbly; flimsy, frangible; shaky, unsteady; friable.

vb. break, break easily, split, snap, shatter, fragment, burst, fall to pieces, splinter, crumble.

see also **48**

339 texture

n. texture, pattern, weave, organization, composition, constitution, make-up, form, structure; feel, sense, taste, shape, mould, fibre, fabric, web, weft, tissue.

adj. structural, organizational, constructional, tectonic; textural, granular.

340 powderiness

n. powderiness, pulverulence; crumbling, pulverization; powder, dust, grain, particle, granule, crumb, flake, pollen.

adj. powdery, fine, granulated, pulverized, pulverulent; dusty; impalpable; crumbling, friable.

vb. grind, crush, pulverize, granulate, pound, beat, grate, scrape, crunch, crumble, atomize.

341 friction

n. friction, rubbing, abrasion, erosion, wearing away, grinding, filing, irritation; massage, polishing; stroke.

adj. frictional, abrasive, rubbing.

vb. rub, abrade, scour, grate, graze, rasp, chafe, grind, file, scrape, scrub; wear away, erode; polish, shine, smooth, massage; burnish; brush, clean, wipe.

342 lubrication

n. lubrication, anointment, unction; lubri-cant, grease, oil, wax, fat, ointment, cream, lotion, balm, salve, unguent; petrol, juice (*sl.*).

vb. lubricate, grease, oil, cream, daub, smear, coat, rub, anoint.

343 fluidity

n. fluidity, liquidity, wateriness, juiciness, solubility, dilution; fluid, liquid, liquor, vapour, solution, solvent, drink, flow.

adj. fluid, liquid, running, flowing, molten, liquefied, watery, juicy, liquescent.

vb. flow, run, pour, stream, swell; liquefy.

344 gaseity

n. gaseity, gaseousness, vaporousness, aeration; gas, vapour, steam, fume, air, smoke, fluid.

adj. gaseous, vaporous, vapory, gassy, gas-like, steaming, aeriform, airy, light, windy, volatile.

vb. gasify, aerate.

345 liquefaction

n. liquefaction, solubility, dissolution, thawing; solvent, dissolvent.

adj. runny, molten, liquefied, melted, thawed, disintegrated; liquefacient, soluble.

vb. liquefy, dissolve, melt, run, thaw, defrost, fuse, flux, condense, fluidify, fluidize, deliquesce, disintegrate.

346 vaporization

n. vaporization, evaporation, condensation, sublimation, gasification, volatization, distillation; vapour, moisture, exhalation, mist, smoke, sublimate.

adj. vaporous, steaming, steamy, gassy, volatile.

vb. vaporize, evaporate, sublimate, distil, diffuse, dissipate, gasify, exhale; smoke, fume, steam.

347 water

n. water, liquid, rain, wet, dampness; ice, steam, water vapour.

adj. watery, aquatic, aqueous, hydrated, liquid, fluid, wet, moist, hydrous, aqua-, hydro-.

see also **349**

348 air

n. air, oxygen, fresh air; airing, exposure, ventilation, air conditioning, aeration; atmosphere, stratosphere, ozone, ether, sky; pneumatics, aerodynamics.

weather, climate, elements; meteorology, forecasting.

adj. airy, aerial; exposed, ventilated, open,

aerated; draughty, breezy, windy; pneumatic, aero-; metereological.

vb. air, aerate, ventilate, open, refresh, freshen, cool, aerify, purify, fan.

see also 359

349 moisture

n. moisture, humidity, dampness, wetness, precipitation; drip, damp, dew, rain, wet; moistening, saturation, wettening, humidification.

adj. moist, damp, wet, humid, muggy, dank, misty; saturated, soaked, sodden, waterlogged, awash, drowned, drenched, wet through, like a drowned rat.

vb. moisten, dampen, wet, humidify; sprinkle, dabble, shower, dip, sponge, splash; saturate, drench, soak, bathe, souse, steep, stream, seep, sog; duck, immerse, submerge; waterlog, drown, flood, swamp, inundate, deluge.

350 dryness

n. dryness, aridity, aridness, parchedness, desiccation, dehydration; thirst, drought.

adj. dry, arid, parched, unmoistened, rainless, sapless, evaporated; barren, desert, dusty, baked, scorched, bleached; dried, dehydrated, thirsty; waterproof, rainproof, watertight.

vb. dry, dehydrate, freeze-dry, drip-dry; desiccate, parch, bake, scorch, torrefy; air, evaporate; shrivel, wither; soak up, absorb.

351 ocean

n. ocean, sea, deep, brine, high seas; oceanography.

adj. oceanic, marine, maritime, pelagic; oceanographical.

352 land

n. land, terrain, *terra firma*, mainland, continent; inland, interior; peninsula, neck, isthmus; ground, soil, earth, gravel, sand, rock, pebble; fields, pasture; shore, beach, seaside, strand, bank, coastline, seaboard.

adj. terrestrial, earthy; inland, interior, landlocked, central; coastal, seaside, littoral, riverside, riparian.

353 gulf

n. gulf, inlet, bay, estuary, bight, mouth, harbour, lagoon, sound, fiord, firth, loch, strait, narrows, arm, kyle; cove, cave.

354 lake

n. lake, tarn, loch, lagoon, pool, pond, creek, mere, inland sea, reservoir, basin; puddle.

355 marsh

n. marsh, fen, swamp, mire, bog, quagmire, quicksand, morass, slough, moor, mud.

adj. marshy, soft, fenny, swampy, boggy, wet, waterlogged, squelchy, slushy, muddy, miry, paludal.

356 plain

n. plain, expanse, open country, flat, lowland, champaign, grassland; meadow, field, grass, pasture; steppe, prairie, savannah, pampa, llano; moor, moorland, common, heath, wold; upland, plateau, tableland, downs; tundra, veld.

357 island

n. island, isle, islet, holm, eyot, ait, archipelago; reef, atoll, ridge, sandbank, cay, key.

358 water in motion

n. river, watercourse, waterway, tributary, branch, fork, effluent; stream, brook, rivulet, beck, runnel, rill, runlet, bourn, creek.

tide, current, flow, course, undercurrent; spring, fountain, spout, gush, rush, jet, outpouring, uprising; whirlpool, eddy, vortex, swirl, maelstrom; wash, backwash.

wave, billow, swell, roller, surge, crest, ripple, undulation, breaker, tidal wave, whitecaps, white horses; waterfall, cataract, fall, shoot, cascade, torrent, rapids, weir.

rain, rainfall, precipitation, drizzle, shower, downpour, thunderstorm, cloudburst, flood, deluge, inundation, monsoon; mist.

adj. runny, streaming; rainy, moist, wet, showery, cloudy, thundery, stormy; torrential.

vb. flow, run, stream, sweep, rush; gush, well, spurt, squirt, jet, spout, issue, flood, inundate; wave, undulate, billow, swell, ripple, ebb; swirl, eddy, surge, roll, whirl, tumble; dash, break, splash; drop, drip, seep, leak, trickle, dribble, gurgle; spill, overflow, spew, exude; fall, cascade; drain, empty, clear, tap, expel, deplete, decant, bleed.

rain, pour, patter, spit, drizzle, shower.

359 air in motion

n. wind, draught, current, breeze, whisk, whiff, puff, flutter, waft, zephyr; gust, blast, flurry, flaw; gale, storm, squall, blizzard, whirlwind, cyclone, typhoon, tornado, hurricane, tempest; trade wind, mistral, föhn.

breathing, respiration, inhalation, expiration, exhalation, afflatus; breath, gasp, sigh, pant, cough, sneeze, wheeze.

adj. windy, open, exposed, fresh, blustery,

squally, gusty, stormy, tempestuous; draughty, well-ventilated; wheezy, asthmatic.

vb. blow, breeze, whiff, waft, flutter, flap, buffet, sweep, whisk, fling; blast, rush, roar, howl, wail, stream, whirl; breathe, respire, inhale, exhale, expire, puff, pant, gasp; sigh; cough, sneeze, wheeze; pump, inflate, blow up, swell, fill.

360 water channel

n. conduit, channel, way, passage, bed, ditch, trench, trough, moat; course, canal, aqueduct; tunnel, pipe, pipeline, tube, main, duct, culvert; spout, tap, funnel, siphon; drain, drainpipe, gutter, sewer; flume, gully, cloaca.

361 air-pipe

n. air-pipe, shaft, tube; vent, chimney, flue, ventilator.

362 semiliquidity

n. semiliquidity, viscosity, glutinousness, stickiness, adhesiveness; semiliquid, glue, paste, size, colloid, emulsion, syrup.

adj. semiliquid, semifluid, gelatinous, viscous, viscid, glutinous, coagulated, slimy, syrupy, creamy, sticky, tacky, slushy, gummy, colloid.

363 bubble; cloud

n. bubble, globule, sac, froth, foam, spray, surf, spume; fizz, head; lather, suds; effervescence, fermentation, bubbling.

cloud, haze, haziness, mist, fog, smog, pea-souper (*inf.*), film.

adj. bubbly, foaming, bubbling, soapy, effervescent, sparkling, fizzy, spumous, spumy; cloudy, overcast, dull, grey, unclear, murky, gloomy, dim, misty, hazy, foggy, nebulous.

vb. effervesce, bubble, boil, fizz, foam, ferment.

364 pulpiness

n. pulpiness, sponginess, softness, succulence; pulp, mash, sponge, paste, pap, mulch, mush, jelly, dough, batter, poultice.

adj. pulpy, mushy, doughy, soggy, spongy, pulpous, ripe, fleshy, succulent; thick, smooth.

vb. pulp, mash, crush.

365 unctuousness

n. unctuousness, oiliness, greasiness; oil, fat, grease, blubber; unction, unguent, embrocation, salve, nard, ointment, lubricant, balm, emollient, remedy, cream; resin, gum, pitch, varnish, lacquer, shellac, asphalt, bitumen.

adj. unctuous, oily, greasy, fatty, unguent, creamy.

vb. grease, oil, lubricate; resin, varnish; anoint.

C Organic matter

366 animate matter

n. creation, nature, animals, plants, fauna, flora; creature, organism, cell, protoplasm; biology, natural history, nature study, ecology, genetics, evolution, biochemistry, anatomy, physiology, botany, zoology.

adj. animate, organic, biological.

367 inorganic matter

n. mineral, rock, deposit, ore, metal, coal; geology, mineralogy, metallurgy.

adj. inorganic, inanimate, mineral, metallurgical.

368 life

n. life, existence, being; organism, human, body, creature, man, person, individual, personage, mortal.

soul, spirit, life-blood, breath, heart; élan, verve; vivification, animation, liveliness, vigour, vitality, force, energy.

adj. living, alive, surviving, in the flesh, vital; lively, animated, vigorous, vivacious, forceful, energetic, spirited, alive and kicking, active.

vb. live, exist, be, have life, breathe, respire; move, subsist; be spared, survive.

be born, come to life, come into the world, see the light; bear, beget, conceive, give birth to, bring to life.

vivify, quicken, animate, reanimate, vitalize, enliven, revive, breathe life into.

369 death

n. death, mortality; decease, dying, passing, departure, end, expiration, exit, extinction, parting, separation, release, homecall; loss, bereavement; fatality; demise, dissolution.

last hour, death bed, last breath, swansong; death list, death toll, casualty list; obituary; the dead, departed, deceased, ancestors, forefathers, those gone before.

adj. mortal, sick, perishing, deathly, moribund, at death's door, on one's last legs; dead, deceased, departed, late, lamented; lifeless, breathless; defunct, extinct, cold, extinguished, terminated, ended, exterminated, lost.

vb. die, depart, go, expire, pass away, give up the ghost, breathe one's last, go the way

of all flesh, be taken, kick the bucket (*sl.*);
perish, succumb, come to nothing, be no
more; be killed, lose one's life; push up
daisies (*inf.*).

370 killing

n. killing, slaying, slaughter, destruction,
assassination, murder, homicide, manslaughter; bloodshed, carnage, massacre,
genocide, butchery, holocaust, liquidation,
extermination, annihilation, decimation;
shooting, knifing, lynching,· poisoning,
execution, hanging, strangulation, electrocution, crucifixion, burning, drowning,
vivisection; euthanasia, mercy killing; abortion; suicide, self-destruction, hara-kiri,
kamikaze.

killer, murderer, assassin, slayer, butcher,
cut-throat, poisoner, strangler; gunman,
terrorist, gangster, homicidal maniac; hangman, executioner.

adj. killing, lethal, fatal, mortal, deadly,
destructive; homicidal, murderous, internecine; suicidal.

vb. kill, murder, slay, destroy, take life,
put to death, bump off (*sl.*), knock off (*sl.*),
do in (*sl.*), do away with (*inf.*), slaughter,
assassinate, massacre, butcher, mow down
(*inf.*), gun down (*inf.*), liquidate, annihilate,
decimate, exterminate; execute, behead, guill-
lotine, decapitate; shoot, gun, knife, hang,
lynch; poison; strangle, suffocate, choke,
asphyxiate; put to sleep (*inf.*), put down, put
away.

kill oneself, commit suicide, take one's
life, do oneself in (*sl.*), blow one's brains
out, shoot oneself, cut one's throat.

371 corpse

n. corpse, remains, body, carcass, skeleton,
relics, ashes, dust, mummy, cadaver, stiff
(*sl.*).

adj. cadaverous, corpse-like, deathlike,
deathly, pale.

372 burial

n. burial, funeral, interment, entombment,
sepulture; cremation, incineration; embal-
ment, mummification.

burial service, funeral rites, last rites,
mourning, obsequies; requiem, elegy, last
post, knell, passing bell; epitaph, obituary, in
memoriam, RIP; coffin, urn, sarcophagus,
pall, mummy case.

mortuary, morgue; undertaker, funeral
director; gravestone, headstone, tombstone,
monument, memorial; tomb, grave, sepul-
chre, vault, crypt, mausoleum, barrow; burial
ground, graveyard, churchyard, God's acre,

cemetery, catacomb, necropolis; pyre,
crematorium; war memorial, cenotaph;
exhumation, disinterment.

adj. buried, interred; funereal, funeral,
mourning, mournful, sad.

vb. bury, inter, inhume, entomb, enshrine,
embalm, lay out, lay to rest, sepulture;
cremate; exhume, disinter, unearth.

373 animality; animal

n. animality, fauna, zoology; animal,
creature, beast, vertebrate, invertebrate;
quadruped, biped, man; mammal, marsupial;
carnivore, herbivore, omnivore; fish, amphibian, mollusc, crustacean; bird, fowl, bird of
prey, waterfowl; insect; reptile; cattle, herd,
livestock, poultry, game; pet, domestic
animal; rodent, vermin, parasite.

adj. animal, zoological, mammalian;
piscine, fishy, amphibian; avian, birdlike.

374 vegetability; plant

n. vegetability, vegetation, botany; plant,
shrub; plantation, shrubbery, undergrowth,
corn, grain, cereal, crop, field; flower, bloom,
bud, petal, blossom; flower-bed, garden;
foliage; foliation, leafage; grass, pasture,
verdure, sod, turf, lawn; herb; weed; tree,
sapling, scion; branch, limb, bough, twig,
sprig, spray, shoot, stem, stalk, leaf; wood,
forest, bush, jungle; copse, spinney, coppice,
woodland, thicket, covert, arboretum;
forestry, dendrology, conservation; seed,
root, bulb.

adj. vegetal, vegetative, botanical, horticultural, floral, verdant, grassy, weedy,
arboreal.

375 zoology

n. zoology, life science, anthropology,
anatomy, physiology, ichthyology, ornithology, bird-watching, entomology, embryology, taxonomy.

adj. zoological, ornithological.

376 botany

n. botany, plant science, horticulture,
ecology, phytology.

adj. botanical, horticultural.

377 management of animals

n. animal husbandry, breeding, stock-
breeding, grazing, taming, domestication.

farm, ranch, homestead; fishery, aquarium; zoo, zoological gardens; veterinary
science, vet; shepherd, herdsman, herd,
cattleherd, cowherd.

vb. keep, husband, breed, rear, raise, herd,
drive, ranch, farm, tend, shepherd; feed,

fodder, graze, fatten, market; shear, chip, fleece; milk; tame, domesticate, train; groom.

378 agriculture

n. agriculture, farming, cultivation, horticulture, gardening, growing, crop raising, husbandry; strip farming, rotation crops, contour ploughing; landscape gardening.

farm, ranch, homestead, holding, smallholding, grange; kibbutz; farmland, meadow, grassland, farmstead, estate, croft, enclosure, land, field, soil, patch, plot, allotment, plantation; garden, orchard, nursery; greenhouse, vineyard, arboretum.

farmer, husbandman, agriculturalist, cultivator, tiller, planter, grower, rancher, homesteadman, peasant, serf, hiredman, labourer, farmhand; gardener, nurseryman, horticulturalist, landscape gardener.

adj. agrarian, farming, agricultural, rustic, rural, peasant; horticultural, garden.

vb. cultivate, till; fertilize, manure; water, irrigate; dig, plough, harrow; seed, sow, broadcast, disseminate, plant, drill, bed, transplant; weed, hoe; graft; harvest, reap, gather in, glean, winnow, thresh, mow, cut, scythe, bind, stack, pick, pluck.

379 mankind

n. mankind, humanity, human race, human beings, populace, population, the world, flesh; person, man, human being, individual, creature, mortal, body, earthling, *homo sapiens*, Adam, anthropoid; people, public, folk.

society, community, civilization, politics; nation, state, body politic, nationality, statehood; chauvinism, nationalism, imperialism; anthropology, social anthropology, ethnology, sociology.

adj. human, mortal; individual, personal; social, civilized; political, national, state, general, public, civil, federal, communal, societal, civic; nationalistic, chauvinist, racialist.

380 male

n. male, man, gentleman, sir; chap, fellow, guy (*sl.*), bloke (*inf.*), boy; virility, masculinity, manliness, manhood.

male animal, cock, drake, gander, dog, tom-cat, hart, stag, stallion, billy-goat, ox, bull; gelding.

adj. male, masculine; manly, virile; gentlemanly.

381 female

n. female, woman, lady, girl; madam, miss; fair sex, weaker sex; femininity, womanliness, girlishness, womanhood; feminism, women's lib; effeminacy; womankind.

female animal, hen, duck, goose, bitch, she-dog, filly, ewe, sow, hind, doe, mare, nanny-goat, cow.

adj. female, feminine, girlish, womanly, lady-like; effeminate.

IV Intellect

1 Formation of ideas

A Intellectual operations in general

382 intellect

n. intellect, mind, brain, consciousness, mentality, intelligence, intellectuality, instinct, faculties; perception, conception, capacity, judgment, understanding, reasoning, genius, wisdom; psychology, behaviourism; psychiatry, psychotherapy.

soul, spirit, psyche, heart, individuality, personality, conscience, self, ego, id, superego, unconscious, subconscious.

adj. mental, intellectual, conceptional, abstract, perceptual, critical, rational, conscious, cognitive, cerebral, intelligent; psychological, psychic, subconscious, subliminal; spiritual.

vb. conceive, cognize, perceive, reason, judge; realize, sense, mark, note.

see also **434**

383 absence of intellect

n. unintellectuality, unintelligence, imbecility, stupidity, shallowness, mindlessness, brainlessness.

adj. unintellectual, unintelligent, emptyheaded, mindless, brainless.

see also **435**

384 thought

n. thought, cogitation, concentration, brain-work; reflection, meditation, rumination, contemplation, thoughtfulness, brooding, pondering, absorption, preoccupation, deliberation; consideration, perception, appreciation, discernment, observation, reasoning, concluding.

adj. thoughtful, pensive, contemplative, reflective, studious; absorbed, engrossed, wrapped up in, dreamy; introspective; discerning, penetrating, intellectual.

vb. think, cogitate, consider, give thought to, concentrate, reflect, meditate, deliberate, ponder, muse, ruminate, contemplate, brood, turn over in one's mind, mull, study, examine, bear in mind, put on one's thinking cap (*inf.*), have on one's mind, take it into one's head (*inf.*); esteem, appraise, weigh up; philosophize, reconsider.

occur to, come to mind, strike, suggest itself, enter one's head.

385 absence of thought

n. thoughtlessness, irrationality, incomprehensibility, folly, senselessness, ignorance, inattention, inconsideration, carelessness, neglect.

adj. thoughtless, irrational, unreasoning, incomprehensible, foolish, blank, vacant, switched off (*inf.*).

vb. not think about, ignore, forget, dismiss, get off one's mind, get out of one's mind, get out of one's head; think no more of, not give another thought to, not give a second thought, not enter one's head.

386 idea

n. idea, notion, concept, conception, thought, mental impression, image, impression; conjecture, fancy, guess, theory, hypothesis, postulate; observation, opinion, assessment, plan.

see also **420**

387 topic

n. topic, subject, problem, matter, question; argument, theme, burden, concern, thesis, proposition, thrust, *leitmotif*, issue, point, point in question, moot point.

B Preliminary conditions and operations

388 curiosity

n. curiosity, interest, concern, regard; thirst, quest, desire, eagerness, inclination; inquisitiveness, intrusiveness, nosiness (*sl.*), prying.

questioner; busy-body, snoop, intruder, meddler, Nosy Parker (*sl.*); gossip, backbiter, chatterbox, scandalmonger.

adj. curious, interested, concerned, into (*inf.*), questioning; inquisitive, searching, poking, scrutinizing; intrusive, prying, snooping, meddlesome, nosy (*sl.*).

vb. enquire, question, investigate, seek; show interest, be into (*inf.*), have a thing about (*inf.*); intrude, pry, snoop, meddle, gossip, chatter, backbite.

389 incuriosity

n. incuriosity, apathy, dislike, disinclination.

adj. incurious, unconcerned, inattentive, apathetic, indifferent, uninquisitive, uninterested, bored.

vb. ignore, disregard, be blind to, dismiss, take no interest in, not care less.

390 attention

n. attention, regard, notice, observation, inspection; consideration, study, attentiveness; assiduousness, diligence; mindfulness, heed, heedfulness, vigilance; concentration, preoccupation.

adj. attentive, mindful; heeding, wary, vigilant; considerate, observant; studious, assiduous, diligent.

vb. pay attention, listen, catch, give heed to, observe, notice, take notice, mind, heed, look to, regard, note, take into account; consider, study, inspect, examine, mark, scrutinize, concentrate on; drink in (*inf.*), lap up (*inf.*), hang on someone's every word; lose oneself in; keep one's ear to the ground (*inf.*); attract, draw, pull, focus.

391 inattention

n. inattention, carelessness, inconsideration, unconcern, heedlessness, thoughtlessness; slackness, indolence; neglect, disregard; indifference, coolness, coldness, detachment; absent-mindedness, wandering.

adj. inattentive, careless, inconsiderate, thoughtless, heedless, unobservant; negligent, indifferent, cool, cold, detached; absent-minded, distracted.

vb. be inattentive, dream, day-dream, let one's mind wander; not catch, miss, disregard, overlook, neglect; go in one ear and out the other; distract, divert, draw away, turn away, call away, detract, attract from, beguile; upset, disconcert.

392 care

n. care, concern, regard, thought, heed, consideration, solicitude, thoughtfulness, pains; carefulness, scrupulousness, prudence, judiciousness, wisdom; watchfulness, vigilance, alertness; forethought, precaution, caution.

exactness, particularity, thoroughness, meticulousness, neatness, fastidiousness, conscientiousness; economy, conservation, frugality, management, husbandry, stewardship.

oversight, direction, surveillance, supervision, inspection, protection, guarding.

adj. careful, concerned, thoughtful, considerate, courteous, kind, solicitous; prudent, judicious, wise, discreet, unobtrusive, self-possessed, watchful, sober, alert, awake, circumspect, vigilant; diplomatic, politic.

thorough, rigorous, particular, precise, exact, exacting, discriminating, conscientious, meticulous, punctilious, scrupulous; neat, tidy, fussy, finicky; pedantic, fastidious, religious; assiduous, diligent, painstaking, dependable, faithful; economical, sparing, frugal, thrifty, stingy (*inf.*).

vb. be careful, mind, heed, tend, look after, take care of; watch, observe; superintend, supervise, direct, manage, stand over; baby-sit, chaperon; keep vigil; keep tabs on, follow up, protect, support, guard.

393 neglect

n. neglect, carelessness, unconcern, disregard, inconsideration, negligence, neglectfulness, apathy, indifference, omission, dereliction, failure, procrastination; imprudence, rashness, hastiness.

adj. negligent, careless, inconsiderate, unthinking, thoughtless, unmindful, forgetful, oblivious; remiss, lax, inattentive; lackadaisical, imprudent, unguarded, hasty, rash, unwary, reckless, unheeding, injudicious, unwise; apathetic, indifferent, casual, slipshod, lazy; wasteful, extravagant, immoderate.

vb. neglect, omit, miss, forget, dismiss, reject, leave undone, lose sight of, evade, gloss over, skip, skimp; disregard, ignore, overlook, not look at, pass over, make light of, brush aside, laugh off, pooh-pooh, shut one's eyes to, give the go-by, turn a blind eye to.

see also **920**

394 enquiry

n. enquiry, inquiry, examination, investigation, study, analysis, search, probe, quest, perusal; checking, scrutiny, review, inspection; question, query, request, invitation, petition, challenge, feeler; experiment, quiz, test, exam, viva, questionnaire; interrogation, interview, dialogue, cross-examination, grilling, catechism.

questioner, examiner, enquirer, interrogator, interviewer, researcher, investigator, canvasser, pollster.

adj. inquiring, inquisitive, curious, nosy (*sl.*); exploratory, fact-finding.

vb. enquire, ask, put a question, pose, put it to; call upon, request, invite, challenge, charge, bid, petition, canvass; question, interrogate, quiz, cross-examine, interview, grill; seek, look for, search, hunt, turn inside out, peruse; sniff out (*inf.*), smell out; investigate, examine, study, inspect, analyse, probe, scrutinize, check, review, monitor; try, hear; pry, snoop, spy.

395 answer

n. answer, reply, response, acknowledgement; comeback, feedback, rebuttal, rejoinder, retort; repartee, backchat, retaliation.

answerer, replier, correspondent, examinee, candidate.

adj. answering, responsive.

vb. answer, reply, respond, come back to, write back, acknowledge, remark, rejoin, retort, answer back, rebut.

396 experiment

n. experiment, test, research; observation, analysis, inspection, operation, diagnosis, exercise; check, verification, proof, sifting; rehearsal, practice run, trial run, test case, pilot, pilot scheme; feeler, probe; speculation, guess, conjecture, trial and error, hit and miss, shot in the dark, hypothesis; sounding board, guinea pig.

researcher, research worker, scientist, boffin (*sl.*), back-room boy, experimenter, experimentalist, speculator.

adj. experimental, hypothetical; tentative, trial, provisional, temporary, probationary, preliminary, preparatory, unproved, speculative, trial, test.

vb. experiment, investigate, study, examine, scrutinize, explore, research, search, sound out, prove; analyse, diagnose; check, verify, prove; guess, speculate, hypothesize; put out a feeler, see which way the wind is blowing, spy out the land.

397 comparison

n. comparison, juxtaposition; weighing, estimation, measurement; relation, connection, association, balance, match, parallel, parallelism, correspondence, equation; identification, resemblance, similarity, likening, analogy, illustration, example, picture, metaphor, simile, allegory; contrast, opposition.

vb. compare, juxtapose, parallel, draw a parallel between, put side by side; measure, weigh, confront, collate; liken, relate, associate, link, balance, match, equate; contrast, oppose, separate.

398 discrimination

n. discrimination, discernment, acumen, astuteness, keenness, shrewdness, penetration; distinction, nicety, differentiation; diagnosis, appreciation, critique, judgment, sense, sensitivity, tact, feel, refinement, taste, selection, choice.

adj. discriminating, careful, selective, particular, exacting, choosy (*inf.*), judicious, tactful, discerning, perceptive, sensitive, critical, tasteful, refined.

vb. discriminate, differentiate, discern, tell apart, tell from, distinguish; compare and contrast; choose, pick carefully, select, separate, set apart.

399 indiscrimination

n. indiscrimination, uncriticalness, insensitiveness, tastelessness.

adj. indiscriminate, undiscriminating, unselective, uncritical, undiscerning, careless; mixed, blanket, promiscuous; random, haphazard; aimless, chaotic, confused.

vb. not discriminate, draw no disctinction, disregard differences, lump together; confuse, confound, mix, muddle, jumble together.

400 measurement

n. measurement, mensuration; quantification; estimation, determination, computation, calculation, assessment, evaluation, reckoning; graduation, calibration; measure, dimension, distance, degree, pitch, time; size, length, depth, height, width, breadth, thickness; area; mass, weight, density, volume, capacity, pressure, intensity, speed, strength, calibre, viscosity; quantity, magnitude, range, extent; amplitude, frequency, ratio, diameter, radius; temperature.

meter, gauge, scale, rule, ruler, tapemeasure, slide-rule, calculator, computer; scales, balance, mark, grade, step, point, limit, standard, criterion; weights and measures, imperial system, avoirdupois, apothecary, troy, metric system, SI unit; metrication.

adj. mensural, dimensional; measurable, assessable, calculable, computable.

vb. measure, quantify, estimate, compute, assess, count, reckon, determine, evaluate, appraise, calculate; gauge, calibrate, graduate; take a reading; level, square; survey, map; average; check; go metric, metricate.

C   Materials for reasoning

401 evidence

n. evidence, fact, clue, reason, justification, explanation, grounds, data, case; support, foundation, backing; sign, indication, trace; document, documentation, information; testimony, witness, statement, plea, asser-

tion, allegation, attestation, exhibit, reference, affidavit; confirmation, corroboration.

adj. suggestive, indicative, symptomatic, corroborative, supporting.

vb. evidence, show, suggest, indicate, evince, illustrate, demonstrate, document, manifest, imply; confirm, verify, support, substantiate, attest, corroborate; testify, bear witness to, witness, affirm; speak for itself (*inf.*), speak volumes (*inf.*).

see also **413**

402 counter-evidence

n. counter-evidence, counterclaim, defence, rebuttal, answer, reply.

adj. rebutting, defending, conflicting; uncorroborative, countervailing; contradictory, contrary, answering, replying.

vb. weigh against, contradict, rebut, refute, squash, deny; be contrary to; cancel out.

see also **414**

403 qualification

n. qualification, modification, limitation, restriction; proviso, exception, reservation; allowance.

adj. qualifying, qualificatory, provisional, contingent, conditional, mitigating, extenuating.

vb. qualify, modify, adjust; limit, restrict, restrain, moderate, mitigate, lessen, temper; condition, colour, make exceptions, exempt, allow for, make allowances for.

see also **700**

404 possibility

n. possibility, potentiality, practicability, feasibility, plausibility, reasonableness, virtuality.

adj. possible, likely, probable; virtual, potential; able, capable, viable, feasible, plausible, practical, practicable, available, attainable, within reach, obtainable, within the bounds of possibility; conceivable, thinkable, imaginable, credible.

vb. be possible, can, may, might, stand a chance; make possible, enable, admit of.

see also **406**

405 impossibility

n. impossibility, impracticability, unavailability, inaccessibility; unreasonableness, no hope, hopelessness, no chance.

adj. impossible, unbelievable, inconceivable, umimaginable, unthinkable; prohibited; insoluble, difficult; unable, implausible, unpracticable, unavailable, insurmountable, insuperable, inaccessible, unobtainable, out of the question, beyond the bounds of possibility.

vb. be impossible, defy possibilities; not dream of (*inf.*); make impossible, exclude.

adv. no way (*inf.*).

see also **407**

406 probability

n. probability, likelihood, likeliness, expectation; prospect, promise, chance, possibility, good chance, hope, opportunity.

adj. probable, likely, expected; reasonable, presumable, on the cards, supposable; promised, well-founded, seeming; feasible, practicable, workable, plausible, credible.

vb. be probable, may well happen, show signs of; make likely, increase the chances of, hope for.

adv. probably, likely, no doubt, in all probability, quite possibly, most likely, to be expected, to be supposed, as likely as not, everything being equal.

407 improbability

n. improbability, unlikelihood, implausibility, inconceivableness, unreasonableness; rarity, infrequency; bare possibility, million to one chance.

adj. improbable, unlikely, unexpected, unreasonable, impracticable, unworkable, implausible, unbelievable, hardly possible, unheard of, doubtful, dubious, questionable; absurd, extraordinary.

vb. be improbable, probably not happen.

408 certainty

n. certainty, certitude; conviction, assurance; reliance, confidence, trust; truth, accuracy, genuineness; dogmatism; unambiguity, conclusiveness; necessity, inevitability, inexorability.

foregone conclusion, safe bet, sure thing (*inf.*), dead cert (*sl.*).

adj. certain, settled, decided, final, definite; absolute, sure, conclusive, solid, irrefutable, indubitable, indisputable, unquestionable, unmistakable, incontrovertible, unassailable, undisputed; reliable, unfailing, unshakable, inerrant, infallible, sound, authoritative, unerring, trustworthy; unambiguous, unequivocal, incontestable; unconditional; ascertained, certified, verified, attested, confirmed, ratified; self-evident, axiomatic.

vb. make certain, guarantee, authenticate, certify, check, confirm, test, prove, verify, corroborate, ratify; ensure, secure, settle, attest, endorse, clinch; commit, engage, take sides; seal, sign, shake hands.

adv. certainly, without doubt, of course, definitely, at all events, sure thing (*inf.*); in the bag (*inf.*).

409 uncertainty

n. uncertainty, incertitude; unreliability, questionableness, unpredictability, untrustworthiness, ambiguity; vagueness, obscurity; inconclusiveness, indeterminateness, improbability, unlikelihood.

doubt, disbelief, unbelief, suspicion, misgiving, scepticism, agnosticism, faithlessness, doubtfulness, incredulity; indecision, equivocalness, wavering, hesitancy, suspense; perplexity, bewilderment; puzzle, problem, maze, dilemma, quandary, enigma; fog, haziness; anybody's guess.

adj. uncertain, doubtful, undecided; unsure, inconclusive, ambiguous, vague, unclear, indeterminate, unpredictable, unlikely, possible; risky, chancy, insecure; haphazard, random, casual; questionable, unreliable, fallible, erring; shakable, precarious; puzzling, perplexing.

controversial, open, debatable, contentious, problematical, moot; uncertified, unverified, unattested, unconfirmed, unratified.

doubting, unbelieving, suspicious, sceptical, faithless, distrustful, agnostic.

vb. be uncertain, doubt, flounder, grope, fumble; suspect, smell a rat; not know where one stands, not know which way to turn; sit on the fence, waver; fall between two stools; puzzle, bewilder, perplex.

adv. in the air, in question, open to question.

D Reasoning processes

410 reasoning

n. reasoning, rationalizing; judgment, argumentation; reason, rationality, logic, rationalism; thinking, brainwork, cogitation, knowing, realizing; insight, discernment, acumen, penetration, understanding, comprehension, grasp; reflection, deliberation; concluding.

conclusion, inference, deduction, induction, derivation; syllogism; problem, proposition, premise, postulate, thesis, theorem.

discussion, conversation, exchange, dialogue, interview, disputation, argument, dispute, debate, controversy, symposium; apologetics.

adj. rational, reasoning, logical, sound, rationalistic, reasonable; thoughtful, deliberate, collected; arguing, discursive, controversial, polemical; argumentative.

vb. reason, argue, discuss, converse, dispute, talk about, explain; defend, justify, plead, make out a case, support, contend; philosophize; conclude, put two and two together (*inf.*), deduce, infer, derive, syllogize; be reasonable, add up (*inf.*), make sense, hold water.

411 intuition

n. intuition, instinct, sentiment, feeling, sense; insight, inspiration, extra-sensory perception, ESP, sixth sense; automatic reaction, reflex action, hunch, presentiment, premonition, impression.

adj. intuitive, instinctive; involuntary, reflex, automatic, mechanical, unthinking; spontaneous, inspired, impulsive.

vb. feel, sense, feel in one's bones, guess, just know, have a funny feeling, have the feeling, follow one's nose.

412 false reasoning

n. sophistry, irrationality, unreasonableness, unsoundness, invalidity; delusion, deceit, deception, erroneousness, speciousness, evasion.

fallacy, sophism, ambiguity, solecism, illogicality, paralogism; inconsistency, *non sequitur*, contradiction; circular argument, vicious circle; misinterpretation; miscalculation; preconception; perversion, prejudice, deviation, aberration.

adj. sophistic, fallacious, illogical, specious, inconsistent, loose, contradictory, ambiguous, solecistic; irrational, unreasonable, unsound, untenable, invalid, deceptive, erroneous, heretical.

vb. reason falsely, evade the issue, beat about the bush, miss the point, beg the question; cavil.

413 demonstration

n. demonstration, proof, verification, justification, establishment, affirmation, validation, corroboration; averment; explanation, elucidation, interpretation, illustration; exhibition, presentation, display.

adj. demonstrative; demonstrated, clear, evident, conclusive, certain, decisive; established, concluded, upheld, valid; demonstrable, verifiable, deducible, inferable.

vb. demonstrate, prove, show, verify, make evident, establish, confirm, substantiate, bear out, affirm, authenticate, attest, validate, test, check; declare, testify, witness, document; have a case; settle, determine; justify; explain, illustrate, describe; manifest, exhibit, display.

414 disproof

n. disproof, confutation, refutation, invalidation, rebuttal, contradiction, denial; upset; exposure; clincher.

adj. disproved, confuted, invalidated; shown up, exposed; contradicted.

vb. disprove, prove false, rebut, invalidate, repudiate, contradict, deny; contend, debate, argue, oppose, dispute; show up (*inf.*), discredit, expose; overthrow, overturn, defeat, finish, confound, overwhelm, crush, floor, silence; knock the bottom out of (*inf.*), cut the ground from under one's feet, get the better of.

E   Results of reasoning

415 judgment

n. judgment, consideration, contemplation, appraisal, examination, review, weighing, sifting, assessment, estimation, appreciation, evaluation, determination; adjudication, arbitration; report, opinion, view, belief, idea, decree, decision, finding, recommendation, pronouncement, verdict, ruling, resolution.

judge, assessor, examiner, valuer, surveyor, adjudicator, arbitrator, referee, umpire.

adj. judicial, judicious; critical; unprejudiced, unbiased.

vb. judge, consider, contemplate, size up (*inf.*), examine, review, appraise, survey, analyse, weigh, sift, assess, evaluate, estimate, appreciate; decide, conclude, find, recommend, pronounce, rule, decree, settle, adjudicate, arbitrate.

416 misjudgment

n. misjudgment, miscalculation, misconception, misunderstanding, misinterpretation, distortion, overestimation, preconception; underestimation; prejudice, bias; narrow-mindedness, pettiness, narrowness, bigotry.

adj. misjudging, wrong; uncritical, unrealistic; injudicious, unwise, ill-judged; partial, unfair, one-sided, biased, prejudiced, intolerant; narrow-minded, petty, mean, narrow, short-sighted, bigoted, insular.

vb. misjudge, miscalculate, misconceive, misconstrue, misapprehend, misunderstand, bark up the wrong tree (*inf.*); undervalue, overvalue, overrate; prejudge, presume, suppose, preconceive, jump to conclusions; prejudice, bias, jaundice, twist, sway, warp, influence.

see also **916**

417 overestimation

n. overestimation, overvaluation, overrating, exaggeration, overstatement; optimism.

adj. overestimated, exaggerated.

vb. overestimate, exaggerate, overvalue, overrate; maximize, emphasize, make a mountain out of a molehill, make too much of, paint in glowing colours.

see also **481**

418 underestimation

n. underestimation, undervaluation, understatement, minimization; pessimism.

adj. underestimated, understated; deprecatory; modest.

vb. underestimate, underplay, play down, underrate, understate, minimize; depreciate, disparage, slight; make light of, not do justice to, think too little of.

419 discovery

n. discovery, finding, disclosure, uncovering; manifestation, revelation; detection, identification, catching; invention; exploration.

adj. on the right track, near, close, warm (*inf.*).

vb. discover, find, hit upon; realize, see, perceive, understand, become aware of, get wise to, get on to, twig (*inf.*); meet, come across, happen upon; expose, disclose, detect, spot, lay bare, reveal, uncover, unearth, bring to light, run to earth (*inf.*), run to ground (*inf.*), track down; catch in the act, catch red-handed.

420 belief

n. belief, credence, trust, acceptance, faith, credit; reliance, dependence, conviction, confidence, persuasion; certainty, surety, assurance, hope; admission, confession, avowal.

creed, doctrine, dogma, credo, revelation; tenet, canon, principle; articles of faith, catechism.

opinion, thought, view, sentiment, idea, notion, conception, impression, assumption; attitude, way of thinking; point of view, position, outlook, angle, stand, stance.

adj. believing, accepting, reliant, dependent, convinced, persuaded, certain, confident; believable, credible, tenable, plausible, trustworthy, reliable, unfailing.

vb. believe, accept, hold, trust, depend, rely, be convicted of, be persuaded of, take at one's word, take on trust, take one's word for; think, consider, regard as, suppose, presume, surmise, fancy, assume, deem,

conclude; come round to, change one's views, be converted; have faith in, be a believer, profess, confess.

convince, persuade, bring round, prove, argue, assure, satisfy, make realize, bring home to; teach; captivate, have a way with (*inf.*).

see also **854**

421 unbelief

n. unbelief, disbelief, doubt, uncertainty, incredulity, scepticism, misgiving, suspicion, mistrust, distrust, qualm, hesitation, reservation, apprehension, irresolution; faithlessness, rejection; agnosticism, atheism.

adj. unbelieving, disbelieving, doubting, questioning, sceptical, distrusting, incredulous; unbelievable, untenable, unreliable, doubtful, dubious, suspicious, questionable, implausible.

vb. disbelieve, doubt, hesitate, waver, not believe, give no credence to, lack confidence in, set no store by; mistrust, suspect, question, challenge.

422 gullibility

n. gullibility, credulity, simpleness, unsophistication.

adj. gullible, credulous, trusting, unsuspecting, simple, naive, unsophisticated, inexperienced, guileless, green.

vb. be gullible, fall for (*inf.*), be easily persuaded.

423 incredulity

n. incredulity, suspicion, scepticism; sophistication.

adj. incredulous, unbelieving, sceptical, unresponsive, ungullible, sophisticated.

vb. refuse to believe, distrust, doubt; reject, turn a deaf ear to.

see also **421**

424 assent

n. assent, affirmative, yes; approval, agreement, acceptance, support, approbation; authorization, permission, consent, empowering, legalization, authority, sanction, guarantee, warrant, authentication, ratification, endorsement, affirmation, go-ahead (*inf.*), green light (*inf.*), nod (*sl.*).

like-mindedness, unanimity, consensus, general agreement; supporter, follower, assenter, signer, subscriber, ratifier, signatory, aye.

adj. assenting, acquiescent; approved, accepted, voted, carried, passed; unanimous, of one mind.

vb. assent, say yes to, agree, concur, affirm,

accept, support, subscribe to, approve, vote for, pass, rubber-stamp (*inf.*), put up with (*inf.*), go along with, tolerate, stand for (*inf.*), bear, endure, acquiesce; acknowledge, admit, concede, grant, yield, recognize, defer to.

authorize, grant permission, empower, legalize, ratify, sign, endorse, authenticate, seal.

425 dissent

n. dissent, disapproval, disagreement, dissidence, disapprobation; difference, variance, discord, dissension, protest, controversy, vendetta, animosity, division; nonconformity; non-acceptance, withdrawal, secession; objection, reservation, negative, no.

dissenter, objector, protester, rebel, nonconformist, caviller; interrupter, heckler; separatist; recusant.

adj. dissident, disagreeing, differing; protesting, objecting.

vb. dissent, disagree, disapprove, differ, agree to differ, protest, object, oppose, challenge, heckle, shout down, take exception; reject, refuse, contradict; withdraw, secede.

426 knowledge

n. knowledge, knowing, awareness, consciousness, recognition, realization, understanding, grasp, cognition; intelligence, education, instruction, learning, erudition, scholarship, culture, bookishness; accomplishments, attainments; facts, information, encyclopedia; expertise, know-how, skill, proficiency; wisdom, maturity, experience.

adj. knowing, conscious, mindful, aware, cognizant; discerning, perceptive; acquainted, familiar, well versed in, well grounded in, *au fait;* clever, intelligent, informed, instructed, trained, knowledgeable, educated, well-taught, well-read, learned, erudite, scholarly, cultured, intellectual; mature, wise, experienced.

known, widely known, common, proverbial, commonplace, household name, hackneyed; infamous, notorious.

vb. know, realize, understand, grasp, see, perceive, apprehend, be aware of, discern, appreciate, recognize; experience; be well-informed, be well up on, be into (*inf.*), know backwards, know inside out, know like the back of one's hand.

see also **434, 460**

427 ignorance

n. ignorance, unawareness, unconsciousness, unknowingness, nescience; unenlighten-ment, incomprehension, darkness, fog, haziness, vagueness; inexperience, immaturity, greenness, naivety, simplicity, emptyheadedness, stupidity; unlearnedness, unintellectuality, illiteracy; unskilfulness, awkwardness.

smattering, shallowness; unknown, unknown quantity, unexplored ground, virgin territory, mystery, closed book, sealed book.

adj. ignorant, unaware, unknowing; unmindful, unconscious, disregarding; inexperienced, immature, green, inept, simple, stupid, thick, dense; unenlightened, in the dark, unfamiliar with, not conversant, a stranger to, none the wiser; untaught, illiterate, uneducated, untrained, backward, unscholarly, unlearned, uncultivated, unread, uncultured, Philistine, unintellectual; unknown, untold, unseen, mysterious, secret, undiscovered, virgin, uncharted.

vb. not know, be ignorant, be in the dark, not have any idea, not have the foggiest idea (*inf.*); pass (*inf.*).

see also **435**

428 student

n. student, scholar, schoolchild, learner, disciple; philosopher, scientist, researcher, expert, man of letters, wise man, savant, sage; professor, don, teacher, doctor; bookworm, intellectual, egghead (*inf.*); genius, brain, know-all, mine of information, walking encyclopedia.

see also **473, 474**

429 ignoramus

n. ignoramus, know-nothing, dunce, fool, blockhead; greenhorn, raw recruit, babe, simpleton.

see also **437**

430 truth

n. truth, fact, reality, the case, gospel truth, plain truth, real thing, real McCoy (*inf.*).

trueness, verity, correctness, exactitude, accuracy, precision, perfection, rectitude, faithfulness, sincerity, honesty; authenticity, infallibility, genuineness, validity.

adj. true, truthful, veracious, real, right, factual, correct, objective, actual; historical; genuine, authentic, original, official, veritable; unadulterated, unmixed; attested, valid, guaranteed; undisputed, conclusive, final; accurate, exact, precise, faithful, infallible; sincere, honest, upright.

vb. be true, be the case; ring true; hit the

nail on the head (*inf.*); come true, come about, happen, occur.

see also **476**

431 error

n. error, mistake, fault, blunder, failure, fall, flaw, lapse, omission, lie, untruth, wrong, deviation, sin; *faux pas*, slip, slip-up (*inf.*); misjudgment, misunderstanding, misconception, inaccuracy, mismanagement; misprint, literal; bloomer (*sl.*), clanger (*sl.*), howler (*sl.*).

erroneousness, falsity, inaccurateness, inexactness.

adj. wrong, incorrect, unreal, untrue; unauthentic, unoriginal, spurious; inaccurate, inexact, imprecise; erroneous, mistaken, lying, untruthful, in error; unfaithful, disloyal, deceitful, corrupt, unsound; deceptive, fallacious, misleading, pretended, sham, counterfeit, faked, mocked; misunderstood; fallible.

vb. go wrong, make a mistake, err, blunder, slip up (*inf.*), bungle; be wrong, be mistaken; misconceive, misunderstand; not hold water, fall down, fall to the ground; mislead, lead astray, lead up the garden path (*inf.*), pervert, deceive, trick, hoax.

see also **477, 478**

432 maxim

n. maxim, proverb, saying, truth, text, dictum, motto, slogan, watchword, moral, aphorism, adage, axiom; banality, truism, platitude, commonplace, cliché; epigram, witticism.

adj. aphoristic, proverbial, epigrammatic; brief, concise, pithy, terse; trite, commonplace.

433 absurdity

n. absurdity, ridiculousness, ludicrousness, outrageousness, folly, silliness, stupidity, nonsense; spoonerism, malapropism; jest, trick, practical joke, prank, farce, buffoonery, clowning, wildness; extravaganza.

adj. absurd, ridiculous, crazy, farcical, nonsensical, senseless, inane, wild, foolish, silly, stupid, bizarre, extravagant, fantastic.

vb. be absurd, talk nonsense, fool around; play tricks.

see also **451**

434 intelligence; wisdom

n. intelligence, understanding, brightness, cleverness, brilliance; genius, talent, brains, grey matter, intellect, sense, common sense, wit.

wisdom, experience, erudition, sagacity,

sapience; shrewdness, discernment, judgment, acumen, insight, perspicacity, sharpness, acuteness, penetration, prudence, foresight.

adj. intelligent, clever, bright, brilliant, able, knowledgeable; wise, sagacious, shrewd, prudent, knowing, contemplative, reasoning, thoughtful, sober, sensible, judicious, circumspect, discreet, considerate, astute, perceptive, perspicacious, far-sighted, discerning, quick, acute, sharp, penetrating, keen, discriminating, having one's wits about one, not born yesterday (*inf.*).

vb. be wise, understand, discern; have one's head screwed on the right way (*inf.*).

see also **426**

435 unintelligence; folly

n. unintelligence, stupidity, dullness, slowness, heaviness; foolishness, folly, weakness, shallowness, silliness, simplicity, childishness, puerility, imbecility; imprudence, short-sightedness, indiscretion.

adj. unintelligent, unthinking, unreasoning; stupid, dull, slow, weak, shallow, superficial, vacant, simple, dumb, thick, dense, empty-headed, slow-witted, feeble-minded, simple-minded, weak-minded, half-witted, blockish, oafish, feather-brained, doltish; foolish, crazy, silly, insane, inane, idiotic, imbecile, puerile, childish; backward, retarded, handicapped, subnormal, deprived; unwise, imprudent, short-sighted, undiscerning.

vb. be foolish, act the fool, fool around, lark about (*inf.*).

see also **427**

436 sage

n. sage, wise man, man of learning, savant, pundit, expert, doctor, scholar, master, great thinker, authority, oracle, elder statesman, connoisseur, luminary; wiseacre, know-all, sciolist.

see also **428, 473**

437 fool

n. fool, simpleton, dunce, idiot, ignoramus, scatterbrain, half-wit, fat-head, thickhead, blockhead, nitwit, nincompoop, moron, cretin, imbecile, numskull, bore, dolt, ass, buffoon, chump (*sl.*), lout, oaf, ninny, jerk (*sl.*), twit (*sl.*).

see also **429, 630**

438 sanity

n. sanity, saneness, balance, normality, clearmindedness, lucidity, wholesomeness, *mens sana*, rationality, reason.

adj. sane, normal, sound-minded, healthy-minded, sound, right-minded, sober, lucid, in one's right mind, self-possessed, all there (*inf.*).

439 insanity

n. insanity, insaneness, madness, lunacy; imbecility, cretinism, idiocy; phobia, mania, craze, passion, obsession, infatuation, fixation, compulsion; mental illness, nervous breakdown, nervous disorder; nervousness, nerves; hysteria, frenzy, fever, attack, fit, rage; peculiarity, eccentricity, abnormality, oddity.

adj. insane, mad, unsound, unbalanced, crazy, deranged, confused, demented, rabid, berserk, out of one's mind, off one's head, off one's rocker (*sl.*); obsessed, infatuated; frenzied, wild, raging, furious; eccentric, odd, cranky, peculiar.

vb. be mad, wander, ramble; go mad, lose one's sanity, take leave of one's senses, go out of one's mind, crack up (*inf.*), go off one's rocker (*sl.*); madden, drive mad, unbalance.

440 madman

n. madman, lunatic, mental case, loony (*sl.*), bedlamite; maniac, psychopath, psychotic, paranoid, hysteric, neurotic, manic-depressive, melancholic, hypochondriac, kleptomaniac; imbecile, idiot, moron, cretin, mongol; fool, crank, nut (*sl.*), eccentric, freak, weirdo (*inf.*), crackpot (*inf.*).

F Extension of thought

441 memory

n. memory, recollection, reminiscence, retrospection, recall, review, flashback, afterthought, hindsight, reconsideration, reflection, thought; retention, good memory, photographic memory, *déjà vu.*

memorandum, memo, reminder, record, note, jotting, scribble, mark; notes, summary; agenda, minutes; mnemonic, aid to memory; souvenir, memento, token, keepsake, relic, trinket; testimonial, memorial, monument, trophy, commemoration; warning, advice, suggestion, hint; prompt, prompter; memoirs, reminiscences, recollections, memories, memorabilia; diary, journal, album, scrapbook, notebook.

adj. remembered, recalled, retained, unforgotten, fresh, vivid; half-remembered, at the back of one's mind; reminiscent, reminding, evocative; memorable, unforgettable, indelibly fixed on one's mind; commemorative, memorial.

vb. remember, recollect, recall, bring to mind, be reminded of, think of, not forget; review, retrace, go back, flash back, look back, turn one's thoughts back, reminisce, call up, revive, rake up the past, drag up (*inf.*), dredge up (*inf.*); recognize, identify, know again, make out.

come to mind, ring a bell, stay in the memory, never be forgotten, haunt, recur, penetrate, stay in one's mind, not leave one's thoughts, not get out of one's mind.

memorize, learn, commit to memory, know by heart, learn by rote, master, impress, retain, fix in the mind; keep always, hold dear, treasure, cherish, commemorate, enshrine in the memory, keep the memory alive.

remind, prompt, suggest, hint, bring back, make one think of, jog one's memory, refresh one's memory; warn, throw the book at (*inf.*).

442 oblivion

n. oblivion, forgetfulness, unmindfulness, absent-mindedness, amnesia, memory like a sieve, loss of memory, blankness, complete blank, mental block; insensibleness, indifference, carelessness.

adj. forgotten, unremembered, lost, out of one's mind, clean forgotten, unrecalled, unretained, in one ear and out the other; out of sight, out of mind; almost remembered, on the tip of one's tongue.

oblivious, forgetful, unmindful, heedless, inattentive, preoccupied, distracted, absent-minded.

vb. forget, fail to remember, have no recollection, put out of one's mind, have a short memory, think no more of, not give another thought, one's memory be a blank, escape one; be forgotten, sink into oblivion, fade from one's memory.

443 expectation

n. expectation, expectancy, looking forward, contemplation, anticipation, prospect, outlook; confidence, trust, hope, high hopes; preparedness; suspense, apprehension, pessimism.

adj. expectant, waiting, in anticipation, looking forward to, in suspense, on tenterhooks, itching, on edge, with bated breath; hoping, hopeful, confident; eager, watchful, vigilant, prepared; apprehensive, pessimistic.

expected, awaited, anticipated, foreseen,

predicted, prophesied, longed for, looked for; on the cards, prospective.

vb. expect, look forward to, promise oneself, hope for, anticipate, contemplate, foresee, long for, bargain for (*inf.*), predict, prophesy, forecast, see coming, take for granted; wait for, await, bide one's time, mark time, hold one's breath, be in suspense; rely on, bank on, count on; be expected, lead one to expect, not put it past (*inf.*), be just like one.

444 non-expectation

n. inexpectation, unpreparedness, unexpectedness; surprise, shock, start, jolt, blow, bombshell, bolt from the blue, thunderbolt; turn-up for the book (*sl.*).

adj. unexpected, unforeseen, sudden, surprising, astonishing, staggering; unheralded, unpredicted, uncontemplated; unheard of, not thought of; more than one bargained for, not on the cards, without warning, out of the blue.

surprised, startled, thunderstruck, off one's guard, unready, unprepared, caught napping.

vb. not expect, not bargain for; surprise, take by surprise, catch unawares, catch in the act, catch red-handed, make one jump, startle, astonish, bowl over (*inf.*), knock down with a feather; come unexpectedly, turn up.

445 disappointment

n. disappointment, foiling, bafflement; discouragement, despondency, dissatisfaction, unfulfilment, discontent, frustration, disillusionment, regret, distress, displeasure.

bad news, setback, adversity, defeat, failure, anti-climax, miscarriage, let-down (*inf.*).

adj. disappointed, discouraged, dissatisfied, thwarted, baffled, unsuccessful, defeated, foiled, let-down (*inf.*), disconcerted, depressed, frustrated, disillusioned, full of regrets, despondent; disappointing, unsatisfactory, inadequate, insufficient, not up to expectations.

vb. disappoint, fail, let down (*inf.*), thwart, foil, baffle; come short of, dash one's hopes, not come up to expectations, leave much to be desired; frustrate, disconcert, disillusion, dissatisfy, let the side down (*inf.*).

446 foresight

n. foresight, second sight, foresightedness, anticipation; forethought, premeditation, preconsideration, preconception.

adj. foreseeing, foresighted, looking ahead, anticipatory.

vb. foresee, prophesy, forecast, anticipate; see ahead, look into the future, have a premonition, feel in one's bones.

447 prediction

n. prediction, forecast, foretelling, prophecy, prognostication, prognosis, foresight, forethought, foreknowledge, precognition, prescience, prevision; augury, divination, vaticination, astrology, clairvoyancy, soothsaying, fortune-telling, crystal-gazing, palmistry, casting lots; parapsychology, extrasensory perception; telepathy, telesthesia.

omen, sign, indication, symptom, portent, clue, hint, auspice, writing on the wall; warning, forewarning, foreboding, presentiment; guess, estimate, conjecture, budget; foretoken; presage; horoscope, fortune; herald, harbinger.

oracle, forecaster, prognosticator, prophet, prophetess, seer; fortune-teller, soothsayer, clairvoyant, augur, diviner, palmist, astrologer, crystal-gazer, gipsy; witch, wizard, medium; sibyl, haruspex; thought-reader, mind-reader, telepath, parapsychologist; weatherman, meteorologist.

adj. predicting, predictive, prognostic, divinatory, clairvoyant, portentous, significant; auspicious, favourable; ominous, foreboding; psychic, second-sighted; supernatural, paranormal, parapsychological; predictable, foreseen, expected, likely; divinable.

vb. predict, forecast, prognosticate, foresee, foretell, prophesy, vaticinate; forewarn; promise; bode, forebode, betoken, portend, foreshadow, presage; divine, augur, tell the future, tell fortunes, cast lots, read one's hand, read one's palm, read tea leaves.

see also **984**

G Creative thought

448 supposition

n. supposition, guesswork, speculation, theorizing, postulation.

guess, surmise, notion, fancy, conjecture, inkling, hint, intimation, shrewd idea, vague idea, sneaking suspicion, rough guess, wild guess, shot in the dark.

premise, presupposition, postulate, proposition; inference, deduction, conclusion; thesis, hypothesis, working hypothesis, theory.

theorist, scientist, theorizer, academic, thinker, speculator, backroom boy, boffin (*sl.*).

adj. suppositional, unproved, tentative,

speculative, conjectural, hypothetical, theoretical; supposed, assumed, presupposed, presumed, reputed, alleged, postulated, putative.

vb. suppose, believe, imagine, think, fancy, deem, guess, venture a guess, conjecture, speculate, estimate, divine, surmise, suspect, gather, assume, presume, presuppose; postulate, posit; infer, imply, deduce, theorize.

449 imagination

n. imagination, inventiveness, creativity, originality, visualization; fantasy, diversion, whimsy, day-dreaming, castle-building, pipe-dreaming, wishful thinking, escapism; utopia, paradise, world of fantasy, cloud-cuckoo land, dream world.

idea, figment of the imagination, invention, notion, fancy, whim, caprice, vagary, chimera, will-o'-the-wisp, vision, appearance, day-dream, castles in the air, romance, flight of fancy, dream, nightmare.

visionary, prophet, seer, idealist, escapist, Quixote, dreamer, day-dreamer.

adj. imaginative, inventive, creative, resourceful, inspired, visionary, idealistic, with one's head in the clouds, quixotic, impractical, unrealistic; imaginary, fanciful, fantastic, capricious, whimsical, chimerical, dreamlike, ideal, utopian, fictitious, pretended, make-believe, illusory, fabulous.

vb. imagine, picture, conjure up, envisage, conceive, suppose, visualize; invent, create, make up, think of, devise, fabricate, coin, hatch; dream, muse, fancy, fantasize, idealize, romanticize, build castles in the air, daydream, pretend, make believe.

2 Communication of ideas

A Nature of ideas communicated

450 meaning

n. meaning, sense, significance, interpretation, implication, explanation; intent, aim, import, drift, tenor, thrust, purport; substance, essence, content.

meaningfulness, expressiveness; signification, connotation, denotation, reference, referendum, definition; unambiguity, equivalence, synonymity; synonym, related word.

adj. meaningful, significant, indicative, expressive, suggestive, evocative; substantial, pithy, full of meaning, pregnant; unambiguous; literal, verbal, word for word, verbatim, exact, faithful, true; semantic, linguistic.

vb. mean, signify, designate, refer to, drive at (*inf.*), denote, connote, indicate, symbolize, suggest, express, convey, declare, state, assert, spell; intimate, hint, betoken, bode, purport, import; imply, involve, speak of, touch on, point to.

451 meaninglessness

n. meaninglessness, senselessness, inexpressiveness, expressionlessness, nonsensicalness; misinterpretation, illogicality, ambiguity.

nonsense, balderdash, rubbish, twaddle, blather, rot (*sl.*), poppycock (*sl.*), trash, inanity, drivel, bunkum, prattle, baloney (*sl.*), bunk (*sl.*), ballyhoo, piffle (*sl.*); hot air (*sl.*), empty talk, humbug; cliché, truism, platitude.

adj. meaningless, insignificant, unindicative, inexpressive, unevocative; insubstantial, empty, void, vacant, blank; irrelevant, unimportant; senseless, aimless, purposeless; vague, ambiguous, tautological; trite, trivial, absurd, nonsensical, foolish; unintended, misinterpreted.

vb. be meaningless, mean nothing; talk nonsense, babble, prattle, blather, twaddle; talk through one's hat (*sl.*).

452 intelligibility

n. intelligibility, comprehensibility; recognizability, cognizability; lucidity, clarity, transparency; precision, plainness, explicitness, unambiguousness; readability, legibility, decipherability; audibility; plain speech; plain English.

adj. intelligible, comprehensible, understandable; clear, obvious, lucid, precise, plain, explicit, clear-cut, distinct, unambiguous, unequivocal; simple, straightforward, popular, made simple, for the beginner, made easy, without tears, for the million; recognizable, readable, legible, decipherable; audible.

vb. understand, apprehend, comprehend, grasp, follow, take in, figure out (*inf.*), catch on (*inf.*), get the meaning of, get the hang of (*inf.*), twig (*inf.*); fathom, penetrate, get to the bottom of, read between the lines, get the idea, get the gist of; know, have knowledge of, realize, perceive, appreciate; discern, distinguish, make out (*inf.*), work out (*inf.*); conceive, be aware of, recognize, sense, be conscious of.

be intelligible, make sense, be clear, click (*sl.*); make clear, put in plain English, put in words of one syllable.

see also **502**

453 unintelligibility

n. unintelligibility, incomprehensibility, meaninglessness, unrecognizability, unsearchableness, impenetrability; unclearness, obscurity, illegibility, ambiguity, indecipherability, unreadability; inaudibility; gibberish, incoherence, double Dutch, Greek; puzzle, mystery, enigma, sealed book, closed book.

adj. unintelligible, incomprehensible, meaningless, beyond one's comprehension; indistinct, vague, indefinite, hazy, inexact, ill-defined, loose, unclear, ambiguous, equivocal; incoherent, mixed up; obscure, puzzling, hard, complicated, intricate, profound, academic, over one's head, abstruse, recondite; concealed, mysterious, hidden, enigmatic, esoteric; illegible, indecipherable, unreadable; inaudible; unrecognizable, impenetrable, unsearchable, inexplicable; inscrutable, unfathomable, unutterable, ineffable.

vb. not understand, not have the first idea, not get the hang of (*inf.*), not make head or tail of, be baffled, be beyond one, get hold of the wrong end of the stick (*inf.*); be unintelligible, talk above someone's head; not make sense, escape one, be all Greek to one.

see also **503**

454 ambiguity

n. ambiguity, equivocalness; vagueness, uncertainty; ambivalence, equivocation, incongruity, inconsistency, prevarication; play on words, pun, *double entendre*.

adj. ambiguous, ambivalent, equivocal, uncertain, vague, vacillating, prevaricating; two-edged, backhanded; incongruous.

vb. cut both ways; play on words, pun; quibble, equivocate, prevaricate.

455 figure of speech

n. figure of speech, metaphor, transference, figurativeness; symbolism, imagery; rhetoric; comparison, simile, likeness, allegory, trope, fable, parable, allusion, personification; euphemism, irony, satire; understatement; onomatopoeia.

adj. figurative, metaphorical, extended, transferred, allusive; rhetorical; symbolic; comparative, allegorical, parabolic; euphemistic, euphuistic, ironical, satirical.

456 interpretation

n. interpretation, explanation, exposition, commentary, elucidation, clarification, illumination, explication; background, reason; analysis, diagnosis, review, criticism, critique, survey, investigation, appraisal, evaluation; significance, importance; annotation, note, comment; example, illustration, instance.

translation, equivalent, dynamic equivalent, paraphrase, rendering, rendition, adaptation, rewording, restatement, gloss, transcription, transliteration, version, reading.

interpreter, commentator, reviewer, critic, analyst, exponent, writer, editor, annotator, expositor, preacher, exegete; translator, linguist, polyglot; hermeneutics, exegetics, homiletics.

adj. interpretive, explanatory, expository, explicatory; analytical, diagnostic, critical, evaluatory; defining, descriptive, illuminating, discursive, exegetical; exemplary, illustrative; editorial, glossarial; literal, faithful, word-for-word; free, rough.

vb. interpret, explain, account for, give reasons for, give reasons why, make sense of; expound, lay bare the meaning, give an account of, state the significance of, read between the lines; make clear, elucidate, make plain, clarify, illuminate, throw light on, cast light on; simplify, expand on, emphasize; demonstrate, illustrate, exemplify, show by example; set forth, reveal, expose, lay bare, unfold, spell out.

translate, render, put in other words, put into, reword, restate, rephrase, paraphrase; transliterate, transcribe; decipher, decode, crack, solve; annotate, comment on, remark on, edit, gloss.

457 misinterpretation

n. misinterpretation, misreckoning, misconception, misunderstanding, misconstruction, falsification, distortion, perversion, delusion, error, mistake; mistranslation.

vb. misinterpret, misunderstand, get hold of the wrong end of the stick (*inf.*), misquote, falsify, distort, pervert, read into, misconstrue, not give a true account of, give a false impression of.

see also **453**

B Modes of communication

458 manifestation

n. manifestation, revelation, showing, demonstration, disclosure, expression, presentation, exhibition; publishing, telling, announcement; divulgence, betrayal.

appearance, vision, apparition; exhibit, show, layout, example, specimen, showpiece; parade, procession, pageant; evidence, sign, miracle, theophany.

adj. manifest, apparent, clear, visible,

perceptible, observable, obvious, patent, open, evident, self-evident, unmistakable, crystal-clear, staring one in the face, written all over one, express, explicit, conspicuous, noticeable, prominent, bold, striking, pronounced, flagrant, glaring, salient.

vb. manifest, appear, reveal, show, disclose, express; present, produce, publish, tell, announce, proclaim, betray, divulge, demonstrate, exemplify, indicate, show signs of, evince; make manifest, make plain, lay bare, expose, show forth; display, exhibit, set out, uncover, unfold, unmask, parade; promote, publicize.
see also **462, 823**

459 latency

n. latency, secrecy, subtlety, dormancy; insidiousness; undercurrent, implication, suggestion, hint, allusion, connotation, inference, more than meets the eye, snake in the grass.

adj. latent, hidden, veiled, dormant, quiescent, lurking, subtle, insidious, beneath the surface, between the lines, underlying, undercover; underdeveloped, potential, possible; implied, inherent, inferred, suggested, intimated, hinted, supposed, tacit, understood, unmentioned, unspoken, unexpressed; suggestive, indicative, provocative.

vb. be latent, be beneath the surface, lurk, lie low; imply, indicate, infer, suggest, mean, intimate, hint, insinuate, involve, provoke, entail.
see also **461**

460 information

n. information, knowledge, facts, info (*inf.*), gen (*sl.*), low-down (*sl.*); briefing, run-down (*inf.*); proof, evidence, notes, details, results, figures, tables, statistics, data; intelligence; news, message, report, notice, communication, notification, declaration, presentation, proclamation, broadcast, transmission; narration, account, description, story, tale, paper; tidings, discovery, revelation, enlightenment; dispatch, release, hand-out, announcement; telephone call, telex, telegram, cable, wire, teletext.

hint, mention, advice, aside, wink, whisper, word in one's ear, tip-off (*inf.*), warning, intimation, suspicion, glimmer, indication, suggestion.

informant, spokesman, narrator, storyteller, messenger, newsman, reporter, authority, announcer, broadcaster, correspondent, journalist; dispatcher, courier, herald, emissary, envoy, ambassador, carrier; guidebook, manual, chart, itinerary, map, timetable.

informer, spy, secret agent, observer, wire tapper, snoop, grass (*sl.*), squealer (*sl.*); gossip, tell-tale, eavesdropper, newsmonger, tattler, scandalmonger.

adj. informative, instructive, enlightening, educational, enriching, newsy (*inf.*), chatty (*inf.*), communicative.

vb. inform, speak, say, tell, notify, let know, communicate, give the facts, put over, put across, get across, get over, present, give to understand, convey, declare, announce, express, proclaim; relate, narrate, recite, report, describe, set forth, make known, let in on, tip off (*inf.*), have a word in someone's ear; enlighten, put in the picture; broadcast, spread the news, circulate, disseminate, promulgate; telephone, ring, call, telex, cable, wire; report back, debrief (*inf.*).

bring up to date, fill in on (*inf.*); keep up with, keep tabs on (*inf.*), keep track of, keep one's finger on the pulse, keep up to date, keep posted; hint, suggest, get at, insinuate, intimate, advise, warn; tell on, inform on, betray, grass on (*sl.*), squeal (*sl.*).
see also **464, 597**

461 concealment

n. concealment, covering, hiding, confinement, burying, secretion; suppression, evasion; seclusion, privacy, isolation, solitude; camouflage, disguise, shroud, veil, curtain, screen, mask, cloak, purdah; cabal.

adj. concealed, hidden, out of sight, behind the scenes, covered, eclipsed, buried, obscured, unseen, unexposed; disguised, camouflaged, incognito; furtive, stealthy, secret, hush-hush, clandestine, underhand, sly.

vb. conceal, hide, cover, bury, suppress, screen, cloak, shroud, veil, curtain, evade, withhold, pull the wool over someone's eyes (*inf.*), keep secret, lie low, keep in the dark, keep under one's hat (*inf.*), sweep under the carpet (*inf.*), secrete; cloud, obscure, envelop, ensconce, camouflage, disguise, dissemble; confine, store, harbour, cache, shelter, stash (*inf.*); close, seal, lock.

sneak, prowl, creep, lurk, steal, slink.
see also **463, 466, 826**

462 disclosure

n. disclosure, exposure, opening, uncovering, revelation, apocalypse; show-down; betrayal, manifestation, give-away; acknowledgement, admission.

adj. disclosed, uncovered, exposed, conspicuous, open; indicative, betraying, tell-tale.

vb. disclose, reveal, give away, expose, divulge, lay open, lay bare, make plain,

uncover, unfold, unveil, unfurl, unmask, take the wraps off; not contain oneself for, bring into the open; declare, make known, spit it out (*inf.*); put one's cards on the table, nail one's colours to the mast, show one's colours; open up (*inf.*), unburden oneself, unbosom, confide, get out of one's system (*inf.*), get off one's chest (*inf.*); come out of one's shell.

confess, admit, acknowledge, concede, grant, own up (*inf.*), come clean, avow, plead guilty, make a clean breast of; one's sins will find one out.

betray, not keep a secret, blurt out, let on, let out, blabber, leak, let the cat out of the bag (*inf.*), spill the beans, come out with, talk out of turn, give the game away.

see also **458, 460**

463 hiding

n. hiding, deceit, faking, deception; hiding place, hide-out, hidey-hole, refuge, retreat, covert, den, shelter.

disguise, camouflage, mask, blind, masquerade, cloak, cover, veil, guise, façade, envelope, shade, blackout, masking; ambush, snare, trap, pitfall, net, noose.

vb. ambush, trap, ensnare, waylay, lay in wait, set a trap for, decoy.

see also **459, 801**

464 publication

n. publication, announcement, communication, revelation, disclosure, notification, proclamation, declaration, promulgation, broadcasting, dissemination.

broadcast; book, booklet; newspaper, periodical, magazine, journal; publicity, promotion, canvassing, advertisement, poster, sign, bill, placard, notice, broadsheet, leaflet, folder, brochure, pamphlet, circular, hand-out, handbill, flysheet, blurb, plug (*inf.*).

adj. published, in print, available, obtainable, in circulation; current, public.

vb. publish, issue, bring out, put into circulation, print, distribute; reissue, reprint; be published, come out, circulate, get around.

make known, announce, notify, proclaim, declare, pronounce, impart, send forth, communicate, reveal, disclose, spread, broadcast, diffuse, pass the word round, put about, blazon, promulgate, disseminate; publicize, promote, advertise, canvass, circularize, sell, plug (*inf.*), tell the world.

465 news

n. news, tidings, information, facts, events, current affairs; headlines, front-page news,

stop press, newsflash, scoop, sensation; description, account, report, story, bulletin, message, release, communiqué, press release, announcement, hand-out, dispatch.

rumour, gossip, hearsay, scandal, whisper, popular report, fabrication, tale, chit-chat; grapevine, bush telegraph.

vb. report, tell, broadcast, publish, circulate, spread; make news, hit the headlines.

466 secret

n. secret, mystery, puzzle, riddle, brainteaser, enigma, arcanum; code, cipher, cryptogram, hieroglyph; confidence; skeleton in the cupboard; suppression, blackout, censure.

adj. secret, strange, mysterious, hidden, unknown, puzzling, mystical, cryptic, enigmatic; private, confidential, classified, top secret, hush-hush; secretive, reticent, taciturn; secluded.

vb. keep secret, keep to oneself, not tell, hide, conceal, keep mum (*inf.*), suppress, stifle, sit on (*inf.*), hush up, censor.

adv. in secret, in private, confidentially, under one's breath, between ourselves; between you, me, and the bedpost.

see also **461**

467 messenger

n. messenger, dispatcher, dispatch bearer, carrier, courier, runner, crier, bearer, office-boy, message-boy, errand-boy, page-boy, buttons; spokesman, intermediary, go-between, ambassador, envoy, emissary, internuncio; herald, forerunner, precursor, harbinger, trumpet; minister, angel, prophet.

post, mail, correspondence; post office; telecommunications, telephony, telegraphy; broadcasting, radio, transistor, wireless, television, the box; telephone, phone, receiver; radio set, two-way radio, intercom (*inf.*), pocket radio, walkie-talkie, field radio; telegram, wire, cable, cablegram, telegraph; teleprinter, telex, teletext, semaphore, flag, beacon, smoke-signal.

468 affirmation

n. affirmation, assertion, statement, declaration, proposition, profession, pronouncement, explanation, answer, report, observation, expression, formulation; admission, acknowledgement, attestation, avowal; agreement, ratification, endorsement.

swearing, asseveration; oath, vow, testimony, sworn statement, affidavit, promise, contract, pledge.

adj. affirmative, assertive, affirmatory, declarative; emphatic, strong, forceful, dogmatic, positive, assured, solemn, sworn, on oath.

vb. affirm, assert, state, declare, profess, pronounce, express, explain, maintain, contend, submit, asseverate, aver; confirm, endorse, ratify; admit, acknowledge; emphasize, stress, underline, highlight, impress, urge, reinforce, rub in (*inf.*), make much of, plug; speak out, have one's say, put one's foot down (*inf.*); swear, vow, promise, pledge, testify, attest, assure, guarantee, vouch; swear in, put on oath, charge, adjure.

see also **514, 698**

469 negation

n. negation, denial, contradiction, repudiation, refusal, renunciation, disclaimer, disavowel; abnegation, recusance.

adj. negative, denying, contrary, contradictory, disavowing, recusant, repugnant.

vb. negate, deny, belie, give the lie to, contradict, contravene, gainsay, renounce, repudiate, disown, disavow, disclaim, abjure, abnegate; refuse, reject; cancel, nullify, invalidate.

see also **694**

470 teaching

n. teaching, education, pedagogy, pedagogics, didactics; instruction, training, study, schooling, direction, guidance, tuition, tutoring, coaching, tutelage; preparation, discipline, cultivation, enlightenment, edification; indoctrination, brainwashing, inculcation, conditioning, propagandism, proselytism; spoon-feeding.

course, curriculum, class, lesson, lecture, talk; catechism, sermon; homework, prep (*inf.*), assignment, exercise, task, work.

adj. educational, informative, instructive, enlightening, edifying; academic, pedagogical, didactic, scholastic.

vb. teach, educate, instruct, impart, inform, acquaint, familiarize, direct, guide, discipline, advise, counsel; convince, explain; prepare, initiate; school, coach, cram, prime, put through the mill (*inf.*); enlighten, edify; cultivate, nurture, train, exercise, practise, groom, drill, ground, bring up, foster, rear, breed, lick into shape (*inf.*); indoctrinate, inculcate, din into, force down someone's throat, ram down someone's throat (*inf.*), instill, imbue, condition; proselytize; catechize; hold classes, lecture, hold forth, expound, preach, sermonize, moralize.

471 misdirection

n. misdirection, misguidance, misinstruction, misteaching, misrepresentation, falsification, perversion, mistake, error, blind leading the blind.

vb. misdirect, misinform, mislead, misrepresent, pervert, distort, deceive.

472 learning

n. learning, knowledge, scholarship, training, erudition, lore; self-improvement, self-education, self-instruction; attainments, study, reading, application, studiousness, industry; lesson, class, course, classwork, homework, prep (*inf.*), assignment; revision, refresher course.

adj. knowledgeable, academic, studious, well-read, learned, industrious, scholarly, erudite; self-taught, self-instructed, self-made.

vb. learn, acquire, pick up, attain; experience, understand, grasp, discover, appreciate; master, become familiar with, get off pat (*inf.*), get the hang of (*inf.*); memorize, learn by heart; study, read, go into, go in for, specialize; absorb, assimilate, digest, drink in, imbibe; read up on, revise, review, refresh oneself, cram, prepare, get up, brush up, improve; pore over, bury oneself in; contemplate; burn the midnight oil; browse, scan, thumb through, flick through (*inf.*), dip into; improve one's mind, teach oneself; study under, sit at the feet of.

see also **426**

473 teacher

n. teacher, educator, advisor, guide, counsellor; school-teacher, headmaster, principal, head; professor, lecturer, don, reader, fellow, doctor, dean; tutor, instructor, pedagogue, coach, trainer, guru, governess.

see also **436**

474 learner

n. learner, pupil, scholar, student, schoolchild; undergraduate, fresher, freshman, graduate, postgraduate; swot, bookworm; follower, disciple, adherent; apprentice, trainee, probationer, novice, beginner, recruit, newcomer, tyro; class, set, form, grade, stream.

see also **428**

475 place of learning

n. school; nursery, kindergarten, crèche; college, polytechnic, university, academy, institute, institution, seminary, varsity (*inf.*), *conservatoire, lycée, gymnasium;* classroom, schoolroom, study, lecture theatre, auditorium; library, carrel.

476 truthfulness

n. truthfulness, veracity, integrity, frankness, openness, candour, straightforwardness, forthrightness; accuracy, honesty, reliability, sincerity, uprightness, guilelessness, impartiality.

adj. truthful, veracious, sincere, guileless, impartial; frank, open, candid, unreserved, plain, direct, straight, straightforward, forthright, blunt, ingenuous.

vb. be truthful, not lie; speak plainly, tell someone straight, not hesitate, make no bones about, speak one's mind, paint in its true colours, call a spade a spade, tell all; not to put too fine a point on it (*inf.*).

see also **430, 508**

477 falsehood

n. falsehood, fraudulence, falsification, fabrication, inaccuracy, deception, dishonesty, lying, mendacity, perjury; misrepresentation, distortion, perversion; double dealing, two-facedness, duplicity, hypocrisy, insincerity, guile; mockery, pretence, make-believe, façade.

adj. false, lying, untruthful, mendacious; fabricated, inaccurate, misrepresented, distorted, put on (*inf.*), make-believe, counterfeit, bogus, pretended, fake, invented, spurious; fraudulent, dishonest, insincere, hypocritical; double-dealing, two-faced; roguish, corrupt, oily, smooth, disingenuous, perfidious.

vb. falsify, lie, fib, exaggerate, understate, tell a white lie, bear false witness, perjure oneself, forswear; prevaricate, equivocate; deceive, mislead, misrepresent, distort, manipulate, doctor, adulterate, make up, invent, concoct, construct, contrive, fabricate, hatch, get up (*inf.*), trump up, spin a yarn; fake, counterfeit, forge; feign, put on (*inf.*), put on a brave face, go through the motions, play, pretend, make believe, sham, simulate, dissemble; laugh off (*inf.*).

see also **431**

478 deception

n. deception, misleading, deceit, misrepresentation, cheating, trickery, craftiness, treachery, fraudulence, dishonesty; lying, guile, furtiveness, beguilement, betrayal, treason; hoax, crying wolf, delusion, self-deception, wishful thinking, hallucination, illusion.

trick, dodge, ruse, trap, artifice, stratagem, subterfuge; fraud, swindle, fiddle, rip-off (*sl.*), bamboozle (*inf.*), skulduggery (*inf.*), underhand dealing, sharp practice, sleight of hand, legerdemain.

adj. deceiving, deceptive, illusory, false, sham, fake, fraudulent, dishonest, underhand, behind someone's back, furtive, treacherous, crafty, wily, cunning, shifty.

vb. deceive, mislead, delude, fool, trick, trap, trip up, catch, entrap, ensnare, hoodwink, beguile, dupe, pull the wool over someone's eyes (*inf.*); outwit, outmanoeuvre; go behind someone's back.

cheat, trick, defraud, swindle, fleece, rip off (*sl.*), bamboozle (*inf.*), chisel (*sl.*), cozen; go down (*inf.*), diddle (*sl.*), cross (*sl.*), double-cross, pull a fast one (*sl.*), stack the cards against, put one over on (*inf.*), victimize; take advantage of, get the better of, take for a ride (*inf.*); hoax, cry wolf; play a joke on, kid (*sl.*), pull someone's leg, have on (*inf.*); trifle with, cajole; betray, commit treason.

479 dupe

n. dupe, fool, victim, sucker (*sl.*), sitting duck, simpleton, greenhorn, gull.

480 deceiver

n. deceiver, beguiler, dodger, trickster, swindler, crook, cheat, rogue, impostor, con man (*sl.*), phoney (*sl.*), wolf in sheep's clothing, charlatan, chisel (*sl.*), knave, cozener, sharper; hypocrite, actor, dissembler, Tartuffe; liar, fibber, story-teller; betrayer, traitor, quisling, rat (*sl.*), informer, double-crosser, victimizer; underground, fifth columnist, saboteur, terrorist.

481 exaggeration

n. exaggeration, overstatement, extravagance, hyperbole, misrepresentation, misjudgment, stretching; storm in a teacup, much ado about nothing, stretch of the imagination, fantasy, tall story.

adj. exaggerated, extravagant, preposterous, fabulous, hyperbolic, excessive, superlative, overdone, out of all proportion, coloured, high-falutin, boastful, bombastic.

vb. exaggerate, overstate, overestimate, overplay, hyperbolize, make too much of, overdo, strain, misrepresent; amplify, enlarge, magnify, emphasize, highlight, maximize, heighten, intensify, aggravate; colour, embroider; make a mountain out of a molehill, stretch a point, lay it on thick, pile it on (*inf.*), out-herod Herod.

see also **417**

C Means of communicating ideas

482 indication

n. indication, calling, identification,

designation, symbolization, signification; sign, badge, emblem, figure, design, symbol, representation, type, token, logo; colophon, flag, banner, pennant, standard, ensign, colours, pendant, bunting, streamer, Union Jack, Stars and Stripes; coat of arms, crest, insignia, medal, regalia.

label, ticket, name, card, notice, bill, stub, counterfoil, docket, form, voucher, counter, chip, tab, tag; indicator, marker, pointer, needle, arrow, index, gauge; stamp, seal, imprint, impression, fingerprint, footprint; signature, autograph, initials, monogram.

signal, gesticulation, gesture; wink, nod, wave, call, shout, whistle, nudge; alarm, siren, hooter, bell; light, beacon.

evidence, hint, suggestion, note, explanation, proof, clue, intimation, symptom, hallmark.

adj. indicative, suggestive, symptomatic, symbolic, typical, representative.

vb. indicate, call, mean, signify; identify, designate, show, name, specify, appoint, assign, symbolize, point to; manifest, express, imply, bear the marks of, evince, intimate, denote, betoken; mark, point, gauge, brand, score, scratch, spot.

label, tag, docket, tab, earmark; stamp, seal, print, punch, impress, emboss, emblazon; sign, initial, autograph; annotate, number, letter, paginate.

gesticulate, gesture, signal, motion, wave, beckon, wink, nod, hoot, ring, shout, whistle, nudge.

483 record

n. record, register, catalogue, account, document, report, statement; brief, memo, memorandum, note; newspaper, bulletin, gazette, almanac; diary, journal, log; certificate, ticket; archives, public records, proceedings, minutes, annals, chronicle, scroll, inscription, manuscript; tape-recording, photograph, film, videotape.

souvenir, memento; relic, mark, trace, remains, evidence; trail, footprint, impression, scent; wash, wake; monument, testimony, witness, memorial, statue, column, cenotaph, remembrance, testimonial, mausoleum, shrine.

adj. recorded, documented, noted, reported.

vb. record, note, mark, report, account, write down, take down, jot down; register, write in, enter, fill in, insert, inscribe, enrol, matriculate; document, list, catalogue, minute, chronicle; tape, tape-record, photograph, film.

adv. on record, in black and white, in writing, on the books.

484 recorder

n. recorder, registrar, secretary, clerk, accountant; diarist, chronicler, annalist, historian, biographer, journalist, archivist, scribe, amanuensis.

tape-recorder, stereo-recorder, cassette-recorder, video-recorder; record, disc.

485 obliteration

n. obliteration, deletion, erasure, effacement, blotting out, eradication, cancellation, expunction; eraser, rubber, sponge, duster.

vb. obliterate, wipe out, rub off, delete, efface, erase, blot out, black out, strike out, write out, leave no traces, remove, iron out, raze, cancel, expunge.

486 representation

n. representation, description, depiction, illustration, portrayal, exemplification, enactment, personification; reproduction, copy, imitation, image, likeness; picture, sketch, diagram, chart, map, model; art, painting, sculpture; photography, photograph, photo, snapshot, slide, transparency.

adj. representative, characteristic, typical, illustrative.

vb. represent, stand for, stand in the place of, serve as; render, realize, draw, depict, describe, portray, illustrate, picture, reproduce, delineate; reflect, mirror; exemplify, typify, embody, symbolize; designate, express.

487 misrepresentation

n. misrepresentation, distortion, perversion, twisting, falsification, exaggeration, understatement; caricature, parody, travesty, burlesque, counterfeit; misinterpretation.

vb. misrepresent, distort, twist, garble, warp, pervert, falsify, caricature, parody, give the wrong impression; misinterpret, misstate.

488 painting

n. painting, art, graphics, fine art; picture, illustration, mural, depiction, canvas, fresco, wall-painting, collage; work, study, sketch, drawing, outline, silhouette, cartoon, representation, copy, composition, likeness; abstract painting, landscape, portrait, self-portrait, still-life; watercolour, oil painting, miniature, masterpiece, old master.

technique, treatment, design, pattern, atmosphere, tone, shadow, values, perspective.

adj. graphic, visual, pictorial, picturesque, scenic.

vb. paint, portray, depict, compose, illustrate, draw, sketch, design, represent, copy, crayon, pencil, silhouette, ink, shade, tint, limn.

489 sculpture

n. sculpture, carving, stone-carving, cutting, casting, moulding; ceramics, pottery; statue, bust, cast, embossment, relief, marble, plaque, cameo; figure, representation, image.

adj. carved, sculptured, glyptic, glyphic.

vb. sculpture, sculpt, carve, chisel, cut, hew, shape, fashion, model, mould, emboss, cast.

490 engraving

n. engraving, etching, carving, chiselling, incising, printing, photogravure, lithography; inscription, print, lithograph, block, woodcut, linocut, plate.

vb. engrave, etch, inscribe, cut, carve, chisel, incise, chase, print, impress, stamp.

491 artist

n. artist, creator, composer, painter, designer, draughtsman, architect, drawer, sketcher, cartoonist, photographer, cameraman; sculptor, carver, modeller, statuary, lapidary; potter, ceramist; engraver, etcher, lithographer, printer, typographer.

492 language

n. language, communication, speech, tongue, talk, style, diction, parlance; utterance, expression, voice, articulation; idiom, dialect, provincialism, *patois*, jargon, pidgin, *koine*, *lingua franca;* mother tongue, vernacular, common speech, British English, American English, Standard English, Queen's English, Received Pronunciation; artificial language, world language, Esperanto; Babel, confusion of tongues.

linguistics, grammar, syntax, semantics, phonetics, phonology, historical linguistics, comparative linguistics, etymology, philology, dialectology, lexicography; linguist, polyglot, philologist, grammarian, lexicographer.

adj. linguistic, lingual, grammatical, standard, current, vernacular, idiomatic.

see also **514**

493 letter

n. letter, symbol, consonant, vowel; capital, upper case, large letter, majuscule; small letter, lower case, minuscule; rune, cuneiform, hieroglyph; syllable, character, ideogram, pictogram; alphabet, ABC; orthography, spelling, spelling-pronunciation.

adj. literal, alphabetical, orthographic, syllabic.

vb. spell, letter, form letters; syllabify.

494 word

n. word, expression, term, name, designation, vocable, sound, syllable, utterance, phrase, construction, locution; neologism, slang, colloquialism, jargon, provincialism, cliché, vogue word, catch phrase, slogan; archaism; root, derivative, derivation; synonym, antonym, homonym.

vocabulary, lexicon, wordlist, dictionary, glossary, thesaurus, concordance, index; lexicology, lexicography, etymology, terminology.

adj. verbal, literal, lexical, lexicographical.

495 neologism

n. neologism, new word, new usage, coinage, neology; formation, translation, loan-word, borrowing, calque, portmanteau, blend, hybrid; corruption, barbarism, nonce word; cliché, vogue word, slang, vulgarism, argot, cant, colloquialism, informal usage, journalese, Americanism, Anglicism, Briticism.

adj. newly-coined, newfangled, colloquial, informal, slang, foreign, borrowed, translated, nonce, vogue.

496 nomenclature

n. nomenclature, naming, calling, appellation, designation, identification, terminology, classification.

name, title; Christian name, first name, given name, forename; surname, last name, family name, signature; sign, style, label, tag; nomen, denomination; nickname, description, epithet.

adj. nominal, titular; named, known as.

vb. name, call, designate, identify, specify, term, title, dub, label, tag, style; classify, characterize, describe, define, nominate, denominate; christen, baptize; be known as, be called, go by the name of, go under the name of.

497 misnomer

n. misnomer, misnaming, malapropism; nickname, pet name, pen name, pseudonym, fictitious name, assumed name, alias, *nom de plume,* stage name, sobriquet, *nom de guerre.*

anonymity, namelessness; what's-its-name, thinggamy (*inf.*), thingumabob (*inf.*), what-d'you-call-it, so-and-so, A. N. Other, Mr. X.

adj. misnamed, in name only, professed, pretended, pseudo-, quasi-, self-styled, so-called, *soi-disant;* anonymous, unidentified, nameless, unknown.

vb. misname, nickname, dub, mislabel, mistake.

498 phrase

n. phrase, clause, sentence, group of words; idiom, figure of speech; expression, utterance, locution; slogan, maxim, saying, formula, cliché.

vb. phrase, word, reword, express, state, put into words, formulate, verbalize.

499 grammar

n. grammar, usage, syntax, word order, sentence structure, analysis, parsing; inflection, case-ending, morphology, accidence.

part of speech, noun, substantive, proper noun, collective noun, mass noun, count noun, case, gender, number, declension; pronoun; verb, participle, gerund, copula, infinitive, split infinitive, person, tense, active, passive, conjugation; adjective, qualifier, modifier, comparative, superlative, comparison; adverb, particle; preposition; interjection; conjunction; article, definite article, indefinite article, determiner; subject, predicate; affix, prefix, suffix, infix.

adj. grammatical, syntactic, correct, proper, well-formed, acceptable, appropriate.

vb. parse, analyse, inflect, conjugate, decline.

500 solecism

n. solecism, ungrammaticalness, bad grammar, misusage, mistake, error, barbarism, blunder; mispronunciation, slip of the tongue; malapropism, spoonerism, cacology, catachresis.

adj. ungrammatical, incorrect, solecistic; slovenly, slipshod, loose; inappropriate, unacceptable, badly-formed.

vb. use bad grammar, make a mistake, murder the language.

see also 511

501 style

n. style, manner, characteristics, presentation; command, fluency, mastery, skill; manner of speaking, diction, phrasing, phraseology, wording, composition, writing; usage, mode of expression, expression, vocabulary, word-power, parlance, choice of words, way of putting it, feeling for words, *sprachgefühl;* mannerism, idiosyncrasy, intonation.

see also 510, 514

502 lucidity

n. lucidity, clearness, clarity, perspicuity, transparency, unambiguousness, intelligibility, directness, plain speech, simplicity, exactness, precision.

adj. lucid, clear, perspicuous, unambiguous, distinct, obvious, direct, plain, intelligible, explicit, easily understood, limpid, pellucid.

see also 452, 802

503 obscurity

n. obscurity, imperspicuity, vagueness, opaqueness, ambiguity, imprecision, unintelligibility, complexity, abstruseness.

adj. obscure, cloudy, blurred, fuzzy, vague, unclear, imperspicuous, imprecise, indistinct, ambiguous, unintelligible, incomprehensible, complicated, involved, intricate, abstruse.

see also 453, 803

504 conciseness

n. conciseness, succinctness, brevity, terseness, curtness, pithiness, laconism; contraction, ellipsis.

adj. concise, brief, succinct, condensed, compressed, shortened, short, precise, pithy, terse, compact, summary, laconic, sententious; elliptic, telegraphic.

vb. be concise, condense, compress, shorten, abridge, abbreviate, summarize, come to the point, put in a nutshell.

adv. in short, in brief, in a nutshell, to the point, to cut a long story short.

505 diffuseness

n. diffuseness, profuseness, abundance; wordiness, verbosity, discursiveness; digression, departure, deviation, excursus; tautology, redundancy, verbiage, repetition, padding, circumlocution, periphrasis, pleonasm.

adj. diffuse, discursive, wordy, lengthy, long-winded, verbose, tedious, rambling, digressive, redundant, repetitious, protracted, prolix, pleonastic, roundabout, periphrastic, circumlocutory.

vb. amplify, enlarge on, develop, expatiate; digress, ramble, wander, deviate, go off at a tangent, go off the subject, get off the point, get sidetracked, beat about the bush (*inf.*); go on and on, talk at length, repeat oneself.

see also 516

506 vigour

n. vigour, power, strength, intensity, force, effectiveness, forcefulness, urgency, piquancy; sparkle, spirit, punch (*sl.*), fervour, vehemence, verve, animation, vitality, fire, glow, warmth.

adj. vigorous, powerful, strong, forceful, trenchant, incisive, bold, tough, lively, inspired, sparkling, racy, fervent, vehement, insistent, impassioned, fiery, ardent, passionate, persuasive; vivid, graphic; pointed.

see also **173, 755**

507 feebleness

n. feebleness, weakness, faintness, frailty, flaccidity, enfeeblement, pauperism, barrenness, lifelessness.

adj. feeble, weak, faint, frail, thin, poor, limp, lifeless, flaccid, insipid, meagre, scant, slight, shallow, diluted, wishy-washy, uninspired, stale, flat, tame, forced.

see also **162**

508 plainness

n. plainness, simplicity, plain speech, naturalness, straightforwardness, modesty, unpretentiousness, severity.

adj. plain, simple, natural, unaffected, artless, naive, straightforward, modest, ordinary, undramatic, severe, restrained, unadorned, unpretentious, unsophisticated, common, homely, homespun, unimaginative, matter-of-fact; direct, frank, open, blunt.

vb. speak plainly, call a spade a spade, come straight to the point.

see also **476**

509 ornament

n. ornamentation, adornment, embellishment, elaboration, enrichment, enhancement, decoration, embroidery, floweriness.

ornament, colour, frills, rhetoric, metaphor, euphemism, verbosity, grandiloquence, bombast, fustian.

adj. ornate, adorned, embellished, grand, rich, lofty, elaborate, lavish, grandiose; vivid, dazzling, scintillating; fancy, extravagant, pretentious, showy, flashy, loud, flaunting, boastful, big, high-falutin, high-flown, big-sounding, magniloquent; rhetorical, voluble, pompous, flowery, euphemistic, euphuistic, grandiloquent.

vb. embellish, adorn, enrich, colour; talk big, lay it on (*inf.*).

see also **846**

510 elegance

n. elegance, tastefulness, style, grace, graciousness, dignity, beauty, correctness, refinement, propriety, polish, finish; harmony, balance, proportion, rhythm; artificiality, affectation.

adj. elegant, tasteful, gracious, graceful, dignified, artistic, delicate, refined, pure, stylized, polished; proper, appropriate, happy, well-expressed, right, correct, felicitous, seemly; harmonious, balanced, well-proportioned, well-turned, mellifluous; affected, artificial.

see also **848**

511 inelegance

n. inelegance, tastelessness, bad taste, gracelessness, impropriety; barbarism, coarseness, vulgarity; incorrectness, stiltedness, formality, awkwardness, clumsiness.

adj. inelegant, tasteless, graceless, unseemly, improper, incorrect, laboured, stilted, forced, heavy, stiff, formal, ponderous, clumsy, awkward, inappropriate; coarse, crude, vulgar, rude, uncouth.

see also **849**

512 voice

n. voice, sound, speech, language, utterance; vocal organs, vocal chords, tongue, lips, larynx, lungs, breath; articulation, pronunciation, vocalization, enunciation, delivery, inflection, intonation, pitch, rhythm, tone, accent, timbre, stress, emphasis; vowel, consonant, phoneme; phonetics.

adj. vocal, expressed, uttered, spoken, oral, lingual, vocalic, phonetic, voiced, sonant, sounded; clear, distinct, articulate.

vb. voice, speak, express, sound, pronounce, utter, articulate, get one's tongue round, vocalize, enunciate; nasalize, palatalize, aspirate; roll, trill, burr; stress, emphasize.

513 muteness

n. muteness, aphonia, voicelessness, inarticulation, dumbness, silence.

adj. mute, voiceless, speechless, tongueless, unsounded, unvoiced, unvocal, surd, inarticulate, tongue-tied, dumb, silent, mum, inaudible.

vb. mute, silence, dumbfound, strike dumb, still, soften, deaden, muffle, suppress, smother.

see also **517, 779**

514 speech

n. speech, language, talk, discourse, utterance, articulation, expression, pronunciation, communication; eloquence, fluency, expressiveness, facility, vivacity, style, poise, delivery, rhetoric, vigour, force, gift of the gab (*inf.*).

speaker, talker, conversationalist; public speaker, orator, lecturer, after-dinner speaker, expositor, rhetorician, declaimer, preacher; spokesman, mouthpiece.

adj. speaking, talking, verbal, oral; articulating; eloquent, fluent, voluble, expressive, forceful, meaningful.

vb. speak, say, talk; vocalize, pronounce, voice, enunciate; express, utter, tell, affirm, converse, communicate, chat; repeat, rattle off, trot out (*inf.*).

address, discuss, lecture, teach, instruct, plead, argue, make a speech, give a talk, deliver a lecture, have the floor, hold forth, preach, speechify (*inf.*), rant, spout.

see also **468, 516**

515 imperfect speech

n. imperfect speech, speech defect, aphasia, impediment, stammer, stutter, faltering, hesitation, mispronunciation, lisp, twang, nasalization, drawl.

adj. inarticulate, indistinct, throaty, shaking, stuttering, stammering, hesitant.

vb. stammer, stutter, hesitate, pause, falter, stumble, lisp, drawl, slur, speak through one's nose, mispronounce, mumble, mutter, garble, swallow one's words.

516 talkativeness

n. talkativeness, gift of the gab (*inf.*), loquacity, garrulity, verbosity, long-windedness.

chatter, chat, jabber, babble, prattle, blather, prittle-prattle (*inf.*), chit-chat, idle talk, chinwag (*sl.*), palaver, small talk; nonsense, drive, twaddle, hot air (*sl.*), yap (*inf.*), yackety-yack (*sl.*); gossip, scandal.

chatterbox, prattler, jabberer, tattler, windbag (*inf.*), gasbag (*sl.*); gossip, muckraker (*inf.*).

adj. talkative, chatty, voluble, loquacious, garrulous; chattering, babbling; glib, eloquent, fluent; long-winded, verbose; gossipy.

vb. chat, keep on, go on about (*inf.*), chatter, talk idly, waffle, ramble on; babble, jabber, prattle, gabble, yackety-yack (*sl.*), yack (*sl.*), yap (*inf.*); gossip, tell tales.

see also **505**

517 taciturnity

n. taciturnity, reserve, reticence, silence, uncommunicativeness, no comment, curtness, brusqueness; modesty, hesitance.

adj. taciturn, reserved, reticent, silent, dumb, mute, quiet, uncommunicative, secretive, tight-lipped, close-lipped, mum, restrained, hesitant, modest, retiring; curt, brusque, laconic; aloof, distant.

vb. say nothing, refuse to comment, keep quiet, keep one's mouth shut, hold one's tongue, save one's breath; stand aloof.

see also **779**

518 address

n. address, speech, talk, lecture, oration, discourse, reading, recitation, recital, exhortation, paper, pep talk (*sl.*), spiel (*sl.*), appeal, invocation, homily, sermon, allocution; harangue, tirade, declamation.

inaugural address, opening; greeting, salutation; farewell address, goodbye, valediction.

oratory, rhetoric, speech-making, public speaking, elocution, preaching, homiletics.

519 conversation

n. conversation, chat, talk, discussion, interview, exchange of views, interchange, expression, repartee, colloquy, interlocution; chatter, chit-chat, prattle; *tête-à-tête*, heart-to-heart.

conference, debate, dialogue, consultation, conflab (*inf.*), powwow, summit conference, summit, congress, symposium, convention, seminar, parley, council, audience, hearing.

vb. converse, chat, discuss, hold a conversation, communicate, counsel, confer, exchange views, debate, negotiate, put one's heads together, confabulate.

520 monologue

n. monologue, soliloquy, monody; apostrophe, aside.

vb. soliloquize, talk to oneself.

521 writing

n. writing, script, lettering, calligraphy, stroke, flourish; handwriting, hand, fist, longhand; graphology, chirography; mark, scribble, scrawl; transcription, inscription, printing, copying, shorthand, stenography, typing; correspondence, letter-writing; journalism, reporting.

written matter, copy, work, composition, document, paper, manuscript, transcript, typescript, parchment, scroll.

writer, calligrapher, scribe, copyist, transcriber, secretary, stenographer, typist; author, novelist, journalist.

adj. written, graphic, in writing, handwritten, in black and white, roman, italic.

vb. write, pen, compose, prepare, draft, write out, report, document, write down, record, put pen to paper; scribble, scrawl; transcribe, inscribe, copy, engrave, print, type.

522 printing

n. printing, typography; composition, typesetting; publishing; print, impression, stamp, page, sheet, copy, printed matter; type, lead, leading, rule, letter, fount, space; galley, proof, slip, bromide.

printer, typographer, typesetter, compositor; proofreader, reader; copy editor.

adj. printed, in print, typographical.

vb. print, impress, imprint, stamp, engrave; compose, set type, set up; run off, go to press, put to bed; publish, issue, bring out.

523 correspondence

n. correspondence, communication, exchange of letters, post, mail; letter, postcard, note, message, report, missive, dispatch, epistle, chit, acknowledgement, reply, answer; business letter, love letter, valentine, fan letter, poison pen letter, chain letter, round robin, circular; address, destination.

correspondent, letter-writer, pen-friend, pen-pal (*inf.*), addressee, recipient.

adj. epistolary, postal.

vb. correspond, write to, communicate, exchange letters, drop a line, send, post, mail, dispatch.

524 book

n. book, publication, work, volume, tome, copy, text, manuscript, bestseller, paperback, hardback, booklet, edition, reprint, offprint; study book, course book, textbook, set book, primer, workbook; reader, companion volume, selected readings; complete works, omnibus edition.

magazine, periodical, journal, review, gazette; back number, back issue.

reference book, encyclopedia, cyclopedia, handbook, manual, dictionary, bible, guidebook; index, concordance; bibliography, reading list.

library, collection of books, lending library, public library, mobile library, interlibrary loan.

writer, author, novelist, biographer, essayist, reporter, ghost-writer, hack; editor, publisher, reviewer, critic; man of letters, man of learning, bookworm, scholar, bookcollector, bibliophile.

525 description

n. description, account, report, statement, record, summary, information, explanation, characterization, specification; portrayal, sketch, portrait, representation, illustration, picture, image, profile; narrative, story, tale, yarn, anecdote, saga, epic; fiction, myth, legend, fairy-tale, fairy story, fantasy, fable, parable, allegory; plot, story-line, subject, argument.

narrator, reciter, story-teller, novelist, raconteur, anecdotist, fabricator.

adj. descriptive, narrative, expressive; graphic, vivid, true-to-life, lifelike, telling, detailed, pictorial; fictional, made-up, legendary, mythical, fabulous, parabolic, allegorical.

vb. describe, portray, sketch, set forth, represent, outline, trace, illustrate, picture, draw, paint, imagine, delineate, characterize, define, specify, mark out, express; account, report, state, record, explain, summarize; narrate, tell, recount, relate, recite, rehearse.

526 dissertation

n. dissertation, essay, paper, composition, commentary, exposition, thesis, treatise, monograph, discourse, disquisition; survey, review, analysis, examination, enquiry, investigation, study, discussion, story, comment, write-up, critique.

essayist, expositor, commentator; critic, reviewer.

vb. discuss, treat, handle, concern, deal with, consider, comment; analyse, survey, examine, explain, interpret; review, criticize, write up.

527 compendium

n. compendium, summary, resumé, precis, abridgment, abstract, summing up, syllabus, survey, outline, synopsis, skeleton, reduction, analysis, conspectus, epitome; core, essence; digest, miscellany, anthology, selections, readings.

adj. compendious, concise, brief, succinct, abbreviated.

vb. summarize, sum up, abstract, abridge, condense, reduce, shorten, digest, outline, survey; boil down to.

see also **504**

528 poetry; prose

n. poetry, song, rhyme, poem, verse, stanza, sonnet, ode, lyric, idyll, epic, ballad, jingle, limerick; chorus, refrain; prosody, versification, scansion, rhythm, metre, stress, beat, foot; prose, writing, literature, composition, story.

poet, writer, composer, versifier, poet laureate, bard, minstrel, troubadour.

adj. poetic, rhythmic, lyrical, idyllic, tuneful.

vb. poetize, sing, versify; rhyme, scan; write, conceive, imagine, compose.

529 drama

n. theatre, the stage; hall, opera house, cinema, playhouse; play, drama, show, opera, melodrama, tragicomedy, tragedy, comedy, farce, slapstick, pantomime, mime, variety, cabaret, pageant, revue, spectacle, carnival; presentation, appearance, exhibition, production; dramatics, stagecraft, showmanship, acting, performance, histrionics.

actor, actress, performer, player, role, part, character, Thespian, lead, star, understudy, extra; cast, characters, *dramatis personae.*

adj. dramatic, theatrical; impressive, spectacular.

vb. dramatize, direct, present, stage, produce, put on, perform, enact, play.

V Volition

1 Individual volition

A Volition in general

530 will

n. will, volition, intention, resolution, power, mind, conviction, determination, willpower, choice, free will, discretion, conation; desire, wish, inclination.

adj. volitional, willing, minded, voluntary, free, intentional, wilful, deliberate, wished, premeditated, conative.

vb. will, wish, want, desire, incline, choose, resolve, make a decision, decide, make up one's mind, determine, purpose, see fit, take it into one's head to (*inf.*), have one's own way; conclude, come to the conclusion.

adv. at will, at pleasure, as one thinks, of one's own accord.

531 necessity

n. necessity, compulsion, obligation; inevitability, unavoidability, certainty, inexorableness, inescapableness; determinism, predestination, foreordination, fatalism; involuntariness, spontaneity, reflex action, instinct, intuition.

no choice, no alternative, Hobson's choice, six of one and half a dozen of the other; must (*inf.*), essential, prerequisite; fate, the inevitable, whatever will be shall be, *che sara, sara.*

adj. necessary, inevitable, unavoidable, inescapable, inexorable, certain, sure, foreordained, predetermined, destined, predestined, irresistible; essential, indispensable, imperative; compulsory, obligatory; deterministic,

fatalistic; involuntary, unintentional, instinctive, unconscious, automatic, reflex, mechanical.

vb. necessitate, compel, oblique, constrain, force, dictate; destine, foreordain; need, require, cry out for.

adv. of necessity, necessarily, inevitably, certainly, willy-nilly.

532 willingness

n. willingness, readiness, disposition, inclination, compliance; eagerness, enthusiasm, zeal, earnestness.

adj. willing, prepared, ready, disposed, inclined, game, desirous, compliant, eager, enthusiastic, zealous; voluntary, uninvited, unasked, unprompted.

vb. be willing, like to, want, desire, choose, feel like, show willing (*inf.*), be inclined towards; volunteer, take on the responsibility, offer oneself; be eager, enthuse, jump at, leap at, lean over backwards (*inf.*), fall over oneself to (*inf.*); gush over, go overboard about (*inf.*), go to town on (*inf.*).

adv. willingly, gladly, eagerly, readily; voluntarily, of one's own accord; off one's own bat.

see also **611**

533 unwillingness

n. unwillingness, disinclination, unreadiness, hesitation, reluctance, scruple, qualm, aversion, demur; non-cooperation, protest, abstention.

adj. unwilling, unready, disinclined, reluctant, hesitant, averse, opposed, loath, not in the mood, unenthusiastic, indifferent, halfhearted.

vb. be unwilling, not feel like, not want to, would rather not, refuse, hesitate, hold back, balk at, shirk, demur, fight shy of, shy away, shrink, dodge, evade; force oneself.

adv. unwillingly, without enthusiasm, against one's will, against one's better judgment, under protest, grudgingly.

see also **612**

534 resolution

n. resolution, determination, resolve, certainty, persistence, constancy, doggedness, conviction, perseverance, boldness, tenacity, fortitude, steadfastness; firmness, willpower, strength of will, mettle; selfcontrol, self-reliance, self-possession.

adj. resolute, determined, steadfast, firm, steady, strong, certain, serious, strong-willed, iron-willed, inflexible, bold, persistent, tenacious, constant, dogged; single-minded, wholehearted, committed, decided; unyielding, unhesitating, unflinching, unwavering, unswerving, unbending.

vb. be resolute, determine, resolve, decide, be bent on; have one's heart set upon, stand fast, take one's stand, hold one's ground, not give in, stick to one's guns, stand no nonsense, put one's foot down; take the bull by the horns; commit oneself, dedicate, put one's heart and soul into.

535 perseverance

n. perseverance, tenacity, steadfastness, firmness, persistence, continuance, constancy, endurance, indefatigability, undauntedness, doggedness; stamina, guts (*inf.*), staying power, backbone, stickability (*sl.*), moral fibre, stiff upper lip.

stayer, bulldog.

adj. persevering, persistent, determined, tenacious, steadfast, constant, steady, firm, unmoved, undaunted, indefatigable, untiring, obstinate, enduring, continuing; diligent, industrious, assiduous.

vb. persevere, remain, persist, endure, continue to the end, go on, carry on, have what it takes, keep at it, keep going (*inf.*), stick at it (*inf.*), soldier on, plod (*inf.*), plug away (*inf.*), slog away, see it through (*inf.*), stick it out (*inf.*); stick out for, hold out for; hold a job down (*inf.*).

536 irresolution

n. irresolution, indecision, vacillation, wavering, fluctuation; inconstancy, hesitation, fickleness, instability.

adj. irresolute, indecisive, undecided, fluctuating, wavering, vacillating, fickle, hesitant, in two minds, unstable, infirm, inconstant, changeable.

vb. be irresolute, vacillate, waver, fluctuate, hesitate, falter, shilly-shally, dilly-dally (*inf.*).

537 obstinacy

n. obstinacy, stubbornness, inflexibility, rigidity, tenacity, hardness, relentlessness, obduracy, intransigence, intractableness; bigotry, dogmatism, narrow-mindedness, intolerance, fanaticism.

dogmatist, bigot, fanatic, die-hard, mule, intransigent; pedant, stickler.

adj. obstinate, stubborn, inflexible, tenacious, uncompromising, intransigent, unyielding, unrelenting, hardened, hard, intractable, headstrong, self-willed, set in one's ways; stiff-necked, pig-headed, recalcitrant, refractory, obdurate, pertinacious; dogmatic.

vb. be obstinate, not give in, stick to one's guns; resist, oppose, dig one's heels in.

see also **534, 535**

538 change of mind

n. change of mind, second thoughts, afterthought, change of heart, *volte-face*, repentance; retraction, withdrawal, backing out, reversal, abandonment, desertion, defection, renunciation, recantation; tergiversation, backsliding, apostasy.

turncoat, time-server, rat, renegade, traitor, deserter, apostate.

adj. fickle, irresolute, unfaithful, inconstant.

vb. change one's mind, have second thoughts, think beter of, change one's tune; take back, withdraw, back out, back down, climb down (*inf.*), disown, deny, retract, revoke, recant, disclaim; nullify; trim; apologize, eat humble pie, eat one's words; fall away, apostasize.

539 caprice

n. caprice, whim, fancy, vagary, notion, quirk, prank, crotchet, freak, craze, whimsy, whim-wham, flash; jest, witticism; capriciousness, whimsicality; fickleness, inconstancy.

adj. capricious, whimsical, fanciful, inconstant, fickle, changeable, flighty, frivolous, freakish, crotchety, unpredictable, erratic, fitful.

540 choice

n. choice, option, decision, determination, selection, adoption; alternative, preference, substitute.

vote, ballot, poll, election, representation, referendum, plebiscite; suffrage, franchise; voter, elector, electorate, constituency, ward.

adj. optional, elective, selective, discretional, discriminating, choosy (*inf.*), fastidious; electoral, voting.

vb. choose, pick, decide on, opt, adopt, sort, prefer, take up, go for, plump for (*inf.*), like, fancy, favour, appoint, co-opt, elect, nominate, commit oneself; separate, select, isolate, segregate, cull, glean, sift, winnow, divide the sheep from the goats, separate the wheat from the chaff; weigh, judge, discriminate, make up one's mind; vote, cast votes, poll, ballot, draw lots, vote in, return.

541 absence of choice

n. no choice, Hobson's choice, first come first served; impartiality, neutrality, no preference, indifference; abstention, don't know.

adj. choiceless, neutral, impartial, disinterested, unbiased, indifferent.

vb. be neutral, abstain, not commit oneself, sit on the fence, not take sides.

542 rejection

n. rejection, dismissal, repudiation, denial, refusal, renunciation, rebuff, disownment, disapproval, exclusion, expulsion.

adj. rejected, repudiated, excluded, renounced, spurned.

vb. reject, not accept, dismiss, exclude, repudiate, renounce, deny, refuse, disapprove, rebuff, spurn, decline, disown, disclaim, despise, turn up one's nose at (*inf.*), expel, jettison, discard, brush aside, have nothing to do with, turn one's back on, laugh in someone's face (*inf.*).

see also **556, 694**

543 predetermination

n. predetermination, predestination, preordination, inevitability, necessity, finality; prediction, forecast; doom, fate; premeditation, predeliberation, foregone conclusion.

adj. predetermined, planned, proposed, designed, fixed, deliberate.

vb. predetermine, foreordain, predestine, appoint, destine, predestinate; predict, forecast, foretell, determine beforehand; premeditate, preconceive.

544 spontaneity

n. spontaneity, spur of the moment; improvisation, extemporization; involuntariness, reflex action; impetuosity, impulsiveness, hastiness, suddenness, rashness; impulse buying.

adj. spontaneous, impulsive, unpremeditated, unthinking, unconsidered; involuntary, automatic, instinctive, reflex; extempore, impromptu, improvised, ad lib (*inf.*); hasty, sudden, rash, precipitate; casual, offhand, throwaway.

vb. act impulsively; blurt out, say the first thing that comes into one's mind; improvise, extemporize, ad lib (*inf.*), play by ear.

adv. on impulse, on the spur of the moment, impulsively, rashly, instinctively, automatically.

see also **613, 859**

545 habit

n. habit, custom, mode, practice, wont, usage, fashion, style, rule, procedure; tendency, propensity, bent, disposition, predisposition, weakness, bias, penchant, second nature, instinct; routine, ritual, rut, groove, treadmill, regularity; convention,

precedent, tradition, etiquette, protocol, the done thing; conditioning, accustoming, adaptation, familiarization, training, acclimatization.

addict, habitué, fiend, creature of habit, devotee, client, patron, regular (*inf.*).

adj. usual, customary, normal, common, general, accepted, expected, prevalent, current, conventional, orthodox, established; habitual, frequent, regular, routine, stereotyped; mechanical, seasoned, inveterate; confirmed, ingrained, deep-seated; besetting, clinging, persistent; accustomed, used to, adapted.

vb. accustom, get used to, take to, adapt, adjust, accommodate, condition, train, familiarize, orientate, acclimatize, harden, season, inure, habituate; catch on.

be wont to, be in the habit of, make a practice of.

adv. usually, as is usual, generally.

546 absence of habit

n. disuse, unaccustomedness, desuetude; cessation, relinquishment; decay, neglect, deterioration.

adj. unused, unaccustomed, not used to, not in the habit of; unskilled, inexperienced.

vb. break a habit, abandon, neglect, relinquish, discard, discontinue, rid oneself of, throw off, wean from; not get used to, not take to; not catch on.

see also **607**

547 motive

n. motive, cause, reason, purpose, ground, basis, spring, spur, impetus, urge, prod, goad, carrot, lure, bait; influence, stimulus, incentive, inspiration, prompting, instigation; persuasion, inducement, coaxing, cajolery, wheedling; charm, attraction, glamour; enticement, temptation, bribery.

motivator, instigator, prompter, animator, coaxer, wheedler; pressure group, lobby, lobbyist.

adj. motivating, persuasive, convincing, impelling, forceful; provocative, stimulating, rousing; fascinating, alluring, charming, captivating, enthralling; enticing, tantalizing.

vb. motivate, cause, inspire, stimulate, prompt, instigate, insist, induce, drive, push, egg on, spur, urge, prod, goad; provoke, elicit, call forth, evoke; influence, encourage, support; persuade, sway, prevail on, talk into, win over, wear down resistance, brainwash (*inf.*), twist round one's little finger (*inf.*), pull strings; coax, cajole, wheedle; captivate, fascinate, charm, attract, interest, entice, tempt, tantalize, beguile, enrapture;

lobby, put pressure on; bribe, buy, get at (*inf.*), oil, corrupt.

548 dissuasion

n. dissuasion, discouragement, hindrance, deterrent, disincentive, damper, restraint, cold water, wet blanket; spoilsport, killjoy.

adj. dissuasive, discouraging.

vb. dissuade, deter, hinder, prevent, advise against, discourage, talk out of, wean from, dampen, stifle, disparage, pour cold water on.

549 pretext

n. pretext, excuse, plea, apology, justification, pretence, gesture, show, guise, veil, cloak, mask, appearance, alibi.

adj. ostensible, alleged, specious.

vb. allege, pretend, claim, profess, excuse; apologize, make excuses, bluff.

550 good

n. good, benefit, gain, profit, success, advantage, service, boon, windfall, godsend, pennies from heaven, providence, blessing, good turn; well-being, welfare, prosperity, fortune, happiness, weal; improvement, betterment, edification, progress.

adj. good, beneficial, advantageous, helpful, useful, edifying.

see also **899, 935**

551 evil

n. evil, misfortune, ill, harm, ruin, nuisance, disadvantage, bane, accident, tragedy, disaster, catastrophe, calamity, affliction, trial, crying shame, raw deal; foul play, wrong, injury, pain, anguish, hurt; wickedness, corruption.

adj. evil, bad, wicked; unfortunate, ill, tragic, catastrophic, disastrous, painful, distressing, hurtful.

see also **900, 936**

B Prospective volition

552 intention

n. intention, purpose, aim, intent, meaning; goal, object, end, objective, mark, destination, target; plan, design, idea, proposal; dream, desire, aspiration, expectation, ambition.

adj. intended, designed, planned, proposed, deliberate; intending, purposeful, teleological.

vb. intend, aim, go for, attempt, try for, pursue; plan, propose, project, design, purpose, mean; dream, expect, hope, aspire,

have designs on (*inf.*); consider, think about, contemplate, study, have in mind, have in view, calculate, work out, decide, determine, resolve.

553 chance

n. chance, randomness, uncertainty, fortuity; fate, fortune, luck, coincidence, fluke, toss-up (*inf.*); speculation, venture, risk, hazard; bet, gamble, wager, stake, flutter, draw, lottery.

speculator, gambler, better, backer, punter; bookmaker, turf accountant, bookie (*inf.*).

adj. chance, lucky, fortuitous, unintentional, haphazard, aimless, random, risky, hazardous, touch-and-go.

vb. chance, risk, venture, hazard, speculate, gamble, bet, wager, back.

see also **158**

554 pursuit

n. pursuit, hunt, chase, race, pursuance, quest, search, tracking; hunter, chaser, pursuer, seeker, quester, follower.

adj. pursuing, following.

vb. pursue, look for, search, follow up, seek, quest, prosecute; hunt, go after, chase, give chase, hound, tail, trail, stalk, shadow, track, sniff out (*inf.*), smell out, dog.

prep. after, in pursuit of, on the track of.

555 avoidance

n. avoidance, evasion, escape, flight, withdrawal, retreat, shunning, abstinence, circumvention; shirker, fugitive, runaway, absconder, eloper, deserter, refugee, truant.

adj. avoiding, evasive, elusive.

vb. avoid, escape, evade, elude, keep away, keep off, boycott; flee, shrink, flinch; get out of, shun, shirk, dodge, flunk, turn away, duck, hedge; steer clear of, keep one's distance, take no part in, leave alone, not get involved in, disregard, give the go-by; abstain, refrain; retreat, withdraw.

556 relinquishment

n. relinquishment, abandonment, giving up, surrender, renunciation, discontinuance, withdrawal, desertion, quitting.

vb. relinquish, abandon, give up, renounce, forgo, abdicate, waive, surrender, throw in the towel; turn over to, turn in; leave, quit, withdraw, back out, go back on, retreat, secede, forsake; discontinue, break with, break off with, drop, let go, throw away, cast off, discard, part with, shed, desert, chuck (*inf.*), ditch, jilt; leave in the lurch, have done with (*inf.*), walk out on (*inf.*).

see also 542, 713

557 business

n. business, affairs, dealings, trade; job, employment, post, appointment, position, situation, engagement, incumbency; vocation, calling, pursuit, occupation, profession, line of business, speciality, *métier*, craft; career, life-work, life, mission; work, task, undertaking, activity, assignment, affair, concern; function, office, role, capacity, responsibility, duty, charge, commission, terms of reference, scope, area, field, realm, province, portfolio.

adj. businesslike, efficient, professional, official, prompt; busy, tied up with (*inf.*).

vb. employ, occupy, appoint, select, recruit, engage, contract, take on, give a job to, commission, enlist, hire, rope in (*inf.*), take on the payroll; work, undertake, be busy, be occupied with, be engaged on, be about.

558 plan

n. plan, scheme, project, design, programme, proposal, schedule; scope, outline, sketch; method, procedure, guidelines, principles; policy, course of action, strategy; representation, chart; master-plan, long-range plan; blueprint, draft, rough draft, pilot scheme, dummy run; plot, conspiracy, intrigue, cabal, little game (*inf.*).

planner, director, designer, organizer, architect, engineer, administrator; conspirer, plotter, schemer.

adj. planned, projected, prospective, on the drawing board, procedural.

vb. plan, design, work out, draw up, organize, arrange, propose, devise, create, dream up (*inf.*), frame, undertake, proceed, outline, sketch, draft; forecast, project, think ahead, phase; scheme, plot, conspire, concoct, hatch.

559 way

n. way, manner, fashion; method, means, procedure, process; tactics, measures, steps; direction, passage, entrance, access, approach, route, itinerary, course.

path, track, footpath, walk; road, street, avenue, lane, drive, crescent, close, alley, terrace, park, garden, green, hill, grove, boulevard, square, place, court, circus, arcade, piazza, market, mall, embankment; ring-road, by-pass, arterial road, motorway, dual carriageway, clearway, primary route, trunk road, highway.

railway, underground, tube; main line, branch line, feeder.

560 mid-course

n. centre, mean, middle course, middle of the road, half-way house.

adj. middle, central, medial, neutral, middle-of-the-road, unextreme, moderate, intermediate, midway, half-way.

561 circuit

n. circuit, detour, by-pass, roundabout way; digression, deviation.

adj. circuitous, roundabout, indirect, out-of-the-way.

see also 250

562 requirement

n. requirement, requisite, stipulation, need, want, demand; condition; essential, imperative, necessity, must (*inf.*), desideratum; needfulness, obligation, compulsion, indispensability, emergency, urgency, matter of life and death, essentiality.

adj. necessary, essential, imperative, indispensable, vital, needful, urgent; wanted, in demand.

vb. require, need, want, wish; lack, be in need of, miss; demand, call for, ask, invite, cry out for; necessitate, force, compel.

563 instrumentality

n. instrumentality, mediation, subservience, intervention; help, aid, assistance, agency, medium, vehicle, intermediary, organ.

adj. instrumental, intermediate, conducive, assisting, subsidiary, auxiliary, subservient, contributory, helpful; effective.

vb. be instrumental, help, aid, mediate.

see also 172

564 means

n. means, wherewithal, resources, ways and means, equipment, supplies, assets, reserves, provisions; power, potential; factor, agent, medium, channel, organization.

vb. find the means, provide, equip, supply.

565 instrument

n. instrument, implement, apparatus, equipment, appliance, gadget, device, invention, contrivance, contraption; machine, mechanism, machinery, engine; tool, utensil; computer, robot, automaton.

adj. instrumental, mechanical, automatic.

566 materials

n. materials, resources, supplies, assets, means, wherewithal, stuff, raw materials.

567 store

n. store, collection, accumulation, heap, pile, stack, load, mass, stock, hoard, bulk, deposit, bundle; crop, harvest; treasure, reserves, savings, nest-egg; backlog; fountain, well, spring, gold-mine, reservoir; abundance, profusion, fullness.

storage, safekeeping; warehouse, stockroom, storeroom, depot, depository; library, museum, archives.

adj. stored, accumulated, saved, kept.

vb. store, keep, put away, put aside, put by, stow away, stash away (*inf.*); accumulate, pile up, heap, stack, amass, bulk, bundle, stockpile, lay in; collect, save, deposit, invest, hoard, salt away (*inf.*); harvest, gather; put by for a rainy day.

adv. aside, in store, in reserve, in stock.

568 provision

n. provision, equipment, supply, furnishings, fittings, fixtures, reserve, store, facilities, belongings, accessories, accompaniments, outfit, paraphernalia, apparatus, appliance; catering, purveying.

adj. provided, furnished, equipped, well-equipped.

vb. provide, equip, supply, furnish, fit, prepare, rig, dress, assemble, deck; give, afford, lend, invest, endow; maintain, stock, cater; supplement, complement; replenish, fill up.

569 waste

n. waste, ruin, decay, devastation, desolation, dilapidation, deterioration, erosion, wear and tear, loss, exhaustion, depletion, decline; consumption, disuse, misuse, squandering, uselessness, dissipation; extravagance, wastefulness, prodigality; excess.

adj. wasteful, extravagant, prodigal, squandering, spendthrift; wasted, squandered, depleted, worthless.

vb. waste, consume, expend, eat up, eat away, exhaust, reduce, deplete, empty, drain, devour, dissipate; squander, lavish, abuse; destroy, erode, decay, dry up, dwindle, wither, run dry, wear out; be of no avail, come to nothing.

570 sufficiency

n. sufficiency, adequacy, enough to go on with; right amount.

adj. sufficient, adequate, enough, satisfactory, acceptable; plenty, abundant, generous, liberal, full, complete, replete.

vb. be sufficient, suffice, be enough, avail, do, comply with, qualify, fill the bill, come up to, live up to, satisfy requirements, make the grade, prove acceptable; lick into shape (*inf.*).

571 insufficiency

n. insufficiency, inadequacy, deficiency, scarcity, meagreness, scantiness, slightness, poverty, paucity, dearth, lack.

adj. insufficient, inadequate, not enough, unacceptable, meagre, thin, slight, scanty, poor, bankrupt, sparing, unsatisfactory, wanting, lacking, missing, failing, disappointing; miserly, parsimonious.

vb. be insufficient, not come up to, fall short, come short, fail, want, need, lack, require.

prep. without, in want of, short of.

see also 35

572 excess

n. excess, redundance; exorbitance, inordinacy, superfluity, oversufficiency, abundance, plenty, lavishness, plethora, profusion, glut, surfeit, surplus, over-supply, saturation, exuberance, superabundance, inundation, flood, deluge, torrent, avalanche, bounty, bonanza, cornucopia, congestion; enough and to spare, more than enough; luxury, extravagance, too much of a good thing.

adj. excessive, inordinate, exorbitant, extravagant, immoderate, unreasonable, saturated, plentiful, superfluous, overfull, congested, surplus, redundant, to spare, extra; plenty, abundant.

vb. abound, teem, swarm; overdo; saturate, glut, inundate, flood, overwhelm, choke, drench.

573 importance

n. importance, significance, consequence; seriousness, gravity; substance, matter, weight, moment, import; prominence, eminence; be-all and end-all, priority, urgency.

adj. important, significant, momentous, decisive, critical, relevant, consequential, crucial, considerable, valuable; great, extensive; serious, grave, weighty, ponderous, heavy, solemn; famous, well-known, eminent, notable, distinguished, prominent, impressive, imposing, influential, illustrious, extraordinary, outstanding, exceptional, top-notch (*inf.*), heavyweight (*inf.*), mainline (*inf.*); basic, essential, fundamental; chief, main, primary, principal, foremost, leading, paramount, salient.

vb. be important, carry weight, influence,

matter, deserve attention; make important, emphasize, underline, stress; value, prize, set great store by, think much of.

574 unimportance

n. unimportance, insignificance, triviality, worthlessness, immateriality, paltriness, irrelevance; red herring, trifle, nothing to speak of, nothing to write home about, nonentity, drop in the ocean.

adj. unimportant, insignificant, immaterial, inconsequential, irrelevant, trivial, worthless, paltry, petty, trifling, inconsiderable, slight, common, ordinary, superficial.

vb. be unimportant, not matter; play second fiddle, make light of, play down, make nothing of.

575 utility

n. utility, usefulness; utilization, employment, helpfulness, efficacy; suitability, applicability, practicability, serviceableness.

advantage, benefit, profit, worth, value, merit; service, application, convenience.

adj. useful, valuable, beneficial, profitable, advantageous, suitable, practicable, convenient, helpful, handy, available, applicable; utilitarian, functional, sensible, pragmatic.

vb. be useful, help, serve a purpose, perform a function, come in handy; profit, benefit, stand one in good stead, avail.

use, employ, have the use of, exploit, exercise, utilize, take advantage of, turn to, take up, adopt, practise, apply, avail oneself of; handle, operate; spend, consume.

see also **606**

576 inutility

n. inutility, uselessness, worthlessness, fruitlessness, ineffectiveness, unsuitability, impracticability; futility, hopelessness, vanity.

lost labour, waste of time, wild-goose chase; dead wood; waste, refuse, rubbish, waste-product, litter, dregs, dust, muck.

adj. useless, of no use, worthless, purposeless, futile, vain, pointless, empty, ineffective, incompetent, counter-productive; thankless, unrewarding; unusable, unsuitable, impracticable, inconvenient, unhelpful, disadvantageous, unavailable; out of order, broken down, inoperative; unnecessary, uncalled for.

vb. be useless, be of no help, come to nothing; flog a dead horse, labour in vain, have no future, beat the air.

577 expedience

n. expedience, suitability, appropriateness,

fitness, rightness, advisability, propriety, desirability, advantageousness, usefulness.

adj. expedient, advantageous, suitable, fitting, appropriate, apposite, desirable, advisable, seemly; practical, useful, convenient; wise, politic.

vb. suit, fit; help, do, benefit.

see also **136, 915**

578 inexpedience

n. inexpedience, unsuitability, inappropriateness, inadvisability, undesirability, unfitness, impropriety, inconvenience, disadvantage, prejudice.

adj. inexpedient, unsuitable, inappropriate, undesirable, inadvisable, unfitting, unseemly, unwise, inopportune, imprudent, unfavourable, detrimental, disadvantageous, inconvenient.

vb. not do, not help; inconvenience, put out, embarrass, bother, trouble, hinder.

see also **137, 916**

579 goodness

n. goodness, excellence, fineness, greatness, magnificence, superiority; quality, value, price, worth, merit.

top people, elite, cream, pick of the bunch, salt of the earth, treasure, gem, one in a million, champion, corker (*sl.*).

adj. good, excellent, fine, great, superb, splendid, magnificent, marvellous, wonderful, attractive, lovely; masterly, skilled, competent; praiseworthy, commendable; admirable, desirable, enticing, surprising, astonishing; super, terrific, out of this world (*inf.*), cool (*sl.*), neat (*sl.*), magic (*sl.*).

best, first-class, first-rate, optimum, premium, prime, highest, supreme, superlative, A-1, top-notch (*inf.*), tops; exceptional, incomparable, surpassing, incredible, unbelievable, excelling, exemplary; choice, select, exquisite, superior, capital (*inf.*); valuable, priceless, inestimable.

fair, pretty good, not bad, all right, O.K., passable, tolerable, adequate, middling, fair to middling.

vb. be good, have value, have quality; do good, benefit, help, edify.

see also **550, 844**

580 badness

n. badness, nastiness, wickedness, vileness, foulness; inferiority, unsatisfactoriness, mediocrity; bane, ill wind, woe, spanner in the works, fly in the ointment.

adj. bad, wrong, awful, nasty, terrible, horrid, horrible; inferior, imperfect, defective, worthless, poor, second-rate, below average, deficient, unsatisfactory, mediocre, ordinary, unwholesome, shoddy, trashy, crummy (*sl.*), shabby; lousy (*sl.*), rotten; pitiful, contemptible, paltry.

harmful, damaging, detrimental, hurtful, destructive, fatal, deadly, corrupting, poisonous, corroding, toxic, venomous, subversive.

vb. be bad, have no value; do bad, harm, injure, hurt, wound, ruin, destroy, corrupt, subvert; vex, trouble, wrong.

see also **551**

581 perfection

n. perfection, excellence, impeccability, faultlessness, stainlessness; maturity, completion, culmination, consummation.

ideal, standard, model, paragon, summit, ultimate, height, acme; showpiece, masterpiece, *pièce de résistance.*

adj. perfect, faultless, pure, flawless, impeccable, immaculate, untainted, unblemished, untarnished, stainless, spotless, unstained, uncontaminated, unadulterated, irreproachable, beyond compare, brilliant; supreme, ideal.

whole, sound, complete, entire, finished, developed, fulfilled, completed, accomplished, consummate.

vb. perfect, develop, complete, finish, bring to fruition, get down to a fine art, consummate.

582 imperfection

n. imperfection, impurity, defectiveness, inadequacy, immaturity; disfigurement, defacement, deformity, discoloration.

blemish, flaw, stain; fault, mistake, defect, lack, drawback, snag, loophole, weak spot, weak link in the chain.

adj. imperfect, flawed, defective, deficient, malformed, distorted, tainted, adulterated, blemished, damaged, injured, impaired.

incomplete, unfinished, unsound, uneven, unsatisfactory, faulty, inadequate, fallible.

vb. be imperfect, show faults, fall short, not come up to, be found wanting.

see also **847**

583 cleanness

n. cleanness, cleanliness, pureness, spotlessness, whiteness; neatness, tidiness, orderliness, trimness; cleaning, washing, scrubbing, scouring, sprinkling; sterilization, disinfection; cleansing, purification, purgation, ablution.

adj. clean, tidy, neat; immaculate, white, spotless, stainless, untarnished, unblemished, unstained, unsullied, unpolluted, unsoiled, dirtless, spick and span, starched, laundered, polished; germ-free.

vb. clean, tidy, clear; wash, lather, shampoo; bathe, scrub, scour, sponge, mop, swab; brush, sweep; freshen, ventilate; disinfect, fumigate; sterilize, pasteurize; launder, starch, iron; cleanse, purify, sprinkle, purge, expurgate.

584 uncleanness

n. uncleanness, impurity, untidiness, disorderliness, muckiness, filthiness, pollution, defilement.

dirt, filth, spot, stain, smear, smudge, blot, muck, grime, grease, slime; squalor.

adj. unclean, dirty, soiled, polluted, tarnished, sullied, spotted, smeared, daubed, smudged, besmirched; filthy, grimy, greasy, muddy, sooty; squalid, foul, mucky; contaminated, decayed, rotten, rancid, putrid; sloppy, untidy, messy, slovenly, dishevelled, bedraggled, unkempt, like something the cat brought in (*inf.*), unwashed; defiled, unrefined, unpurified.

vb. be dirty, rust, decay, rot, collect dust; dirty, soil, sully, tarnish, daub, bedaub, smudge, blot, pollute, foul; mess up, untidy; corrupt, defile, debase, taint, contaminate, infect.

585 health

n. health, wholeness, soundness, healthfulness, healthiness, salubrity, wholesomeness, balance, vitality; sanity; fitness, strength, well-being, good health, rosy cheeks.

hygiene, sanitation, public health, cleanliness.

adj. healthy, well, sound, whole, wholesome, fit, strong, robust, vigorous, energetic, hale, hearty; all right, rosy-cheeked, flourishing, never feeling better, in fine fettle, in good shape, fighting fit.

healthful, invigorating, stimulating, bracing, beneficial, salubrious; nutritious, nourishing, body-building, restorative, therapeutic, corrective; good for one, what the doctor ordered; hygienic, sanitary.

vb. be healthy, flourish, feel fine; be good for.

586 ill health

n. ill health, poor health, bad health, frailty, weakness, infirmity, invalidity, unhealthiness, indisposition.

illness, disease, ailment, malady, sickness, complaint, disability, affliction, condition, disorder, breakdown, collapse, relapse; fever, infection, virus (*inf.*), bug (*sl.*), pain; bout, spell; stroke, fit, attack, seizure, spasm, convulsions.

lack of hygiene, insalubrity, uncleanliness, contagiousness, infectiousness.

adj. ill, unwell, ailing, weak, unhealthy, poorly, frail, infirm, sick; suffering, down with, indisposed, disabled; drooping, languishing, declining, bed-ridden, laid up, confined; run down, exhausted; under the weather (*inf.*), out of sorts, seedy (*inf.*), groggy (*inf.*).

unhygienic, insanitary, polluted, bad for, insalubrious; infectious, contagious, endemic; poisonous, toxic, deadly.

vb. be ill, be down with, suffer; fall ill, catch, become ill with, contract, go down with, get, be stricken with; show symptoms of, sicken for; waste away, droop, languish; be bad for, disagree with.

587 improvement

n. improvement, betterment, change, advance, development, refinement, progress, reformation, face-lift, amelioration; enrichment, promotion, furtherance, reform, modernization; revision, correction, amendment.

adj. improved, corrected, amended, revised, reformed, touched up; progressive, reformatory.

vb. improve, develop, further, better, reorganize, promote, reform, straighten out, mend, ameliorate; revise, update, upgrade, correct, rectify; polish, refine, enrich; decorate, beautify, touch up, refurbish; progress, make progress, get better, advance, profit; pick up, come on, rally; pull one's socks up (*inf.*); mellow, mature.

see also **288**

588 deterioration

n. deterioration, impairment, degeneration, decay, rotting, decomposition, erosion, rust; dilapidation, ruin, collapse, decadence, disintegration; impoverishment, adulteration, defilement, corruption, spoiling, detriment, pollution; retrogression; damage, injury, wound, lesion, cut, gash, sore, bruise.

adj. deteriorated, impaired, spoiled, decadent, ruined; damaged, harmed, desolate, ravaged, plundered, robbed, marred, mutilated; decayed, decomposed, rotten, putrified, foul, putrid; worn away, wasting away, emaciated, depleted; ramshackle, tumbledown.

vb. deteriorate, worsen, degenerate, decay, decline, slide, fall, slump, sink, go downhill, fall away, depreciate; go bad, rot, crumble, the rot set in (*inf.*); wither, shrivel; spoil; go

to pieces, break up, decompose, fade away, waste away, die; collapse, break down, founder, go to wrack and ruin, go to the dogs (*inf.*), go to pot (*inf.*); go off the rails (*inf.*).

impair, pervert, ruin, corrupt, distort; lower, pull down, reduce, degrade, dehumanize, adulterate, defile, deprave, infect, contaminate; eat away, erode, corrode.

harm, damage, injure, wound, savage, cripple, lame; maltreat, misuse; disgrace, dishonour, discredit; exacerbate, aggravate; hold against (*inf.*), count against; confuse, mess up (*inf.*).

589 restoration

n. restoration, healing, cure, recovery, convalescence, recuperation; renovation, repair, reconditioning, refurbishing, reconstruction, remaking; rehabilitation, re-establishment, resumption, reinstatement, return, getting back to normal; reparation, restitution, amends; reclamation, salvage, rescue.

revival, renewal, reawakening, reinvigoration, resuscitation, rebirth, regeneration, resurrection, renaissance, resurgence, rejuvenation; Indian summer, face-lift, new look, comeback.

adj. restored, repaired, re-established, back to normal; restorative, corrective, remedial, recuperative, therapeutic, soothing, curative.

vb. restore, rebuild, reconstruct, remodel, refashion, reorganize, recondition, reform, remake, revamp, renovate, modernize; repair, mend, fix; refurbish, touch up; darn, patch, sew.

put right, correct, rectify, amend, redress; return, recompense, refund, make amends, make restitution, reinstate, put back, reinstall, re-establish, resume, return to normal; reclaim, salvage, rescue, retrieve, redeem.

revive, refresh, renew, recreate, reanimate, regenerate, resurrect, resuscitate, rejuvenate, reawaken, revitalize, rekindle.

cure, heal, treat, minister to, nurse, rehabilitate, put on one's feet again.

be restored, recover, convalesce, recuperate, get well, get better, fall on one's feet (*inf.*), pick up, rally, pull through, gain strength, get back into circulation (*inf.*); come up smiling (*inf.*).

see also **618**

590 relapse

n. relapse, return, reversion, retrogression, regression; deterioration, declension; apostasy.

vb. relapse, regress, retrogress, deteriorate,

degenerate, sink back, slip back, revert, suffer; backslide, fall from grace, apostasize.
see also **289**

591 remedy

n. remedy, cure, relief, assistance, treatment, medication; medicine, medicament, preparation, prescription, pharmaceutical, drug; mixture, dose, potion, linctus; pill, tablet, capsule, lozenge; vaccine, injection, inoculation, jab (*inf.*), shot (*inf.*); lotion, ointment, balm salve; tonic, pick-me-up, stimulant, restorative, refresher, tranquillizer. sedative; panacea, cure-all, elixir; operation, surgery.

adj. remedial, therapeutic, healing, medicinal, corrective, curative, restorative.

vb. remedy, cure, heal, restore; treat, attend, practise; relieve, support, help, mitigate, soothe, palliate; send for the doctor, send to hospital, dial 999, hospitalize, operate; undergo treatment, take pills, take one's medicine.

592 bane

n. bane, curse, plague, evil, scourge, affliction, trial, cross, thorn in the flesh; pain in the neck (*inf.*); weakness, besetting sin; poison, venom, virus; blight, mildew, rust, mould, rot, fungus, gangrene, cancer.

adj. baneful, evil, pestilent; deadly, poisonous, venomous; harmful, destructive.

593 safety

n. safety, security, surety, impregnability, invulnerability, immunity; protection, defence, safekeeping, custody, guardianship, supervision, care; law and order.

protector, guard, defender; custodian, warden, curator, keeper, trustee; life-guard, bodyguard, guardian; patrol, lookout, scout, night watchman, watchdog, vigilante, sentry, policeman.

adj. safe, secure, impregnable, invulnerable, unassailable; protected, guarded, safeguarded, defended, shielded, sheltered; unharmed, unhurt, safe and sound, unscathed; waterproof, bulletproof.

vb. make safe, safeguard, protect, keep, guard, defend, shelter, screen, shield, harbour; supervise, care for, mind, look after, take charge of, keep an eye on, attend to, take under one's wing; keep order, patrol, police, be on the lookout, keep vigil, keep cave (*sl.*); hide, lie low, go to earth.

adv. out of danger, in the clear, out of harm's way, in safe hands, under one's wing, under lock and key.
see also **595**

594 danger

n. danger, peril, risk, hazard, jeopardy; menace, threat; dangerousness, perilousness, riskiness, insecurity, precariousness, vulnerability, exposure, openness, helplessness; weak spot.

adj. dangerous, perilous, hazardous, risky, insecure, precarious, alarming, unsafe, treacherous, slippery, shaky, unstable; unsheltered, unshielded, vulnerable, exposed, open, naked, unfortified; menacing, threatening, ominous; critical, serious, delicate, explosive.

vb. endanger, jeopardize, put in jeopardy, expose, lay open to, risk, run the risk of, render liable to, court disaster, tempt providence.

595 refuge

n. refuge, shelter, sanctuary, asylum, retreat; home, ivory tower, port, harbour, haven; den, lair, nest, covert; castle, fortress, stronghold; safeguard, protection, defence; cover, screen, shade, shield, umbrella, windbreak; escape, way out, recourse, last resort.
see also **593, 646**

596 pitfall

n. pitfall, trap, snare, ambush, booby-trap; reef, rock, sandbank, quicksand, undercurrent; danger spot, black spot, trouble spot; trouble-maker, wrecker, snake in the grass.

597 warning

n. warning, caution, lesson, example, advice, counsel, caveat; alert, hint, intimation, admonition, tip-off (*inf.*), early warning, writing on the wall, symptom, sign, omen, augury; foreboding, premonition; notice, indication, notification; call, cry, shout.

adj. warning, cautionary, advisory, instructive.

vb. warn, caution, advise, alert, admonish, counsel, encourage, exhort, hint, prompt, suggest; forewarn, tip off (*inf.*); notify, inform, give notice, apprise.
see also **460**

598 indication of danger

n. alarm, alert, bell, alarm bell, fire alarm; siren, horn, fog-horn, klaxon, tocsin; light, red light, warning light; red alert; SOS, distress signal; beacon; war-cry, drum-beat; false alarm, hoax, scare.

vb. give the alarm, raise the alarm, dial 999, alert, put on the alert; cry wolf.

599   preservation

n. preservation, protection, maintenance, saving, keeping, conservation; storage, canning, freezing, refrigeration, dehydration.

adj. preservative, protective; preserved, kept, intact, protected; fresh, well-preserved.

vb. preserve, maintain, keep, protect, look after; conserve, keep fresh, bottle, can, tin, season, cure, salt, dry, smoke, freeze, refrigerate, freeze-dry, dehydrate, pickle, spice, marinade; embalm, mummify.

600   escape

n. escape, flight, departure, getaway; evasion, avoidance, abdication, desertion, disappearance; freedom, release, deliverance, rescue; retreat, withdrawal; narrow escape, close shave, near miss, near thing.

exit, way out, overflow, vent, waste-pipe, exhaust, leak, leakage, life-line, loophole.

escaper, runaway, truant, dodger, fugitive, refugee.

adj. escaped, free, out, at large, at liberty, missing, wanted.

vb. escape, flee, take flight, abscond, leave, depart, break loose, break out, decamp, free, get clear of, get away with, make one's getaway, make oneself scarce, give the slip, slip through one's fingers, elude, avoid, evade, elope, play truant; emerge, issue, burst out.

see also **921**

601   deliverance

n. deliverance, saving, rescue, release, freeing, liberation, relief; extrication, unbinding, loosening, disentanglement; ransom, forgiveness, pardon; remission, discharge, acquittal, reprieve, exoneration; emancipation, affranchisement, manumission.

vb. deliver, rescue, release, free, discharge, relieve; remit, acquit, let off (*inf.*), exonerate; extricate, loosen, untie; emancipate, liberate; salvage, retrieve; save, redeem, ransom, pardon, forgive.

see also **680, 911**

602   preparation

n. preparation, plan, step, arrangement; outline, draft, scheme, foundation, groundwork, spadework; rehearsal, practice, training, dummy run; approach, run-up (*inf.*); preparedness, readiness, fitness, experience, all systems go (*inf.*); red alert.

adj. preparatory, introductory, initial; prepared, ready, alert, waiting, on call, standing by, all set; experienced, skilled, qualified, versed, seasoned, broken in.

ready-made, prefabricated, ready-mixed, treated; frozen, pre-cooked, processed, dehydrated, ready-to-eat, oven-ready, instant; off-the-peg.

vb. prepare, get ready, arrange, plan, make preparations; settle, decide; adapt, adjust, fit, equip, supply, deck out, fit out, provide; take steps, take measures; practise, rehearse, train, study, hold in readiness; clear the decks, lay the foundations, prepare the ground, pave the way, smooth the way, blaze a trail, do the groundwork, do one's homework, break the ice.

see also **558**

603   non-preparation

n. non-preparation, unpreparedness, lack of training, inexperience; immaturity, rawness, naivety.

adj. unprepared, unready, napping, surprised, taken aback, unguarded, off one's guard, with one's pants down (*sl.*); unorganized, makeshift, hasty, rush (*inf.*); thoughtless; inexperienced, unskilled, uninstructed, untrained, unqualified, unequipped; new, naive, raw, immature; undeveloped, half-baked; backward, developing; fallow, virgin.

vb. be unprepared, be taken unawares, be caught napping; not plan, make no provision for; improvise.

604   attempt

n. attempt, try, effort, trial, experiment, endeavour, essay, undertaking, enterprise, venture.

adj. experimental, probationary, tentative, trial.

vb. attempt, try, have a try, make an effort, endeavour, venture, seek, aim for, strive, contend, risk, aspire, contest, have a go, lift a finger, put oneself out, have a crack at (*inf.*), have a shot at (*inf.*), have a stab at (*inf.*).

605   undertaking

n. undertaking, enterprise, project, plan, programme, cause, pursuit, campaign, operation, exercise, venture, exploit, feat; occupation, business, job, task, work, concern, matter in hand, proposition, engagement, commitment, obligation.

adj. enterprising, adventurous, venturesome, daring, go-ahead, pioneering, progressive, up-and-coming; ambitious, aspiring.

vb. undertake, engage in, go in for, do, take part in, participate in, devote oneself to; manage, engage, promise, contract; take upon oneself, put one's hand to, commit oneself to, take on, assume, shoulder, bear the burden of, tackle, embark on, enter upon, get down to (*inf.*), launch into, plunge into, commence, begin, start, set to, broach, set about; get down to business, get one's teeth into (*inf.*), take the bit between the teeth (*inf.*), get down to brass tacks (*inf.*), get to grips with.

adv. in hand, under control, in order.

see also **88**

606 use

n. use, usage, application, practice, exercise, employment, management, conduct, realization, adoption, conversion, treatment, handling, performance, control; method, technique; utility, usefulness.

adj. used, applied, utilized, adopted, accepted, practised; in use, in service, in force; old, second-hand.

vb. use, employ, apply, utilize, put to use, put into service; realize, adopt, draw on, take advantage of; adapt, convert, relate, bring to bear, resort to, have recourse to, fall back on; manage, conduct, deal with, treat, handle; exploit, use to the full, get the most out of, cash in on (*inf.*), capitalize, get the benefit of.

see also **575**

607 disuse

n. disuse, non-use, discontinuance, suspension, abolition, rejection, relinquishment, abandonment, unemployment, abeyance; obsolescence.

adj. disused, neglected, abandoned, idle, abolished, deserted, derelict; unused, unemployed, unspent; out of order, out of service, inactive; extra, spare.

vb. disuse, suspend, abolish, put aside, have done with, reject, get rid of, throw out, jettison, discard, scrap, throw on the scrapheap, neglect, abandon, desert, relinquish.

608 misuse

n. misuse, abuse, misapplication, misemployment, mishandling, mismanagement, misappropriation; perversion, debasement, degradation, prostitution, desecration, defilement, profanation, pollution; outrage, violation; error, mistake.

vb. misuse, abuse, mistreat, ill-treat, maltreat, mishandle, misemploy, misappropriate; pervert, prostitute, debase, desecrate, defile, violate, deprave, profane; wrong, insult, injure, hurt, harm, malign; squander, waste.

C Voluntary action

609 action

n. action, doing, execution, commission, operation, management, handling.

act, deed, thing, work, job, activity, feat, exploit; performance, achievement, undertaking, accomplishment; move, step, measure; blow, stroke.

doer, performer, worker, workman; instrument.

adj. doing, in operation, in process, operative.

vb. act, do, conduct, operate, work, function.

achieve, accomplish, complete, fulfil, carry out, bring about, execute, realize, effect, perform, dispose of, commit, transact, put into effect, put into action, put into operation.

take action, take steps, do something about, specialize in, concern oneself with, make it one's business, go in for; persist, persevere, keep going.

see also **611, 615**

610 inaction

n. inaction, rest, waiting, inertia, suspension, abeyance; laissez-faire, dormancy, neglect, stagnation.

adj. inoperative, idle, unemployed; suspended, in abeyance.

vb. not act, wait, pause, hang fire, bide one's time, twiddle one's thumbs, hold your horses (*inf.*); wait and see, do nothing, abstain, refrain; leave alone, have nothing to do with, let sleeping dogs lie.

see also **612**

611 activity

n. activity, liveliness, agility, nimbleness, alertness, alacrity, readiness, keenness, eagerness; energy, life, vigour, spirit, verve, zest, dynamism, enthusiasm, get-up-and-go (*inf.*); hurry, bustle, flurry, rush, commotion, rat-race.

industry, diligence, assiduousness, perseverance, resolution, determination, application, concentration; enterprise, initiative; activism, militancy, aggressiveness.

busy person, enthusiast, zealot, activist, fanatic, militant, live wire.

adj. active, lively, energetic, dynamic; busy, hard at it, eventful, bustling, dashing, raring to go; alert, agile, nimble, sharp, spry, wire, alive; restless, fidgety.

enthusiastic, keen, zealous; pushy (*inf.*), ambitious, aggressive, forceful, activist, militant, go-ahead, enterprising; industrious, diligent, hard-working, studious.

vb. be active, be busy, rush around, bustle about, have one's hands full, have a finger in every pie; have many irons in the fire; busy oneself in, stir oneself, rouse onself; persevere, keep going, keep at it; work hard, not have a moment to spare, never stop, overwork, overdo it, have no time to call one's own.

see also **532, 609**

612 inactivity

n. inactivity, stillness, inertia; lethargy, slackness, sluggishness, torpor, lifelessness, listlessness; apathy, indifference, carelessness; idleness, laziness, indolence, sloth.

fatigue, tiredness, weariness, sleepiness; sleep, slumber, rest, doze, nod, snooze, shuteye, catnap, forty winks, siesta, repose, dormancy; breather, pause, holiday, vacation.

lazy person, idler, loafer (*inf.*), good-for-nothing, lazy-bones, bum (*sl.*), tramp, sluggard, wastrel, parasite, sponger.

adj. inactive, still, stable; unemployed, unoccupied, fallow, barren; idle, lazy, slothful, indolent, lethargic, slack, sluggish, listless, torpid, languid; unadventurous, unenterprising, stay-at-home; apathetic, indifferent, uninterested.

tired, weary, drowsy, sleepy, fatigued, somnolent, dormant; exhausted, run down, overworked, worn out, washed out, drooping, faint, weak, stale.

vb. be inactive, rest, relax, pause, bide one's time; drift, vegetate, stagnate.

idle, loaf about (*inf.*), mooch about (*sl.*), loiter about, hang about (*inf.*), bum around (*sl.*); dilly-dally, shilly-shally, languish; kill time, waste time, while away the time.

sleep, slumber, doze, drowse, snooze, take a nap, nod off, have forty winks, yawn, dream; go to bed, turn in, kip down (*sl.*), hit the sack (*sl.*).

see also **533, 617, 841**

613 haste

n. haste, rush, hurry, scramble, scurry, flurry, hurly-burly; dash, spirit, spurt, run, burst, sprint, bolt, race; hurriedness, hastiness, urgency, promptness, precipitation, rashness, impulsiveness, impetuosity.

adj. hasty, quick, fast, swift, speedy, hurried, dashing; impetuous, impulsive, rash, inconsiderate, reckless, foolhardy, precipitate, headlong, impatient.

vb. hasten, quicken, speed up, accelerate, expedite, dispatch, stimulate, fillip, urge,

goad, whip, incite, push through, rush through, railroad through (*inf.*).

rush, sprint, spurt, scurry, scuttle, dash, bustle, zoom, tear, bomb (*inf.*), go all out (*inf.*), step on it (*inf.*).

see also **280, 544, 859**

614 leisure

n. leisure, free time, spare time, time off, recreation, relaxation, rest, respite, breather, break, pause, lull, recess; holiday, leave, leave of absence, vacation, sabbatical, furlough, home leave.

adj. leisurely, resting, unoccupied.

vb. have time to spare, be off, take one's ease, relax, rest.

adv. off, off duty, on holiday; at leisure, at one's convenience, at an early opportunity.

see also **281, 840**

615 exertion

n. exertion, effort, panic, trouble, toil, labour, work, travail, strife, strain, tension, elbow grease, drudgery; hard work, handful (*inf.*), uphill task, sweat (*sl.*), drudge.

adj. laborious, arduous, hard, difficult, strenuous, onerous, painstaking, gruelling, punishing, uphill, back-breaking.

vb. exert oneself, try, attempt; take pains, work, labour, fight, toil, contend, struggle, strive, sweat blood; knuckle down (*inf.*), get down to it (*inf.*), buckle down (*inf.*); drudge, grind, plod (*inf.*), plug away (*inf.*), slog away, sweat one's guts out (*sl.*); make heavy weather of, make a meal of; put oneself out, do one's best, do one's utmost, go to all lengths, go all out, leave no stone unturned, move heaven and earth, pull out all the stops (*inf.*); overdo it, have one's work cut out.

see also **535, 611**

616 repose

n. repose, rest, relaxation, inaction; breather, break, pause, coffee-break, tea-break, lunch-break, lunch-hour, rest period; day of rest, Sabbath, Lord's Day; ease, quiet, quietness, tranquillity.

adj. restful, tranquil, quiet, calm, peaceful; sabbatical.

vb. rest, be quiet, stop, halt; take a rest, take it easy, let up, ease off, slow down, stretch one's legs, have a break; get away from it all (*inf.*).

see also **610, 618**

617 fatigue

n. fatigue, tiredness, weariness; sleepiness, heaviness, drowsiness, doziness, somnolence;

faintness, weakness. exhaustion, collapse, staleness, jadedness; lassitude, languor.

adj. tired, weary, exhausted, run down, fagged out (*inf.*), worn out, ready to drop (*inf.*), dog-tired, dead beat, all in, whacked (*inf.*); heavy, dozy (*inf.*), drowsy, sleepy; weak, faint, dropping, haggard; washed out, drained, stale, jaded.

vb. be tired, drop, collapse, flag, jade, peg out (*inf.*), flake out (*sl.*); faint, pass out (*inf.*), lose consciousness; work too hard, overdo it.

weary, tire, fatigue, wear out, exhaust, take it out of (*inf.*), fag out (*inf.*), strain; bore.

see also **612, 841**

618 refreshment

n. refreshment, enlivenment, invigoration, recovery, restoration, convalescence, recuperation, relief.

adj. refreshing, restoring, invigorating, exhilarating, bracing, stimulating, arousing; refreshed, invigorated, like a new man.

vb. refresh, restore, arouse, revive, enliven, animate, strengthen, stimulate, invigorate, renew, reawaken, bring round, give new life to, energize, improve, relieve, resuscitate, vivify; encourage, cheer.

recover, recuperate, pick up, perk up, recharge one's batteries, get one's breath back.

see also **589, 616**

619 agent

n. agent, doer, actor, performer, participant, instrument, medium, practitioner, executor; worker, workman, operator, mechanic, labourer, operative, craftsman, skilled worker; apprentice; hack, drudge, slave, fag.

workforce, employees, staff, personnel, labour, payroll, manpower, resources.

620 workshop

n. workshop, workplace, establishment, installation, institution, plant, factory, works, foundry, yard; shop, house, office, bureau, branch, station, laboratory; firm, company, concern, industry.

621 conduct

n. conduct, behaviour, manner, deportment, demeanour, air, carriage, bearing, posture, attitude, comportment, mien, delivery, appearance, guise; guidance, control, oversight, supervision, superintendence, execution, government, management, organ-

ization; strategy, tactics, policy, campaign, programme.

adj. behavioural; tactical, strategical.

vb. behave, act, conduct; acquit oneself, bear oneself, comport onself, pose, appear, seem; behave oneself, mind one's manners, mind one's P's and Q's, be on one's best behaviour; manage, guide, supervise, direct, regulate, administer.

622 management

n. management, conduct, guidance, direction, control, order, charge, power, execution, government, organization, administration, decision making, handling, regulation, legislation, jurisdiction; oversight, supervision, superintendence, surveillance, command, authority, leadership; stewardship, husbandry, housekeeping, economics.

adj. directive, managerial, controlling, supervisory; executive, administrative, governmental, gubernatorial, legislative; official, bureaucratic.

vb. manage, conduct, run, guide, direct, lead, control, regulate, order, govern, command, steer, point the way, decide; handle, execute, administer, organize, legislate; supervise, superintend; steward.

623 director

n. manager, director, controller, leader, executive, governor, politician, minister, legislator, commander; dictator; superintendent, supervisor, inspector, overseer, foreman; steward; administrator, official, bureaucrat, functionary, secretary; guide, organizer.

see also **34, 675**

624 advice

n. advice, suggestion, opinion, view, counsel, guidance, encouragement, information, instruction, recommendation; warning, admonition, criticism, dissuasion, caution, notice; notification.

advisor, counsellor, right-hand man, friend, confidant, teacher, informant, helper, consultant; think-tank.

adj. advisory, consultative.

vb. advise, guide, direct, tell, have a word with, suggest; exhort, urge, prompt, encourage, persuade, recommend, counsel; warn, admonish, dissuade; inform, notify, acquaint.

consult, ask, discuss, talk over, seek the opinion of, seek advice, turn to, confide in.

625 council

n. council, cabinet, committee, government, parliament, board, directorate, board of governors; congress, conference, assembly, convention, synod, convocation, diet; panel, forum, brains trust.

councillor, minister, member of parliament, back-bencher, parliamentarian, statesman, senator, congressman; delegate, representative, officer.

626 precept

n. precept, maxim, command, direction, instruction, prescription, principle, statute, commandment, rule; canon, doctrine, law, charge, mandate, injunction, edict; formula, recipe.

see also **103, 954**

627 skill

n. skill, capability, proficiency, competence, skilfulness, expertness, ability, aptitude, talent, gift, genius, endowment, flaw, strong point, forte, what it takes, knack; experience, practice, training, qualifications, expertise, know-how, judgment; adeptness, deftness, adroitness, facility.

adj. skilful, capable, able, proficient, competent, effective, clever; experienced, trained, qualified, fit, suited, cut out for (*inf.*), accomplished, well-versed, expert, veteran; gifted, endowed; handy, adept, deft, adroit, agile, dexterous; all-round, versatile; enterprising, inventive.

vb. be good at, shine at, have what it takes; be expert, know backwards, know the ropes (*inf.*), know the ins and outs (*inf.*).

628 unskilfulness

n. unskilfulness, inability, ineptitude, inexperience, greenness, weak point, incompetence, inefficiency, mismanagement; awkwardness, clumsiness; botch-up, hash, mess, cock-up (*inf.*).

adj. unskilful, inexperienced, uneducated, unqualified, incompetent, amateur, unsuited, unused to, lay, amateurish, unprofessional, do-it-yourself, scratch; butterfingers; awkward, clumsy, heavy-handed, bungling, maladroit; impracticable, home-made, Heath Robinson; unwieldy, cumbersome, bulky.

vb. be no good at (*inf.*), spoil, bungle, ruin, botch, mismanage, mishandle, make a mess of, make a hash of, mess up (*inf.*), louse up (*sl.*), screw up (*sl.*), cock up (*sl.*), put one's foot in it; misfire, go off at half-cock (*inf.*).

629 expert

n. expert, master, adept, proficient, handyman, Jack-of-all-trades, man of many parts, man of many talents; professional, authority,

specialist, scholar, genius, whizz-kid (*inf.*), veteran, old hand; man of the world.

see also **436**

630 bungler

n. bungler, fumbler, botcher, muddler, dunce, idiot, blockhead, scatterbrain, ignoramus; butterfingers; beginner, novice, greenhorn; amateur, layman; lout, lubber.

see also **437**

631 cunning

n. cunning, craftiness, intrigue, deceit, guile, artfulness, craft, subtlety, slyness, wiliness, cleverness, shrewdness, chicanery, finesse.

stratagem, artifice, trick, deception, plot, scheme, ruse, wile, dodge, trap, little game (*inf.*), con (*sl.*), hoax, fabrication, double-dealing, casuistry.

artful dodger, hypocrite, fraud, cheat, plotter, con-man (*sl.*), trickster, slippery customer (*inf.*), smooth talker (*inf.*).

adj. cunning, shrewd, crafty, artful, sly, wily, deceptive, subtle, dishonest, fraudulent, unscrupulous, underhand, shifty, smart, shady, smooth, slippery, sharp, clever (*inf.*), too clever by half (*inf.*).

vb. be cunning, trick, deceive, fraud, cheat, trap, hoax, con (*sl.*), plot, scheme, contrive, pull a fast one (*sl.*), put one over on (*inf.*), put one across (*inf.*), outwit, get the better of.

632 artlessness

n. artlessness, simplicity, innocence, naivety, simple-mindedness, guilelessness, ingenuousness; child, babe.

adj. artless, innocent, simple, naive, simple-minded, guileless, unaffected, natural, uncomplicated, straightforward, ingenuous, childlike, unsophisticated, genuine, frank, open, candid, forthright.

vb. be natural, wear one's heart on one's sleeve; speak one's mind, not mince words.

D Antagonism

633 difficulty

n. difficulty, problem, headache (*inf.*), trouble, tall order, handful, heavy going; dilemma, predicament, quandary, strait, plight, embarrassment, fix, pickle (*inf.*), scrape, tight spot (*inf.*), hole (*sl.*); hardship, arduousness, laboriousness, troublesomeness; perplexity.

adj. difficult, hard, tough, laborious, arduous, uphill, strenuous; awkward, burdensome, trying, troublesome, bothersome, wearisome; unclear, obscure, knotty, thorny, baffling, perplexing, complicated, intricate.

vb. be in difficulties, flounder, have a hard time, strike a bad patch, make heavy weather of, make a meal of, not keep one's head above water; get into difficulty, get into hot water; put one's foot in it (*inf.*); beset, trouble, harm, disconcert, discourage, inconvenience, embarrass; baffle, perplex, put on the spot (*inf.*).

adv. in deep water, in difficulty, on the horns of a dilemma, in a quandary, in a spot, in hot water, in trouble.

see also **615, 635**

634 ease

n. ease, facility, straightforwardness; child's play, plain sailing, piece of cake (*inf.*), nothing to it (*inf.*), walk-over (*inf.*), push-over (*inf.*), cinch (*sl.*).

adj. easy, simple, cushy (*inf.*), manageable, facile; obvious, apparent; pleasant, comfortable; clear, uncomplicated; effortless.

vb. be easy, require no effort, present no difficulties, give no trouble, run smoothly, go like clockwork; take in one's stride.

ease, facilitate, smooth the way, free, relieve, rid, get rid of, lighten, release, disentangle; take a weight off someone's mind (*inf.*).

635 hindrance

n. hindrance, impedance, intervention, interruption; restriction, prohibition, restraint, check, blockage; retardation, curb, arrest, drag; inconvenience, hitch, setback, hold-up, bottleneck, catch, snag, spanner in the works (*inf.*), encumbrance, chain, menacle.

obstacle, obstruction, barrier, impediment, interference, stumbling-block, barricade, hurdle, bar, impasse, cul de sac.

adj. hindering, restraining, preventive.

vb. hinder, prevent, thwart, frustrate, hamper, trammel; stop, check, restrain, foil, confine, retard, arrest; deter, prohibit, restrict, bar, forbid, encumber, burden, chain, fetter, shackle; interfere, meddle; obstruct, block, impede, barricade; spoil, gum up the works (*sl.*).

see also **633, 665**

636 aid

n. aid, help, assistance; helping hand, leg up; encouragement, comfort, relief, succour, alleviation, mitigation; favour, benevolence, service; advice, backing, guidance.

financial aid, giving, support, maintenance, charity; compensation, allowance, grant, subsidy, benefit, stipend, honorarium, expenses; patronage, sponsorship, promotion, advancement.

adj. helpful, beneficial, assisting; auxiliary.

vb. help, aid, assist, cooperate; encourage, stand by, back up, sustain, bolster, relieve, comfort, succour, save, rescue, abet; lend a hand, play one's part; befriend, advise, serve, minister to, take under one's wing.

patronize, finance, support, keep, maintain, promote, subsidize, foster, shoulder, sponsor, sanction.

see also **217, 639**

637 opposition

n. opposition, antagonism, confrontation, repugnance, defiance, hostility, abhorrence, aversion, incompatibility, polarity; dislike, dissension, contradiction.

adj. opposing, antagonistic, defiant; hostile.

vb. oppose, counter, conflict with, fly in the face of, run counter to; confront, fight, combat, hinder, obstruct, thwart; object, dispute, contradict; resist, defy; deny, not have any part in, part company with, disapprove, disagree.

see also **648, 883**

638 opponent

n. opponent, antagonist, adversary, enemy, foe, the opposition, competitor, challenger, candidate, entrant, rival, contestant.

see also **883**

639 cooperation

n. cooperation, collaboration, participation, partnership, fellowship, brotherhood, harmony; give and take, teamwork, solidarity; amalgamation, merger, fusion, affiliation, membership; help, assistance.

adj. cooperative, collaborative, participatory; associated.

vb. cooperate, collaborate, give and take, help each other out, play ball with; contribute, help.

join, combine, unite, merge, club together, affiliate, join forces, pool together, pool resources, stand together, stick together (*inf.*), pull together; share, take part in, participate, throw in one's lot, go along with, team up with, take sides; gang up against (*inf.*); put one's heads together (*inf.*).

see also **180, 709**

640 auxiliary

n. auxiliary, helper, assistant, aid, ancillary, collaborator, helping hand, partner, associate, colleague, fellow-worker, co-worker, team-mate, sidekick (*inf.*); accomplice, confederate; friend, companion, ally, comrade; follower, adherent, disciple; hanger-on; patron, backer, supporter; right-hand man, stalwart, tower of strength.

see also 636

641 party

n. party, group, movement, organization, society, band, body; council, congress, alliance, association, confederation, federation, league, coalition, union; community, fellowship, brotherhood; company, firm, establishment, concern, cooperative, cartel, syndicate.

faction, sect, denomination, tradition, splinter-group, clique, coterie, inner circle.

adj. federal, allied, confederate, cooperative; exclusive, cliquish, partisan, sectarian.

vb. join, enrol, become a member of, affiliate, subscribe; associate with, side with.

642 discord

n. discord, dissension, trouble, difference, disagreement, misunderstanding, cross purposes, variance, ill feeling, tension, friction; divisiveness, troublesomeness, quarrelsomeness, rivalry.

dispute, quarrel, row, fight, argument, squabble, bickering, tiff, vendetta, feud; schism, split, rift, parting of the ways.

adj. discordant, disagreeing, divisive; contradictory; quarrelsome, troublesome, violent, factious, pugnacious, harsh, uncooperative, bolshie (*sl.*).

vb. differ, clash, conflict, dissent; fall out with, part company with; break up.

dispute, contend, fight, struggle, strive, come to blows, complain, object, argue, disagree; quarrel, wrangle, squabble, bicker; have a bone to pick with, have words with, take issue with; look for trouble (*inf.*), ask for it (*inf.*), rub up the wrong way (*inf.*), tread on someone's toes.

adv. at loggerheads, at odds, at variance, at sixes and sevens, not on speaking terms.

see also 25, 893

643 concord

n. concord, agreement, harmony, conformity, understanding, consonance, rapport, goodwill, friendship, amity, concert, accord, consensus, unanimity, unity, *détente, rapprochement,* entente, entente cordiale.

adj. agreeing, harmonious, friendly, peaceful, amicable, reconciled, unanimous, united.

vb. agree, get on with, get along with, hit it off (*inf.*), see eye to eye, be at one with; come to an understanding.

see also 24, 699

644 defiance

n. defiance, disobedience, rebellion, insubordination, insolence, obstinacy; mutiny, revolt, revolution; challenge, dare.

adj. defiant, bold, daring, proud; unruly, rebellious, disobedient, insubordinate; independent, lawless, anarchistic, militant.

vb. defy, confront, brave, challenge, dare, fling down the gauntlet, call one's bluff; resist, disobey, oppose, disregard, flout, spurn, laugh at, scorn, taunt; rebel, revolt, insult, protest, kick against, kick against the pricks.

see also 648

645 attack

n. attack, assault, onslaught, aggression, advance, charge, push, thrust, drive, outbreak, outburst, raid, offensive, storm, skirmish, foray, sally, sortie; invasion, intrusion, inroad, incursion, encroachment; siege, barrage, bombardment, blitz; mugging, rape.

attacker, aggressor, assailant, fighter, raider, stormer, invader, enemy, intruder, sniper, ravager; mugger, rapist.

adj. attacking, assaulting, aggressive.

vb. attack, assault, advance, charge, rush, push, thrust, assail, fight; raid, invade, storm, sally, sortie, foray; intrude, encroach; besiege, lay siege to, blockade; ravage, lay waste; fire, shoot, snipe; bomb, bombard; beat up, do over (*sl.*), smash somone's face in (*inf.*), mug, rob, rape.

646 defence

n. defence, protection, guarding, security; fortification, castle, fort, fortress, stronghold, keep, bastion, citadel, garrison; trenches, ditch, moat; embankment, rampart, battlement, earthworks; armour.

defender, guard, watch, sentry; protector, champion.

adj. defended, guarded, safe; defensive, armed, watchful.

vb. defend, protect, guard, keep, keep safe, safeguard, secure, shield, shelter, screen; withstand, beat off, ward off, fend off, drive back, take evasive action; spring to someone's defence; strengthen, reinforce, fortify; arm, cover, camouflage.

see also 593

647 retaliation

n. retaliation, reprisal, revenge, reaction, backlash, counterattack, counterinsurgence, second-strike capability; measure for measure, an eye for an eye, tit for tat, just deserts; requital, repayment, vengeance, punishment, retribution; recrimination; retort, riposte.

adj. retaliatory, retributive, reciprocal.

vb. retaliate, hit back, strike back, fight back, get back (*inf.*), defend oneself; requite, avenge, revenge, punish, return, repay, vindicate, pay back, settle up, get square, get one's own back, give tit for tat, get even with; reciprocate, return the compliment, give someone a dose of his own medicine; retort, counter, recriminate.

see also **912**

648 resistance

n. resistance, withstanding, defence, stand, check; steadfastness, renitence.

adj. resisting, recalcitrant, hard-hearted.

vb. resist, withstand, not give in, not submit, repel, stand up to, not take lying down, stand fast; stay, defend, hold off, oppose, prevent, thwart, foil, frustrate, obstruct, attack; counteract, neutralize; endure, suffer, tolerate; persevere, hold out, stick it out (*inf.*); maintain, take one's stand, stand one's ground, stick one's heels in (*inf.*), stick to one's guns, hold one's own.

see also **535, 644**

649 contest

n. contest, engagement, fight, battle, war, encounter, confrontation, action, skirmish, feud, *mêlée*, set-to, tussle, scrap (*sl.*), brush, affray, altercation; duel, joust, warfare, hostilities; conflict, strife, struggle, bloodshed, onslaught, carnage.

game, match, event, rally, race, challenge; competition, round, tournament; sport, recreation.

adj. contending, contestant; competitive.

vb. contend, fight, oppose, combat, confront, challenge, encounter, engage in battle, campaign, battle, brush with, dispute, strive, struggle, scrap (*sl.*), set to, take on, tussle, joust, assert oneself; compete, contest, race, vie with.

see also **651, 655**

650 peace

n. peace, absence of hostilities, armistice, truce, treaty; pacification, conciliation, reconciliation, love, friendship, agreement, harmony, accord; cold war, peaceful coexistence.

adj. peaceful, quiet, tranquil; bloodless, nonaggressive, pacifist; appeasing, conciliatory, peace-making.

see also **24, 652**

651 war

n. war, hostilities, combat, fighting, warfare, attack, battle, campaign, operation, mission, action, contention.

aggressiveness, warlikeness, belligerence, militancy, warmongering, pugnacity.

adj. warlike, aggressive, militant, pugnacious, belligerent, martial, threatening, contentious, warmongering, unfriendly, bellicose, up in arms, on the warpath; fighting, warring.

vb. wage war, engage in hostilities, attack, invade, contend, strive; declare war, go to war; mobilize, call up, recruit, enlist, conscript, muster.

see also **645, 649**

652 pacification

n. pacification, peace-making, appeasement, conciliation, reconciliation, reparation, satisfaction, assuagement, alleviation, mollification, soothing, calming; propitiation, atonement.

peace-offering, sacrifice, placation, gift; white flag, olive branch.

adj. pacificatory, placatory, propitiatory; irenic.

vb. pacify, conciliate; appease, satisfy, sacrifice, atone, propitiate; quiet, calm, still, moderate, quell, soften, alleviate, assuage, mollify, placate, tranquillize; reconcile, harmonize, bring together, bring to terms, settle one's differences, accommodate; make peace, bury the hatchet; make it up, shake hands.

see also **650**

653 mediation

n. mediation, arbitration, interposition, intervention, shuttle diplomacy.

mediator, arbitrator, go-between, intermediary, arbiter, negotiator, peace-maker, trouble-shooter, intercessor, third party; judge, referee, umpire; adjudicator, assessor; neutral, independent.

adj. mediatory, intercessory.

vb. mediate, arbitrate, negotiate, reconcile, hear both sides, intercede, interpose, intervene; judge, umpire, rule; interfere, meddle.

see also **230**

654 submission

n. submission, yielding, obedience; acquiescence, resignation, deference; submissiveness, docility, meekness, humility, passivity.

adj. submissive, obedient; compliant, amenable, tractable, mouldable; resigned, subdued; acquiescent, reconciled, patient; docile, humble, lowly, tame.

vb. submit, give in, yield, surrender, capitulate, resign, relinquish, give up, throw in the towel, admit defeat.

obey, defer, bow to, comply, acquiesce; take the line of least resistance.

see also **673, 679**

655 combatant

n. combatant, fighter, contender, opponent, serviceman, soldier, conscript, recruit, pressed man; casual, irregular; mercenary, hireling; warrior, veteran.

armed forces, services, troops, forces, military force, army, infantry, cavalry, artillery; navy, air force; unit, group, division, section, squad, troop, patrol; party; task force; formation, column, line, array.

656 non-combatant

n. non-combatant, pacifist, conscientious objector, neutral, dove, flower people, conchie (*sl.*); peace-maker.

657 arms

n. arms, weapons, armament, munitions; armour, mail, panoply; small arms, firearm, gun; revolver, rifle, shotgun, machine gun, automatic; cannon, mortar; bazooka; hand-grenade bomb, explsoive, dynamite, gunpowder; atomic bomb, hydrogen bomb, H-bomb, neutron bomb; armoury, arsenal; ballistics.

658 arena

n. arena, battlefield, battleground, scene of action, field of action, theatre of war, trenches, front; field, ground, centre, scene, sphere, track, court, course; stadium, gymnasium, playground, campus, coliseum, amphitheatre, circus, forum, pit.

E Results of action

659 completion

n. completion, finish, end, conclusion, achievement, performance, accomplishment, fulfilment, perfection, realization, execution.

finishing touch, crown, *coup de grâce;* last straw, limit (*sl.*).

adj. complete, finished, accomplished, fulfilled, perfect, entire, whole; conclusive, final, last.

vb. complete, finish, end, conclude, terminate; achieve, perform, carry out, implement, bring off (*inf.*), pull off (*inf.*), succeed; knock off (*inf.*), polish off (*inf.*), wrap up (*inf.*); get over with (*inf.*), get over

and done with (*inf.*); accomplish, work out, hammer out, see through, go through with, realize, effect, fulfil, discharge, settle; be resolved, things work out, perfect, consummate, ripen, mature; culminate, come to a head.

see also **56, 609**

660 non-completion

n. non-completion, failure, non-performance, neglect, defeat; fault, blemish, deficiency, defect.

adj. uncompleted, failed, neglected, incomplete, half-done, partial, imperfect, deficient.

vb. not complete, leave undone, neglect, miss, fail, drop out, leave, not stay the course.

see also **57, 582**

661 success

n. success, completion, achievement, attainment, accomplishment; successfulness, happy ending, favourable outcome, prosperous issue; triumph, victory, conquest, push-over (*inf.*), walk-over (*inf.*); breakthrough, advance, progress; prosperity, luck, happiness, bed of roses; success story, hit, smash hit (*sl.*).

winner, victor, champion, hero, titleholder, conqueror.

adj. successful, winning, victorious, triumphant, champion, in the lead, unbeaten, invincible; beneficial, advantageous; fruitful, prosperous, fortunate, thriving, flourishing.

vb. succeed, make a success of, achieve, attain, accomplish, reach, complete, fulfil, obtain, get, capture, gain, pull off (*inf.*), bring off (*inf.*); be successful, come off (*inf.*), do the trick (*inf.*); advance, get on, make it (*inf.*), make a go of (*inf.*), make a breakthrough, proceed, progress, benefit, reap, profit, prosper, flourish, thrive, prevail, score a hit, hit the jackpot.

win, beat, conquer, defeat, get the better of, gain the upper hand, clobber (*sl.*), overcome, ride out the storm, crush, overwhelm, win hands down, walk away with (*inf.*), come out on top (*inf.*), come off with flying colours; survive, get by, hang on.

662 failure

n. failure, misadventure, breakdown, collapse, fiasco, disaster, débâcle, disappointment, flop (*inf.*), wash-out (*inf.*); defeat, overthrow, downfall, ruin, landslide; unsuccessfulness, ineffectiveness, defectiveness; neglect, omission, shortcoming; no-go (*inf.*), wild goose chase, utter defeat, clobbering (*sl.*), rout.

loser, underdog, has-been (*inf.*), also-ran (*inf.*), non-starter, dud.

adj. unsuccessful, futile, vain, useless, fruitless, profitless; unfortunate, disastrous; inadequate, ineffective, abortive; overthrown, defeated, fallen, outmatched, thwarted, frustrated, foiled, pipped at the post, outvoted.

vb. fail, go amiss, fall down, let one down; abandon, neglect, miss; thwart, frustrate; fall short, break down, fall through (*inf.*), miscarry, come to nothing, flounder, falter, go on the rocks, flop (*inf.*), fizzle out (*inf.*); lose, be defeated, suffer defeat, go down, go under; bark up the wrong tree (*inf.*), not get to first base (*inf.*); get no change out of (*inf.*).

663 trophy

n. trophy, prize, reward, award, honour, medal, badge, cup, memorial, decoration, ribbon, order, crown, palm, laurel, accolade, mention, citation; consolation prize, booby prize, wooden spoon.

booty, loot, spoil, plunder, premium, capture.

see also **724**

664 prosperity

n. prosperity, good fortune, happiness, welfare, well-being, successfulness, luckiness, affluence, wealth, riches, luxury, benefits, blessings; golden age, good old days, heyday, boom, bed of roses, halcyon days, summer.

adj. prosperous, flourishing, thriving, successful, well-to-do, well-off, comfortable, rich, auspicious; up-and-coming, born with a silver spoon in one's mouth; golden, glorious, cloudless, sunny, halcyon.

vb. prosper, thrive, flourish, increase, blossom, be successful, fare well, turn out well; get on in the world, make one's mark, be rich, make a fortune; Fortune smile upon.

see also **661**

665 adversity

n. adversity, misfortune, trouble, hardship, unluckiness, bad luck, hard times, bad patch, ill wind, deep water, difficulty, misadventure, unhappiness; disaster, distress, catastrophe, crisis, calamity, burden, pressure, affliction, blight, curse, plague, scourge.

adj. adverse, unfavourable, hostile, unfriendly, sinister; disastrous, catastrophic; afflicted, troubled, wretched, stricken; unfortunate, unlucky, unhappy, ill-starred, ill-fated, down on one's luck, in a bad way, in the wars.

vb. be in trouble, hit a bad patch, be in for it (*inf.*), have a hard time of it, feel the pinch, fall on hard times, decline, sink, stew in one's own juice, go under, get out of one's depth, fall flat on one's face (*inf.*), fall by the wayside.

see also **633**

666 mediocrity

n. mediocrity, commonness, ordinariness, averageness, passableness, tolerableness.

adj. mediocre, average, ordinary, indifferent, middling, fair, poor, feeble, common, commonplace, dull, monotonous, stale, insipid, wishy-washy, tolerable, fair-to-middling, passable, humdrum, run of the mill, so-so, nothing to write home about, much of a muchness.

vb. make do, just exist, struggle along, muddle through, scrape through, manage somehow, get by, just keep one's head above water, stagnate, vegetate.

2 Intersocial volition

A General

667 authority

n. authority, power, control, right, prerogative, command, rule, sway; dominion, sovereignty, ascendancy, upper hand, supreme authority, last word; influence, prestige, power behind the throne, arm of the law.

government, democracy, *vox populi*, officialdom, bureaucracy, administration, establishment, them, powers that be; open government, devolution.

adj. authoritative, commanding, dominant, lawful, powerful, sovereign; in office, in power; official, executive, administrative, bureaucratic, governmental, democratic, gubernatorial, political.

vb. rule, govern, control, direct, dominate, lord it over, domineer, command, sway, reign; assume control, take over, take the reins, have power, rule the roost; authorize, empower, back, devolve, decentralize.

see also **671**

668 laxity

n. laxity, slackness, looseness, flexibility; anarchy, lawlessness, mob rule, disorder, chaos, turmoil.

adj. lax, slack, loose, remiss, soft, flabby, relaxed, flexible; anarchic, uncontrolled, lawless, chaotic, rebellious.

vb. be lax, tolerate, not enforce, stretch a point; misrule, misgovern; give a free hand to, give free rein to; take the law into one's

own hands, do what is right in one's own
eyes.

see also **670**

669 severity

n. severity, strictness, austerity, firmness,
rigidity, inflexibility, rigour; hardness,
cruelty; firm hand, strong hand, heavy hand,
rod of iron, tight rein, pound of flesh, letter
of the law.

tyranny, oppression, despotism, fascism;
tyrant, dictator, despot, autocrat, taskmaster,
authoritarian, disciplinarian.

adj. severe, stern, strict, harsh, hard,
austere, extreme, puritanical; firm, rigid,
unbending, inflexible, immovable, unchanging; rigorous, exacting, uncompromising,
stringent; grim, cruel, forbidding; unfeeling,
hard-hearted; tyrannical, overbearing, dom-
ineering, despotic, totalitarian, authoritarian,
oppressive, heavy-handed.

vb. be severe, be hard on, discipline, come
down on (*inf.*), deal harshly with, insist,
crack down on (*inf.*), clamp down on (*inf.*),
put one's foot down (*inf.*), keep a tight rein
on, rule with an iron hand, domineer, lord it
over, dominate, oppress, tyrannize.

see also **963**

670 lenience

n. lenience, softness, tolerance, mildness,
forbearance; mercy, clemency, forgiveness,
pardon; kindness, compassion, favour.

adj. lenient, soft, gentle, mild, kind,
compassionate, loving, soft-hearted, tender,
sympathetic, easy-going; tolerant, forbearing,
long-suffering; merciful, forgiving, clement.

vb. be lenient, go easy on, spare the rod;
pass over, forbear, refrain; forgive, pardon;
tolerate, bear.

671 command

n. command, direction, rule, charge,
ordinance, mandate, directive, dictate,
injunction, behest; bidding, call, summons;
decree, ruling, law, act, fiat, canon, edict,
bull, proclamation; writ, warrant, subpoena;
demand, claim, request, requirement; final
demand, ultimatum.

adj. commanding, powerful, authoritative.

vb. command, rule, direct, dictate, order,
charge, decree, proclaim, ordain; lay down,
prescribe; demand, claim, request, ask,
require, exact; bid, call, summon, invite,
send for.

see also **667, 954**

672 disobedience

n. disobedience, violation, disregard,
neglect, non-observance, infringement, transgression, sin; misbehaviour, naughtiness;
waywardness, stubbornness, insubordination,
defiance, intractableness, unruliness; mutiny,
revolt, rebellion, revolution, desertion, riot,
insurgence.

rebel, revolutionary, radical, anarchist,
reactionary, extremist, insurrectionist, insurgent, rioter, terrorist, mutineer, deserter;
trouble-maker, brawler.

adj. disobedient, insubordinate; naughty,
misbehaving; defiant, refractory, unsubmis-
sive, disloyal, rebellious, intractable, unruly,
lawless, uncontrollable, obstreperous; stubborn, wayward, insolent; revolutionary,
mutinous, riotous, anarchistic, dissident,
factious, insurgent.

vb. disobey, defy, fly in the face of, disregard, neglect, ignore, pay no attention to, not
heed, violate, infringe, transgress, sin, break
rules; misbehave; revolt, rebel, mutiny.

673 obedience

n. obedience, submission, compliance,
loyalty, devotion, faithfulness, fidelity,
constancy; meekness, docility.

adj. obedient, submissive, complaisant;
law-abiding, well-behaved, good; devoted,
loyal, faithful, respectful, dutiful, subservient, docile, acquiescent; round one's little
finger (*inf.*), at one's beck and call, on a
string, henpecked.

vb. obey, submit, do, keep, observe, follow,
pay attention to, bow to, heed, comply, fulfil,
agree, behave, do what one is told, do one's
duty, do what is expected of one.

see also **654, 679**

674 compulsion

n. compulsion, force, drive, necessity,
need, obligation, pressure, constraint, coer-
cion, violence, strong arm, duress; urgency;
conscription.

adj. compelling, compulsive, necessary,
driving, pressing, coercive, unavoidable,
irresistible, compulsory, urgent.

vb. compel, force, drive, coerce, constrain,
impel, dictate, necessitate, oblige, require,
urge, bring pressure to bear on, inflict.

675 master

n. master, mistress, chief, leader, head,
superior, principal, lord; director, manager,
supervisor, boss, management, overseer,
authority, officer, official, mayor, mayoress;
governor, governess, ruler, president, executive, sovereign, king, queen, prince, princess, emperor, empress, regent; captain,

commander, lieutenant; big Chief (*sl.*), bigwig.

see also **34, 623**

676 servant

n. servant, dependant, assistant, righthand man, subordinate, employee, worker, staff, personnel; slave, serf, vassal, captive, bondman, fag; orderly, menial; drudge, hack; chauffeur, butler, domestic, housekeeper, maid, nurse; porter, janitor, doorman; steward, stewardess, waiter, waitress, barman, barmaid; charwoman, cleaner.

adj. serving, ministering, attending, helping.

vb. serve, work for, be in the employment of, minister, aid, help, wait upon, care for, look after, nurse, mother; attend, do for (*inf.*).

677 sign of authority

n. badge of office, insignia, symbol, emblem, livery, uniform, regalia, rod, sceptre, mace, crown, staff, wand, rod, sword, stripe, decoration, flag.

678 freedom

n. freedom, liberty, independence, autonomy, democracy, self-determination; freedom of choice, free will; immunity, exemption, privilege, *carte blanche*, blank cheque, unrestraint; range, scope, play, field, room, leeway, latitude, opportunity, full play, free rein, elbow room.

adj. free, released, liberated, freed, at liberty, at large, let out, scot free; clear, extricated, unshackled, unfettered, unattached, unengaged, unconfined, unimpeded, unhindered, unrestrained; independent, autonomous, self-governing, democratic, enfranchised.

vb. free, have a free hand, have the run of; be independent, please oneself, do as one wishes, fend for oneself, stand on one's own two feet, go it alone.

see also **680**

679 subjection

n. subjection, subservience, servitude, dependence, subordination, inferiority; allegiance, service; bondage, slavery, serfdom, servility, thrall.

adj. subject, dependent, subordinate, submissive, inferior, junior, accessory, subsidiary, satellite, auxiliary; accountable, answerable, liable, contingent.

vb. subject, enslave, dominate, subordinate, master, rule, hold captive, conquer, tame, subdue, subjugate, hold under one's thumb; repress, suppress, sit on.

be subject to, depend on, lean on; be at the mercy of, serve.

see also **35**

680 liberation

n. liberation, release, discharge, deliverance, rescue; extrication, disengagement, unravelling, loosing, unfettering, loosening, untying; emancipation, enfranchisement, manumission.

adj. freed, liberated, released, loose.

vb. liberate, free, release, discharge, deliver, save, rescue, set at liberty, restore, let out; extricate, loose, remove fetters, unfetter, untie, remove, unbind, undo, cut loose, disengage, unravel, let slip; ransom, pardon, dismiss, acquit; emancipate, enfranchise; shake off, free oneself of, get rid of, lose.

see also **601, 961**

681 restraint

n. restraint, control, constraint, discipline, self-control, self-discipline, self-restraint, reticence, reserve, caution; repression.

restriction, limitation, barrier, check, hindrance, impediment, obstacle, block, bar, curb, blockade, embargo, ban, veto; curfew; closed shop; censorship, news blackout; monopoly, cartel, protectionism.

custody, detention, imprisonment, confinement, impounding; chain, bond, irons, fetter, shackle.

adj. restraining, restrictive, controlling, limiting, strict, narrow, repressive; restrained, under control, in check, controlled, disciplined, reserved, cautious, calm, reticent, withdrawn, repressed, pent-up, bottled-up.

in custody, under arrest, imprisoned, detained, confined, in prison, in detention, behind bars, inside (*sl.*), in jug (*sl.*), in clink (*sl.*).

vb. restrain, control, limit, govern, check, arrest, curb, keep in check, hold back, narrow; discipline, bridle; repress, suppress, keep back, bottle up, muzzle, gag, subdue, quell, quash; hinder, impede, restrict, hamper; control oneself, pull oneself together, take a grip on oneself (*inf.*), sort oneself out (*inf.*), get organized.

take into custody, apprehend, help police with their inquiries, run in, turn in (*inf.*), turn over to, pick up, arrest, convict, take prisoner; imprison, detain, confine, put into prison, put away (*inf.*), shut up, lock up, put behind bars, intern, impound; tie, bind, chain, fetter, manacle.

682 prison

n. prison, gaol, jail, lock-up, nick (*sl.*), clink (*sl.*), jug (*sl.*), maximum-security prison, police station; cell, cage, guardroom; dungeon; detention camp, internment camp, concentration camp; Borstal, detention centre, approved home, remand centre.

683 keeper

n. keeper, custodian, warden, curator, attendant, official, guard; caretaker, porter, janitor, concierge, housekeeper, gatekeeper; watchman, lookout, patrol, scout; baby-sitter, governess, nurse, nanny, guardian; escort, bodyguard; gamekeeper, ranger; jailer, warder, prison governor, screw (*sl.*).
see also 593

684 prisoner

n. prisoner, convict, culprit, con (*sl.*), inmate, star, gaolbird, young offender, captive, prisoner of war, internee; defendant, the accused, detainee; criminal, rogue.
see also 906, 940

685 vicarious authority

n. commission, delegation, deputation, representation, authorization, committal, trusteeship; appointment, nomination, assignment; mission, embassy, envoy, legation, agency; devolution, decentralization; inauguration, installation, investiture, induction, ordination, coronation; accession.
trust, charge, mandate, authority, warrant; task, duty, errand, employment.

adj. commissioned, delegated, vicarious, deputed.

vb. commission, delegate, appoint, empower, grant authority to, authorize, charge, commit, assign, entrust; devolve, decentralize; name, nominate; inaugurate, invest, induct, ordain, install, place, establish; crown, enthrone; employ, engage, hire, contract.
represent, deputize, act on behalf of, stand in for.

686 annulment

n. annulment, cancellation, abrogation, dissolution, revocation, retraction, invalidation, nullification, reversal, repeal, abolition, countermand.
dismissal, removal, displacement, the sack (*inf.*), the boot (*sl.*), the push (*sl.*); retirement, lay-off, redundancy, natural wastage; deposal, dethronement, impeachment; demotion, downgrading, degradation.

adj. annulled, cancelled, null and void; rained off, abandoned, postponed.

vb. annul, cancel, abolish, repeal, revoke, dissolve, rescind, quash, render void, nullify, invalidate; refute, counteract, reverse, repudiate, countermand.
dismiss, oust, overthrow, unseat, remove from office, discharge, depose, dethrone, displace, suspend, sack (*inf.*), fire, give the push to (*sl.*), give the boot to (*sl.*), give papers to, show the door to, strike off the register, write out, pension off; relieve, replace, recall; impeach, unfrock; demote, degrade, downgrade.

687 resignation

n. resignation, abdication, retirement, relinquishment, renunciation, withdrawal, departure, leaving, surrender, desertion; pension, golden handshake, leaving gift, leaving present, gratuity, superannuation.

adj. resignatory; retired, former, previous, outgoing, one-time, sometime, emeritus.

vb. resign, quit, leave, depart, vacate office, relinquish, abandon, step down, stand down, stand aside, retire, abdicate, give up office, walk out of, hand in one's notice, tender one's resignation, hand in one's papers.

688 consignee

n. consignee, delegate, representative, substitute, deputy; trustee, executor, nominee, proxy; intermediary, middleman, negotiator, broker; committee, board, panel, group, organization, deputation, cabinet, decision maker.
ambassador, envoy, commissioner, delegation, emissary, diplomat, consul, attaché, plenipotentiary, nuncio; embassy, consulate, mission.
see also 619, 689

689 deputy

n. deputy, assistant, second-in-command, right-hand man; delegate, substitute, representative, proxy, surrogate, stand-in, agent, proxy, vicar; ambassador, commissioner; spokesman, mouthpiece.

adj. deputy, deputizing, vice, pro, acting.

vb. deputize, substitute, represent, stand in for, act on behalf of.

B Special

690 permission

n. permission, liberty, leave, freedom, consent; authorization, legalization, confirmation, endorsement, affirmation, sanction;

authority, permit, grant, charter, licence, certificate, concession, allowance; pass, passport, visa, password; letter of commendation; go-ahead, green light (*inf.*), all-clear, clearance, nod; free hand, free rein, *carte blanche*, blank cheque.

adj. permitting, allowing; tolerant, lenient, permissive; permitted, granted, allowed, authorized, approved.

vb. permit, let, allow, grant, give permission; consent, approve, favour, have no objections; authorize, warrant, legalize, sanction, certify, charter, franchise, license; give the go-ahead, give the green light (*inf.*), give clearance, rubber-stamp (*inf.*); tolerate, concede, bear, suffer.

691 prohibition

n. prohibition, forbiddance, obstruction, suppression, repression, refusal, interdiction, injunction, disallowance, countermand, ban, veto, embargo, boycott, taboo.

adj. prohibiting, forbidding; prohibitive, excessive, restrictive; prohibited, forbidden, illegal, illicit, unlawful, taboo, impermissible.

vb. prohibit, forbid, refuse, withhold, deny, disallow, prevent, hinder, hamper, preclude, restrain, interdict; ban, veto, boycott, say no to, debar, exclude, shut out; obstruct, oppose, suppress, repress, restrict, stop, halt.

692 consent

n. consent, acceptance, agreement, allowance, permission, approval, assent, concurrency, acquiescence, compliance.

adj. consenting, agreeable, willing, acquiescent.

vb. consent, accept, allow, agree, approve, assent, say yes to, be in favour of, concur, acquiesce, accede; concede, grant, yield, acknowledge, vouchsafe.

see also **690**

693 offer

n. offer, tender, bid, submission; approach, advance, overture; proposal, proposition, presentation, suggestion.

adj. on offer, available, for sale, advertised.

vb. offer, hold out, present, suggest, propose, submit, extend, move, put forward, put forth, tender, bid, approach; make overtures, make advances; lay at one's feet, sacrifice, proffer.

volunteer, offer oneself, come forward, stand for.

694 refusal

n. refusal, rejection, denial, declension; rebuff, snub, slap in the face, insult; veto, ban, exclusion.

adj. refusing, unwilling, uncompliant, resisting, hard-hearted, reluctant.

vb. refuse, reject, not want, decline, resist, ignore, turn down, say no to, not hear of, exclude, disallow, shun, repudiate, repel, spurn, rebuff, scorn, snub, repulse, turn one's back on, turn a deaf ear to, set one's face against, wash one's hands of, harden one's heart against; slam the door in someone's face (*inf.*); withhold, deny, hold back.

see also **469, 542**

695 request

n. request, call, petition, invitation, bid, application, demand, appeal, plea, address; inquiry, question; offer, proposal, proposition; prayer, entreaty, intercession, invocation, supplication; importunity, urgency.

adj. requesting, petitioning, supplicatory, imprecatory, invocatory, prayerful, begging, on bended knees; urgent, importunate, persistent, clamorous.

vb. request, call, ask, express a wish, apply for, summon, demand, implore, beseech, beg, appeal, entreat, pray, call on, petition, crave, plead, adjure; inquire, invite.

urge, ply, press, persist, pester, bother, coax, clamour.

canvass, solicit, importune, tout, hawk; appeal for money, pass the hat round (*inf.*), have a whip-round (*inf.*), make a collection.

696 protest

n. protest, deprecation, disapproval, objection, complaint, dissent, expostulation, remonstrance.

demonstration, demo (*inf.*), rally, sit-in, mass meeting, march, protest march, strike, hunger strike.

adj. protesting, deprecatory, expostulatory, remonstrative.

vb. protest, depreciate, speak against, lodge a protest, ask not to, disapprove, object, disagree, oppose, criticize, demur, remonstrate, expostulate; groan, jeer, murmur, heckle, sneer; demonstrate, march, strike, go on strike, picket.

see also **144**

697 petitioner

n. petitioner, supplicant, suppliant, applicant, claimant, candidate, bidder; inquirer, advertiser; lobby, lobbyist, pressure group, canvasser, hawker, tout, pedlar, vendor;

beggar, scrounger, cadger, sponger, loafer, idler, vagabond, tramp, down-and-out.

C Conditional

698 promise

n. promise, covenant, pledge, contract, pact, undertaking, commitment, consent, word, vow, word of honour; gentleman's agreement.

engagement, betrothal; fiancée, fiancé, intended (*inf.*).

adj. promised, committed, pledged, bound; engaged, betrothed.

vb. promise, agree, undertake, commit, declare, covenant, pledge, contract, consent, vow, swear; warrant, guarantee; bind onself, give one's word, pledge one's honour; become engaged, betrothe.

699 contract

n. contract, agreement, covenant, undertaking, pact, concordat, promise, pledge, understanding, arrangement, settlement, transaction, bargain, deal (*inf.*); negotiation, compromise, give and take; treaty, convention, alliance, league, charter, entente; gentleman's agreement.

adj. contractual, conventional, promissory.

vb. contract, agree, covenant, undertake, pledge, promise, arrange, bargain, deal, negotiate, hammer out, stipulate; sign, sign on the dotted line, agree on terms, settle, come to an agreement, accept an offer, shake on it (*inf.*); ratify, confirm.

see also 24, 643

700 conditions

n. conditions, terms, provisions, specifications, frame of reference, strings, proviso, contingencies, arrangements, limitations, restrictions, reservations, exceptions, escape clause, *sine qua non*.

adj. conditional, provisional, contingent, with strings attached, granted on certain terms, dependent on, subject to.

vb. negotiate, discuss; propose conditions, postulate, stipulate, attach strings, insist on, impose.

see also 403

701 security

n. security, surety, warranty, covenant, bond, promise, pledge, earnest, token, certainty; deposit, caution money, money in advance, forfeit, stake, insurance, bail, pawn,

mortgage, collateral; liability, responsibility; hostage, captive, prisoner.

adj. guaranteed, pledged, pawned, on deposit.

vb. give security, guarantee, pledge, sign for, insure, assure, underwrite, mortgage, stake, pawn; give bail, go bail; stand surety, bail out; stand for, back.

702 observance

n. observance, attention, performance, doing, carrying out, keeping, heeding, practice; obedience, compliance, devotion.

adj. observant, practising, professing; diligent, conscientious; exact, scrupulous, pedantic; dependable, responsible; loyal, faithful, devoted, obedient.

vb. observe, heed, keep, do, carry out, follow, adhere to, perform, discharge, practise, adopt, conform to, fulfil, comply; keep on the right side of the law; hold fast, stand by, embrace, profess, give allegiance to, be loyal to.

703 non-observance

n. non-observance, neglect, disregard, omission; breaking, infringement, violation, transgression, trespass, breach, sin; disobedience, disloyalty, infidelity; inattention, carelessness, indifference, irresponsibility.

adj. non-observant, negligent, careless, indifferent; unfaithful, disobedient.

vb. not observe, not practise, not keep; break, disobey, violate, infringe, transgress, breach, contravene; neglect, disregard, omit; break faith, be faithless.

704 compromise

n. compromise, bargaining, agreement, understanding, settlement; give and take, concessions, mutual concessions; middle course, middle ground, half-way house; composition; *modus vivendi*.

vb. compromise, make concessions, give and take, meet half-way, go fifty-fifty, steer a middle course, split the differences; negotiate, come to an agreement, come to an understanding, reconcile, settle, adjust, agree to differ.

D Possessive relations

705 acquisition

n. acquisition, getting, obtainment, procuration; recovery, retrieval, redemption.

gain, benefit, advantage, reward, income, earnings, wages, salary, grant, profit, receipts, proceeds, emolument; collection, gathering, produce, output, yield, fruit, harvest, crop; addition, accrual, accumulation.

adj. obtainable, available; acquisitive, hoarding, grasping.

profitable, fruitful, productive, advantageous, worthwhile, lucrative, paying its way, remunerative.

vb. acquire, get, obtain, take possession of, make one's own, appropriate, lay hold of, procure; force from, grab, seize, capture, pocket, secure, draw, tap; gain, accept, receive, make, collect, earn, benefit, win, accumulate; gather, harvest, glean, reap.

get back, recover, retrieve, regain, redeem.

buy, purchase; profit, capitalize on, cash in on (*inf.*); inherit, come into, be left.

see also 716

706 loss

n. loss, mislaying, misplacement; dispossession, deprivation, forfeiture, want, bereavement; insolvency, bankruptcy.

adj. lost, missing, misplaced, mislaid, nowhere to be found, hidden, obscured, vanished, strayed, gone; lacking, wanting, deprived of, bereft; overdrawn, insolvent, bankrupt; unprofitable, disadvantageous, wasted, irretrievable, desperate, hopeless, futile.

vb. lose, mislay, misplace, not find; let slip, drop, miss, fail, forfeit; deprive, displace; waste, squander; incur losses, go bankrupt.

707 possession

n. possession, ownership, occupancy, residence, tenancy, tenure; possessorship, proprietorship; hold, mastery, grasp, control, custody; purchase.

adj. possessing, having, owning; possessive, exclusive, monopolistic, selfish; possessed, owned, purchased, enjoyed, in possession of.

vb. possess, own, have, hold, keep, retain, grasp, occupy, control, maintain, use, boast of, enjoy; have title to, have rights to, have claim upon; monopolize, hog (*inf.*), have all to oneself, corner; include, comprise, contain; belong, appertain.

708 non-possession

n. non-possession, loss, deprivation, surrender of rights; lease; no man's land.

adj. not owning, lacking; destitute, poor, impoverished, penniless; unowned, unoccupied, unpossessed, unattached, free, ownerless, virgin, unclaimed, lost, independent, unbound.

see also 706

709 joint possession

n. joint possession, co-ownership, cooperation, participation, partnership, sharing; socialism, communism, public ownership, nationalization, worker participation, profit-sharing; community, cooperative, collective, kibbutz; joint fund, kitty, pool; share, portion.

participator, partner, member, partaker, shareholder, worker-director.

adj. cooperative, joint, participatory, common, communal, profit-sharing; involved, committed, dedicated, connected with.

vb. participate, share, cooperate, join, take part in, partake, go halves.

see also 639

710 possessor

n. possessor, owner, holder, master, partner; buyer, purchaser; occupant, occupier, tenant, resident, lodger, lessee, landlord, landlady, landowner, landholder, proprietor, proprietress; heir, heiress, inheritor.

711 property

n. property, land, assets, resources, means, goods, riches, wealth, valuables, inheritance, capital, investment, equity, land, holding, estate.

belongings, equipment, paraphernalia, things, trappings, fixtures, furniture, furnishings, goods and chattels; appurtenances, accoutrements; personal effects, luggage, baggage; burden, encumbrance, impedimenta.

712 retention

n. retention, holding, keeping; hold, grasp, clench, clinch, grip, hug, embrace, clasp; confinement, stranglehold, tight grip, straitjacket.

adj. retentive, holding; retained, held, kept.

vb. retain, hold, keep, keep hold of, grasp, clench, grip, clinch, clasp, clutch, embrace, hug, squeeze, press; cling to, stick to, fasten on, secure, hold fast; contain, restrain, enclose, confine; maintain, preserve; cherish, nurture, harbour; detain, reserve, withhold.

713 non-retention

n. relinquishment, abandonment, renunciation, disposal; exemption, dispensation, release; divorce, dissolution.

adj. abandoned, thrown away, rejected, marooned.

vb. not retain, relinquish, abandon, renounce, let go, part with, dispose of, discard, throw away, jettison, release; waive, lift restrictions, derestrict, exempt.

see also **556, 921**

714 transfer

n. transference, conveyancing, assignation; changeover, change of hands; devolution, delegation; exchange, conversion, interchange; sale, lease; bequest, endowment, legacy.

adj. transferable, negotiable, interchangeable, exchangeable; transferred, made over.

vb. convey, transfer, sell, sign, consign, assign, change over, deliver, make over; entrust, commit; exchange, convert; devolve, delegate, decentralize; bequeath, will, make a will, pass on, hand down.

see also **268**

715 giving

n. giving, bestowal, conferral, granting, imparting, delivery.

gift, present, donation, grant, award, presentation, prize; allowance, subsidy, aid, assistance; tip, gratuity; bounty, largesse, windfall; leaving present, golden handshake; charity, hand-out, alms; bequest, legacy; blessing, favour, grace, mercy.

sacrifice, worship, dedication, consecration; offering, collection, offertory.

giver, donor, contributor.

adj. giving, charitable, generous, liberal, sacrificial; given, free.

vb. give, donate, grant, award, present, contribute, render, remit, convey, supply, furnish, provide, afford, dispense, hand out, dole out, distribute, administer, deal out, mete out, subsidize, give towards; bestow, confer, endow, invest with, impart, communicate; expend, spend, lavish; offer, sacrifice.

716 receiving

n. receiving, reception, acquisition, acceptance, admission, collection; receipts, proceeds, dues, monies, toll.

recipient, receiver, beneficiary; object, target, victim, guinea pig; customer, client; trustee, payee, addressee, earner; heir, heiress.

adj. receiving, receptive, welcoming, hospitable, sensitive.

vb. receive, accept, admit, be given, get, gain, acquire, collect, obtain, draw, take in, derive, come by, attract, come in for, be on the receiving end; take up, levy, charge; be received, accrue, come in, fall to one.

see also **302, 705**

717 apportionment

n. apportionment, allotment, sharing, division, distribution, dealing, rationing.

portion, share, allocation, section, piece, part, fraction, fragment; helping, serving, slice, ration; proportion, quota, allowance; cut (*sl.*), split, parcel, lot.

vb. apportion, allot, distribute, divide, share out, hand out, dole out, dish out (*inf.*), farm out, parcel out, deal, assign, dispose, administer, give away, dispense, ration.

see also **55**

718 lending

n. lending; loan, advance, mortgage, allowance, credit, investment, credit card, credit account, hire purchase, never-never (*inf.*).

bank, building society, pawnbroker, popshop (*sl.*); banker, bank manager, lender, financier, money-lender, creditor; usurer, shark, angel (*sl.*), Shylock.

vb. lend, let out, allow to borrow, trust with, entrust, hire out, let, lease, charter; loan, finance, support, back, advance, grant, lend on security, put out at interest, give credit, risk.

719 borrowing

n. borrowing, rental, hire, loan; assumption; appropriation, adoption, importation; imitation, copy.

vb. borrow, rent, hire, lease, charter; take on tick (*inf.*), raise money, pawn, cadge; touch for (*sl.*); obtain, use, adopt.

720 taking

n. taking, possession, acceptance, appropriation, requisition; seizure, grab, capture; kidnapping, abduction; dispossession, deprivation, extortion, confiscation; recovery, retrieval.

taker, possessor; seizer, grabber, raider; kidnapper, abductor.

adj. taking, grasping, greedy, rapacious, extortionate, ravenous.

vb. take, possess, accept, receive, get, obtain, win, gain; seize, lay hold of, appropriate, take for oneself, acquire, avail oneself of, adopt, assume; grip, clasp; catch, apprehend, grasp; grab, trap, snatch, capture, raid; take away, steal, kidnap, abduct; confiscate, commandeer; recover, retrieve; take from, remove, deprive of, divest of, dispossess, extort, strip, disinherit.

see also **722**

721 restitution

n. restitution, restoration, return, giving back, reinstatement; retrieval, recovery, repossession, repatriation; recompense, repayment, refund, amends, compensation, reimbursement, remuneration, reparation, indemnification, redemption, satisfaction.

adj. restitutive, restoring, compensatory, redemptive.

vb. restore, return, give back, reinstate, reinstall; rehabilitate, repair; recover, get back, retrieve, recoup, regain, retake, reclaim.

make restitution, refund, make amends, reimburse, repay, compensate, indemnify, redeem, ransom.

see also **589**

722 stealing

n. stealing, theft, larceny, robbery, burglary, house-breaking, shop-lifting; vandalism, looting, pilfering, ransacking, pillage, plunder, sacking; hijacking, skyjacking (*inf.*); kidnapping, abduction; hold-up, stick-up (*inf.*), mugging (*inf.*), hit-and-run-raid, smash-and-grab-raid, job (*sl.*); embezzlement, misappropriation, extortion, fraud.

adj. thieving, light-fingered.

vb. steal, take, burgle, thieve, rob, remove, go off with, get away with, make off with, run off with, seize, pilfer, pick-pocket, pinch (*sl.*), nick (*sl.*), filch, fleece, nobble (*sl.*), knock off (*sl.*), rip off (*sl.*), screw (*sl.*), shoplift, purloin; abduct, kidnap, mug (*inf.*), hijack, skyjack; embezzle, misappropriate, defraud, swindle, cheat, fiddle, peculate, smuggle; loot, rifle, sack, raid, ransack, plunder, pillage.

be stolen, fall off the back of a lorry (*inf.*).

723 thief

n. thief, robber, stealer; burglar, housebreaker, shop-lifter, mugger, attacker; pilferer, pick-pocket; hijacker, skyjacker (*inf.*), highwayman; safe-blower, safecracker; kidnapper, abductor; plunderer, looter; embezzler, swindler, cheater, fiddler; crook, rogue, thug, smuggler, pirate.

see also **684**

724 booty

n. booty, prize, haul, loot, swag (*sl.*), takings, plunder, spoil, winnings, stolen goods, goods fallen off the back of a lorry (*inf.*), capture, premium, contraband, prey.

725 business

n. business, trade, commerce, business affairs, traffic; negotiations, bargaining, transactions, marketing, buying and selling; barter, exchange, swap (*inf.*).

adj. business, trading, commercial, mercantile.

vb. transact business, trade, traffic, deal in, handle, market, buy and sell; negotiate, bargain; exchange, barter, swap (*inf.*).

726 purchase

n. purchase, buying, obtaining, acquisition; shopping, payment, investment, marketing.

buyer, purchaser, consumer, shopper, customer, patron, client, clientele, custom, market, patronage.

vb. purchase, buy, get, obtain, gain, acquire; go shopping, pay for, invest, exchange, bargain, sign; patronize; go window-shopping, buy back, redeem.

727 sale

n. sale, disposal, selling, marketing, trading; clearance, sell-out; bazaar, jumble sale, rummage sale; auction, public sale; sales talk, salesmanship, high-pressure salesmanship, sales patter, promotion, advertising.

seller, vendor, retailer, shopkeeper, shop assistant, salesman, commercial traveller, sales rep.

adj. saleable, marketable, in demand; available, on the market.

vb. sell, dispose, market, flog (*sl.*), retail, trade, dump, vend; ask, demand; transfer, transact, exchange; peddle, hawk; reduce prices, sell off; auction, come under the hammer.

728 trader

n. trader, dealer, retailer, shopkeeper, tradesman, middleman, wholesaler, exporter, importer, shipper, trafficker, merchant; businessman, industrialist, capitalist, manager, financier, entrepreneur, tycoon, stockbroker, speculator.

pedlar, hawker, tinker, huckster; tout; rag-and-bone man.

729 merchandise

n. merchandise, commodities, stock, wares, articles, goods, property, product, possessions; things, stuff; line, supplies; consumer goods, consumer durables.

730 market

n. market, mart, square, mall, arcade, shopping centre, shopping precinct, exchange, emporium; shop, store, supermarket, department store, multiple, chain store, boutique, hypermarket; kiosk, stand, stall, booth, barrow, bazaar; place of business, premises, concern, establishment.

731 money

n. money, currency, legal tender, cash, bank notes, bread (*sl.*), dough (*sl.*), lolly (*sl.*); change, small change; cheque, credit card, hire purchase; pay, salary, wages, pocket money, pin money; sum, amount, balance; funds, credit, finance, reserves, capital, wealth, wherewithal.

adj. monetary, pecuniary, financial.

vb. mint, coin, issue, monetize, put in circulation; withdraw, remove from circulation, call in, demonetize.

732 treasury

n. treasury, bank, exchequer, repository, coffer, vault, strongroom, depository, safe, cash box; cash register, till; money-box, piggy bank; wallet, purse, bag.

733 treasurer

n. treasurer, receiver, cashier, banker, purser, bursar, paymaster, accountant, teller, steward, trustee.

734 wealth

n. wealth, riches, money, affluence, luxury, opulence, prosperity, fortune, money to burn; profits, assets, means, resources.

rich man, millionaire, moneybags, man of means, capitalist.

adj. rich, wealthy, affluent, prosperous, luxurious, well-off, in the money, well-to-do, well provided for, made of money (*inf.*), rolling in it (*inf.*).

vb. get rich, make a fortune, come into money, line one's pocket; live comfortably, afford, bear the expense of, make both ends meet.

735 poverty

n. poverty, impoverishment, poorness; destitution, scarcity, privation, penury, pennilessness, pauperism, indigence, insolvency; beggary, mendicancy; poor man, pauper, beggar.

adj. poor, needy, destitute, under-privileged, distressed; impecunious, poverty-stricken, penniless, hard up, broke (*inf.*), bankrupt, insolvent; begging, mendicant; starving, hungry, empty-handed, down-and-out.

vb. be poor, find it hard going, live from hand to mouth, starve; impoverish, ruin, eat out of house and home.

736 credit

n. credit, trust, reliability; loan, account, credit account, credit card; creditor, mortgagee.

vb. credit, charge, charge to an account, credit one's account; give credit, defer payment, lend.

737 debt

n. debt, liability, obligation, claim, commitment, indebtedness, due, duty; debts, bills, amount due, amount owing, accounts outstanding, score, deficit, arrears.

debtor, borrower, purchaser, buyer, mortgagor.

adj. indebted, liable, answerable, responsible, committed, under obligation; owing, in debt, overdrawn, in the red; unpaid, due, outstanding, payable, unsettled, in arrears, overdue.

vb. be in debt, owe, be under obligation, overdraw, run up a bill, fall into debt, be in Queer Street (*sl.*).

738 payment

n. payment, remittance; settlement, clearance, reckoning; recompense, restitution, compensation, reimbursement, refund, subsidy; deposit, instalment, down payment, first payment.

pay, wages, salary, earnings, remuneration, emolument; fee, stipend, allowance, expenses, honorarium; pay packet, pay slip; payroll.

adj. paying, remunerative, not owing; paid, discharged, out of debt.

vb. pay, make payment for; repay, reward, remunerate; settle, discharge, defray, meet, bear the cost of, foot the bill; recompense, reimburse, compensate, recoup, refund; subsidize; pay on the nail; contribute, chip in (*inf.*), fork out (*inf.*), cough up (*sl.*); spend, expend; stand, treat.

739 non-payment

n. non-payment, failure to pay, default, bankruptcy, insolvency, liquidation, crash, ruin; overdraft, overdrawn account; debts.

non-payer, defaulter, bankrupt, lame duck; embezzler.

adj. non-paying, defaulting, insolvent, bankrupt, failed, ruined, on the rocks (*inf.*), bust (*inf.*), liquidated.

vb. not pay, default, fall into arrears, go bankrupt, go into liquidation, go to the wall, fold up (*inf.*), fail, be wound up, go bust (*inf.*), crash, go under; write off; bankrupt,

ruin, wind up, put in the hands of a receiver,
liquidate.

740 expenditure

n. expenditure, outlay, payment, disbursement, spending, costs, expenses, outgoings,
investment.

vb. spend, expend, pay, pay out, lay out,
invest, foot the bill; exhaust, discharge,
consume; squander, waste, lavish.

741 income

n. income, receipts, revenue, returns,
earnings, salary, wages, profit, assets,
proceeds, dividends, gains, takings, turnover, box-office receipts, gate-money.

receipt, acknowledgement, slip, voucher,
record.

742 accounts

n. accounts, bookkeeping; account, bill,
invoice, reckoning, statement, balance sheet;
ledger, log, cash-book; budget.

accountant, chartered accountant, auditor,
bookkeeper, actuary, cashier.

adj. accounting, budgetary.

vb. account, keep the books, enter, debit,
credit, balance; budget; cook the books
(*inf.*), falsify, fiddle (*sl.*).

743 price

n. price, cost, expense, amount, charge,
toll, fee, fare; rent, rental, hire charge; value,
face value, worth; evaluation, valuation,
estimate, quotation.

taxation, tax, duty, levy, tariff, inland
revenue; excise, custom, impost, tribute,
dues; rates, rateable value, assessment.

price control, price freeze, austerity,
squeeze; cost of living, price index; price tag,
label, ticket.

adj. priced, marked, charged, valued,
worth.

vb. price, value, charge, assess, estimate,
put a price on, reckon, rate; demand, ask;
reduce, mark down; increase, mark up.

cost, be worth, go for, sell for, fetch, come
to, amount to.

tax, exact, levy, put a tax on, raise taxes;
pay taxes.

744 discount

n. discount, reduction, rebate, allowance,
deduction, cut, subtraction, remission,
concession; depreciation; subsidy.

vb. reduce, lower, rebate, deduct, cut, take
off, knock off, subtract, allow; depreciate.

745 dearness

n. dearness, expensiveness, expense,
costliness; exorbitance, excessiveness, extravagance.

adj. dear, expensive, costly, high-priced,
pricey (*inf.*); exorbitant, too high, overpriced, excessive, prohibitive, extortionate,
immoderate, unreasonable, extravagant,
lavish, steep (*inf.*), stiff (*inf.*).

vb. be dear, cost a lot, cost a pretty penny
(*inf.*); go up, increase, revalue; overcharge,
exploit, bleed, fleece, extort.

746 cheapness

n. cheapness, inexpensiveness, competitiveness, reasonableness; bargain, good value,
good buy.

adj. cheap, inexpensive, low-priced,
moderate, reasonable, fair, peanuts (*sl.*).

family-sized, economy-sized, economy,
bargain, standard; reduced, cut-price, halfprice, marked down, dirt cheap.

free, gratuitous, for nothing, without
charge, complimentary, gratis, on the house,
for love.

vb. be cheap, get one's money's worth;
fall in price, decrease, cheapen, depreciate,
mark down, devalue.

747 liberality

n. liberality, generosity, benevolence,
bounteousness, bounty, largesse; kindness,
giving, charity, hospitality, cordiality.

adj. liberal, generous, big-hearted, openhanded, bountiful, lavish, unsparing, unstinting, munificent; kind, benevolent, unselfish,
charitable, beneficent.

vb. be liberal, give generously, lavish,
heap upon, spare no expense, go beyond
what one can afford.

748 economy

n. economy, thrift, care, prudence,
housekeeping, stewardship, management,
frugality, husbandry, providence; parsimony,
stinginess; saving; retrenchment.

adj. economical, economizing, careful,
prudent, good, saving, thrifty, frugal, sparing;
stingy, mean; convenient, time-saving,
labour-saving.

vb. economize, cut back, keep costs down,
cut costs, cut corners, tighten one's belt
(*inf.*), make ends meet, live within one's
means; manage, steward, husband, save,
conserve.

749 extravagance

n. extravagance, wastefulness, squandering, prodigality, lavishness, immoderateness; money to burn, shopping spree, spending spree, no thought of tommorow; prodigal, wastrel, spendthrift, squanderer.

adj. extravagant, wasteful, squandering, prodigal, lavish, over-generous, immoderate, exorbitant, reckless, careless, profligate.

vb. waste, squander, throw away, have money to burn, spend money like water, hang the expense, blow (*sl.*), blue (*sl.*); fritter away, dissipate; go too far, overdo it.

750 parsimony

n. parsimony, parsimoniousness, stinginess, scrimping, niggardliness, penny-pinching, cheese-paring, meanness, miserliness, penuriousness; niggard, miser, screw; greed, avarice, covetousness, avidity, voracity, gluttony.

adj. parsimonious, stingy, niggardly, miserly, mean, tight-fisted, close-fisted, penny-pinching, scrimping; sparing, chary, greedy, avaricious, voracious, possessive, acquisitive, grasping, grabby (*inf.*), itchy (*inf.*), rapacious, covetous, avid.

vb. be parsimonious, scrimp, stint, skimp; over-economize; be greedy, always want more.

VI Affections

A Affections in general

751 affections

n. affections, qualities, character, nature, make-up; personality, psyche, heart, soul, breast, inner self; temperament, disposition, spirit, temper, mood, state of mind, frame of mind, humour; tendency, inclination, bent, bias.

adj. affected, characterized, formed, moulded, disposed, inclined, predisposed.

see also **5, 58**

752 feeling

n. feeling, emotion, affection, sentiment, passion; experience, sense, impression, consciousness, sensation, perception, sympathy, warmth, tenderness, sensitivity, empathy; fervour, ardour, enthusiasm.

adj. feeling, emotional, sentimental, romantic, passionate, fervent, intense, impassioned, dramatic, burning, earnest, moving, tender; felt, experienced, heart-felt, thrilled, moved, affected, touched.

vb. feel, sense, experience, go through, enjoy, suffer, undergo, bear, endure.

move, affect, touch, stir, impress, excite, influence, quicken, touch one's heart, touch to the quick; appreciate, respond; thrill, tingle.

753 sensitivity

n. sensitivity, sensibility, susceptibility, awareness, consciousness, responsiveness, excitability.

five senses, sight, hearing, smell, taste, touch; sixth sense, intuition, feminine intuition; extra-sensory perception.

adj. sensitive, aware, conscious of, alive to, awake to, susceptible, impressionable, receptive, sensible; sensory, sentient.

raw, tender, bare, sore, bruised, delicate, painful, oversensitive, hypersensitive; exposed, open, vulnerable.

754 insensitivity

n. insensitivity, insensibility, unawareness, unresponsiveness, inexcitability, impassiveness; apathy, indifference, lethargy, aloofness, coldness; hypnosis, numbness, paralysis; dream, trance, coma, stupor; hardness of heart, callousness; stoic, ascetic; iceberg.

adj. insensitive, insusceptible, unimpressionable, unresponsive, inexcitable, unmoved, unaffected, unaware, unconscious, dead to, blind to, oblivious to, lost to, insensible; lethargic, dull, unenthusiastic, apathetic, indifferent, cool, aloof; unfeeling, unemotional, passionless, unresponsive, frigid, cold, numb, paralysed; blank, poker-faced, dead pan, expressionless; thick-skinned, hard-hearted, callous, cold-blooded.

vb. deaden, numb, paralyze, stupefy, stun, harden, sear, blunt, dull, drug; turn off (*inf.*), switch off (*inf.*); be unaffected, leave cold.

755 excitation

n. excitation, stimulation, activation, animation, inspiration, quickening; incitement, provocation, agitation, excitement; captivation, fascination, interest.

adj. exciting, stimulating, inspiring, moving, sparkling, exhilarating, thrilling, delightful; captivating, fascinating, interesting, absorbing, gripping, stirring, tantalizing, compelling, impressive, dramatic, sensational.

vb. excite, stimulate, arouse, activate, move, stir, work up, whip up, incite, influence, affect, provoke, awaken, touch, interest, animate, quicken, inspire; inflame, intensify, kindle, fire, light up; electrify, galvanize, energize.

absorb, fascinate, attract attention, impress, intrigue; tantalize, tease, anger, cause a stir; catch one's attention, come home, arrest, compel, engage; make one's mouth water, whet the appetite; knock for six (*inf.*), take one's breath away; delight, thrill, exhilarate, turn on (*inf.*), switch on (*inf*).

see also **756, 829**

756 excitability

n. excitability, impetuousness, boisterousness, instability, emotionalism, restlessness, agitation, irritability, intolerance.

excitement, exhilaration, thrill, ecstasy, transport; rage, fury, outburst, agony; hysterics, delirium; fuss, big song and dance (*inf.*), hullabaloo, tizzy (*sl.*), tiz-woz (*sl.*), dither (*inf.*), fluster, stew (*inf.*), to-do.

adj. excited, moved, stirred, inspired, thrilled, quickened, enthusiastic, eager, impressed, delighted, pleased, happy, joyful, touched.

excitable, sensitive, highly-strung, nervous, easily excited, emotional; impulsive, quick-tempered, impetuous; moody, temperamental; impatient, irritable, touchy, edgy, jumpy, jittery, restless, fidgety; tense, uptight, all worked up (*inf.*), keyed up, a bundle of nerves (*inf.*); distraught, beside oneself; mad, fuming, raging.

vb. be excited, thrill; let oneself go, get carried away, abandon oneself, freak out (*sl.*); tingle, glow, palpitate, pant; tremble, quiver, shake.

get excited, work oneself up; flap (*inf.*), shuffle, fuss; rage, fume, explode, flare up, boil over (*inf.*).

see also **755**

757 inexcitability

n. inexcitability, imperturbability, stability, composure, calmness, coolness, level-headedness, even temper, steadiness; peace of mind, serenity, tranquillity; self-possession, self-control, self-restraint, self-assurance; detachment, aloofness; stoicism.

patience, endurance, forbearance, long-suffering, submission, humility, meekness, resignation.

adj. inexcitable, calm, cool, composed, collected, self-possessed, dispassionate, imperturbable, unflappable (*inf.*), unruffled, immovable, stable, level-headed, even-tempered, easy-going, moderate, sedate, serene, tranquil, placid, inoffensive, mild, phlegmatic; patient, forbearing, uncomplaining, meek, submissive, philosophic, stoical; detached, aloof, disinterested, spiritless, nonchalant, blasé, casual.

vb. keep calm, keep one's temper, keep one's cool (*sl.*), keep one's shirt on (*sl.*), not

bat an eyelid; calm down, compose oneself, control oneself, relax, take hold of oneself, pull oneself together, cool it (*sl.*), simmer down (*inf.*), cool off.

bear, tolerate, endure, put up with, stomach (*inf.*), stick it out (*inf.*), swallow, brook, resign oneself to, grin and bear it, submit to, make the best of.

B Sensation

758 touch

n. touch, feeling, contact, tactility; feel, touching, stroking, massage, manipulation; tickle, titillation, itching, scratching, pricking, stinging, shivers.

adj. tactile, tactual, tangible, touchable, palpable.

vb. touch, feel, press, squeeze, stroke, rub, finger, paw, smooth, caress, fondle, massage, manipulate, lick, kiss, tap, pat, hit. strike; explore, feel for, grope, fumble, grasp, grip, grab, grapple, clasp, clutch; tickle, titillate, itch; graze, scratch, prick, sting.

759 heat

n. heat, hotness, warmth, tepidity; temperature, thermometer; thermostat, hot weather, summer, heatwave, scorcher (*inf.*), dog days; fire, blaze, glow, light, sparkle, flicker, conflagration; ardour, fervour, zeal, passion, intensity.

adj. thermal; hot, very warm, torrid, parched; burning, fiery, blazing, ignited, lit, alight, on fire, in flames, glowing, incandescent, smoking; heated, molten; sweltering, baking, scorching, sizzling, scalding, grilling, roasting; tropical, humid, sticky, close, sultry, muggy, stifling, oppressive; warm, tepid, lukewarm, temperate, mild, fair, sunny, summery; bright, clear; intense, fervent, vehement, passionate, ardent, excited.

vb. be hot, burn, flame, burst into flames, catch fire, flare up, flicker, glow; smoke, fume, reek, smoulder, smother, suffocate; cook, boil, scald, seethe, fry, sizzle, roast, parch, scorch, bake, swelter.

760 cold

n. cold, coldness, chilliness, frigidity, frozenness, iciness, frostiness, congelation; chill, nip, shivers, shivering; cold snap, arctic conditions; ice, icicle, glacier, iceberg, black ice; frost, rime, hoar-frost; hail, hailstorm; snow, snowflake, snowdrift, snowstorm, blizzard, avalanche, sleet, slush.

adj. cryoscopic, cold, cool, chilly, fresh, crisp, brisk, nippy, frigid; piercing, biting, cutting, numbing, stinging; raw, sharp, keen; wintry, brumal, bleak, Siberian, arctic, polar; freezing, icy, gelid, frosty, hoary.

vb. be cold, freeze, shiver, shudder, quiver; chatter.

761 heating

n. heating, warming; combustion, burning, incineration, flaming, kindling, ignition, scorching, incandescence.

adj. heating, warming, calefactory; combustible, flammable; glowing, incandescent.

vb. heat, warm, heat up, reheat, put on the fire; ignite, kindle, set fire to, strike a light, put a match to, touch off; burn, scorch, consume, scald, incinerate, reduce to ashes, cremate; fire, smelt; thaw, defrost, de-ice, unfreeze, melt, liquefy; insulate.

762 refrigeration; incombustibility

n. refrigeration, cooling, chilling, freezing, glaciation, glacification.

incombustibility, non-flammability; asbestos, safety curtain.

adj. cooled, chilled; frozen, icy.

incombustible, non-flammable, fireproof.

vb. refrigerate, cool, chill, make cold, freeze, deep-freeze, ice, frost, congeal, glaciate.

extinguish, put out, blow out, quench, stifle, smother, damp, choke, snuff, douse, drown.

763 furnace

n. furnace, boiler, kiln, stove, cooker, oven; incinerator, crematorium; fire, heater, radiator, hearth, fireplace, fireside, grate, hob.

764 refrigerator

n. refrigerator, fridge, freezer, deep-freeze, icebox, icepack, cool-bag, cool-box, cooling apparatus, cold storage; air-conditioning, fan, ventilator.

765 fuel

n. fuel, combustible; coal, coke, charcoal, briquette, wood, log, gas, oil, petrol, electricity, juice (*sl.*), hydro-electricity, nuclear power, solar energy.

match, lighter, firelighter, fuse, touchpaper, vesta, detonator, torch, firebrand, tinder, flint.

adj. combustible, flammable, explosive.

vb. fuel, fire, power; feed, stoke.

766 thermometer

n. thermometer, calorimeter, thermostat, mercury, clinical thermometer, pyrometer,

thermocouple, thermopile, thermograph; Fahrenheit, centigrade, Celsius, Réamur, kelvin; degree.

767 taste

n. taste, flavour, relish, savour, smack, sapor; tang, after-taste; tongue, palate, taste buds; gustation.

adj. tasty, palatable, delicious, appetizing, gustatory.

vb. taste, relish, enjoy, eat, smack one's lips; try, sample, sip; taste of, savour of.

768 tastelessness

n. tastelessness, insipidity, flavourlessness, dullness, flatness, staleness.

adj. tasteless, unsavoury, insipid, flavourless, dull, flat, bland, stale, wishy-washy, unseasoned, unspiced, plastic (*inf.*), uninteresting.

see also 507, 843

769 pungency

n. pungency, piquancy, sharpness, keenness, spiciness, tanginess; zest, bite, edge, tang, kick (*inf.*), zing (*sl.*), punch (*sl.*).

adj. pungent, sharp, piquant, penetrating, poignant, strong, tangy, racy; spiced, curried, hot; tart, sour, bitter.

see also 307

770 savouriness

n. savouriness, palatability, deliciousness, tastiness, richness, lusciousness.

delicacy, luxury, treat, rarity, delight, titbit, dainty, *bonne bouche*, chef's special, dish fit for a king; caviar; ambrosia, nectar.

adj. palatable, delicious, savoury, tasty, nice, dainty, delightful, choice, rich, luscious, delectable, exquisite, heavenly (*inf.*), scrumptious (*inf.*), yummy (*inf.*); fit for a king, fit for the gods; well done, done to a turn.

appetizing, mouth-watering, tempting, inviting, enticing, tantalizing, moreish (*inf.*).

vb. taste good; enjoy, like, relish, savour, appreciate.

771 unsavouriness

n. unsavouriness, unpalatability, unpleasantness, flavourlessness; bread and water, bitter pill, yuk (*sl.*).

adj. tasteless, flavourless, bland, dull, inedible; undrinkable; underdone; gone off; yukky (*sl.*); uninteresting, unappealing, unappetizing, uninviting, disagreeable, horrible, revolting.

vb. nauseate, disgust, turn one's stomach; disagree with, turn off (*inf.*); dislike, loathe.

772 sweetness

n. sweetness, sweetening, sugariness; sweet, sweetener, sugar, honey, molasses, syrup, treacle, saccharin.

adj. sweet, sweetened, sugared; sugary, saccharine, syrupy, rich, luscious, delicious; sticky; bitter-sweet, sweet-and-sour.

vb. sweeten, make sweet, sugar; dulcify.

773 sourness

n. sourness, acidity, bitterness, sharpness, acid, vinegar, gall, wormwood.

adj. sour, acid, tart, bitter, caustic, cutting, pungent, sharp, biting, dry; acidulous, vinegary, acetous, unsweetened, unsugared, unripe.

vb. sour, turn sour, set one's teeth on edge; ferment, curdle, tartarize.

774 odour

n. odour, smell, scent, trace, trail, exhalation, emanation, effluvium; fragrance; stench.

sense of smell, smelling, olfaction, detection.

adj. smelling, scented, odorous; strong, pungent, redolent; olfactory.

vb. smell, smell of, give out, give off, emit, scent, exhale; sniff, whiff, detect, perceive, smell out.

see also 776, 777

775 inodorousness

n. inodorousness, no smell; deodorization, ventilation, fumigation; deodorant, deodorizer; fumigant, fumigator, cleanser.

adj. inodorous, odourless, unscented, scentless.

vb. deodorize, fumigate, aerate, clean, purify.

776 fragrance

n. fragrance, aroma, bouquet, scent, perfume, spice, balm.

adj. fragrant, aromatic, scented, perfumed, spicy, sweet-scented, sweet-smelling, redolent, odoriferous, odorous, ambrosial.

vb. smell, scent, be fragrant; scent, perfume, embalm.

777 stench

n. stench, smell, stink, fetor, reek, fume, mephitis, miasma; foulness, uncleanness, smelliness, mustiness, rancidity; B.O. (*inf.*), body odour; skunk, polecat; stink-bomb.

adj. smelly, stinking, foul, unclean, fetid, strong-smelling, foul-smelling, nasty, vile, repulsive, offensive, rank, noxious, noisome; stale, musty, rancid, putrid, decaying, high, putrescent.

vb. smell, stink, reek, smell to high heaven (*inf.*).

778 sound

n. sound, noise, vibration, resonance, report, reverberation, echo, ringing; loudness, softness; note, level, accent, cadence, tenor, intonation, tone, timbre; acoustics, phonetics.

adj. sounding, heard, audible, distinct, within earshot; loud, resonant, sonorous; auditory, acoustic, phonetic.

vb. sound, make a noise, give out, emit, produce; hear, listen.

see also 795

779 silence

n. silence, inaudibility, quietness, stillness, noiselessness; peace, quiet, still, hush; loss of signal, blackout, news blackout, security blackout, censorship.

adj. silent, inaudible, noiseless, hushed, quiet, still, soundless, unuttered, unspoken, unvoiced; soundproof.

vb. silence, hush, quiet, still, calm, muffle, reduce to silence, mute, stifle; subdue, deaden, repress, tone down, put the lid on.

see also 513, 517

780 loudness

n. loudness, noisiness, audibility, rowdiness; noise, racket, roar, boom, blast, swell, din, clamour, tumult, outcry, uproar, hubbub, hullabaloo, pandemonium.

adj. loud, noisy, clamorous, vociferous, loud-mouthed; boisterous, rumbustious, rowdy, obstreperous; thundering, deafening, ringing, booming, ear-splitting, resounding, piercing, blaring, crashing, stentorian, enough to wake the dead.

vb. be loud, boom, roar, thunder, fulminate, resound, bellow, blare, peal, crash, rattle, deafen, be unable to hear oneself think.

781 faintness

n. faintness, softness, inaudibility; whisper, breath, undertone, murmur, mutter, sigh, rustle, ripple, hum.

adj. faint, soft, quiet, hushed, inaudible; indistinct, stifled, muted, muffled, deadened, subdued; feeble, weak, low, distant, muttering.

vb. whisper, speak softly, murmur, mutter, sigh, hum, rustle, purr, creak, squeak.

782 sudden and violent sound

n. bang, blast, shot, report, boom, detonation, eruption, explosion; thud, whack, knock, slap, tap, rap, snap; crash, crackle; shout, cry, yelp.

vb. crash, crack, knock, slap, smack, whack, tap, rap, snap; click; plop, plonk, thud; thunder, boom, detonate, bang, pop, slam, burst, explode, blow up, set off.

783 repeated and prolonged sound

n. roll, clang, clatter; rattle, rustle; chuckle, cackle; whistle, hum, whirr, purr, buzz, strum; throb.

vb. roll, clang, clatter; rattle, rustle, ripple, swish, hum, drone, whirr, purr, buzz, strum, whistle, trill; thump, throb, palpitate, tick, beat, pound, patter; chime, peal, toll; chuckle, cackle, rumble, grumble, growl.

784 resonance

n. resonance, vibration, tintinnabulation; ringing, clanging, echo, resounding, thunder, boom; chime, bell, gong, jingle, tinkle.

adj. resonant, vibrant, reverberating, loud, echoing, ringing, clanging, chiming, deep-sounding.

vb. resound, reverberate, boom, vibrate, echo, re-echo, ring, gong, chime, tinkle, jingle, clang, whirr, buzz, drone, whine, purr, hum.

785 non-resonance

n. non-resonance, thud, bump, plop, plump, thump, plonk, clonk, clunk.

adj. non-resonant, deadened, muffled, dead, heavy, dull.

vb. thud, bump, plonk, plump, plop, thump, clonk, clunk; muffle, stifle, dull, damp, deaden.

786 hissing sound

n. hiss, hissing, sibilance, buzz, swish, rustle, whirr, whistle, splash, squelch, whoosh, zip.

adj. hissing, sibilant.

vb. buzz, hiss, swish, rustle, whistle, splash, whoosh, zip, fizz, whiz, whirr, squelch, sizzle, sneeze, wheeze, effervesce, sibilate.

787 harsh sound

n. harshness, hoarseness, gruffness, discord, dissonance, cacophony; shrillness, whistle, croak, squawk, squeal, screech, shriek.

adj. strident, shrill, high-pitched, piercing, sharp, penetrating; squealing, creaking, grating, scratchy, tinny, metallic; clanging, clashing, screeching, jarring, discordant, dissonant; hoarse, gruff, harsh, raucous, loud, husky, throaty, guttural, dry.

vb. clang, clatter, clunk, crash, bang, clash, jangle; croak, quack, squawk, caw, cluck; saw, grind; shrill, whistle, shriek, screech, scream, squeal, yelp, squeak, creak; grate, rasp, irritate, jar, set one's teeth on edge, get on one's nerves.

788 human sound

n. cry, exclamation, utterance, shout, call, noise, shouting, clamour, outcry; scream, shriek, yell, moan, groan, wail, bellow, howl, whimper.

adj. clamorous, noisy, loud, yelling, vociferous.

vb. cry, exclaim, call, speak, utter, shout, scream, yell, shriek, screech, squeal, squeak, caterwaul, bawl, bellow, hoot, vociferate, whoop, hoop, hollo; groan, moan, complain, howl, wail, whine, whimper, sob.

cheer, chant, clamour, support; shout down, hiss, boo, ridicule, disapprove, censure.

789 animal sound

n. call, cry, ululation, barking.

vb. cry, yelp, yap, squeal, squawk; cackle, cluck, quack; caw, crow; screech, croak; coo, cuckoo; gobble, gaggle; chuckle, chirp, chirrup, cheep; tweet, twitter, whistle, pipe, trill, sing, warble; purr, miaow, mew, caterwaul, hum, drone, buzz; bark, bay, howl, woof, roar, bellow, bell; grunt, snort, snap, growl, snarl, whine, oink; neigh, bray, whinny; bleat, baa; moo, low.

790 melody

n. melody, melodiousness, tunefulness, concord, consonance, euphony, harmony, unison, accord, concert, music, blending.

adj. melodious, musical, euphonic, tuneful, rhythmical, melodic, lyrical, harmonious, in tune, accordant; sweet-sounding, dulcet, soothing, pleasing, mellow, soft, rich; catchy, memorable, singable, popular.

791 discord

n. discord, discordance, unmelodiousness, inharmoniousness, dissonance, atonality; noise, din, racket, cacophony.

adj. discordant, dissonant, atonal, unmelodious, inharmonious, unmusical, untuneful, out of tune, off key, flat, sharp; cacophonous, clashing, jarring, grating.

792 music

n. music, composition, work, opus, piece;

arrangement, adaptation, setting, transcription, orchestration, instrumentation; incidental music, background music, accompaniment; record, recording; concert, recital.

classical music, chamber music, light music, country and western, folk music, pop music, electronic music, jazz, blues, reggae, punk, rock, soul, ragtime.

symphony, concerto, suite; overture, prelude; sonata; ballet, dance; opera, operetta; song, air, solo, hymn, strain; tune, chorus, refrain, round; duo, trio, quartet; passage, movement, phrase.

adj. musical, tuneful, pleasing; vocal, choral; scored, arranged, adapted.

vb. compose, write, set to music, arrange, score; perform, render, play, make music, interpret; sing, chant, croon; listen.

793 musician

n. musician, artist, player, performer, virtuoso, soloist, instrumentalist, concert artist; singer, vocalist, chorister, bard, minstrel, artiste, choir, chorus, singing group; orchestra, band, ensemble, symphony orchestra, chamber orchestra; group; dancer, ballerina; composer.

794 musical instrument

n. musical instrument, brass, woodwind, stringed instruments, percussion; record player, gramophone, stereo, hi-fi, music centre, stereogram, juke-box; record, disc, single, L.P; tape-recorder, cassette-recorder; recording tape.

795 hearing

n. hearing, sense of hearing; good hearing, an ear for; earshot, range, carrying distance, sound; listening, auscultation; eavesdropping, wire-tapping.

listener, hearer, auditor, witness; eavesdropper, wire-tapper, peeping Tom; audience, auditorium; audition, interview, reception.

adj. auditory, hearing, auricular.

vb. hear, listen to, catch, take in, pick up, lend an ear, be all ears, give a hearing to, hark; attend to, pay attention to; perceive, detect, get wind of; overhear, listen in, eavesdrop, tap, bug.

796 deafness

n. deafness, inaudibility, deaf-and-dumbness, deaf-mutism; lip reading, deaf-and-dumb alphabet, deaf-and-dumb language, dactylology.

adj. deaf, hard of hearing, stone-deaf, deaf-and-dumb, deaf-mute; deafening, stunning, ear-splitting; deaf to, unaware of.

vb. deafen, stun.

797 light

n. light, illumination, lighting, radiance, brilliance, splendour, brightness, clearness, lightness; luminosity, phosphorescence.

beam, ray, gleam, shaft, streak, laser, pencil, stream, glint, chink; flash, streak, blaze, flame, flare, glow, spark, sparkle, twinkle, flicker, glimmer, glitter, dazzle, shimmer; glare, gloss, shine, lustre; polish, reflection; daylight, sunshine; sunrise, daybreak, dawn.

adj. luminous, light, bright, clear, shining, brilliant, beaming, glowing, glittering, sparkling, gleaming, dazzling; shiny, glossy, sheeny; illuminated, lighted, lit; cloudless.

vb. shine, burn, glow, blaze, glitter, glimmer, glisten, gleam, sparkle, dazzle, blind; flash, shimmer, flicker, twinkle, scintillate, blink, flare, beam; dance, play, reflect, glare.

illuminate, switch on, lighten, brighten, enlighten, dawn, shed light on, light up, irradiate; polish, burnish.

798 darkness

n. darkness, dark, night, nightfall, Cimmerian gloom, blackness, blackout, eclipse, shade, shadow, umbra, penumbra, adumbration, obscuration; gloom, sombreness.

adj. dark, unlit, unlighted, unilluminated; black, starless, dull, overcast, cloudy; indistinct, obscure, shady, nebulous, shaded, shadowy; tenebrous, obfuscous; dismal, gloomy, sombre, dreary, bleak, desolate, murky, dim.

vb. darken, blacken, black out, switch off, cover, eclipse, obscure, overshadow, becloud, place in shadow, cast a shadow over, obfuscate, adumbrate.

799 dimness

n. dimness, murkiness, shadiness, obscurity; dusk, twilight, half-light, gloaming, gloom.

adj. dim, dull, faint, vague, indistinct, obscure, blurred, opaque, fading, evanescent; grey, cloudy, foggy, hazy, misty, shadowy, gloomy.

vb. dim, dull, fade out, blur, obscure, shade, becloud, cloud over, dull, vanish, wane, evanesce.

800 source of light

n. light, luminary, sun, moon, planet, star, halo, aurora, corona, nimbus; meteor, shooting star; lightning, flash; fireworks.

lamp, torch, bulb, spotlight, searchlight, flashlight, floodlight, headlamp, side-light, indicator; neon light, fluorescent tube, strobe light, lantern; beacon, lighthouse.

candle, wick, spill, taper, wax; match, flame, flare; coal, ember, brand.

801 shade

n. shade, covering, veil, shield, screen, blind, curtain, shutter, drape; sunglasses, blinkers, goggles; visor, hood; shelter, awning, canopy; umbrella, parasol.

adj. shady; screened.

vb. shade, cover, veil, screen, shield, shelter, protect, curtain, blinker.

see also **463, 593**

802 transparency

n. transparency, clearness, glassiness, vitreosity, translucence, lucidity.

adj. transparent, translucent, clear, see-through, revealing, unobstructed, glassy, vitreous, crystal, lucid, diaphanous, pellucid, limpid.

vb. be transparent, see through, show, show through.

see also **502**

803 opacity

n. opacity, opaqueness, cloudiness, murkiness, obscurity, darkness; smoke, mist, cloud, film.

adj. opaque, non-transparent, absorbing light, impervious, dark, unclear, smoky, misty, cloudy, muddy, blurred, filmy, dull, murky, dim, darkened, turbid.

vb. make opaque, devitrify, obscure, darken, cloud, smoke, obstruct one's vision.

see also **503**

804 semitransparency

n. semitransparency, translucence, pearliness, milkiness; smoked glass, frosted glass, opal glass; dark glasses, sunglasses.

adj. semitransparent, semitranslucid, semiopaque, frosted, pearly, smoked, milky.

805 colour

n. colour, hue, shade, tinge, tone, dash, touch, tint, tincture, cast; paint, pigment, dye, wash, stain, lake; prism, spectrum; glow, brilliance, warmth, intensity; coloration, colouring, pigmentation, complexion, chromatism.

adj. coloured, chromatic, tinted, tinged, touched, dyed, painted, stained; constant, fast.

colourful, bright, warm, glowing, intense, strong, deep, rich, brilliant; garish, glaring,

gaudy, loud, showy, flashy, lurid, harsh, clashing, painful.

soft, pastel, subdued, refined, tender, delicate, matt; faded, dingy, dull, drab, cold, uninviting.

vb. colour, shade, tinge, paint, touch up, stain, wash, coat, put on, lay on; contrast, set off, throw into relief; clash, not go with, conflict, grate.

806 absence of colour

n. colourlessness, achromatism, discoloration, fading, paleness, dullness, dimness, faintness, flatness; anaemia, sallowness, whitening, bleaching.

adj. colourless, hueless, toneless, lacklustre, dull, lifeless, cold, dim, faint, weak; faded, washed out, pale, pallid, sallow, ashen, white, anaemic, pasty; transparent.

vb. fade, lose colour, lose brightness, bleach, blanch, wash out, whiten, drain, turn pale, discolour, grow dim, etiolate.

807 white

n. white, whiteness, whitishness, lightness, fairness, paleness; milkiness, chalkiness, silveriness, snowiness.

adj. white, fair, light, blonde, hoary; snowy, snow-white, frosted, milky, lactescent, chalky, silvery, pearly, ivory, albescent; whitish, cream, off-white; pale, ashen, anaemic, sallow, wan; clean, spotless, pure.

vb. whiten, whitewash, bleach, blanch, snow; clean, purify.

808 black

n. black, blackness, darkness, inkiness, sootiness.

adj. black, blackish; jet-black, pitch-black, coal-black, inky, sooty, stained; dark, murky; sable, swarthy.

vb. blacken, ink, ink in, darken, shade.

809 grey

n. grey, greyness, dinginess, drabness, dusk, shade.

adj. grey, greyish, shaded, dull, drab, dingy, sombre, neutral; dusty, smoky; silver-haired, hoary; speckled, pepper-and-salt.

810 brown

n. brown, tan, beige, mahogany.

adj. brown, brownish, beige, khaki, maroon, auburn, buff, bronze, copper, chocolate, coffee, rust-coloured, reddish-brown, bay, chestnut, russet, sepia, ochre, hazel.

811 red

n. red, redness, blush, glow, colour, cochineal, carmine.

adj. red, reddish, ruddy, scarlet, crimson, vermilion, ruby, cherry-red, blood-red, coral, brick-red, maroon, rust, magenta, russet, auburn, pink, salmon-pink, rosy; glowing, warm; blushing, embarrassed, burning.

vb. redden, blush; glow, flush.

812 green

n. green, verdure; lawn, turf.

adj. green, greenish, grassy, verdant, leafy, lime, emerald, sage, olive, beryl, blue-green, aquamarine, sea-green, pea-green; bilious, sickly, pale; fresh, unripe.

813 yellow

n. yellow, cream, tan, lemon; buttercup, daffodil, crocus, jasmine.

adj. yellow, yellowish, cream, saffron, sand, gold, golden, buff, tan, khaki, light-brown; sallow, bilious, jaundiced.

814 purple

n. purple; violet, pansy, lavender.

adj. purple, purplish, reddish-blue, bluish-red, violet, indigo, mauve, lilac, lavender, plum-coloured.

815 blue

n. blue, sky, azure, indigo.

adj. blue, bluish, turquoise, azure, royal blue, navy blue; sapphire, sky-blue, indigo.

816 orange

n. orange, tangerine, apricot, peach, mandarin, carrot, salmon, coral.

adj. orange, orangey, reddish-yellow, gold, old gold, copper, bronze, brass, ginger.

817 variegation

n. variegation, diversification, diversity, motley, spectrum, rainbow, kaleidoscope; chequerwork, tartan, mosaic, parquetry, marquetry.

adj. variegated, kaleidoscopic, many-coloured, multi-coloured; spotted, mottled, motley, patched, piebald, pied, dappled, speckled, freckled; striped, streaked, checked.

vb. diversify, variegate, chequer, checker; stud, mottle, spatter, dapple, speckle, stipple, streak.

818 vision

n. vision, sight, eyesight, perception, recognition; observation, inspection, scru-

tiny, investigation, notice, once-over (*inf.*); bird's eye view, survey, panorama, overview.

viewpoint, standpoint, position, outlook, perspective, attitude; lookout, observation point, watch-tower, gallery, grandstand.

adj. visual, ocular, opthalmic, optical; observant; watchful, vigilant.

vb. see, look at, view, watch, look on, observe, perceive, discern, recognize, notice, catch sight of, set eyes on, eye; glance, glimpse, catch a glimpse of, peep; blink, wink, twinkle; gaze, gape, stare, fix one's eyes on; leer, ogle, glare, glower.

scrutinize, investigate, survey, inspect; scan, look through, look over, flick through (*inf.*), thumb through (*inf.*).

819 blindness

n. blindness, sightlessness, colour-blindness, night-blindness, snow-blindness; blind spot, blind side, failing, mote in one's eye.

adj. blind, sightless, unseeing, eyeless, colour-blind; blinded, blindfold, blinkered, hoodwinked, in the dark.

vb. be blind, lose one's sight, strike blind, put someone's eye out; obscure, hide, mask, screen, blindfold, blinker, hoodwink.

820 imperfect vision

n. imperfect vision, partial vision; short-sightedness, myopia; longsightedness, presbyopia; double vision; colour-blindness; squint, strabism, cross-eye, astigmatism, conjunctivitis, cataract.

adj. dim-sighted, purblind, half-blind; shortsighted, myopic; longsighted, presbyopic; colour-blind, astigmatic, cross-eyed, squinting, strabismic.

vb. see double, squint, screw up one's eyes, see blurred.

821 spectator

n. spectator, viewer, onlooker, observer, watcher, eye-witness, bystander, passer-by, looker-on, beholder; sightseer; peeper, peeping Tom; spy, snoop, meddler.

spectators, crowd, public, supporters, fans, followers, turn-out, audience.

822 optical instrument

n. glasses, spectacles, bifocals, goggles, specs (*inf.*), contact lenses, monocle, eye-glasses, lorgnette, pince-nez; binoculars, opera glasses, field glasses, telescope; microscope, magnifying glass, lens; camera; mirror, looking glass, reflector, glass, speculum.

823 visibility

n. visibility, perceptibility, clarity, distinctness, plainness, prominence, conspicuousness.

adj. visible, apparent, in view, in sight, observable, perceptible, noticeable, before one's very eyes; evident, clear, plain, obvious, patent; prominent, conspicuous, pronounced, standing out; unmistakable, glaring; open, exposed; distinct, well-defined, definite, clear-cut.

vb. show, show through, show itself, manifest itself, be revealed, come into sight, come into view; stand out, stand out a mile (inf.), stick out like a sore thumb (sl.), hit in the face, leap to the eye.

see also 458, 825

824 invisibility

n. invisibility, concealment, seclusion, latency, obscurity, indistinctness, imperceptibility, indefiniteness, vagueness, indiscernibility, cloudiness, darkness, haziness, fuzziness.

adj. invisible, imperceptible, indiscernible; hidden, out of sight, concealed, obscure; inconspicuous; indistinct, unclear, ill-defined, vague; intangible, unseen, spiritual; cloudy, nebulous, shadowy, mysterious, hazy, blurred, fuzzy.

see also 461, 826

825 appearance

n. appearance, look, aspect, feature, shape, form, outline, profile, face; condition, presentation, expression; posture, pose, bearing; mien, countenance, manner, behaviour; externals, appearances, outward show, first impression, face value.

phenomenon, spectacle, display, exhibition, show, demonstration, scene, parade, pageant.

adj. apparent, visible, manifest; seeming, ostensible, supposed, specious, plausible, alleged, outward, superficial, external, to look at (inf.).

vb. appear, look, seem, show, take the form of; emerge, arise, come into view, be revealed, turn up, show up, put in an appearance, crop up (inf.), pop up (inf.), occur, happen, present itself, express itself, manifest itself, materialize, come to light, come into the picture, come onto the horizon, see the light of day.

adv. apparently, to all appearances, superficially, at first sight, on the face of it, for show, to all intents and purposes.

see also 222, 458, 823

826 disappearance

n. disappearance, vanishing, fading, fade-out, evanescence, evaporation, dematerialization; departure, retirement, flight, escape, removal, withdrawal, loss.

adj. disappearing, fading, evanescent; disappeared, vanished, missing.

vb. disappear, vanish, fade, evaporate, dematerialize, dissolve; pass out of sight, leave no trace, disappear into thin air, go up in smoke, vanish from sight, be eclipsed, be swallowed up, be lost to view.

go away, depart, remove, withdraw, retire, escape, flee; cease, be no more, die, perish, sink.

see also 824

C Personal

827 pleasure

n. pleasure, joy, happiness, gladness, delight, enjoyment, satisfaction, fulfilment; serenity.

enchantment, bewitchment, exultation, relish, gusto, zest, glee, cheer, thrill, kick (inf.), ecstasy, elation, bliss, rapture, euphoria, transport; luxury, ease, convenience, comfort, paradise, bed of roses, golden age, halcyon days, lap of luxury.

gratification, indulgence, self-indulgence, revelry, hedonism, sensuousness, sensuality, sexuality.

adj. pleasant, satisfying, enjoyable, delightful, exciting, adorable, welcome; comfortable, snug, cosy, homely, comfy (inf.), congenial, convenient, palatial, luxurious; gratifying, pleasurable, sensuous, bodily, physical, hedonistic, voluptuous, self-indulgent, carnal.

happy, pleased, joyful, glad, delighted, joyous, satisfied; thrilled, excited, tickled pink (inf.), exhilarated, starry-eyed, bubbling over, in the seventh heaven; smiling, laughing, genial, convivial, delirious; merry, in good spirits, cheery, jolly, blithe, gladsome, blissful; overjoyed, ecstatic, in ecstasies, enraptured, in raptures, enthusiastic, carried away; peaceful, contented, at peace.

vb. enjoy, like, take delight in, derive pleasure from, rejoice in, love, fancy, be keen on, appreciate, relish, revel in, get a kick out of (inf.), rave about (inf.), enjoy oneself, have a good time, tread on air.

see also 829, 836, 840

828 pain

n. pain, hurt, distress, discomfort, affliction, anguish, misery, agony, shock, blow, injury, suffering, unhappiness, sorrow, grief, sadness, regret, melancholy, despair, broken heart, weeping, wretchedness, tribulation, trial, ordeal, torment, torture, martyrdom, crucifixion, hell; bereavement, sense of loss, mourning, grieving; ache, twinge, pang, spasm, stitch, wound, sting, burn, illness, sickness.

worry, anxiety, heartache, vexation, fretting, uneasiness, discontent, disquiet, dissatisfaction; problem, care, burden.

sufferer, victim, prey, scapegoat, wretch, guinea pig.

adj. painful, hurtful, tormenting, excruciating, suffering, writhing, agonizing, harrowing; unpleasant, extreme, sharp, severe, grievous, sore, sensitive.

unfortunate, unhappy, sad, miserable, troubled, afflicted, heavy-laden, burdened, anxious, worried, vexed, uneasy; sorrowful, weeping, mournful, wretched, cut up (*inf.*), heart-broken.

vb. undergo, suffer, go through, bear, endure, put up with (*inf.*), persevere; ache, smart, throb, sting, burn; be tender, be sore, be bruised; regret, despair, mourn, weep.

see also **830**

829 pleasurableness

n. pleasurableness, pleasantness, niceness, enjoyableness, loveliness; charm, fascination, glamour, prestige, attractiveness, winsomeness, allurement.

delight, treat, surprise, amusement, fun, gift, joy, honeymoon, benefit, refreshment, titbit, feast, banquet, manna.

adj. pleasant, nice, enjoyable, agreeable, pleasing, lovely, charming, fascinating, attractive, beautiful, picturesque; glamorous, prestigious, appealing, enchanting, winsome, luring, seductive; delightful, exquisite, delicious, luscious, tasty.

vb. please, satisfy, delight, gladden, rejoice, thrill, gratify; turn on (*inf.*), turn on to (*inf.*), switch on (*inf.*), stimulate, excite; interest; attract, charm, enchant, enthrall, captivate, bewitch, enrapture; amuse, tickle, titillate.

see also **755, 827**

830 painfulness

n. painfulness, hurtfulness, unpleasantness, bitterness, disagreeableness; sorrow, pain, disappointment, irritation, annoyance, nuisance, difficulty, problem, care, burden, trouble, load, cross, concern, nightmare, bitter cup, bitter pill; embarrassment.

adj. unpleasant, disagreeable, bothersome, upsetting, disturbing, troublesome, annoying, irritating, trying, tiresome; distressing, awful,

grim, shocking, appalling, tragic, extreme, dreadful.

vb. hurt, grieve, injure, wound, afflict, pain; distress, worry, trouble, outrage, bother, upset, disturb, annoy, irritate, vex, needle; torment, harass, pester, tease, pick on (*inf.*), have it in for (*inf.*); harrow, agonize, excruciate, crucify, martyr, torture, obsess, haunt, plague; lose sleep over (*inf.*), discomfort, put out, inconvenience.

see also **828, 893**

831 content

n. content, contentment, peace, peace of mind, happiness, satisfaction; self-satisfaction, complacency; ease, rest, comfort, serenity, solace.

adj. contented, content, pleased, peaceful, satisfied, happy, carefree, without cares, uncomplaining.

vb. be content, be satisfied, sit pretty, have one's wishes granted, have all that one could wish for, have nothing to worry about, have nothing to complain of, can't complain.

satisfy, gratify, indulge, suffice; go down well, put at ease; appease, reconcile.

832 discontent

n. discontent, dissatisfaction, unhappiness, sadness, depression, resentment, regret, unrest, uneasiness, tension, strain; grudge, chip on one's shoulder.

complainer, grumbler, fault-finder, grouch; reactionary, radical, protester, angry young man.

adj. discontented, unhappy, uneasy, restless, disgruntled, dissatisfied, cheesed off (*sl.*), browned off; grumbling, complaining, critical, hyper-critical, hard to please, never satisfied.

vb. be discontented, grumble, criticize, find fault, go on about, pick holes in (*inf.*), speak out against, moan; dissatisfy, disappoint, disconcert, disgruntle, discourage, dishearten.

833 regret

n. regret, sorrow, misgiving, compunction, scruple, qualm, pang of conscience, apology, repentance, change of heart, contrition, penitence, self-reproach, remorse, soul-searching.

adj. regretful, apologetic, penitent, humble, sorry, remorseful, contrite, repentant, broken, conscience-stricken.

vb. regret, apologize, be sorry for, cry over, repent, humble oneself, admit, own up, grieve, weep over, mourn, bewail, bemoan; rue.

834 relief

n. relief, alleviation, mitigation, assuagement; help, aid, comfort, consolation, relaxation, ease, load off one's mind; remedy, cure.

adj. relieving, easing, comforting, consoling, consolatory, soothing, comfortable, breathing easily.

vb. relieve, alleviate, mitigate, ease, soften, comfort, cushion, assuage, soothe, lighten, ease the strain, console, cheer up.

be relieved, feel better, recover; heave a sigh of relief, breathe again.

see also 176

835 aggravation

n. aggravation, exacerbation, worsening, heightening, intensification, sharpening, deepening, strengthening, inflammation; annoyance, irritation, exasperation.

adj. aggravated, worsened, made worse, not improved.

vb. aggravate, worsen, exacerbate, make things worse, complicate, increase, magnify, multiply, heighten, intensify, deepen, go from bad to worse, get worse and worse; annoy, irritate.

836 cheerfulness

n. cheerfulness, good humour, happiness, gladness, joy; high spirits, vitality, animation, sparkle, liveliness, jollity, merriment, mirth, gaiety, glee; laughter, fun and games; light-heartedness, levity, breeziness; stoicism, stiff upper lip.

adj. cheerful, glad, happy, joyful; genial, animated, lively, in good humour, sparkling, vivacious, exuberant, full of beans (*inf.*), in high spirits, high-spirited, on top of the world, jolly, merry, gay, jovial, jocular, playful, sporty; light-hearted, perky, chirpy, breezy, carefree, debonair.

cheering, heartening, encouraging, inspiring, heartwarming.

vb. cheer, gladden, cheer up, perk up (*inf.*); brighten, encourage, comfort; enliven, animate, inspire; uplift, raise the spirits, warm the heart.

be cheerful, take heart, snap out of it (*inf.*); persevere, keep smiling (*inf.*), grin and bear it, keep one's chin up (*inf.*), keep a stiff upper lip, keep one's end up (*inf.*).

see also 827, 838

837 dejection; seriousness

n. dejection, despondency, melancholy, sorrow, sadness, grief, depression, despair, gloom, misery, heaviness of spirit, low spirits, blues, dumps, doldrums, mopes, *weltschmerz*.

seriousness, earnestness, solemnity, gravity, sedateness, sobriety, coolness; dead pan (*inf.*), straight face.

adj. dejected, unhappy, despondent, downcast, sad, sorrowful, down-hearted, depressed, low, troubled, desolate, dispirited, broken-hearted, crushed, heart-broken, upset, cut up (*inf.*), discouraged, crestfallen, blue, down, moping, down in the mouth, down in the dumps, in the doldrums (*inf.*), out of sorts; melancholy, world-weary, careworn, gloomy, miserable, dismal, forlorn, doleful, wretched, cheerless, dull; suicidal, despairing.

serious, earnest, grave, sober, solemn; thoughtful, pensive; stern, strict; straight-faced, dead pan (*inf.*), expressionless.

vb. be dejected, lose heart; regret, grieve, mourn, sorrow; fret, brood, mope; languish, droop, wilt, pull a long face, beat one's breast.

sadden, oppress, break a person's heart, cut up (*inf.*), discourage, deject, depress, unnerve, dismay, demoralize, get down (*inf.*); cast down; drive to drink (*inf.*); dampen, pour cold water on.

be serious, keep a straight face, take life seriously, not see the joke.

see also 828, 839

838 rejoicing

n. rejoicing, happiness, celebration, congratulation, jubilation, exultation, revelry, festivity, merrymaking, mirth, thanksgiving; cheers, shouts, hurrahs, applause; laughter, laugh, chuckle, chortle, giggle, snigger, cackle, titter, roar, guffaw; smile, grin, smirk, beam.

adj. rejoicing, jubilant, elated, exultant, rollicking.

vb. rejoice, be happy, sing for joy, leap for joy, dance, exult, celebrate, revel, have a party; clap one's hands, applaud, say thank you to, congratulate.

laugh, chuckle, chortle, guffaw, giggle, titter, snigger; burst out laughing, roar, fall about laughing, double up with laughter, be convulsed with laughter, split one's sides, roll in the aisles (*inf.*), be in stitches (*inf.*); smile, beam, smirk, grin, twinkle; laugh at, ridicule, poke fun at, deride.

see also 840, 842

839 lamentation

n. lamentation, mourning, grief, sorrow, weeping, sobbing, tears, waterworks (*sl.*); cry, weep, good cry, sob, bawl, wail, whimper; lament, elegy, requiem, dirge, funeral oration.

adj. lamenting, sad, mournful; weeping, sobbing, in tears, tearful.

vb. lament, grieve, sorrow; cry, weep, burst into tears, break down, dissolve into tears, shed tears, turn on the waterworks (*sl.*), sob, cry one's eyes out (*inf.*), sob one's heart out (*inf.*), blubber, snivel, whimper, whine, howl, bawl, wail.

see also **837**

840 amusement

n. amusement, pleasure, fun, good time; leisure; hobby, pastime, diversion, relaxation, entertainment, recreation, sport, play, game; television, radio, cinema, concert, theatre; meal, picnic, party, barbecue, banquet, feast; fete, fair, carnival, gala, fiesta, festivity; holiday, excursion, outing, pleasure trip, jaunt.

adj. entertaining, amusing, engaging, diverting, pleasant, witty; amused, entertained.

vb. amuse, entertain, delight, cheer, enliven, brighten up.

amuse oneself, enjoy oneself, relax, play games, go out, have fun, have a good time, let off steam (*inf.*), have a ball (*sl.*), let one's hair down (*inf.*), paint the town red (*sl.*), carouse, revel.

see also **614, 827, 842**

841 weariness

n. weariness, tiredness, exhaustion, fatigue, lassitude; tedium, boredom, apathy, listlessness, world-weariness, ennui, monotony, sameness, humdrum, the same old thing (*inf.*).

misery, wet blanket, drip; pain in the neck.

adj. wearisome, tiresome; tedious, boring, uninteresting, uninspiring, heavy, monotonous, dreary, flat, stale, repetitious, repetitive, soporific; tired, weary, exhausted, drowsy, jaded, worn out.

vb. weary, fatigue, tire, tire out, send to sleep, bore, exhaust, depress, leave cold; flag, droop.

see also **612, 617, 843**

842 wit

n. wit, wittiness, humour, joking, fun; jocularity, whimsicality, facetiousness, flippancy, drollery.

joke, witticism, repartee, pun, play on words, quip, jest, Spoonerism, *double entendre*, whimsy, sally, wisecrack, gag, funny story, shaggy-dog story, chestnut, aphorism, epigram; satire, sarcasm, irony; banter, burlesque, badinage.

humorist, comedian, joker, wag, life and soul of the party, jester, clown, buffoon, satirist.

adj. witty, humorous, funny, amusing, jocular, quick-witted, whimsical, quick, keen, lively, nimble; waggish; clownish; teasing, bantering.

vb. be witty, crack a joke, joke, jest, pun, bring the house down (*inf.*), sparkle, scintillate; tease, pull a person's leg, banter, rib (*inf.*), rag (*sl.*), make fun of, ridicule, kid (*sl.*).

843 dullness

n. dullness, heaviness, tediousness, mediocrity, insipidity, colourlessness, drabness, dreariness, tameness, flatness, dryness, stuffiness, slowness; familiarity, triteness, banality.

adj. dull, heavy, ponderous, tedious, boring, uninteresting, dry, stuffy, stodgy, sluggish, mediocre, flat, uninspired, lifeless, dead, drab, dreary, gloomy; long-winded, prosaic; conventional, stereotyped, common, commonplace, trite, banal, pointless.

844 beauty

n. beauty, elegance, attractiveness, good looks, loveliness, prettiness, fairness, handsomeness, shapeliness, pulchritude; glamour, grace, charm, appeal; magnificence, gloriousness, splendour, brilliance; beautification, face-lift, hair-dressing, adornment; cosmetics, make-up; plastic surgery.

good looker, smasher (*inf.*), stunner (*inf.*), belle, raving beauty, peach (*sl.*), pin-up (*inf.*), dream, Venus; ornament, masterpiece, showpiece.

adj. beautiful, attractive, good-looking, lovely, pretty, swell (*inf.*), smashing (*inf.*), glamorous, fair, handsome, appealing, pleasing, sightly, graceful, elegant, refined, comely, charming; shapely, well-formed, well-proportioned.

splendid, magnificent, brilliant, wonderful, glorious, marvellous, gorgeous, grand, fine, resplendent, excellent, impressive, exquisite.

vb. beautify, improve the appearance of, pretty up (*inf.*), doll up (*inf.*), tart up (*sl.*), dress up (*inf.*), adorn, decorate, ornament, trim, embellish.

see also **579, 846**

845 ugliness

n. ugliness, hideousness, unloveliness, uncomeliness, inelegance, disfigurement, offensiveness; mutilation, deformity, distortion.

eyesore, defacement, horror, mess, blemish, blot, graffiti, slum.

adj. ugly, hideous, inelegant, unbecoming, unprepossessing; frightful, horrid, shocking, offensive; unlovely, unseemly, uncomely; disfigured, deformed, misshapen, monstrous, grotesque.

vb. make ugly, disfigure, deface, distort, mutilate.

see also 245

846 ornamentation

n. ornamentation, decoration, adornment, embellishment, enhancement, trimming, frill, foil; embroidery, needlework; illumination, lettering, illustration; jewellery, jewel, gem, stone, precious stone; tinsel, ribbon, lace, gilt, tassel, bunting.

adj. ornamental, decorative, adorning, embellishing, garnishing, cosmetic; florid, dressy, ornate, fancy, gaudy, garish.

vb. decorate, adorn, beautify, enhance, brighten up, embellish, garnish, embroider, deck, bedeck, gild, festoon, array, set off.

see also 509, 844

847 blemish

n. blemish, defect, flaw, stain, smudge, blot, blur, taint, daub, spot, speck, smirch, blotch, tarnish, rust, stigma, dent, impurity, disfigurement, deformity.

adj. blemished, spoilt, disfigured, defective, imperfect.

vb. blemish, stain, smudge, blot, daub, smear, smirch, tarnish, sully, soil, spoil, mar, damage, deface, disfigure.

see also 582, 845

848 good taste

n. good taste, refinement, tastefulness, elegance, grace, polish; discrimination, good judgment, culture, sophistication; decorum, decency, soberness, seemliness, properness, restraint, simplicity, delicacy, daintiness.

good judge, connoisseur, expert, critic, gourmet, *bon vivant.*

adj. tasteful, in good taste, refined, polished, elegant, dignified, graceful, delicate; decent, sober, becoming, seemly, proper, simple, aesthetic; cultured, discriminating, sophisticated, cultivated.

see also 510

849 bad taste

n. bad taste, tastelessness; vulgarity, coarseness, rudeness, barbarism; pretension, artificiality; showiness, gaudiness; ugliness, unloveliness, hideousness; dowdiness, unfashionableness; cad, bounder (*sl.*).

adj. tasteless, in bad taste, unrefined, unpolished; vulgar, coarse, rude, gross, crass,

uncouth; pretentious, artificial, florid, ostentatious, flashy, showy; inelegant, ugly, unsightly, unlovely; dull, tawdry, shoddy, low, common, plebeian.

see also 511

850 fashion

n. fashion, style, mode, trend; new look, latest style, the latest; fad, craze, rage, all the rage, the last word; society, high society, set, right people; upper cut, upper crust.

adj. fashionable, stylish, trendy, latest, in fashion, in vogue, in (*inf.*), all the rage (*inf.*), modern, up-to-the-minute.

vb. catch on (*inf.*), become popular, grow in popularity, find favour; jump on the bandwagon (*inf.*), follow the crowd.

851 ridiculousness

n. ridiculousness, ludicrousness, funniness, outrageousness, absurdity.

adj. ridiculous, funny, comic, droll, amusing, hilarious, farcical, whimsical, side-splitting, too funny for words, rich, priceless (*sl.*), killing (*sl.*), absurd, ludicrous, preposterous, outrageous, fantastic.

vb. be ridiculous; laugh; bring the house down (*inf.*); play the fool, look silly.

see also 853

852 affectation

n. affectation, pretentiousness, pretence; artificiality, unnaturalness; show, sham, foppery, put-on (*sl.*), play-acting, front, façade, act, airs, airs and graces.

pretender, actor; play-actor; charlatan, impostor, humbug, dandy, fop.

adj. affected, pretentious, put-on, tongue in cheek, pretended, assumed, artificial, unnatural, theatrical; showy, for effect; awkward; superficial, shallow, hollow; insincere.

vb. be affected, pretend, assume, put on, feign, simulate, act out the part of, pose, fake, sham, go through the motions of; talk big; put up a front.

853 ridicule

n. ridicule, mockery, contempt, scorn, disdain, derision, sneering, jeering, scoffing; satire, parody, caricature, burlesque; irony, sarcasm.

laughing-stock, target, victim, butt, dupe, fool.

adj. derisory, contemptuous; scoffing; ironical.

vb. ridicule, mock, laugh at, deride, sneer, jeer, scoff, revile, gibe; boo, hiss, hoot; pour scorn on, run down, make fun of, pull a person's leg; banter, taunt; laugh on the other side of one's face (*inf.*); parody, caricature, satirize.

see also **924**

854 hope

n. hope, faith, trust, reliance, confidence, assurance; promise; expectation, anticipation; aspiration, dream, vision, pipedream, desire, wish, longing, yearning, ambition; optimism, cheerfulness, high hopes; false optimism, wishful thinking, pious hopes, fool's paradise.

hoper, aspirant, competitor, candidate, optimist, idealist.

adj. hoping, trusting, expecting, hopeful, assured, expectant, optimistic, relying on, confident, sanguine, bold, fearless, ambitious; promising, auspicious, favourable.

vb. hope, trust, believe, have faith in, rely, rest on, depend, lean on, bank on, rest assured, expect, anticipate; aspire, dream, wish, desire, long for, yearn for, contemplate; look on the bright side, see things through rose-coloured spectacles.

raise one's hopes, inspire, promise, lead one to expect, have the makings of, show signs of promise, bid fair, bode well.

see also **420, 836**

855 hopelessness

n. hopelessness, despair, desperation, despondency; irrevocability, irredeemability; defeatism, pessimism; pessimist, Job's comforter.

adj. hopeless, irrevocable, irredeemable, incurable, irreversible, beyond hope, vain, to no avail, futile; unfortunate, bad, disastrous, impossible, helpless, lost, gone; pessimistic, defeatist.

vb. despair, lose heart, give up hope, abandon all hope, give up; dash one's hopes.

see also **837**

856 fear

n. fear, fright, terror, horror, dread, scare, tremor, panic, despair, alarm, blue funk (*sl.*), consternation, awe, trepidation; timidity, fearfulness, timorousness.

anxiety, hesitation, worry, concern, uneasiness; nervousness, apprehension, cold feet, butterflies (*inf.*), nerves, jitters (*inf.*), willies (*sl.*), heebie jeebies (*sl.*), cold sweat.

adj. afraid, frightened, terrified, dreading, scared, scared stiff, shocked, in awe, trembling, panicking, panic-stricken, startled, petrified, shrinking.

uneasy, worrying, anxious, troubled, bothered, disturbed, hesitant, timid, shy,

timorous, cautious; nervous, apprehensive, fidgety, jittery (*inf.*), jumpy, edgy, on edge, tense.

terrible, frightful, awful, dreadful, horrifying, ghastly, atrocious, frightening, terrifying, appalling, harrowing, traumatic, inconceivable; disturbing, disquieting.

vb. fear, be afraid, panic; dread, shake, quiver, quake, cringe, tremble, shudder, one's knees be knocking, be scared out of one's wits, break out in a cold sweat; funk, shrink, clinch; go to pieces, crack up (*inf.*), break down.

frighten, scare, terrify, shock, startle, make one jump; intimidate; give cause for alarm, appal, petrify, frighten out of one's wits, make one's hair stand on end, make one's blood run cold; put the fear of God into (*inf.*); disturb, trouble, bother, concern, dismay, daunt, disquiet, unnerve, worry, torment.

see also **858**

857 courage

n. courage, valour, bravery, fearlessness, boldness, intrepidity, audacity, daring, fortitude; pluck, mettle, heart, backbone, guts (*inf.*), what it takes, stamina, staying power, spunk (*inf.*), grit (*inf.*); Dutch courage; gallantry, chivalry, heroism, prowess, manliness, self-reliance, resolution, determination, firmness, strength; enterprise, initiative.

brave person, hero, heroine, stalwart.

adj. courageous, brave, valiant, bold, confident, fearless, intrepid, audacious, daring, dauntless, undaunted, unflinching; determined, resolute, strong, tough; plucky, heroic, chivalrous, gallant; game; enterprising, adventuresome.

vb. be courageous, have what it takes; keep one's chin up (*inf.*); face, brave, encounter, confront, handle, look in the face, face up to, meet face to face, take the bull by the horns; have the nerve to; make a stand, risk.

pluck up courage, take heart, summon, muster, nerve oneself.

hearten, encourage, strengthen, fortify, inspire, assure, boost.

see also **534, 535**

858 cowardice

n. cowardice, cowardliness, faint-heartedness, weakness, shrinking, funk, cold feet, week knees, yellow streak; fear, apprehension; shyness, timidity.

coward, scaredy-cat (*inf.*), cry-baby; deserter, shirker, slacker; poltroon, dastard, sneak.

adj. cowardly, craven, faint-hearted, timid,

shy, weak, weak-kneed, scared, lily-livered, yellow (*inf.*), chicken (*sl.*); dastardly, pusillanimous.

vb. lose one's courage, get cold feet, back out, chicken out (*inf.*), funk, shrink, quail, show the white feather.

859 rashness

n. rashness, temerity, imprudence, impulsiveness; hurriedness, overhastiness, carelessness, recklessness, foolhardiness; indiscretion; daring, presumption; flippancy, levity; dare-devil, harum-scarum (*inf.*).

adj. rash, impulsive, impetuous, hurried, sudden, precipitous, overhasty, premature, breakneck, headlong, frenzied, furious; reckless, foolhardy, careless, thoughtless, imprudent, inconsiderate; headstrong, unthinking, heedless; wild, brash, illconsidered.

vb. be rash, stick one's neck out (*inf.*), jump to conclusions, rush to conclusions, play with fire, burn one's fingers, court danger, court disaster, ask for trouble (*inf.*), ask for it (*inf.*), fools rush in where angels fear to tread, throw caution to the winds, tempt providence.
see also **544, 613**

860 caution

n. caution, prudence, cautiousness, care, heed, alertness, vigilance, wariness, suspicion; discretion, circumspection, deliberation, forethought, precaution, presence of mind, foresight.

adj. cautious, watchful, wary, circumspect, careful, prudent, vigilant.

vb. be cautious, play safe, take precautions, take care, look out, provide for, look before one leaps, watch one's step.

861 desire

n. desire, wish, need, want; liking, fondness, fancy, weakness, predilection, inclination, urge, aspiration, ambition; ardour, longing, yearning, pining; nostalgia, homesickness; craze, frenzy, lust, covetousness.

hunger, thirst, ravenousness, craving, voracity, relish, appetite, famine, drought.

adj. desiring, wanting, wishing, liking, desirous, fond, inclined, partial, longing, yearning, pining, itching (*inf.*), dying; eager, keen, crazy, mad keen, craving; covetous.

hungry, greedy, ravenous, starving, famished, voracious, dry, parched; unsatisfied; peckish (*inf.*).

vb. desire, want, wish, need; like, be fond of, enjoy, choose, fancy, take a fancy to, incline towards, love, take to, be sweet on, have a soft spot for, go for in a big way, set one's heart on (*inf.*), set one's sights on, prize, esteem; aspire, dream; long for, crave, yearn, pine, hanker, make one's mouth water, lust, covet; relish.

be hungry, hunger, starve, famish; be thirsty, be dry, thirst.
see also **889**

862 dislike

n. dislike, distaste, disinclination, dissatisfaction; hate, hatred, loathing, aversion, repugnance.

adj. disliking, disinclined, averse to, loath to, fed up with, allergic, squeamish.

disliked, objectionable, repugnant, loathsome, abhorrent, abominable, disagreeable, unpopular.

vb. dislike, not feel like, not care for, hate, loathe, detest, not take kindly to, have nothing to do with, avoid, turn up one's nose at (*inf.*), not go for, not stomach.
see also **892**

863 indifference

n. indifference, unconcern, apathy, coldness, insensitivity, neutrality; half-heartedness, lukewarmness; unambitiousness.

adj. indifferent, cold, neutral; lukewarm, half-hearted; unconcerned, impassive, dispassionate, unresponsive, unmoved, uninvolved, lackadaisical, listless, inattentive; isolated, uncommunicative.

vb. be indifferent, not mind, not care, not care less, not give a damn (*inf.*), take no interest in, not matter, be all the same to, leave one cold; take it or leave it.
see also **754**

864 fastidiousness

n. fastidiousness, fussiness, meticulousness, scrupulousness, punctiliousness, pedantry, conscientiousness; perfectionism, idealism.

perfectionist, idealist, stickler, purist, pedant; fuss-pot (*inf.*).

adj. fastidious, particular, exact, precise, meticulous, exacting, scrupulous, rigorous, choosy (*inf.*), discriminating, selective, squeamish, finicky, pernickety (*inf.*), overscrupulous, overparticular, overprecise, hypercritical; hard to please; pedantic; delicate, nice.

vb. be fastidious, fuss, be hard to please, split hairs, pick and choose; make a fuss about, make a song and dance about (*inf.*).

865 satiety

n. satiety, repletion, saturation, fill, surfeit,

glut, plethora, jadedness, too much of a good thing.

adj. sated, satiated, replete, gorged, glutted, cloyed, overfull, overflowing; full, satisfied.

vb. satiate, fill, surfeit, glut, gorge, stuff, cloy, overfill, overfeed, satisfy, gratify; have one's fill, have enough.

866 wonder

n. wonder, surprise, amazement, awe, astonishment, bewilderment, fascination, stupefaction, incredulity.

sensation, miracle, sign, phenomenon, portent, spectacle, freak, marvel, drama, the unbelievable, prodigy, curiosity, oddity, rarity, something to write home about.

adj. surprising, amazing, astonishing, marvellous, fantastic, unbelievable, incredible, dramatic, remarkable, sensational, phenomenal, miraculous, stupendous, unprecedented, unparalleled, extraordinary, unusual, freakish, unique.

surprised, amazed, astonished, lost in wonder, bewildered, flabbergasted, spellbound, speechless, dumbfounded, thunderstruck, aghast.

vb. wonder, marvel, be surprised, be amazed, be taken aback, stare, gape, not believe, not get over.

amaze, astonish, surprise, bewilder, stupefy, dumbfound, flabbergast, overwhelm, take one's breath away.

867 absence of wonder

n. non-wonder, blankness; expectation; ordinariness, just as one thought, nothing much to write home about.

adj. unastonishing, expected, common, ordinary, usual; unamazed, unsurprised, unimpressed.

vb. not wonder, not be surprised, not bat an eyelid, not turn a hair; expect, take for granted, presume.

868 repute

n. repute, good standing, reputation, name, good name, renown, character, credit, respectability, reliability, trustworthiness, dependability; respect, favour, prestige, honour, glory, regard, kudos (*inf.*); fame, distinction, eminence, prominence, popularity; greatness, dignity, superiority, exaltation, majesty; rank, position, station, status.

big name, somebody, celebrity, star, dignitary, VIP, bigwig, big shot (*sl.*), grand old man.

adj. reputable, respectable, reliable, trustworthy, dependable, respected, well thought of, esteemed, acclaimed; renowned, of renown, famous, popular, celebrated, notable, leading, well-known; prestigious, honourable, distinguished, illustrious, eminent, prominent.

dignified, noble, great, grand, superior, high, exalted, elevated, sublime, majestic.

vb. be somebody, have a name, leave one's mark, make a name for oneself, go down in history.

honour, regard, respect, esteem, hold in high regard, admire, revere, praise, worship; exalt, glorify, crown, enthrone, ennoble, knight, immortalize.

869 disrepute

n. disrepute, disfavour, dishonour, ill-repute, bad name, bad character, unreliability, poor reputation; notoriety, infamy; disgrace, disrespect, reproach, shame, humiliation, degradation, abasement, ignominy, contempt.

scandal, gossip, backbiting, slander, calumny, defamation; slur, slight, insult, stain, stigma, brand, blot.

adj. disreputable, dishonourable, discreditable, ignominious; humiliating, lowering, degrading; notorious, infamous, shady, questionable; disgraceful, scandalous, shameful, outrageous, shocking, contemptible, despicable, corrupt, offensive, flagrant, base, mean, low, shabby, shoddy.

disgraced, humiliated, unable to show one's face.

undistinguished, obscure, unknown, unheard of, unrenowned.

vb. disgrace oneself, lose one's reputation, lose face, lapse from grace, fall from grace, fade; condescend, stoop, descend, lower oneself.

put to shame, disgrace, discredit, dishonour, expose, mock, show up; ridicule, embarrass, humiliate, humble; debase, degrade, snub, confound, unfrock; stain, tarnish, smear, sully, blot; take down a peg or two (*inf.*), cut down to size (*inf.*), drag through the mire (*inf.*).

870 nobility

n. nobility, dignity, grandeur, greatness, distinction, eminence; rank, descent, birth, blood, high birth, blue blood; royalty, majesty, court; aristocracy, gentry, landed gentry, peerage, ruling class, privileged class, elite, gentility; society, high society, upper classes, upper ten thousand, upper crust (*inf.*), higher-ups (*inf.*).

nobleman; peer, peeress, archbishop; duke, duchess; marquis, marchioness; earl; count, countess; viscount, viscountess;

bishop; baron, baroness; lord, lady; baronet; knight, dame; life peer; dowager.

adj. noble, dignified, grand, great, magnificent, lofty, imposing, distinguished; royal, majestic, monarchic, regal, reigning, princely; aristocratic, courtly, titled, lordly; highborn, of gentle birth, born in the purple.

871 common people

n. common people, commonalty, commons; people, the masses, general public, rank and file, grass roots; bourgeoisie, middle class; working class, lower class, have-nots, underdogs, proletariat; rabble, crowd, herd, riff-raff, *hoi polloi*, ragtag and bobtail, the great unwashed, scum, dregs.

commoner, plebeian, citizen, civilian, man in the street, Mr. Average; countryman, rustic, yokel, country bumpkin, peasant, serf.

adj. common, plebeian, bourgeois, ordinary, average, lowly, humble, of low estate, mean, ignoble; rustic.

872 title

n. title, name, designation; courtesy title, handle (*inf.*), honorific; order, privilege, honour; decoration, ribbon, medal, crest, emblem.

873 pride

n. pride, self-respect, self-regard, self-esteem, dignity, self-love; conceit, vanity, haughtiness, vainglory; self-exaltation, self-glorification; ego-trip; arrogance, insolence.

proud person, bighead (*inf.*), swank (*inf.*), boaster, bragger.

adj. self-respecting, pleased with oneself, self-assured, self-satisfied; dignified, lofty, stately, elevated, highfalutin; egotistic, conceited, bigheaded (*inf.*), patronizing.

vb. be proud, hold one's head high; take pride in, pride oneself on, glory in, boast.

see also **875**

874 humility

n. humility, humbleness, self-abasement, self-effacement; submission, obedience, meekness, lowliness, modesty, subservience, subjection; unobtrusiveness.

humiliation; abasement; mortification; come-down (*inf.*), let-down (*inf.*), deflation, crushing, shame.

adj. humble, lowly, meek, submissive, modest, self-effacing, subservient, servile; unassuming, unpretentious; humiliated, humbled, let down (*inf.*), deflated, squashed, crushed, crestfallen, chastened; embarrassed, ashamed.

vb. humble oneself, submit, obey; condescend, stoop, deign; eat humble pie, come down from one's high horse; be humiliated, not dare show one's face, feel small, feel squashed.

humiliate, humble, shame, embarrass, deflate, crush, squash, let down (*inf.*), bring low, put to shame, disconcert, make one feel small, take down a peg or two (*inf.*), teach one his place, reduce to tears.

see also **881**

875 vanity

n. vanity, conceit, self-importance, self-glorification, egotism, vainglory, self-applause, boastfulness; self-worship, narcissism; futility, emptiness, uselessness.

egotist, show-off, exhibitionist, know-all, smart aleck (*inf.*), toffee-nose (*sl.*), Narcissus.

adj. vain, conceited, haughty, self-centred, self-important, self-glorifying, self-applauding, full of oneself, boastful, cocky, swollen-headed, stuck up (*inf.*), puffed up, too big for one's boots (*sl.*), swanky (*inf.*), snooty (*inf.*), high and mighty (*inf.*), pompous, arrogant, insolent, supercilious, pretentious, snobbish, toffe-nosed (*sl.*), stand-offish; showy, exhibitionist.

vb. be vain, be puffed up, get too big for one's boots (*sl.*), have a high opinion of oneself, think too much of oneself, come the high and mighty with (*inf.*), know it all, boast, show off; turn up one's nose at (*inf.*); go to one's head, puff up.

see also **879**

876 modesty; shyness

n. modesty, unassumingness, unpretentiousness, unobtrusiveness, restraint, meekness, retiring nature; chastity, purity, virtue.

shyness, timidity, bashfulness, reserve, reticence, coyness; inhibition, nervousness.

adj. modest, retiring, restrained, meek, unassuming, unobtrusive, diffident, shrinking; restrained, tasteful, undecorated; chaste, pure, innocent.

shy, timid, bashful, quiet, reserved, coy, reticent, reluctant, backward, inhibited, secretive, demure, proper; blushing, embarrassed, red.

vb. hold back, hide one's face, keep in the background, take a back seat, hide one's light under a bushel, retire into one's shell; blush, go red.

877 ostentation

n. ostentation, exhibitionism, showiness, pretension; pomp, pompousness, magnificence, splendour, grandeur, majesty, pageantry; blatancy, flagrancy, flashiness, gaudiness, loudness; flourish, parade, fuss, splurge, showing off; bravado, histrionics, theatricality, sensationalism, effect, showmanship; exhibitionist, show-off, showman.

adj. ostentatious, showing off, proud, pompous, grandiose, extravagant, bombastic, high-flown, fancy, jazzy, showy, garish, gaudy, flashy, flamboyant, flaunting, blatant, flagrant, obtrusive, conspicuous, loud, screaming; spectacular, sensational, theatrical, histrionic, for effect, for show.

vb. show off, flaunt, parade, flourish, splurge, play to the gallery, do for show, make an exhibition of oneself, give oneself airs; sensationalize.

878 celebration

n. celebration, commemoration, honouring, keeping, observance; anniversary, jubilee, birthday, red-letter day, centenary, bicentenary, tercentenary; ceremonial; solemnization; ceremony, function, occasion, festive occasion, do (*inf.*); clapping, applause, praise, acclaim, cheers, hurrahs, cries, ovation, standing ovation, salute.

adj. celebrative, commemorative, anniversary, congratulatory, ceremonial, festive.

vb. celebrate, commemorate, observe, keep, remember, honour, congratulate, crown; throw a party, make merry, kill the fatted calf.

879 boasting

n. boasting, self-glory, self-glorification; boast, brag, empty talk, big talk, hot air, bombast, bluster, braggadocio, gasconade.

boaster, big mouth, swank (*inf.*), gas-bag (*sl.*), braggart, Gascon.

adj. boastful, bragging, big-mouthed, pretentious, inflated, self-glorifying, vaunting.

vb. boast, vaunt, brag, show off, talk big, bounce, exaggerate; blow one's own trumpet, have a high opinion of oneself, pat oneself on the back, congratulate oneself, flatter oneself.

880 insolence

n. insolence, rudeness, boldness, audacity, effrontery, impudence, impertinence, arrogance, presumption, forwardness, shamelessness, officiousness, sauciness, defiance, lip (*sl.*), cheek, nerve (*inf.*), sauce, brass.

upstart, wise guy (*sl.*), pup.

adj. insolent, impudent, impertinent, arrogant, high-handed, disrespectful, insulting, rude, offensive, officious, outrageous, defiant,

cheeky, saucy, uppity (*inf.*); presumptious, forward.

vb. be insolent, have the cheek, have a nerve (*inf.*), get fresh, come the high and mighty with (*inf.*), get on one's high horse (*inf.*); give lip (*sl.*), brazen it out, answer back, presume, take for granted.

881 servility

n. servility, obsequiousness, meniality, sycophancy, toadyism; sycophant, toady, back-scratcher, yes-man, sponger, parasite, hanger-on, boot-licker.

adj. servile, menial, beggarly, slavish, subservient, obsequious, cringing, toadyish, boot-licking, ingratiating, fawning, grovelling, snivelling.

vb. be servile, suck up to (*sl.*), crawl (*inf.*), grovel, go down on one's knees, lick the boots of, ingratiate oneself with, toady, fawn, curry favour; flatter.

D Sympathetic

882 friendship

n. friendship, companionship, amity, comradeship, fraternity, intimacy, familiarity; friendliness, affection, amicability, sociability, good terms, neighbourliness, understanding, compatibility, matiness, warmth, cordiality.

friend, companion, mate, pal, chum, buddy, comrade; boy-friend, girl-friend; acquaintance, neighbour; close friend, best friend, bosom friend, confidant, intimate.

adj. friendly, close, familiar, intimate, inseparable, confiding; faithful, loyal, devoted, true, trusted, staunch, firm; amicable, sympathetic, compatible, sociable, affectionate, warm-hearted, brotherly, matey, pally; kind, benevolent.

vb. be friendly, know, be acquainted with, be on good terms with; befriend, get to know, make friends with, get in with (*inf.*), get pally with, chum up with, break the ice; go out with (*inf.*), go with, knock about with (*inf.*), go around with, keep company with, go together, see (*inf.*), run after (*inf.*), go after (*inf.*), chase, try to get, take out, accompany, court, woo, make advances; be just good friends.

see also **889**

883 enmity

n. enmity, hostility, inimicality; antipathy, unfriendliness; hatred, antagonism, dislike, repugnance, animosity; ill-feeling, hard feelings; separation, estrangement, alienation; bitterness, acrimony, coolness.

enemy, foe, antagonist, opponent, adversary, arch-enemy, invader; public enemy; rival, informer.

adj. inimical, hostile, antagonistic, unfriendly, ill-disposed, opposed; irreconcilable, alienated, estranged; at odds, at daggers drawn, at loggerheads, not on speaking terms, on bad terms; cool, cold, chilly, uncordial; opposite, contrary, conflicting; quarrelsome, unsympathetic, grudging, resentful.

vb. be opposed to, differ, be at odds with, conflict, clash; antagonize, provoke, alienate, estrange.

see also **637, 638**

884 sociability

n. sociability, geniality, friendliness, cordiality, gregariousness, conviviality, affability, hospitality, open house, social intercourse.

party, social, get-together, ball, meeting, reunion, rendezvous, reception, at home, soirée; visit, call, appointment, engagement, date, interview, stay; arrangement.

visitor, dropper-in, guest, caller; mixer, good mixer, life and soul of the party; gate-crasher, uninvited guest.

adj. sociable, friendly, genial, cordial, affable, gregarious, neighbourly, hospitable.

vb. be sociable, invite, welcome, receive, entertain, throw a party; keep open house; visit, drop in on, look in, call by.

885 unsociability

n. unsociability, unfriendliness, uncommunicativeness, shyness; distance, unapproachability, aloofness; seclusion, privacy, separateness, isolation, retirement, withdrawal, solitariness, loneliness; backwater, back of beyond, backwoods, refuge, retreat, cloister, ivory tower, shell, desert island.

recluse, hermit, monk, anchorite, backwoodsman; loner, stay-at-home; outcast, castaway; refugee, evacuee; outlaw, bandit; orphan, leper.

adj. unsociable, unfriendly, distant, shy, uncommunicative, unapproachable, aloof, stand-offish, antisocial, inhospitable; lonesome, solitary, lonely, friendless, desolate, retiring, withdrawn; secluded, forsaken, isolated, rustic, out-of-the-way, remote, God-forsaken, unexplored, uninhabited, deserted.

vb. be unsociable, stand aloof, keep oneself to oneself, keep one's distance, go into seclusion, shut oneself up, retire into one's shell; seclude, exclude, expel, excommunicate, repel, cold-shoulder, keep at arm's length, keep at bay, beat off.

886 courtesy

n. courtesy, thoughtfulness, consideration, politeness, manners, good manners, civility, culture, refinement, breeding, gentility, respect, kindness, friendliness, generosity, gallantry, chivalry; condescension, flattery, oiliness.

good turn, favour, compliment; greeting, handshake, smile, embrace, hug, kiss.

adj. courteous, polite, well-mannered, civil, amiable, affable, thoughtful, considerate, kind, friendly, generous, obliging; cultivated, cultured, refined, polished, well-bred; politic, diplomatic; gentlemanly, ladylike; gallant, chivalrous; condescending, obsequious, ingratiating, patronizing.

vb. be courteous, behave oneself, mind one's P's and Q's, be on one's best behaviour; give one's regards, give one's compliments, send best wishes, pay one's respects, compliment; greet, welcome, hail, exchange greetings, hold out one's hand, shake hands, smile, wave, hug, embrace, kiss.

887 discourtesy

n. discourtesy, impoliteness, bad manners, misbehaviour, incivility, ill breeding; disrespect, impudence, unfriendliness, brusqueness; meanness, nastiness, unpleasantness, rudeness, vulgarity, boorishness, coarseness, grossness, shamelessness.

adj. discourteous, impolite, bad-mannered, uncivil, uncultured, unrefined, unbecoming, misbehaved, ungentlemanly, rude, unfriendly, unkind, ungracious, unpleasant, nasty, obstreperous, disrespectful, offensive, crude, coarse, vulgar, shameless; loutish, rowdy, disorderly, boorish; thoughtless, careless, inconsiderate, tactless, gauche, outspoken; brusque, abrupt, curt, offhand, rough, gruff, surly, difficult; audacious, brash; cheeky, high-handed.

vb. be rude, insult, affront, outrage; give the cold shoulder; irritate, annoy, shout down, interrupt; snub, disregard, ignore.

888 congratulation

n. congratulation, felicitation, best wishes, compliments, happy returns; applause, appreciation, bouquet, praise, acknowledgment, toast.

adj. congratulatory, complimentary.

vb. congratulate, compliment, felicitate, pay one's respects, offer one's congratulations, salute, praise, honour, acclaim, sound the praises of, appreciate, admire, adulate; toast, celebrate; mob.

889 love

n. love, fondness, affection, attachment, devotion, adoration; passion, Eros, ardour. amorousness, lust, infatuation, crush (*sl.*), pash (*sl.*); first love, calf-love, puppy love; emotion, sentiment; attractiveness, charm, winsomeness, appeal, sex-appeal, fascination; love affair, affair, romance, liaison, relationship, flirtation, amour, eternal triangle.

lover, admirer, suitor, wooer, boy-friend, girl-friend, date (*inf.*), steady (*inf.*), blind date; Romeo, Juliet, fiancé, fiancée; mistress; cohabitant.

adj. loving, fond, affectionate, devoted, adoring, attached; emotional, sentimental, tender, soft; yearning, longing, passionate, ardent, amorous, glowing.

enamoured, attracted, enchanted, fascinated, caught, charmed, captivated, enraptured, taken with, sweet on, keen on, infatuated, gone on, crazy, wild, mad, smitten, in love, head over heels in love.

lovable, winsome, attractive, charming, appealing, captivating, irresistible, dear; loved, beloved, cherished.

vb. love, like, be fond of, care for, delight in, adore, fancy; treasure, hold dear, take to one's heart (*inf.*), admire, regard, cherish, appreciate, esteem, value, prize; be in love, dote on, be enraptured by; fall in love, fall for, be crazy about, have it bad (*inf.*); lose one's heart to, have a crush on, be swept off one's feet (*inf.*), be infatuated with; long, yearn; copulate, have intercourse, make love to, have sex with (*inf.*), sleep with (*inf.*), sleep together (*inf.*), go to bed with, have it off with (*sl.*); live with, live together, cohabit, live in sin (*inf.*).

attract, appeal, fascinate, captivate, charm, enchant, allure, draw, rouse, enrapture, infatuate, sweep off one's feet (*inf.*).

see also **861, 882**

890 endearment

n. endearment, affection, attachment, fondness, love, sweet nothings, embrace, kiss, cuddle, stroke, fondling, petting, necking (*sl.*); courtship, courting, wooing, pass, advance, dating, flirtation, amorous intentions; love-letter, Valentine; proposal, offer of marriage, engagement.

vb. woo, court, go out with (*inf.*), run after (*inf.*), pursue, chase, date, pay attentions to, make overtures, make advances, make passes, make eyes at (*inf.*), ogle, flirt; propose, pop the question (*inf.*).

be fond of, cherish; embrace, hug, clasp, draw close, snuggle, kiss, cuddle; stroke, fondle, caress, pat, pet, neck, smooch (*inf.*).

see also **882**

891 darling; favourite

n. darling, dear, love, beloved, dearest, sweetheart, angel, pet, sweet, sweetie (*inf.*), sweetie-pie (*inf.*), sugar (*inf.*), honey (*inf.*), precious (*inf.*), treasure (*inf.*), jewel (*inf.*); favourite, mother's darling, teacher's pet, blue-eyed boy, apple of one's eye.

892 hate

n. hate, hatred, dislike, antipathy, aversion, loathing, abhorrence, repugnance, repulsion, disgust, scorn, detestation, nasty look.

anathema, abomination, menace, pest, *bête noire*, bitter pill.

adj. detestable, hateful, odious, abominable, abhorrent, loathsome, accursed, offensive, repugnant, disgusting, revolting, repulsive, vile; averse to, hostile, antagonistic.

vb. hate, dislike, loathe, abhor, detest, abominate, denounce, condemn, object to, spurn, spit upon, curse, reject, have it in for (*inf.*).

offend, rub up the wrong way, repel, disgust, shock, alienate, estrange, antagonize, make one's blood run cold.

see also **295, 862**

893 resentment; anger

n. resentment, bitterness, hurt, soreness, malice, grudge, bone to pick; sore point.

anger, indignation, displeasure, antagonism; rage, fury, wrath, vehemence, passion, vexation, exasperation, annoyance, impatience, ire; bad temper, outburst, fit, tantrum, huff, tiff, quarrel, argument, fight.

adj. resentful, indignant, sore, hurt, grudging, bitter, embittered, with a chip on one's shoulder, acrimonious.

angry, cross, irate, furious, raging, fiery, mad (*inf.*), hopping mad (*inf.*), fuming, displeased; antagonized, enraged, exasperated, infuriated, annoyed, irritated, peeved (*sl.*), impatient, irritable, ratty (*sl.*), shirty (*sl.*), provoked, affronted, riled, vexed, worked up, het up (*inf.*); up in arms, in a huff, hot under the collar, foaming at the mouth (*inf.*).

vb. resent, feel bitter towards, take umbrage, take exception, be insulted, bear a grudge, bear malice, have a bone to pick.

get angry, get cross, lose one's temper, blow one's top (*inf.*), hit the roof (*inf.*), fly off the handle (*inf.*), blow up (*inf.*), explode;

get worked up, get het up (*inf.*), get hot under the collar, go up the wall (*inf.*), go off the deep end (*inf.*).

be angry, burn, roar, rage, rant and rave, fume, storm, boil, seethe, foam at the mouth (*inf.*); snap, bite someone's head off (*inf.*), jump down someone's throat (*inf.*); criticize, nag, get at.

anger, enrage, incense, infuriate, madden, antagonize, exasperate, provoke, bother, harass, vex, annoy, incite, irritate, needle, nettle, rankle, rile, stir, get someone's back up (*inf.*), get someone's blood up, make one's blood boil, send up the wall, rub up the wrong way (*inf.*), tread on someone's toes (*inf.*), get on someone's nerves, get under someone's skin, get someone's goat (*sl.*), upset, ruffle, discompose, put out.

see also **642**

894   irritability

n. irritability, sensitivity, nervousness, uneasiness, exasperation, impatience, touchiness, bad temper.

adj. irritable, sensitive, susceptible, touchy, oversensitive, prickly, edgy, short-tempered, ratty (*sl.*), shirty (*sl.*), uptight, gruff, grumpy; nervous, anxious, jumpy, jittery (*inf.*); temperamental, moody; irritated, annoyed, needled, riled, rankled, nettled, rubbed up the wrong way, with a chip on one's shoulder; irascible, choleric, querulous, cantankerous.

895   sullenness

n. sullenness, moroseness, glumness, moodiness, unsociability, sourness, bad temper, gruffness, spleen; frown, scowl, grimace, sneer, dirty look (*inf.*), wry face.

adj. sullen, morose, glum, silent, unsociable; moody, surly, grouchy, churlish, sulky, cross, mopish, ill-humoured, ill-natured, disagreeable, sour, mournful, saturnine; scowling, frowning; gloomy, dismal, sad, dim, dark, cheerless, sombre.

vb. scowl, frown, grimace, make a face, pull a face, glower, growl, sulk, grouch, mope, sneer.

896   marriage

n. marriage, matrimony, wedlock, conjugality, union, match, alliance, marriage tie, marriage bed; wedding, pledging, ceremony, nuptials, espousals; church wedding, civil marriage, registry-office wedding; elopement, abduction; shotgun wedding; reception, wedding breakfast, party, dance; honeymoon, consummation.

man and wife, bride and groom, bridal pair, newlyweds, honeymooners; partner, spouse, mate; husband, man; wife, helpmeet, better half (*inf.*), the missus (*sl.*).

adj. matrimonial, marital, nuptial, conjugal, married, wed, united, matched; newlywed; honeymooning, going-away, marriageable, eligible, suitable, of marriageable age.

vb. marry, get married, wed, espouse, take to oneself, lead to the altar, plight one's troth, become one, get hitched (*sl.*), get spliced (*sl.*), make an honest woman of (*inf.*); honeymoon, go away, consummate; run away, leave home, elope; join, unite, pronounce man and wife, marry, give in marriage, give away; marry into, marry out of; marry off, match, matchmake, find a match for, find a mate for; catch, find, hook (*sl.*).

see also **889**

897   celibacy

n. celibacy, singleness, bachelorhood, virginity, spinsterhood; celibate, bachelor, confirmed bachelor; spinster, bachelor girl, old maid, virgin.

adj. celibate, single, unmarried, unwed, not the marrying kind; eligible, unattached, free; virgin.

898   divorce; widowhood

n. divorce, separation, annulment, dissolution, decree nisi, desertion; breakdown of marriage.

widowhood; survivor, widow, dowager, relict; widower; grass widow, golf widow.

adj. divorced, parted, separated, living apart.

vb. divorce, get a divorce, annul, cancel, put asunder, sue for a divorce, desert, split up (*inf.*), separate, live apart; widow, bereave; leave, survive.

899   benevolence

n. benevolence, kindness, helpfulness, thoughtfulness, kindheartedness, graciousness, courtesy, charity, altruism, philanthropy, fellow-feeling, the golden rule; service, good deed, good turn, aid, relief, favour, benefit, alms.

kind person, good Samaritan, good neighbour, altruist, humanitarian, do-gooder, philanthropist, heart of gold.

adj. kind, benevolent, charitable, helpful, careful, thoughtful, well-meaning, well-intentioned, well-meant, gracious, good, pleasant, generous, obliging, neighbourly, kindhearted, warm-hearted, compassionate, sympathetic, unselfish, altruistic, humanitarian, philanthropic; merciful, pitying.

vb. be kind, help, do a good turn, do a favour, benefit, support, encourage, comfort, relieve, bless, mean well, wish well, do as one would be done by, bend over backwards to help.

see also **550, 905, 935**

900 malevolence

n. malevolence, unkindness, hate, animosity, malice, malignity, spite, bitterness, acrimony; cruelty, abuse, inhumanity, wickedness, ruthlessness, relentlessness, harshness, severity, callousness; tyranny, oppression, despotism, intolerance; brutality, beastliness, savagery, barbarousness, brutishness, monstrousness.

ill, harm, misfortune, mischief, blow, outrage, foul play, catastrophe, disaster, atrocity, torture.

adj. unkind, unfriendly, unloving, uncharitable, inconsiderate, thoughtless; spiteful, malicious, catty, hateful, resentful, bitter, acrimonious, caustic.

cruel, malevolent, malicious, inhuman, wicked, harsh, severe, relentless, fierce, savage, barbarous, brutal, beastly; pitiless, unmerciful, intolerant, ruthless, cold, callous, hardhearted, oppressive, despotic, devilish, diabolical.

vb. be malevolent, hurt, harm, abuse, maltreat, damage, injure, oppress, tyrannize, be intolerant, persecute, torture, torment, victimize, have it in for (*inf.*), take it out on (*inf.*).

see also **551, 906, 936**

901 curse

n. curse, malediction, denunciation, exercration, abuse, vilification, vituperation, scurrility; profanity, swearing, oath, imprecation, expletive, swearword, naughty word, bad language, blasphemy, sacrilege, profanation.

adj. maledictory, imprecatory, damnatory; abusive, scurrilous, profane, sacrilegious, blasphemous, blue, naughty, indecent, obscene.

vb. curse, wish on (*inf.*), invoke, summon, call down on; abuse, defame, denounce, pour abuse, call names, revile, vituperate, vilify, damn; swear, swear like a trooper, blaspheme.

902 threat

n. threat, menace, warning, intimidation, blackmail; writing on the wall, danger signal, distress signal; threatening, commination.

adj. threatening, menacing, intimidating, frightening; ominous, imminent.

vb. threaten, menace, intimidate, blackmail, frighten, scare, torment, bully, push around (*inf.*), order about (*inf.*); be brewing, loom, be imminent.

see also **154**

903 philanthropy

n. philanthropy, humanitarianism, utilitarianism, altruism, social conscience; welfare state, social services; patriotism, love of one's country, loyalty, public spirit; nationalism, chauvinism; internationalism.

philanthropist, humanitarian, do-gooder; idealist, altruist, visionary, man with a vision, missionary; patriot, lover of one's country, loyalist, nationalist, chauvinist; internationalist, citizen of the world, cosmopolitan.

adj. philanthropic, humanitarian, humane, kind, altruistic, patriotic; chauvinistic; public-spirited, reforming.

vb. have a social conscience, be public-spirited, show public spirit; love one's country.

904 misanthropy

n. misanthropy, selfishness, egotism, cynicism, unsociability, incivism; misanthrope, man-hater, misogynist, woman-hater, cynic, egoist.

adj. misanthropic, antisocial, unsocial, unsociable, inhuman, cynical; unpatriotic.

see also **885**

905 benefactor

n. benefactor, benefactress, helper, good neighbour, do-gooder, giver, donor, contributor; protector, guard, watch, champion, guardian; patron, supporter, backer; rescuer, deliverer, liberator, redeemer; angel, guardian angel.

see also **640**

906 evildoer

n. evildoer, wrongdoer, trouble-maker, mischief-maker; criminal, law-breaker, offender, transgressor, sinner, public enemy; crook, villain, rogue; thief, gangster, con man (*inf.*); murderer, assassin; ruffian, thug, hooligan, layabout (*inf.*), nasty piece of work (*inf.*); beast, brute, monster, vampire, viper.

see also **684, 723, 940**

907 pity

n. pity, compassion, goodness, kindliness, benevolence, understanding, charity; tenderness, soft-heartedness, warm-heartedness; condolence, sympathy, commiseration, fellow feeling, comfort, solace, consolation; mercy, favour, grace, clemency, forbearance, forgiveness, second chance.

adj. pitying, compassionate, kind, tender, gentle, lenient; merciful, gracious, clement, forbearing, forgiving, generous; sympathetic, consoling, commiserating, comforting, sorry; pitiful, pitiable.

vb. pity, show mercy, take pity on, pardon, spare, forgive, reprieve, give a second chance; relent, relax, repent; put out of one's misery.

sympathize, feel for, feel with, put oneself in someone's shoes, be understanding, express sympathy, commiserate, share another's sorrow, grieve with, weep for, love, console, comfort, support, uphold, encourage, sit by, put one's arm around.

908 pitilessness

n. pitilessness, ruthlessness, mercilessness, relentlessness, cruelty, heartlessness, callousness, hardness of heart; letter of the law, pound of flesh.

adj. pitiless, unpitying, unmerciful, merciless, relentless, unrelenting, unforgiving, barbarous, tyrannical, vindictive, revengeful; rough, harsh, severe; cruel, brutal, savage; cold, unsympathetic, unfeeling, unmoved, inflexible; hard-hearted, stony-hearted, cold-blooded.

vb. show no pity, stop at nothing (*inf.*), harden one's heart, turn a deaf ear to, give no quarter, exact one's pound of flesh; one's heart bleeds for (*inf.*).

909 gratitude

n. gratitude, thankfulness, appreciation, gratefulness, sense of obligation; thanks, thank-you, acknowledgement, response, recognition, praise, tribute, vote of thanks, honour, credit; blessing, grace, prayer, benediction; bread-and-butter letter; reward, trip; leaving-present.

adj. grateful, thankful, appreciative, responsive; indebted, obliged, much obliged; pleased, gratified, overwhelmed.

vb. thank, say thank you, show one's gratitude, respond, appreciate, show one's appreciation, acknowledge, recognize, praise, pay a tribute to, never forget, applaud; reward, tip; give thanks, say grace, return thanks.

910 ingratitude

n. ingratitude, ungratefulness, lack of appreciation, thanklessness, no sense of obligation; thoughtlessness, rudeness.

adj. ungrateful, unappreciative, unmindful, forgetful, rude; thankless, unrewarding, unprofitable, worthless; unthanked, unacknowledged, unrewarded.

vb. be ungrateful, not thank, take for granted, presume upon.

911 forgiveness

n. forgiveness, pardon, free pardon, absolution; remission, acquittal, release, discharge; exoneration, exculpation; justification, reconciliation, redemption, atonement; reprieve, amnesty, indemnity; grace, mercy, patience, forbearance.

adj. forgiven, pardoned, excused, absolved, let off, acquitted, free, not guilty, released, reinstated, reconciled, restored, taken back, welcomed home; redeemed, justified, adopted.

vb. forgive, pardon, excuse, remit, reprieve, clear, absolve, discharge, acquit, free, declare not guilty, let off (*inf.*), let go; let pass, disregard, ignore, shut one's eyes to, grant amnesty to; show mercy, tolerate, forbear; redeem, reconcile, justify; purge, blot one's sins out, wipe the slate clean; bury the hatchet, make it up, kiss and make up; forgive and forget, let bygones be bygones.

see also **921, 961**

912 revenge

n. revenge, vengeance, requital, reprisal, retaliation; vindictiveness, spitefulness, rancour; avenger, vindicator.

adj. revengeful, vengeant, spiteful, retaliatory, unrelenting, rancorous, unappeasable, implacable.

vb. avenge, take revenge, take vengeance, requite, vindicate, retaliate, get even with, get one's own back.

see also **647**

913 jealousy

n. jealousy, resentment, intolerance, distrust, suspicion, green eye, green-eyed monster; rivalry, unfaithfulness, hostility; vigilance, watchfulness, possessiveness.

adj. jealous, green-eyed, resentful, distrustful, suspicious, vigilant, watchful, possessive.

914 envy

n. envy, covetousness, resentment.

adj. envious, covetous, jealous.

vb. envy, covet, lust after, desire, crave, hanker; grudge, begrudge.

E Moral

915 right

n. right, justice, rightfulness, lawfulness,

legality, legitimacy, fairness, equity, impartiality, poetic justice; suitability, reasonableness, fittingness; the right thing, what is right, the proper thing, square deal, fair play.

adj. right, correct, precise, true, valid, accurate; appropriate, proper, suitable, apt, fit, on the right track; fair, honest, upright, righteous, just, rightful, lawful, legitimate, equitable, impartial, objective, unprejudiced, unbiased, disinterested, dispassionate, straightforward, plain; fair and square, straight, fair-minded, sporting.

vb. be just, play the game, try to be fair, do justice to, do the right thing, give the Devil his due.

see also 577

916 wrong

n. wrong, wrongness, injustice, wrongfulness, inequity, unfairness, partiality, partisanship, prejudice, bias, favouritism; foul play, raw deal, irregularity; grievance, injury; preferential treatment, discrimination, reverse discrimination, nepotism.

adj. wrong, unjust, wrongful, unreasonable, unfair, inequitable, partial, biased, prejudiced, partisan, uneven, unbalanced; below the belt, not cricket (*inf.*), unsportsmanlike; erroneous, imprecise, inaccurate, on the wrong track, at fault; injurious, harmful; wicked, sinful, unsuitable, unfitting, inappropriate, improper; unjustifiable, inexcusable, unforgivable; inadmissible, illegal, illicit, illegitimate.

vb. do wrong, break the law, wrong, hurt, injure, harm, treat unfairly, maltreat, cheat; discriminate, favour, prefer, show preference, be biased, show partiality; not play the game properly, not play fair, hit below the belt.

see also 416, 578

917 dueness

n. dueness, due; deserts, come-uppance, just deserts, merits; right, human rights, rights of man, women's rights; dues, fees, levy, contribution; reward, compensation; punishment; privilege, responsibility, prerogative.

adj. due, owing, payable, overdue, outstanding, unpaid, unsettled, in arrears, chargeable; deserved, well-deserved, merited, worthy, just, warranted, entitled, deserving, worthy, needy, rightful, meritorious.

vb. be due, become due, mature, deserve, merit, have the right to, be entitled to; be worthy of, warrant, expect, earn, claim, lay claim to; demand one's rights; have it coming to one (*inf.*), have only oneself to thank, serve someone right.

918 undueness

n. undueness, unfittingness; presumption, assumption, overstepping, arrogation, violation, encroachment; dispossession, disentitlement, forfeiture, disfranchisement.

adj. undue, undeserved, unmerited, unwarranted, uncalled for, improper, unnecessary, immoderate; unworthy, unjust, unfair, undeserving; unentitled, unprivileged.

vb. have no right to, presume, venture, overstep, assume, usurp, violate, not be entitled to, take liberties; not expect; disqualify, invalidate, disentitle, disfranchise.

919 duty

n. duty, obligation, liability, responsibility, burden, onus; accountability; engagement, commitment, pledge, contract, debt; call of duty, sense of duty, moral obligation, conscience, still small voice; loyalty, faithfulness, allegiance.

adj. incumbent, up to one, behoving; obliged, duty-bound, under obligation; liable, responsible, answerable, subject to, accountable; obligatory, binding, compulsory, necessary; dutiful, obedient, submissive, tractable, compliant.

vb. be one's duty, be the duty of, should, ought, had better, behove; be responsible for, rest with, devolve on, rest on the shoulders of, fall to, fall to one's lot; accept responsibility, commit oneself; do one's duty, do what is expected of one, perform, fulfil, acquit oneself well, meet one's obligations; impose a duty, call upon, enjoin, look to; oblige, bind, saddle with, put under obligation.

920 neglect of duty

n. neglect, disregard, omission, evasion, non-observance, dereliction, negligence; carelessness, slackness, remissness, slovenliness; absence, absenteeism, truancy; defection, desertion, mutiny; disloyalty, unfaithfulness.

adj. negligent, inattentive, careless, slack, undutiful; disloyal, unfaithful; rebellious, mutinous.

vb. neglect, fail, break, violate; pass over, let slip, let go, omit, ignore, evade, shirk; defer, postpone, procrastinate; suspend, discard, dismiss; rebel, mutiny; absent oneself, play truant; let someone down, not trouble oneself.

see also 393

921 exemption

n. exemption, immunity, privilege; freedom, liberation, release, dispensation, exception, absolution; permission, leave; lifting of restrictions; escape-clause.

adj. exempt, free, clear, non-liable, not subject to, not chargeable; immune, privileged; unaffected, unrestrained, uncontrolled, unbound, unrestricted; outside.

vb. exempt, free, clear, release, acquit, discharge; lift restrictions; shrug off, pass the buck (*inf.*); be exempt, be free, enjoy immunity, get away with murder (*inf.*).

see also 680, 961

922 respect

n. respect, regard, honour, esteem, appreciation, favour, admiration, recognition, high opinion, high regard, deference, liking, love; praise, reverence, veneration, awe, worship; respects, bow, curtsy, salute, greeting, salutation.

adj. respectful, deferential, courteous, polite, admiring, showing respect for; attentive, reverential; on one's knees, prostrate.

respected, highly regarded, valued, appreciated, esteemed, honoured, time-honoured, important, well thought of.

vb. respect, regard highly, think well of, think a great deal of, have a high opinion of, admire, take off one's hat to (*inf.*), value, appreciate, honour, hold dear; praise, extol, revere, worship; pay one's respects, bow, kneel, curtsy, welcome, greet; scrape, grovel; keep in with (*inf.*), keep on the right side of; stand in awe of.

command respect, impress, overawe, awe, stun, overwhelm, humble.

923 disrespect

n. disrespect, discourtesy, impoliteness, irreverence, dishonour, low opinion, low regard; insult, affront, offence, humiliation, slight, snub, rebuff, slap in the face, backhanded compliment.

adj. disrespectful, discourteous, impolite, irreverent, dishonourable, insulting, offensive, slighting, cutting, humiliating, rude, scornful, impertinent, depreciating, pejorative.

vb. have no respect for, show disrespect for, have a low opinion of, have no time for, underrate, dishonour, offend, insult, affront, slight, snub, rebuff, scorn, despise, look down on (*inf.*), humiliate, interrupt.

924 contempt

n. contempt, scorn, disdain, ridicule, mocking, derision, disrespect, disdainfulness, contemptuousness, scornfulness, snobbishness, haughtiness; sneer, slight, scoff, cold shoulder.

adj. contemptuous, disdainful, scornful, disrespectful, haughty, supercilious, insolent, snooty, snobbish; contemptible, mean, poor, base, worthless, shameful, despicable, beneath contempt.

vb. despise, disdain, spurn, scorn, pour scorn on, turn one's nose up at (*inf.*), sneer at, mock, laugh at, ridicule, deride; pity, look down on (*inf.*), look down one's nose at (*inf.*); disregard, cut dead; avoid, shun, steer clear of; cheapen, belittle, pooh-pooh, not care a fig for.

see also 853

925 approval

n. approval, recognition, acknowledgment; satisfaction; agreement, permission, sanction, adoption, acceptance; admiration, esteem, credit, honour; compliment, bouquet, commendation, citation, write-up; praise, glorification; applause, clapping, ovation, acclaim.

adj. approving, favourable, complimentary, commendatory, laudatory; approvable, commendable, laudable, praiseworthy, creditable, acceptable; approved, popular, praised, uncensored.

vb. approve, recognize, acknowledge; agree, give permission, allow, sanction; accept, adopt, favour; not reject, not sniff at; praise, admire, esteem, compliment, commend, speak well of, write up, crack up (*inf.*), take off one's hat to (*inf.*), give full marks to, must hand it to (*inf.*); find no fault with, have nothing but praises for; sing the praises of, rave about (*inf.*); clap, applaud, cheer, acclaim, hail, give a big hand to.

926 disapproval

n. disapproval, disagreement, nonacceptance, objection, criticism, complaint, opposition, rejection, contradiction, denunciation, censure, fault-finding, reprehension, judgment, blame, reproach, sneer, taunt.

rebuke, reprimand, reproof, admonition, talking to, telling off, lecture, piece of one's mind; brickbat; dissatisfaction, discontent, displeasure.

adj. disapproving, critical, hostile, reproachful, sneering, taunting, reproving, chiding, censorious, condemnatory, defamatory; niggling, fault-finding; unfavourable, uncomplimentary, disparaging; shocked, not amused.

objectionable, blameworthy, reprehensible, not good enough, in a person's bad books, not all it is cracked up to be (*inf.*).

vb. disapprove, disagree, not accept, not think much of, not hold with, hold no brief for, frown on; run down, disparage, belittle; object to, oppose, contradict; boo, hiss; blame, reproach, incriminate; snub, taunt, sneer.

criticize, complain, denounce, find fault with, pick holes; reprehend, reprove, rebuke, reprimand, admonish, upbraid, judge, knock (*sl.*), slam (*sl.*), condemn, censure, punish, put someone in his place; tell off, talk to, tick off (*inf.*), speak to, lecture, have words with (*inf.*), dress down (*inf.*), dust down (*inf.*), tear off a strip (*sl.*), chide, scold, take to task, rap over the knuckles (*inf.*), haul over the coals (*inf.*); give a piece of one's mind to, give a person what for (*sl.*).

927 flattery

n. flattery, adulation, compliment, soft soap (*inf.*), eyewash (*sl.*), false praise, insincerity, obsequiousness, fawning, cajolery, wheedling.

flatterer, cajoler, wheedler, hypocrite, toady.

adj. flattering, adulatory, blandishing, complimentary, over-complimentary, unctuous, ingratiating, insincere, smooth, smarmy (*inf.*).

vb. flatter, butter up (*inf.*), suck up to (*sl.*), soft-soap (*inf.*), cajole, wheedle, inveigle; lay it on thick (*inf.*), lay it on with a trowel (*inf.*).

see also **881**

928 disparagement

n. disparagement, depreciation, detraction, degradation, debasement, vilification, discrediting, belittling; defilement, denigration, smear campaign, whispering campaign, muck-raking, mud-slinging, backbiting; slander, libel, calumny, defamation; aspersion, slur, smear, insinuation, innuendo, scandal, gossip.

disparager, critic, slanderer, libeller, backbiter, scandal-monger, muck-raker, mudslinger; mocker, scoffer, cynic, satirist.

adj. disparaging, deprecatory, derogatory, pejorative, denigratory, slanderous, libellous, defamatory, slighting; cynical.

vb. disparage, deprecate, belittle, play down, run down (*inf.*), decry, discredit, cut down to size (*inf.*); denounce, denigrate, blacken; attack, cast aspersions on; criticize, revile, defame, vilify, malign, slight, slur, tarnish, defile, sully, knock (*sl.*), smear; slander, libel; hound; deride, scoff, mock, ridicule.

929 vindication

n. vindication, justification, establishment, support, plea, defence, excuse, extenuation; ground, right, basis; exoneration, exculpation.

adj. vindicating, justifying, excusing; extenuating; justifiable, arguable, defensible, plausible.

vb. vindicate, justify, establish, support, bear out, uphold, confirm, show, prove, demonstrate, maintain, defend, give grounds for; absolve, acquit, clear, exonerate, excuse, make excuses for, make allowances for.

930 accusation

n. accusation, indictment, prosecution, arraignment, impeachment, charge, censure, incrimination, insinuation, slur, exposé, complaint, denunciation, smear, blame, allegation, action, case; frame-up (*inf.*), put-up job.

accuser, plaintiff, prosecutor.

adj. accusing, denunciatory, incriminating, defamatory.

vb. accuse, censure, charge, bring charges, prefer charges, arrest, arraign, impeach, indict, impute, complain, bring a complaint, find fault with, blame, pin blame on, denounce, incriminate, implicate, involve, reprove, slur, attack, recriminate, slander, libel; point the finger at; frame (*sl.*), trump up, concoct, invent, fabricate, construct, bear false witness.

931 probity

n. probity, uprightness, rectitude, honesty, integrity, fidelity, faithfulness, loyalty, morality, goodness, virtue, reliability, conscientiousness, truthfulness, character, principles, high principles.

adj. honourable, upright, moral, right, fair, good, straight, square, virtuous, honest, law-abiding, reputable, reliable, trustworthy, dependable, conscientious, faithful, loyal, straightforward, sincere, frank, candid, principled, scrupulous.

see also **935, 951**

932 improbity

n. improbity, dishonesty, immorality, badness, evil, wickedness, criminality, corruption; cunning, guile; disloyalty, faithlessness, double-dealing, double-crossing, sell-out, duplicity, betrayal, defection, treason, treachery, perfidy, foul play, trick, prank.

adj. dishonest, immoral, bad, wicked, corrupt, evil, criminal, fraudulent; unscrupulous, unprincipled, disreputable; unreliable, undependable, faithless; betraying, treacherous, perfidious, insidious, two-faced, insincere, deceitful, double-dealing; underhand, sly, crafty, devious, shady, dubious, suspicious, questionable, fishy (*sl.*).

vb. be dishonest, lie, cheat, swindle, deceive, betray, double-cross, sell out (*inf.*), two-time (*sl.*).

see also **936, 952**

933 disinterestedness

n. disinterestedness, impartiality, indifference, non-involvement, unconcern, detachment, objectivity, neutrality; selflessness, self-sacrifice, self-denial.

adj. disinterested, impartial, indifferent, unconcerned, unbiased, unprejudiced, dispassionate, objective, fair, unselfish, selfless, self-denying, self-sacrificing, self-effacing, self-forgetful; generous, liberal, magnanimous.

934 selfishness

n. selfishness, self-indulgence, greed, meanness, narrowness; self-worship, narcissism, egoism, vanity, self-interest, self-seeking.

self-seeker, egoist, individualist, timeserver, narcissist, number-one.

adj. selfish, self-centred, self-indulgent, greedy, miserly, mean, narrow; wrapped up in oneself, self-absorbed, self-seeking, egoistic.

vb. be selfish, look after number one.

935 virtue

n. virtue, morality, goodness, uprightness, righteousness, narrow way, sanctity, rectitude; honesty, temperance, kindness, excellence; quality, character, integrity; purity, chastity, innocence; ethics, morals.

adj. virtuous, moral, good, upright, righteous, holy, saintly, angelic; honest, kind, excellent, worthy, proper; perfect, irreproachable, unblemished, immaculate, impeccable; chaste, pure, innocent.

vb. be good, behave oneself, acquit oneself well, keep to the straight and narrow; set a good example.

see also **931, 951**

936 vice

n. vice, wickedness, corruption, iniquity, evil, immorality, perversity, baseness, meanness, malignity, malevolence, grossness, wantonness; degeneration, deterioration; unrighteousness, transgression, ungodliness;

bad habit, besetting sin, failing, weakness, fault.

adj. wicked, evil, bad, corrupt, immoral, wayward, dissolute, perverse, gross, wanton, base, mean, malevolent, perverted, depraved, degenerate, irreligious, sinful, unrighteous, ungodly, unregenerate.

offensive, shocking, outrageous, scandalous, atrocious, abominable, heinous, repugnant, monstrous, unforgivable.

vb. err, stray, fall, lapse, degenerate, transgress, go off the rails (*inf.*); make wicked, corrupt, demoralize, defile, lead astray.

see also **932, 952**

937 innocence

n. innocence, guiltlessness, blamelessness, inculpability, irreproachability, faultlessness, integrity, probity, uprightness, perfection, purity, impeccability; clear conscience, clean hands, clean slate.

adj. innocent, not guilty, above suspicion, in the clear, pure, clean, spotless, unsoiled, untainted, undefiled, blameless, irreproachable, faultless, upright, perfect, impeccable; unoffending, simple, unsophisticated, inexperienced, guileless.

vb. be innocent, have a clear conscience, have nothing to confess.

938 guilt

n. guilt, blame, culpability; responsibility, liability, answerability; criminality, sinfulness; bad conscience, guilty conscience.

crime, offence, transgression, trespass, misdeed, sin, misdemeanour, misconduct, misbehaviour, error, fault, lapse, slip.

adj. guilty, wrong, at fault, offending, to blame, culpable, reproachable; blamed, condemned, judged, incriminated; red-handed, caught in the act.

939 good person

n. good person, good example, model, standard, pattern, ideal, paragon; one in a million, salt of the earth, last word, ultimate; saint, angel, hero, pillar; perfect gentleman; good fellow, good sort, good egg, sport (*sl.*).

see also **905**

940 bad person

n. bad person, wrongdoer, evildoer, sinner, transgressor; reprobate; scoundrel, wretch, villain, miscreant, rogue, rascal, blackguard, knave; bully, scallywag, scamp, scapegrace; wastrel, bum (*sl.*), idler, loafer, prodigal, beggar, tramp; ugly customer, nasty piece of work (*inf.*), bad lot, bad egg; good-for-nothing, ne'er-do-well, black sheep; criminal, crook, liar, cheat, traitor, impostor; rat, louse (*sl.*), worm.

941 penitence

n. penitence, repentance, change of heart, confession, contrition; sorrow, regret, remorse; sackcloth and ashes, hair shirt; penitent, convert, prodigal son.

adj. penitent, repentant, confessing, humble, contrite, conscience-stricken, convicted; regretful, sorry, compunctious, apologetic, full of regrets.

vb. repent, confess, acknowledge, plead guilty, humble oneself, own up, admit; feel shame, deplore; be penitent, be sorry, regret, apologize; turn from sin, see the light, be converted.

942 impenitence

n. impenitence, hardness of heart, heart of stone, seared conscience, obduracy; no regrets; hardened sinner.

adj. impenitent, unrepentant, uncontrite; hard, insensitive, callous, stubborn, obdurate, unashamed; incorrigible, irredeemable; dead, lost.

vb. be impenitent, have no regrets, show no remorse; harden one's heart.

943 atonement

n. atonement, satisfaction, amends, apology, redress, compensation, indemnity, retribution, requital, repayment, restitution, reparation.

propitiation, reconciliation, sacrifice, offering; substitute, representative; scapegoat; expiation; penance; purgatory.

adj. atoning, satisfying, indemnificatory, compensatory; propitiatory, reconciliatory, sacrificial, redemptive; substitutionary, representative, vicarious.

vb. atone, make amends, redress, compensate, indemnify, requite, repay; apologize; propitiate, reconcile, appease, satisfy, redeem.

944 temperance

n. temperance, moderation, abstemiousness, restraint, self-restraint, self-control, self-discipline; self-denial, abstinence, teetotalism; abstainer, total abstainer, teetotaller.

adj. temperate, moderate, restrained, disciplined, careful; self-denying, self-controlled, abstinent; continent; sparing, frugal, plain; abstemious, sober.

vb. be temperate, exercise self-control, control oneself, deny oneself, abstain, refrain; know when to stop, know when one has had enough.

945 intemperance

n. intemperance, excess, extravagance, inordinateness, self-indulgence; sensuality, voluptuousness, carnality, flesh; luxury, high living; dissipation, debauchery; hedonism, epicureanism.

adj. intemperate, immoderate, unrestrained, inordinate, excessive, self-indulgent; sensual, sensuous, voluptuous, carnal, bodily, fleshly, gluttonous, debauched; high-living, pleasure-loving, epicurean, hedonistic.

vb. be intemperate, indulge oneself, have one's fling, sow one's wild oats, paint the town red (*sl.*), not know when to stop, overeat, drink too much.

946 ascetism

n. ascetism, austerity, abstinence, abstemiousness, mortification, plain living.

ascetic, self-denier, recluse, hermit, anchorite, stylite; fakir, dervish, flagellant.

adj. ascetic, austere, plain, severe, rigid, stern, abstemious, puritanical, rigorous.

947 fasting

n. fasting, abstinence, hunger, starvation; fast, bread and water, short commons, diet, slimming; fast-day, Lent, Ramadan.

adj. fasting, abstinent, abstaining, starving, hungry, unfed, famished, Lenten.

vb. fast, eat nothing, go hungry, starve, famish; go on hunger strike; diet, reduce weight, slim, take off weight.

948 gluttony

n. gluttony, greed, voracity, rapacity, insatiability, intemperance, excess, indulgence.

glutton, pig (*inf.*), guzzler, hog, greedy-guts (*sl.*); gourmand, epicure.

adj. greedy, gluttonous, ravenous, devouring, guzzling.

vb. overeat, stuff oneself, make a pig of oneself (*inf.*), eat like a horse, devour, guzzle, gobble, gulp down, bolt down; eat out of house and home.

949 soberness

n. soberness, sobriety, temperance, abstinence, teetotalism, prohibition.

sober person, abstainer, teetotaller, total abstainer, prohibitionist, Band of Hope, Temperance League.

adj. sober, temperate, abstinent, teetotal, on the wagon (*sl.*), off drink, clear-headed, in one's right mind, in possession of one's senses, unintoxicated, stone-cold sober, dry.

vb. be sober, not drink, sign the pledge; hold one's drink, have a good head for drink; sober up, sleep it off (*inf.*).

950 drunkenness

n. drunkenness, intoxication, inebriety, insobriety, intemperance; alcoholism, dipsomania; a drop too much, tipsiness; drinking-bout, pub-crawl, party, celebration, orgy; pink elephants; hangover, head, headache.

drunkard, drinker, heavy drinker, hard drinker, tippler, boozer, alcoholic, drunk (*sl.*).

adj. drunk, intoxicated, inebriated, under the influence, tipsy, befuddled; on the bottle; happy, high, lit up (*inf.*); seeing double, glassy-eyed; groggy; the worse for drink, sloshed (*sl.*), tight (*inf.*), stoned (*sl.*), blotto (*sl.*), canned (*sl.*), sozzled (*sl.*), plastered (*sl.*), under the table.

vb. drink, booze, guzzle, tipple, wet one's whistle (*inf.*), hit the bottle, drink like a fish, drown one's sorrows; be merry, be tipsy, have a drop too much, have one over the eight; be drunk, have more than one can hold, see double, get stoned out of one's mind (*sl.*); intoxicate, inebriate, go to one's head.

951 purity

n. purity, cleanness, cleanliness, whiteness; sinlessness, perfection; untaintedness, unsulliedness, spotlessness, immaculateness.

morality, chastity, virtue, decency, abstemiousness, virginity; prudery, primness, prudishness, overmodesty, false modesty, squeamishness; prude, prig, old maid.

adj. pure, clean, perfect, sinless; unsullied, untainted, spotless, undefiled, unadulterated, uncontaminated; decent, demure, abstemious; edifying; chaste, virtuous; continent, celibate, virgin, platonic; prudish, prim, squeamish, shockable, narrow, strict, Victorian, puritanical, strait-laced, old-maidish; simple, innocent, guileless, artless; inexperienced.

see also **931, 935**

952 impurity

n. impurity, uncleanness, sinfulness, imperfection, taintedness, sulliedness, contamination, pollution, adulteration.

immorality, unchastity, indecency, looseness of morals, permissive society; lewdness, prurience, profligacy, incontinence, lechery, wantonness, licentiousness, dissoluteness, salaciousness, lasciviousness; lust, sensuality, eroticism; obscenity, filth, dirt, smut, pornography; free love, promiscuity, adultery, wife-swapping (*inf.*), sleeping around (*inf.*), fornication, unfaithfulness, infidelity, affair, relationship, liaison, eternal triangle; seduction, rape, assault, violation, defilement; prostitution, street-walking, harlotry, whoredom; homosexuality, lesbianism, sodomy, incest.

adj. impure, unclean, imperfect, tainted, sullied, contaminated, polluted, adulterated; immoral, unchaste, indecent, loose, slack, of loose morals, easy, fast, wild, promiscuous, of easy virtue, permissive; lewd, profligate, lecherous, licentious, lascivious, wanton, dissolute, salacious, debauched; sensual, erotic; vulgar, coarse, risqué, spicy, obscene, filthy, dirty, smutty, lurid, sexy, pornographic, blue, unprintable, unexpurgated; homosexual, gay (*sl.*), queer (*sl.*), lesbian; extramarital, unlawful, illicit, adulterous, incestuous.

vb. be impure, commit adultery, fornicate, sleep around (*inf.*); seduce, take advantage of (*inf.*), rape, assault, violate; go on the streets, walk the streets, prostitute, adulterate, contaminate; sully, taint, pollute.

see also **932, 936**

953 libertine

n. libertine, profligate, Don Juan, rake, womanizer, lecher, adulterer, seducer, rapist, fornicator; homosexual, homo (*inf.*), queer (*sl.*), gay (*sl.*), fairy (*sl.*), pansy (*inf.*), nancy (*sl.*), butch (*sl.*), transvestite, pervert; lesbian.

adultress, woman of easy virtue, loose woman, flirt, tart (*sl.*), slut, pick-up (*inf.*); mistress; prostitute, pro, call-girl, fallen woman, whore, harlot, street-walker, hustler (*sl.*).

954 legality

n. legality, legitimacy, lawfulness, permissibility, validity, constitutionality; legislation, law-giving, law-making, authorization, codification, sanction, enactment; right, authority, justice; jurisprudence.

law, statute, decree, ordinance, act, edict, order, code, regulation, rule, by-law, constitution.

adj. legal, legitimate, lawful, right, just; constitutional; permissible, permitted, valid, sanctioned, codified, authorized, prescribed, within the law, statutory; jurisprudential, nomothetic.

vb. legalize, permit, authorize, sanction, approve, validate, establish, enforce, pass, license, charter, empower; legislate.

see also **103, 626**

955 illegality

n. illegality, unlawfulness, unconstitutionality, miscarriage of justice, injustice; lawbreaking, violation, transgression, trespass, contravention, encroachment, infringement, offence, wrong, crime.

lawlessness, antinomianism, irresponsibility, terrorism, anarchism, mob rule, chaos, disorder, breakdown of law and order.

illegitimacy, bastardy; bastard, illegitimate child, natural child, love child.

adj. illegal, unlawful, illicit, forbidden, prohibited, banned, unauthorized, wrong, against the law, outside the law; stolen, black-market, smuggled, contraband; lawless, wild, chaotic, anarchic, irresponsible; illegitimate, bastard, natural, born out of wedlock, born on the wrong side of the blanket, born without benefit of clergy (*inf.*).

vb. break the law, disobey, commit, violate, transgress, contravene, infringe; take the law into one's own hands, be a law unto oneself; nullify, abrogate, void, annul, cancel.

956 jurisdiction

n. jurisdiction, authority, control, direction, supervision; right, power, responsibility, capacity, competence; executive, corporation, administration; domain, extent, scope, range, territory.

police, police force, constabulary; police officer, policeman, constable, officer, copper (*sl.*), cop (*sl.*), rozzer (*sl.*), fuzz (*sl.*); traffic warden, meter maid.

adj. jurisdictional, judiciary, competent, responsible, judicial, executive.

vb. administer, preside, direct, supervise; judge; police, keep order, control.

957 tribunal

n. tribunal, court, assizes, session, bench, bar; judgment seat, mercy seat, throne; dock, witness-box; courthouse.

958 judge

n. judge, justice, J.P., recorder, magistrate, stipendiary, beak (*sl.*); judiciary; marshal; jury, panel, tribunal; juror, juryman, jurywoman, foreman.

see also **653, 960**

959 lawyer

n. lawyer, legal practitioner; the bar, legal profession; defender, counsel, barrister, advocate, bencher; legal adviser, attorney, procurator, solicitor; prosecution; notary, commissioner for oaths; legist, jurist, jurisconsult; pettifogger.

vb. practise law, plead; be called to the bar, take silk; argue, defend, advocate; allege, prosecute.

960 lawsuit

n. lawsuit, case, suit, action, legal proceedings, hearing, indictment; litigation, judicature; summons, writ, subpoena; affidavit, bill; pleadings, argument, prosecution, cross-examination, defence, plea, summing-up; verdict, finding, decision, ruling, pronouncement, sentence, decree, award, precedent; appeal; litigant, party, suitor, plaintiff, defendant.

vb. go to law, prosecute, sue, litigate, bring an action against, bring to trial, file a claim; try, hear, give a hearing to, judge, arbitrate, adjudicate; rest one's case; sum up; rule, find, pronounce, declare, return a verdict, bring in a verdict, pass sentence, sentence, convict, acquit.

961 acquittal

n. acquittal, discharge, reprieve, release, remission, pardon, clearance, dismissal, exoneration, exculpation; innocence; suspended sentence.

adj. acquitted, not guilty, clear, discharged, released, set free, liberated, justified; forgiven.

vb. acquit, declare not guilty, discharge, pardon, absolve, forgive, clear, dismiss, grant remission, reprieve, release, set free, let off (*inf.*), exempt; exonerate, exculpate; justify, vindicate; save, rescue, redeem.

see also **601, 921**

962 condemnation

n. condemnation, denunciation, conviction.

adj. condemnatory, damnatory.

vb. condemn, find guilty, sentence, pass sentence on, judge, convict, punish, doom, damn, curse; proscribe, denounce, criticize, find fault with, blame, rebuke.

963 punishment

n. punishment, reproof, discipline, chastisement, correction, reprimand, retribution; penalty, imposition, fine, damages, costs, compensation; exile, banishment; hard labour; bread and water.

corporal punishment, slap, rap, cuff, blow, clout; capital punishment, death sentence, execution, decapitation, beheading, hanging, electrocution, strangling, strangulation, poisoning, crucifixion, impalement, drowning; torture; slaughter, genocide, mass murder, massacre, annihilation.

punisher; executioner, hangman, firing squad; inquisition.

adj. punitive, penal, castigatory, disciplinary, corrective.

vb. punish, reprove, discipline, chastise, correct, sentence, take to task, admonish, rebuke, reprimand, dress down (*inf.*), come down on like a ton of bricks (*inf.*), crack down on (*inf.*); make an example of; retaliate, get one's revenge, get even with.

expel, exile, banish, deport, transport, outlaw, isolate, send to Coventry; imprison, jail; penalize, fine, endorse one's licence.

strike, hit, slap, rap over the knuckles, box on the ears; flog, whip, beat, thrash, scourge, flay; spank, give a good hiding (*inf.*), thrash the living daylights out of (*sl.*), lick (*sl.*), tan (*sl.*), belt, strap, clout, wallop (*sl.*), cane, whack (*inf.*).

kill, put to death, shoot, execute, behead, guillotine, decapitate; hang, lynch; hang, draw, and quarter; crucify, impale; electrocute, gas; strangle; burn at the stake; drown; poison; slaughter, annihilate, massacre; torture, martyr, put on the rack, break on the wheel, tar and feather.

be punished, suffer, pay the penalty, get one's just deserts, have it coming, deserve; face the music, take the rap.

see also 926

964   means of punishment

n. scourge, birch, whip, lash, belt, cane, rod, stick, switch, cat-o'-ninetails; pillory, stocks, ducking stool, whipping post; torture chamber, rack, wheel, screw, water torture; axe, guillotine; block, scaffold; cross, stake; gallows, gibbet, noose, rope; electric chair, gas chamber, death chamber; condemned cell.

965   reward

n. reward, pay, payment, compensation, recompense, remuneration, reimbursement, reparation, redress; allowance, expences, honorarium; tip, gratuity; prize, award, trophy, bonus, premium, bounty, accolade, guerdon.

adj. rewarding, remunerative, compensatory; profitable, advantageous, worthwhile; charitable, liberal, generous, open-handed, unsparing.

vb. reward, pay, recompense, reimburse, redress, compensate; award, recognize, pay tribute, present, give, bestow, confer, grant, thank.

see also 663, 715

F   Religious

966   divinity

n. divinity, divineness, deity, godhead; God, Spirit, Supreme Being, Creator, prime mover, Providence.

adj. divine, spiritual; godlike, godly; heavenly, celestial, sublime; transcendent, immanent, self-existent; eternal, everlasting, immortal; almighty, omnipotent, all-powerful, infinite, supreme; omniscient, all-knowing; just, merciful, gracious, loving, personal.

967   God

n. God; Trinity; Father, Lord, Yahweh, Jehovah, Almighty, King of Kings; Son of God, Jesus Christ, Son of Man, Immanuel, Word, Messiah, Saviour, Redeemer; Holy Spirit, Holy Ghost, Comforter, Paraclete.

god, goddess, object of worship; idol, false god; golden calf; pantheon; numen; totem, fetish; mumbo-jumbo.

supreme deity, Zeus, Jupiter; goddess of women and marriage, Hera, Juno; goddess of crops, Demeter, Ceres; god of the sun, Phoebus, god of music, medicine, and poetry, Apollo; god of war, Ares, Mars; god of commerce, eloquence, and cunning, Hermes, Mercury; god of the sea, Poseidon, Neptune; god of metalworking, Hephaestus, Vulcan; god of wine and revelry, Dionysus, Bacchus; god of the underworld, Hades, Pluto, Dis; god of agriculture, Kronos, Saturn; god of love, Eros, Cupid; goddess of love and beauty, Aphrodite, Venus; goddess of the moon and hunting, Artemis, Diana; goddess of wisdom, Athena, Minerva; god of the countryside, Pan, Faunus.

Allah; Brahma, Atman, Vishnu, Shiva, Buddha.

968   good spirit

n. good spirit, angel, ministering spirit, seraph, cherub, host, principalities, authorities, powers, thrones, dominions; archangel.

adj. angelic, ministering, heavenly, celestial.

969   evil spirit

n. devil, Satan, fallen angel, father of lies, Beelzebub, prince of this world, prince of darkness; demon, evil spirit, unclean spirit, powers of darkness; imp, fiend, vampire; adversary.

adj. satanic, devilish, diabolic, diabolical, wicked.

see also 984

970 mythical being

n. fairy, spirit, elf, brownie, goblin, hob, bogle, body, kobold, hobgoblin, dryad, pixie, gnome, peri; sprite, genie, jinnee; nymph; wood-nymph, hamadryad; mountain-nymph, oread; water-nymph, naiad; sea-nymph, nereid; siren, mermaid, water-spirit, water-elf, nix, nixie, kelpie; imp, puck, leprechaun, gremlin, urchin; changeling; sylph; dwarf, troll.

adj. fairy, mythical, imaginary, fabulous; elfin, elfish, impish.

971 ghost

n. ghost, spectre, spook (inf.), apparition, vision, phantom, phantasm, appearance, shade, presence, poltergeist, wraith, doppelgänger, double, fetch, visitant, spirit, departed spirit, zombie.

adj. ghostly, spooky (inf.), supernatural, evil, haunted, eerie, weird, uncanny, phantom.

vb. haunt, visit, walk, return from the dead.

972 heaven

n. heaven, paradise, bliss, glory, kingdom of heaven, Abraham's bosom, heavenly city, next world, world to come, eternal rest, kingdom-come (sl.), happy hunting ground, Elysium; rapture, resurrection, translation, ascension, glorification.

adj. heavenly, celestial, blesssed, glorious, glorified, empyrean.

973 hell

n. hell, perdition, underworld, lower world, nether regions, bottomless pit, abyss, inferno, everlasting fire, lake of fire and brimstone, place of the lost, place of torment, pandemonium; Sheol, Gehenna.

adj. hellish, infernal.

974 religion

n. religion, belief, faith, dogma, teaching, doctrine, creed, tenet, revelation, articles of faith, confession; theology.

deism, theism, monotheism, polytheism, pantheism; animism; gnosticism.

Christianity, Judaism; Islam, Buddhism, Hinduism, Brahmanism, Taoism, Confucianism.

teacher; prophet, apostle; preacher, lay-preacher, exponent, interpreter, commentator, evangelist, missionary.

adj. religious, spiritual, divine, holy, sacred; theological, doctrinal; devout, godly, believing, practising, faithful, regenerate, converted.

see also 980

975 irreligion

n. irreligion, ungodliness, godlessness, unholiness, unspirituality, wickedness, sinfulness; idolatry, heathenism, paganism; atheism, unbelief; disbelief, scepticism, doubt, agnosticism; heresy, antichristianity; rationalism, free thinking, materialism.

unbeliever, atheist; agnostic, doubter, sceptic, doubting Thomas; idolater; heathen, pagan; infidel, heretic, dissenter.

adj. irreligious, ungodly, godless, wicked, sinful, idolatrous, heathen, pagan; unbelieving, atheistic; heretical, unorthodox; disbelieving, sceptical, agnostic; materialistic, secular, worldy, profane; unregenerate, unconverted, lost, damned.

see also 981

976 revelation

n. revelation, disclosure; inspiration, afflatus, prophecy, vision; signs, foreshadowing; Scripture, Bible, Word of God, canon; Talmud, Torah, Ten Commandments; Law, Gospel.

Koran, Vedas.

adj. revelational, inspirational, inspired, revealed, prophetic, biblical, scriptural, canonical; evangelical; authoritative.

977 orthodoxy

n. orthodoxy, soundness, faithfulness, strictness, truth, adherence, observance.

the Church, body of Christ, Church invisible, Church militant, Church triumphant, Christendom; believer, true believer, Christian, practising Christian, church member, the saints, the faithful.

adj. orthodox, sound, correct, right, pure, true, faithful; evangelical, conservative, strict, literal, fundamentalist; practising, believing.

978 heresy

n. heresy, heterodoxy; divergence, aberration, distortion, perversion, unorthodoxy, unauthenticity, apostasy, infidelity.

adj. heretical, heterodox, divergent, different, unorthodox, unsound, unscriptural, unbiblical.

979 sectarianism

n. sectarianism, partisanship, schismatism, separatism; denominationalism; party-spirit.

sect, schism, split, section, faction, division, branch; denomination, communion, tradition, off-shoot, secession; sectarian, party-man, seceder, dissident, non-conformist, rebel.

adj. sectarian, partisan, schismatic, party-minded; denominational; dissident, non-conformist; separatist, secessionist, breakaway; exclusive.

980 piety

n. piety, devoutness; devotion, single-mindedness; trust, faith; loyalty, submission, dedication, commitment, faithfulness, adherence, perseverance, allegiance, zeal, ardour, earnestness; adoration, worship, reverence, fear, awe, prayerfulness; holiness, sanctity, consecration, godliness, saintliness, humility, spirituality.

saint, believer, convert, man of prayer, man of God; follower, disciple, pilgrim; pietist.

adj. pious, devout, devoted, faithful, loyal, dedicated, committed, single-minded, zealous, earnest; believing, practising, holy, godly, saintly, spiritual, sanctified, consecrated, other-worldly, humble, meek.

vb. be pious, repent and believe, have faith, trust, fear God; keep the faith, persevere; worship, pray; sanctify, consecrate, make holy, dedicate, hallow.

981 impiety

n. impiety, godlessness, irreverence, unrighteousness, unholiness, sinfulness, disobedience; worldliness; blasphemy, sacrilege, desecration, defilement, violation.

hypocrisy, sanctimoniousness, false piety, self-righteousness, religiosity, formalism, hallowness, churchianity (*inf.*), religious show, façade, lip service, cant.

sinner, blasphemer; scoffer, mocker; materialist, worldling; hypocrite, Pharisee, scribe.

adj. impious, irreligious, ungodly, godless, irreverent, unholy, unrighteous, sinful, wicked, disobedient; unbelieving, atheistic, agnostic, non-practising; unhallowed, unsanctified, unregenerate, hardened; blasphemous, sacrilegious, profane; sanctimonious, hypocritical, pharasaical, false, deceitful, insincere, dishonest.

vb. be impious, sin, blaspheme; desecrate, profane, pay lip service.

982 worship

n. worship, honour, reverence, praise, adoration, exaltation, homage, veneration; service, devotions; prayer, private devotion, quiet time, meditation; confession; thanksgiving, grace; supplication, request, entreaty, appeal, petition, intercession, rogation;

hymn, song, psalm, chant, anthem, canticle, chorus.

worshipper, church-goer, Christian, communicant; supplicant, petitioner, intercessor, man of prayer; congregation, church, flock, assembly.

adj. worshipping, devoted, reverent, religious, devout, prayerful, on one's knees, supplicant; worshipful, reverential, solemn, holy, serious, dignified, sublime, majestic, glorious.

vb. worship, adore, praise, glorify, bless, exalt, honour, magnify, revere, venerate, pay homage to, laud, bow down, humble oneself; idolize; pray to, seek; confess; thank, give thanks, ask, invoke, entreat, petition, implore, intercede, say one's prayers, beseech; sing; meditate, contemplate, consider, reflect.

see also **977**

983 idolatry

n. idolatry, idolism, idol worship, irreligion, heathenism, paganism, fetishism, demonism, devil-worship, hero-worship, iconolatry, image-worship, mumbo-jumbo; idolization, deification, apotheosis.

idol, false god, image, graven image, icon, statue, golden calf, totem, fetish.

idolater, idolizer, pagan, heathen, image-maker.

adj. idolatrous, heathen, pagan, idol-worshipping.

vb. idolatrize, idolize, worship, enshrine, deify; sing the praises of, put on a pedestal, admire, dote on, treasure.

984 sorcery

n. sorcery, magic, superstition, witchcraft, diabolism, black magic, occultism, cabbala, exorcism, divination; miracle-working, thaumaturgy; spell, incantation, bewitchment, enchantment, influence, possession, trance, hocus-pocus, mumbo-jumbo, open sesame, abracadabra; charm, amulet, talisman, mascot, fetish, goodluck charm.

spiritism, spiritualism, spirit communication; séance, sitting; ouija board, planchette, automatic writing; levitation.

sorcerer, wizard, witch, enchanter, spellbinder, magician, conjurer; soothsayer, clairvoyant; astrologer; shaman, witch-doctor, medicine-man; voodoo; thaumaturgist, miracle-worker; diviner; exorcist; occultist, necromancer, spiritualist.

adj. sorcerous, devilish, diabolical, occult, necromantic; spell-binding; magical, supernatural, weird, uncanny, eerie; charmed, bewitched, enchanted; mystic, esoteric, transcendental.

vb. divine, conjure; wave a wand; exorcise, lay ghosts; call up spirits; bewitch, enchant, charm, fascinate, mesmerize, obsess, possess, put under a curse; hold a séance; go into a trance; materialize, dematerialize.

see also 447

985 churchdom

n. churchdom, Christendom, the church, ministry; call, vocation; office, holy orders; pastorship, pastorate, priesthood, clerical order, cure of souls, spiritual guidance, pastoral case, service, preaching, administration of the sacraments, prayer; fellowship, communion.

adj. ecclesiastical, ministerial, pastoral, cleric, priestly, sacerdotal.

vb. call, ordain, consecrate, present, nominate; take holy orders.

986 clergyman

n. clergyman, servant of God, shepherd; pastor, preacher, minister, incumbent, priest, vicar, parson, rector; curate, chaplain, cleric, padre, father, reverend; abbot, prelate, bishop, archbishop, prior, dean, archdeacon, canon, primate, Pope; metropolitan, patriarch, cardinal; monk, friar; nun, sister; rabbi, teacher.

adj. clerical, ordained.

vb. be ordained, enter the ministry.

987 laity

n. laity, layman, lay people, parish, congregation, church, fold, flock, assembly, church member, parishioner, brethren; elder, deacon; lay-preacher, lay-reader.

adj. lay, unordained, non-clerical, secular, temporal, of the world, civil, profane, unholy, unconsecrated, unsacred.

vb. laicize, secularize, deconsecrate.

988 religious service

n. ceremony, ordinance, rite, ritual, custom, institution, observance; order, form, litany; administration, celebration, officiation.

service, divine worship, service of worship, morning service, matins, evening service, evensong, vespers, compline, fellowship, prayer meeting, Bible Study, Sunday School; Holy Communion, Lord's Supper, mass, Eucharist; baptism.

adj. ritual, ceremonial, customary, formal, liturgical.

vb. observe, keep, celebrate, minister, administer, officiate, perform, dedicate, bless, pray, baptize, worship; encourage, share, fellowship.

989 vestment

n. vestment, cloth, clerical dress, canonicals, robes, surplice, gown, mantle, cassock, rochet, chasuble, cape, hood; mitre, staff, crook, crosier.

990 church building

n. church, chapel, sanctuary, house of prayer, house of God, Lord's house, bethel, kirk, tabernacle; mission, house-church, meeting-house; cathedral, minster, abbey; monastery, priory, friary, convent, nunnery; synagogue; mosque, shrine, temple.

INDEX

A

A-1 *adj.* 579
abacus *n.* 38
abandon *vb.* 546, 556, 607, 687, 713
abasement *n.* 869, 874
abate *vb.* 37, 176, 197
abbey *n.* 990
abbot *n.* 986
abbreviate *vb.* 203, 504, 527
ABC *n.* 88, 493
abdicate *vb.* 556, 687
abduct *vb.* 720, 722
aberrant *adj.* 285
aberration *n.* 412, 978
abet *vb.* 636
abeyance *n.* 607, 610
abhorrence *n.* 637, 892
abhorrent *adj.* 862, 892
abide *vb.* 112, 143, 145, 191
able *adj.* 159, 434, 627
ablution *n.* 583
abnormality *n.* 106, 439
abode *n.* 191
abolish *vb.* 2, 164, 607, 686
abolitionist *n.* 167
abominable *adj.* 862, 892, 936
abomination *n.* 892
aborigine *n.* 190
abortion *n.* 370
abortive *adj.* 662
abound *vb.* 572
about *adv., prep.* 9, 229
about-turn *n.* 147, 220, 289
above *adj.* 118; *adv.* 84
above-mentioned *adj.* 118
abracadabra *n.* 984
abrade *vb.* 341
abreast *adv.* 238
abridge *vb.* 197, 203, 504, 527
abrogation *n.* 686
abrupt *adj.* 115, 887
abscond *vb.* 600
absence *n.* 76, **189**
absence of choice *n.* **541**
absence of colour *n.* **806**
absence of form *n.* **243**
absence of habit *n.* **546**

absence of intellect *n.* **383**
absence of relation *n.* **10**
absence of thought *n.* **385**
absence of time *n.* **108**
absence of wonder *n.* **867**
absent *adj.* 189
absenteeism *n.* 189, 920
absent-minded *adj.* 391, 442
absolute *adj.* 46, 56, 408
absolute difference *n.* **14**
absolutely *adv.* 56
absolute state *n.* 7
absolution *n.* 911, 921
absorb *vb.* 302, 350, 472
absorbed *adj.* 384
absorbent *adj.* 264
absorbing *adj.* 755
absorption *n.* 302, 384
abstain *vb.* 541, 555, 610, 944
abstainer *n.* 944, 949
abstaining *adj.* 947
abstemious *adj.* 944, 946, 951
abstinence *n.* 555, 944, 946, 947, 949
abstract *n.* 527; *adj.* 4, 382; *vb.* 203, 527
abstraction *n.* 101
abstruse *adj.* 453, 503
absurdity *n.* **433**, 451, 851
abundance *n.* 26, 32, 75, 168, 572
abuse *n.* 608, 901; *vb.* 569, 608, 900, 901
abusive *adj.* 901
abut *vb.* 199, 201
abyss *n.* 210, 254, 973
academic *n.* 448; *adj.* 453, 470, 472
academy *n.* 475
accede *vb.* 692
accelerate *vb.* 280, 613
accent *n.* 512, 778
accept *vb.* 420, 424, 692, 716, 925
acceptable *adj.* 302, 499, 570, 925
accepted *adj.* 424, 545, 606
access *n.* 302, 559
accessible *adj.* 262, 292
accession *n.* 40, 41

accessories *n.* 192, 568
accessory *n.* 6, 35, 41, **60**; *adj.* 35, 40, 60, 679
accident *n.* 153, 551
accidental *adj.* 158
acclaim *n.* 878, 925; *vb.* 888, 925
acclaimed *adj.* 868
acclimatize *vb.* 105, 545
acclivity *n.* 219, 316
accolade *n.* 663, 965
accommodate *vb.* 105, 302, 545, 652
accommodation *n.* 191
accompaniment *n.* 60, 792
accompany *vb.* 60, 122, 882
accomplice *n.* 640
accomplish *vb.* 159, 609, 659, 661
accomplished *adj.* 581, 627, 659
accomplishment *n.* 609, 659, 661
accord *n.* 24, 643; *vb.* 16, 24, 105, 180
account *n.*
(description) 460, 465, 483, 525;
(money) 736, 742;
vb. (describe) 157, 456, 483, 525; (pay) 742
accountable *adj.* 679, 919
accountant *n.* 733, 742
accounts *n.* **742**
accretion *n.* 40, 41
accrue *vb.* 36, 40, 705, 716
accumulate *vb.* 36, 40, 94, 567, 705
accurate *adj.* 430, 476, 915
accursed *adj.* 892
accusation *n.* **930**
accuse *vb.* 930
accustom *vb.* 105, 545
ache *n.* 828; *vb.* 828
achieve *vb.* 609, 659, 661
achievement *n.* 89, 609, 659, 661
achromatism *n.* 806
acid *n.* 773; *adj.* 773
acknowledge *vb.* 395, 424, 468, 692, 909, 925, 941
acme *n.* 212, 581

acoustics *n.* 778
acquaintance *n.* 882
acquiesce *vb.* 424, 654, 673, 692
acquire *vb.* 472, 705, 716, 720, 726
acquisition *n.* **705**, 716, 726
acquisitive *adj.* 705, **750**
acquit *vb.* 601, 680, 911, 921, 961
acquit oneself well *vb.* 919, 935
acquittal *n.* 601, 911, **961**
acrimonious *adj.* 893, 900
act *n.* 609, 852, 954; *vb.* 172, 529, **609**, 621
acting *n.* 529; *adj.* 689
action *n.* 172, 266, **609**, 651, 960
activate *vb.* 88, 266, 282
active *adj.* 172, 368, 611
activism *n.* 611
activist *n.* 611; *adj.* 611
activity *n.* 266, 557, 609, **611**
actor *n.* 529, 619
actress *n.* 529
actual *adj.* 1, 3, 120, 430
actuary *n.* 742
acumen *n.* 434
acute *adj.* 255, 434
acute angle *n.* 246
adage *n.* 432
Adam *n.* 379
adapt *vb.* 24, 105, 125, 142, 602, 606
adaptable *adj.* 105, 151
adaptation *n.* 456, 545, 792
add *vb.* 36, **40**
addendum *n.* 41
addict *n.* 545
addition *n.* 38, **40**, 41, 705
additional *adj.* 6, 40
additive *n.* 307
address *n.* 191, **518**, 523, 695; *vb.* 514
addressee *n.* 523, 716
adept *n.* 629; *adj.* 627
adequate *adj.* **570**, 579
adhere *vb.* 50
adherent *n.* 474, 640
adhesive *n.* 49; *adj.* 50
ad infinitum adv. 78
adjacent *adj.* 199, 238
adjective *n.* 499

adjoin *vb.* 199, 201
adjournment *n.* 89, 135
adjudicate *vb.* 415, 960
adjudicator *n.* 415, 653
adjunct *n.* 41, 60
adjure *vb.* 468, 695
adjust *vb.* 24, 105, 142, 403, 704
ad lib *adj.* 544; *vb.* 544
administer *vb.* 621, **622**, 956, 988
administration *n.* 622, 667, 956
administrator *n.* 558, 623
admirable *adj.* 579
admire *vb.* 868, 888, **922**, 925
admissible *adj.* 302
admission *n.* 98, 300, 302, 420, 462, 468, 716
admit *vb.* 98, 262, 300, 302, 424, 462, 468, 716, 833
admit defeat *vb.* 654
admonish *vb.* 597, 624, 926, 963
adolescent *n.* 131; *adj.* 129, 131
adopt *vb.* 540, 575, 606, 702, 720
adopted *adj.* 40, 100, 171, 606
adoption *n.* 171, 540, 606
adorable *adj.* 827
adore *vb.* 889, 982
adorn *vb.* 509, 844, 846
adroit *adj.* 627
adulation *n.* 927
adult *n.* 133; *adj.* 133
adulterate *vb.* 45, 477, 582, 952
adulterer *n.* 953
adultery *n.* 952
adulthood *n.* **133**
adumbrate *vb.* 798
advance *n.* **288**, 292, 587, 645, 693, 718, 890; *adj.* 236; *vb.* **288**, 292, 587, 645, 661, 718
advanced *adj.* 125
advantage *n.* 34, 550, 575
advantageous *adj.* 550, 575, 577, 661, 965
adventure *n.* 153, 269
adventurer *n.* 270
adventurous *adj.* 605
adverb *n.* 499

adversary *n.* 638, 883, 969
adverse *adj.* 14, 665
adversity *n.* 445, **665**
advertisement *n.* 464
advertising *n.* 727
advice *n.* 460, 597, **624**, 636
advisable *adj.* 577
advise *vb.* 460, 597, **624**, 636
advisor *n.* 473, 624
advisory *adj.* 597, 624
advocate *n.* 959; *vb.* 959
aerate *vb.* 344, 348, 775
aerial *adj.* 273, 318, 348
aerodynamics *n.* 348
aeronautical *adj.* 273, 278
aeronautics *n.* 273
aeroplane *n.* 278
aesthetic *adj.* 848
affable *adj.* 884
affair *n.* 153, 557, 889, 952
affect *vb.* 177, 752, 755
affectation *n.* 510, **852**
affected *adj.* 510, 751, 752, 852
affection *n.* 752, 882, 889, 890
affections *n.* **751**
affidavit *n.* 401, 468, 960
affiliate *vb.* 11, 52, 639, 641
affinity *n.* 18, 105, 218, 294
affirm *vb.* 401, 413, 424, 468, 514
affirmation *n.* 413, 424, **468**, 690
affirmative *n.* 424; *adj.* 468
affix *n.* 499; *vb.* 40, 47
afflict *vb.* 830
affliction *n.* 551, 586, **592**, **665**, 828
affluence *n.* 664, 734
afford *vb.* 568, 715, 734
affront *n.* 923; *vb.* 887, 923
affronted *adj.* 893
afloat *adj.* 153
aforementioned *adj.* 84
afraid *adj.* 856
after *adj.* 119; *adv.* 85
after-effect *n.* 87, 156
afterlife *n.* 123
aftermath *n.* 87, 156
afternoon *n.* 128

afterthought *n.* 87, 441, 538
afterwards *adv.* 85
again *adv.* 62, 77
age *n.* 109, **130**; *vb.* 130
aged *adj.* 130
ageless *adj.* 114, 129
agency *n.* 172, 563, 685
agenda *n.* 83, 441
agent *n.* 149, 155, 564, **619**, 689
aggravation *n.* **835**
aggregate *n.* 54; *adj.* 54
aggressive *adj.* 173, 175, 645, 651
aggressor *n.* 645
aghast *vb adj.* 866
agile *adj.* 280, 611, 627
agitation *n.* 80, **326**, 755, 756
agitator *n.* 142, 148
agnostic *n.* 975; *adj.* 409, 975, 981
agnosticism *n.* 409, 421, 975
ago *adv.* 124
agonize *vb.* 830
agonizing *adj.* 828
agony *n.* 756, 828
agrarian *adj.* 378
agree *vb.* **24**, 105, 180, 424, 692, 925
agreeable *adj.* 692, 829
agreed *adj.* 24
agreement *n.* **24**, 105, 424, 643, 650, 692, 699, 704, 925
agriculture *n.* **378**
ahead *adv.* 236, 286
ahead of *adj.* 118
aid *n.* 563, **636**, 640, 834, 899; *vb.* 563, **636**
ailment *n.* 586
aim *n.* 178, 284, 450, 552; *vb.* 178, 284, 552
aimless *adj.* 158, 399, 451, 553
air *n.* 329, 344, **348**, 621, 792; *vb.* 348, 350
air conditioning *n.* 348
aircraft *n.* **278**
airing *n.* 348
air in motion *n.* **359**
airman *n.* 273
air-pipe *n.* **361**
airport *n.* 298
airs *n.* 852
air travel *n.* **273**

airy *adj.* 4, 331, 333, 344, 348
ajar *adj.* 262
akin *adj.* 11
alacrity *n.* 611
alarm *n.* 482, 598, 856
alarming *adj.* 594
album *n.* 441
alcoholism *n.* 950
alcove *n.* 254
alert *n.* 597, 598; *adj.* 392, 602, 611; *vb.* 597, 598
algebra *n.* 38
alias *n.* 497
alibi *n.* 549
alien *n.* 100; *adj.* 100
alienate *vb.* 883, 892
alight *adj.* 759; *vb.* 298
alike *adj.* 13, 18
alive *adj.* 368, 611, 753
all *n.* 54; *adj.* 54, 56
Allah *n.* 967
allegation *n.* 401, 930
allege *vb.* 549, 959
alleged *adj.* 448, 549, 825
allegiance *n.* 679, 919, 980
allegory *n.* 397, 455, 525
all-embracing *adj.* 54, 98
allergic *adj.* 862
alleviate *vb.* 176, 652, 834
alley *n.* 559
alliance *n.* 641, 699, 896
allied *adj.* 11, 47, 180, 641
all-inclusive *adj.* 54, 98
allocation *n.* 717
allot *vb.* 55, 717
allotment *n.* 378, 717
allow *vb.* **690**, 692, 744, 925
allowance *n.* 31, 690, 715, 717, 718, 738, 744, 965
allow for *vb.* 31, 403
alloy *n.* 45; *vb.* 45
all right *adj.* 579, 585; *adv.* 79
all-round *adj.* 627
allure *vb.* 547, 829, 889
allusion *n.* 455, 459
ally *n.* 640
ally with *vb.* 47
almanac *n.* 116, 483
Almighty *n.* 967
almighty *adj.* 159, 966
almost *adv.* 199

appropriate *adj.* 105,
499, 510, 577, 915;
vb. 705, 720
approval *n.* 424, 690,
692, **925**, 954
approximate *vb.* 18,
199, 292
approximately *adv.* 199
apricot *n.* 816
apt *adj.* 179, 915
aptitude *n.* 627
aquarium *n.* 377
aquatic *adj.* 347
aquatics *n.* 271
aqueduct *n.* 360
arbiter *n.* 653
arbitrary *adj.* 10
arbitrate *vb.* 415, 653,
960
arc *n.* 247
arcade *n.* 247, 559, 730
arch *n.* 247; *vb.* 247,
252
archaic *adj.* 126
archaism *n.* 124, 494
archbishop *n.* 870, 986
archetype *n.* 23
architect *n.* 166, 491,
558
archives *n.* 483, 567
archivist *n.* 484
arctic *adj.* 760
ardent *adj.* 506, 759,
889
ardour *n.* 752, 759, 861,
889, 980
arduous *adj.* 615, 633
area *n.* 26, 182, 183,
194, 234, 400, 557
arena *n.* 234, **658**
arguable *adj.* 929
argue *vb.* 410, 414, 420,
514, 642, 959
argument *n.* 25, 387,
410, 525, 642, 893,
960
argumentative *adj.* 410
arid *adj.* 350
arise *vb.* 88, 153, 318,
825
aristocracy *n.* 870
arithmetic *n.* 38
arm *n.* 353; *vb.* 159, 646
armistice *n.* 144, 650
armour *n.* 646, 657
arms *n.* **657**
army *n.* 75, 655
aroma *n.* 776
around *adv.*, *prep.* 229
arouse *vb.* 155, 618, 755
arraign *vb.* 930

arrange *vb.* 58, 81, 242,
558, 602, 699, 792
arrangement *n.* 9, 79,
81, 244, 602, 699,
792, 884
array *n.* 79, 655; *vb.* 81,
846
arrears *n.* 737
arrest *n.* 635; *vb.* 89,
144, 635, 681, 681,
755, 930
arrival *n.* 292, **298**
arrive *vb.* 153, 298
arrogant *adj.* 875, 880
arrow *n.* 290, 482
arsenal *n.* 657
art *n.* 486, 488
artful *adj.* 631
article *n.* 163, 327, 499
articles *n.* 192, 729
articulate *adj.* 512; *vb.*
512
artifice *n.* 478, 631
artificial *adj.* 510, 849,
852
artillery *n.* 655
artist *n.* **491**, 793
artistic *adj.* 510
artlessness *n.* 508, **632**,
951
asbestos *n.* 762
ascend *vb.* 316
ascent *n.* **316**
ascertained *adj.* 408
ascetism *n.* **946**
ascribe *vb.* 157
ashamed *adj.* 874
ashen *adj.* 806, 807
aside *n.* 460, 520; *adv.*
567
ask *vb.* 394, 695
askance *adj.* 219
askew *adj.* 219, 245
asleep *adj.* 267
as long as *adv.*, *prep.*
111
aspect *n.* 5, 7, 55, 825
aspersion *n.* 928
asphalt *n.* 365
asphyxiate *vb.* 370
aspirate *vb.* 512
aspire *vb.* 552, 604, 854,
861
aspiring *adj.* 605
ass *n.* 437
assail *vb.* 645
assassin *n.* 370, 906
assassinate *vb.* 370
assault *n.* 175, 645, 952;
vb. 645, 952
assemblage *n.* 47, **94**

assemble *vb.* 47, 58, 94,
242, 568
assembly *n.* 59, 94, 625,
982, 987
assent *n.* **424**, 692; *vb.*
24, 424, 692
assert *vb.* 450, 468
assert oneself *vb.* 649
assess *vb.* 400, 415, 743
assessor *n.* 415, 653
assets *n.* 564, 566, 711,
734, 741
asseverate *vb.* 468
assiduous *adj.* 390, 392,
535
assign *vb.* 685, 714, 717
assignable *adj.* 157
assignment *n.* 470, 557
assignment of cause *n.*
157
assimilate *vb.* 302, 472
assist *vb.* 636
assistance *n.* 563, 636,
639
assistant *n.* 640, 676,
689
assizes *n.* 957
associate *n.* 640; *vb.* 9,
47, 94, 157, 397
associated *adj.* 60, 157,
639
association *n.* 52, 60,
397, 641
assorted *adj.* 45
assuage *vb.* 176, 652,
834
assume *vb.* 448, 720,
852
assumption *n.* 420, 918
assurance *n.* 408, 420,
854
assure *vb.* 420, 468,
701, 857
asthmatic *adj.* 359
astigmatism *n.* 820
astonish *vb.* 444, 866
astonishing *adj.* 444,
579, 866
astrologer *n.* 447, 984
astrology *n.* 329, 447
astronaut *n.* 274
astronomy *n.* 329
astute *adj.* 434
asylum *n.* 595
asymmetry *n.* 17, 219,
245
atavism *n.* 147
at hand *adj.* 123, 188;
adv. 199
atheism *n.* 421, 975
atheist *n.* 975
athlete *n.* 270

athletic *adj.* 161
at home *n.* 884
atlas *n.* 329
at last *adv.* 89
atmosphere *n.* 8, 229,
329, 348, 488
atoll *n.* 357
atom *n.* 33, 195, 327
atomic *adj.* 195
atomic bomb *n.* 657
atomize *vb.* 53, 164,
340
atonal *adj.* 791
at once *adv.* 115
atonement *n.* 31, 652,
911, **943**
atrocious *adj.* 856, 936
atrocity *n.* 900
attach *vb.* 40, 47
attaché *n.* 688
attached *adj.* 47, 889
attachment *n.* 41, 50,
60, 889, 890
attack *n.* 326, 439, 586,
645, 651; *vb.* 645,
648, 651, 928, 930
attacker *n.* 645, 723
attain *vb.* 472, 661
attainable *adj.* 292, 404
attainments *n.* 426, 472
attempt *n.* **604**; *vb.* 552,
604, 615
attend *vb.* 188, 287,
591, 676
attendant *n.* 60, 287,
683; *adj.* 60, 188
attending *adj.* 60, 676
attend to *vb.* 593, 795
attention *n.* **390**, 702
attentive *adj.* 390, 922
attenuate *vb.* 205, 333
attest *vb.* 401, 408, 413,
468
attested *adj.* 408, 430
at the same time *adv.*
122
attire *n.* 227
attitude *n.* 7, 420, 621,
818
attorney *n.* 959
attract *vb.* 224, 291,
294, 390, 547, 889
attract attention *vb.*
755
attraction *n.* **294**, 330,
547
attractive *adj.* 579, 829,
844, 889
attributable *adj.* 157
attribute *n.* 5; *vb.* 157
atypical *adj.* 19
auburn *adj.* 810, 811

basement *n.* 213
bash *vb.* 282
bashful *adj.* 876
basic *adj.* 88, 155, 213, 573
basin *n.* 193, 213, 254, 354
basis *n.* 23, 155, 547
basket *n.* 193, 275
bastard *n.* 171, 955
baste *vb.* 306
bastion *n.* 646
batch *n.* 26, 94
bathe *vb.* 271, 349, 583
battle *n.* 649, 651
battleground *n.* 658
battlement *n.* 646
battleship *n.* 277
bawl *vb.* 788, 839
bay *n.* 353; *adj.* 810; *vb.* 789
bazaar *n.* 727, 730
be *vb.* 1, 185, 188, 368
beach *n.* 352
beacon *n.* 467, 482, 598, 800
beaker *n.* 193
be-all and end-all *n.* 573
beam *n.* 217, 797, 838; *vb.* 797, 838
beanfeast *n.* 306
bear *vb.* 217, 275, 368, 828
bearer *n.* 275, 467
bearing *n.* 9, 217, 284, 621, 825
bearings *n.* 185
bear in mind *vb.* 384
bear malice *vb.* 893
bear out *vb.* 413, 929
bear upon *vb.* 9
bear witness to *vb.* 401
beast *n.* 175, 373, 906
beastly *adj.* 900
beast of burden *n.* 275
beat *n.* 140, 325, 528; *vb.* 140, 282, 325, 340, 661, 783, 963
beat about the bush *vb.* 412, 505
beat off *vb.* 295, 646, 885
beat one's breast *vb.* 837
beat up *vb.* 645
beautiful *adj.* 844
beautify *vb.* 587, 844, 846
beauty *n.* 510, **844**
becalm *vb.* 267
beck *n.* 358

beckon *vb.* 482
becloud *vb.* 798, 799
become *vb.* 1, 142, 288
become of *vb.* 156
becoming *n.* 1; *adj.* 848
bed *n.* 206, 213, 360; *vb.* 378
bed and breakfast *n.* 191
bedaub *vb.* 584
bedeck *vb.* 846
Bedlam *n.* 80
bedlamite *n.* 440
bed of roses *n.* 661, 664, 827
bedouin *n.* 270
bedraggled *adj.* 584
bed-ridden *adj.* 586
be drunk *vb.* 950
be dry *vb.* 861
bedsitter *n.* 191
beefy *adj.* 161, 194
bee-line *n.* 248
Beelzebub *n.* 969
beer *n.* 309
be excited *vb.* 756
be excused *vb.* 310
befall *vb.* 153
before *adj.* 118; *adv.* 84, 286
beforehand *adj.* 117
be found *vb.* 1, 185
befriend *vb.* 636, 882
befuddled *adj.* 950
beg *vb.* 695
beget *vb.* 163, 368
begetter *n.* 170
beggar *n.* 697, 735, 940
beggarly *adj.* 881
begin *vb.* 88, 605
begin again *vb.* 88
beginner *n.* 474, 630
beginning *n.* **88**, 155
begrudge *vb.* 914
beg the question *vb.* 412
beguile *vb.* 391, 478, 547
beguiler *n.* 480
behave oneself *vb.* 621, 886, 935
behead *vb.* 48, 370, 963
behest *n.* 671
behind *adj.* 135; *adv.* 85, 237
behind bars *adj.* 681
behindhand *adj.* 135
behind someone's back *adj.* 478
behind the scenes *adj.* 461

behind the times *adj.* 126
beholder *n.* 821
behove *vb.* 919
beige *n.* 810; *adj.* 810
being *n.* **1**, 5, 327, 368; *adj.* 1
being according to external form *n.* **6**
being according to internal form *n.* **5**
being around *n.* **229**
being between *n.* **230**
being exterior *n.* **222**
being horizontal *n.* **215**
being interior *n.* **223**
being oblique *n.* **219**
being opposite *n.* **239**
being vertical *n.* **214**
belated *adj.* 135
belie *vb.* 469
belief *n.* 415, **420**, 974
believable *adj.* 420
believe *vb.* **420**, 448, 854
believer *n.* 146, 977, 980
believing *adj.* 420, 974, 977, 980
belittle *vb.* 924, 926, 928
bell *n.* 482, 598, 784; *vb.* 789
belle *n.* 844
belligerent *adj.* 651
bellow *vb.* 780, 788, 789
belong *vb.* 9, 58, 60, 202, 707
belonging *adj.* 9, 60
belongings *n.* 60, 568, 711
beloved *n.* 891; *adj.* 889
below *adv.* 209
below average *adj.* 580
below par *adj.* 35
below the belt *adj.* 916
belt *n.* 49, 207, 250, 964; *vb.* 963
bemoan *vb.* 833
bench *n.* 957
bencher *n.* 959
bend *n.* 219, 247; *vb.* 105, 219, 246, 285
bend over *vb.* 319
bend over backwards to help *vb.* 899
beneath *adv.* 209
beneath contempt *adj.* 924
beneath the surface *adj.* 459

benediction *n.* 909
benefactor *n.* **905**
beneficial *adj.* 550, 575, 585, 636, 661
beneficiary *n.* 716
beneficent *adj.* 747
benefit *n.* 550, 575, 636, 705, 829, 899; *vb.* 575, 577, 579, 661, 705, 899
benevolence *n.* 636, 747, **899**, 907
bent *n.* 178, 545, 751; *adj.* 219, 247, 252
bequeath *vb.* 714
bequest *n.* 714, 715
bereave *vb.* 898
bereavement *n.* 369, 706, 828
bereft *adj.* 706
berry *n.* 306
berserk *adj.* 439
berth *n.* 191, 298
beryl *adj.* 812
beseech *vb.* 695, 982
beset *vb.* 633
besetting *adj.* 545
besetting sin *n.* 592, 936
beside oneself *adj.* 756
besides *adv.* 40
besiege *vb.* 645
be situated *vb.* 1, 185
besmirched *adj.* 584
best *adj.* 34, 579
best friend *n.* 882
bestow *vb.* 715, 965
bestseller *n.* 524
best wishes *n.* 888
be subject to *vb.* 179, 679
bet *n.* 553; *vb.* 553
bête noire *n.* 892
be the duty of *vb.* 919
bethel *n.* 990
betoken *vb.* 447, 450, 482
betray *vb.* 458, 462, 478, 932
betrayer *n.* 480
betrothal *n.* 698
betrothed *adj.* 698
better *n.* 34, 553; *adj.* 34; *vb.* 587
better half *n.* 896
betterment *n.* 550, 587
between *prep.* 230
between ourselves *adv.* 466
between the lines *adj.* 459
be up to *vb.* 159
beverage *n.* 309

bewail *vb.* 833
bewilder *vb.* 409, 866
bewitch *vb.* 829, 984
bewitched *adj.* 984
be worth *vb.* 743
beyond compare *adj.* 34, 581
beyond hope *adj.* 855
bi- *adj.* 61
bias *n.* 178, 416, 545, 751, 916; *vb.* 416
biased *adj.* 416, 916
Bible *n.* 524, 976
biblical *adj.* 976
bibliography *n.* 83, 524
bicker *vb.* 642
bicycle *n.* 276
bid *n.* 693, 695; *vb.* 394, 671, 693
bidder *n.* 697
bide one's time *vb.* 443, 610, 612
bifurcate *vb.* 63, 297
big *adj.* **32**, 161, 194, 509
bigheaded *adj.* 873
big-hearted *adj.* 747
big-mouthed *adj.* 879
big name *n.* 868
bigot *n.* 537
bigoted *adj.* 416
big-sounding *adj.* 509
big talk *n.* 879
bigwig *n.* 675, 868
bike *n.* 276; *vb.* 269
bilateral *adj.* 61
bilious *adj.* 812, 813
bill *n.* 464, 482, 742, 960
billet *n.* 191
billion *n.* 70
bill of fare *n.* 306
billow *vb.* 358
billy-goat *n.* 380
bin *n.* 193
binary *adj.* 39, 61
bind *vb.* 47, 378, 681, 698, 919
binding *adj.* 919
binoculars *n.* 822
biographer *n.* 484, 524
biology *n.* 366
bipartite *adj.* 61
birch *n.* 964
bird *n.* 373
bird's eye view *n.* 818
bird-watching *n.* 375
birth *n.* 88, 155, 870
birthday *n.* 140, 878
biscuit *n.* 306
bisection *n.* **63**
bishop *n.* 870, 986

bit *n.* 33, 55, 59
bit by bit *adv.* 55
bitch *n.* 381
bite *n.* 306, 306, 769; *vb.* 304
bite someone's head off *vb.* 893
biting *adj.* 255, 760, 773
bitter *adj.* 769, 773, 893, 900
bitter-sweet *adj.* 772
bitumen *n.* 365
bizarre *adj.* 139, 433
blabber *vb.* 462
black *n.* **808**; *adj.* 798, 808; *vb.* 99
blacken *vb.* 798, 808, 928
blackguard *n.* 940
black hole *n.* 329
blackish *adj.* 808
blacklist *vb.* 99
black magic *n.* 984
blackmail *n.* 902; *vb.* 902
black-market *adj.* 955
black out *vb.* 485, 798
blackout *n.* 463, 466, 779, 798
black sheep *n.* 940
black spot *n.* 596
blame *n.* 926, 930, 938; *vb.* 157, 926, 930, 962
blameless *adj.* 937
blameworthy *adj.* 926
blanch *vb.* 806, 807
bland *adj.* 768, 771
blank *n.* 2; *adj.* 2, 385, 451, 754
blank cheque *n.* 678, 690
blanket *n.* 225; *adj.* 54, 101, 399
blankness *n.* 442, 867
blare *vb.* 780
blasé *adj.* 757
blaspheme *vb.* 901, 981
blast *n.* 359, 780, 782; *vb.* 175, 359
blatant *adj.* 877
blather *n.* 451, 516; *vb.* 451
blaze *n.* 759, 797; *vb.* 797
blazon *vb.* 464
bleach *vb.* 806, 807
bleached *adj.* 350
bleak *adj.* 760, 798
bleat *vb.* 789
bleed *vb.* 301, 358, 745

blemish *n.* 582, 660, 845, **847**; *vb.* 847
blend *n.* 45, 495; *vb.* 52
bless *vb.* 899, 982, 988
blessed *adj.* 972
blessing *n.* 550, 715, 909
blessings *n.* 664
blight *n.* 53, 167, 592, 665
blind *n.* 225, 463, 801; *adj.* 754, 819; *vb.* 797
blinded *adj.* 819
blindfold *adj.* 819; *vb.* 819
blindness *n.* **819**
blind spot *n.* 819
blink *vb.* 797, 818
blinker *vb.* 801, 819
blinkers *n.* 801
bliss *n.* 827, 972
blithe *adj.* 827
blitz *n.* 645; *vb.* 164
blizzard *n.* 175, 359, 760
bloat *vb.* 196
bloated *adj.* 252
block *n.* 490, 681, 964; *vb.* 263, 265, 635
blockade *n.* 99, 681; *vb.* 234, 265, 645
blockage *n.* 263, 635
blockhead *n.* 429, 437, 630
blonde *adj.* 807
blood *n.* 11, 870
blood relationship *n.* 11
bloodshed *n.* 370, 649
bloom *n.* 374
bloomer *n.* 431
blossom *n.* 374; *vb.* 163, 168, 664
blot *n.* 584, 845, 847, 869; *vb.* 584, 847, 869
blotch *n.* 847
blot out *vb.* 164, 485, 911
blow *n.* 282, 444, 609, 828, 900, 963; *vb.* 359, 749
blowout *n.* 48, 306
blow up *vb.* 196, 359, 782, 893
blubber *n.* 306, 365; *vb.* 839
blue *n.* **815**; *adj.* 815, 837, 901, 952
blue blood *n.* 870
blue-eyed boy *n.* 891
blueprint *n.* 23, 558

blues *n.* 792, 837
bluff *vb.* 549
blunder *n.* 431, 500; *vb.* 431
blunt *adj.* 256, 476, 508; *vb.* 162, 256, 754
bluntness *n.* **256**
blur *n.* 847; *vb.* 799
blurb *n.* 464
blurred *adj.* 243, 503, 799, 803, 824
blurt out *vb.* 462, 544
blush *n.* 811; *vb.* 811, 876
bluster *n.* 879
blustery *adj.* 359
board *n.* 217, 305, 625, 688
boarder *n.* 190
boast *n.* 879; *vb.* 873, 875, 879
boaster *n.* 873, 879
boastful *adj.* 481, 509, 875, 879
boasting *n.* **879**
boat *n.* 193, 277
bode *vb.* 447, 450
bode well *vb.* 854
bodiless *adj.* 4, 328
bodily *adj.* 327, 827, 945
body *n.* 3, 327, 368, 371
body-building *adj.* 585
bodyguard *n.* 593, 683
body odour *n.* 777
boffin *n.* 396, 448
bog *n.* 355
bogie *n.* 217
bogus *adj.* 477
boil *n.* 252; *vb.* 175, 306, 363, 759, 893
boil down *vb.* 203, 527
boiler *n.* 763
boil over *vb.* 756
boisterous *adj.* 175, 756, 780
bold *adj.* 458, 506, 534, 644, 854, 857
boldness *n.* 534, 857, 880
bolshie *adj.* 642
bolster *vb.* 217, 636
bolt *n.* 49, 613; *vb.* 47, 263, 304
bolt down *vb.* 948
bomb *n.* 657; *vb.* 280, 613, 645
bombard *vb.* 164, 645
bombast *n.* 509, 879
bombastic *adj.* 481, 877
bomber *n.* 278

carcass n. 371
card n. 482
cardinal n. 986; adj. 34
cardinal point n. 284
care n. (carefulness)
392, 860; (worry)
828, 830; vb. 593,
676, 889
career n. 557
carefree adj. 831, 836
careful adj. 392, 398,
748, 860
careless adj. 391, 393,
703, 749, 859, 920
caress vb. 758, 890
caretaker n. 683
cargo n. 192
caricature n. 20, 22,
487, 853; vb. 20, 487,
853
carnage n. 370, 649
carnal adj. 827, 945
carnival n. 529, 840
carnivore n. 373
carouse vb. 840
carpet n. 225
carrel n. 475
carriage n. 217, 268,
276, 621
carried away adj. 827
carrier n. 275, 460, 467
carrot n. 547, 816
carry vb. 217, 268, 275
carry on vb. 91, 145,
535
carry out vb. 609, 659,
702
cart n. 276; vb. 268
carte blanche n. 678,
690
cartel n. 641, 681
cartilage n. 337
carton n. 193
cartoon n. 488
cartoonist n. 491
carve vb. 48, 163, 242,
489, 490
carver n. 491
cascade n. 358; vb. 358
case n. 7, 193, 401, 499,
930, 960
cash n. 731
cash-book n. 742
cash box n. 732
cashier n. 733, 742
cash in on vb. 136, 606,
705
cash register n. 732
casserole vb. 306
cassette-recorder n.
484, 794
cassock n. 989

cast n. 22, 94, 489, 529;
vb. 242, 489
castaway n. 885
cast down vb. 321, 837
caste n. 97
castle n. 191, 595, 646
castles in the air n. 449
cast lots vb. 447
cast off vb. 228, 271,
556
castoffs n. 44
castrate vb. 160, 169
casual n. 655; adj. 139,
158, 393, 409
casuistry n. 631
catacomb n. 372
catalogue n. 83, 483;
vb. 83, 483
catalyst n. 142, 173
cataract n. 358, 820
catastrophe n. 153, 551,
665, 900
catastrophic adj. 148,
551, 665
catch n. 635; vb. 478,
720, 795
catch-all n. 54; adj. 54
catch in the act vb. 419,
444, 938
catch on vb. 452, 545,
850
catch sight of vb. 818
catch up vb. 280
catchy adj. 790
catechism n. 420, 470
categorize vb. 97
category n. 97
catenary n. 247
cater vb. 568
catering n. 306, 568
cathedral n. 990
catholic adj. 101
cattle n. 373
cattleherd n. 377
catty adj. 900
cauldron n. 193
causal adj. 155
causation n. 155
cause n. 155, 547, 605;
vb. 155, 547
caustic adj. 773, 900
caution n. 392, 597,
624, 860; vb. 597
cautionary adj. 597
cautious adj. 681, 856,
860
cavalry n. 655
cave n. 254, 317, 353
caveat n. 597
cave in vb. 254
cavity n. 319
caw vb. 787, 789

cease vb. 89, 144, 267,
826
ceasefire n. 144
ceaseless adj. 145
ceiling n. 225, 235
celebrate vb. 838, 878,
888, 988
celebrated adj. 868
celebration n. 838, 878
celebrity n. 868
celestial adj. 329, 966,
968, 972
celestial body n. 329 ◀
celibacy n. 897
celibate n. 897; adj.
169, 897, 951
cell n. 234, 366, 682
cement n. 49; vb. 47
cemetery n. 372
cenotaph n. 372, 483
censor vb. 466
censorious adj. 926
censorship n. 681, 779
censure n. 466, 926,
930; vb. 926, 930
census n. 38
centenary n. 70, 109,
878
central adj. 5, 90, 223,
224
centrality n. 224
centralize vb. 224
centre n. 90, 96, 183,
560; adj. 90, 224; vb.
96, 224
centrifugal adj. 297
century n. 70
ceramics n. 489
ceramist n. 491
cereal n. 306, 374
ceremonial adj. 878,
988
ceremony n. 878, 896,
988
certain adj. 408, 413,
420, 531, 534
certainly adv. 408, 531
certainty n. 408, 420,
531, 534
certificate n. 483, 690
certified adj. 408
certify vb. 408, 690
cessation n. 89, 144,
267
chafe vb. 341
chain n. 49, 85, 635,
681; vb. 635, 681
chalet n. 191
chalky adj. 807
challenge n. 394, 644,
649; vb. 394, 425,
644, 649

challenger n. 638
chamber n. 210
champ vb. 304
champagne n. 309
champion n. 579, 646,
661, 905; adj. 661
chance n. 158, 406, 553;
adj. 139, 553; vb.
158, 553
chance upon vb. 158
chancy adj. 409
change n. 142, 731; vb.
15, 142
changeable adj. 15, 142,
151, 536, 539
changeableness n. 151
change of mind n. 538
change over vb. 714
channel n. 261, 262,
360, 564; vb. 261
chant n. 982; vb. 788,
792
chaos n. 80, 243, 668,
955
chap n. 380
chapel n. 990
chaperon vb. 392
chaplain n. 986
character n. 5, 58, 493,
529, 751, 868, 931
characteristic n. 102;
adj. 5, 102, 486
characterize vb. 525
charcoal n. 765
charge n. 557, 622, 626,
645, 671, 685, 743,
930; vb. 159, 645,
671, 685, 736, 743,
930
charismatic adj. 294
charitable adj. 715, 747,
899, 965
charity n. 636, 715, 747,
899, 907
charlatan n. 480, 852
charm n. 547, 829, 844,
889, 984; vb. 547,
829, 889, 984
charming adj. 547, 829,
844, 889
chart n. 460, 486, 558
charter n. 690, 699; vb.
690, 718, 719, 954
charwoman n. 676
chary adj. 750
chase n. 554; vb. 287,
490, 554, 882, 890
chaser n. 554
chasm n. 200, 254, 317
chassis n. 217
chaste adj. 876, 935,
951

chastened *adj.* 874
chastise *vb.* 963
chat *n.* 516, 519; *vb.* 514, 516, 519
chatter *n.* 516, 519; *vb.* 326, 388, 516, 760
chatterbox *n.* 388, 516
chatty *adj.* 460, 516
chauffeur *n.* 676
chauvinist *n.* 903; *adj.* 379
cheap *adj.* 746
cheapen *vb.* 746, 924
cheapness *n.* **746**
cheat *n.* 480, 631, 940; *vb.* 478, 631, 722, 916, 932
cheater *n.* 723
check *n.* 396, 635, 648, 681; *vb.* 37, 144, 394, 396, **408**, 413, 635, 681
checker *vb.* 817
checklist *n.* 83
cheeky *adj.* 880, 887
cheer *n.* 827; *vb.* 618, 788, 834, 836, 840, 925
cheerfulness *n.* **836**, 854
cheerless *adj.* 837, 895
cheers *n.* 838, 878
cheese *n.* 306
cheesed off *adj.* 832
cheese-paring *n.* 750
cheque *n.* 731
chequer *vb.* 817
cherish *vb.* 441, 712, 889, 890
cherub *n.* 968
chest *n.* 193
chestnut *n.* 842; *adj.* 810
chew *vb.* 304
chicanery *n.* 631
chicken *adj.* 858
chicken out *vb.* 858
chide *vb.* 926
chief *n.* 34, 675; *adj.* 34, 573
child *n.* 11, 131, 171
childhood *n.* 129
childish *adj.* 129, 131, 435
childless *adj.* 169
childlike *adj.* 129, 131, 632
chill *n.* 760; *vb.* 762
chilly *adj.* 760, 883
chime *n.* 784; *vb.* 783, 784
chimney *n.* 361
chink *n.* 200, 797

chip *n.* 33, 55, 482; *vb.* 48, 377
chip in *vb.* 738
chip on one's shoulder *n.* 832
chirp *vb.* 789
chirpy *adj.* 836
chirrup *vb.* 789
chisel *n.* 312, 480; *vb.* 163, 312, 478, 489, 490
chit *n.* 523
chit-chat *n.* 465, 516, 519
chivalry *n.* 857, 886
chocolate *adj.* 810
choice *n.* 398, 530, **540**; *adj.* 579, 770
choiceless *adj.* 541
choir *n.* 793
choke *vb.* 265, 370, 572, 762
choleric *adj.* 894
choose *vb.* 398, 530, 532, **540**, 861
choosy *adj.* 398, 540, 864
chop *vb.* 48, 319
chop and change *vb.* 151
choppy *adj.* 258
choral *adj.* 792
chord *n.* 247
chorister *n.* 793
chortle *vb.* 838
chorus *n.* 528, 792, 793, 982
christen *vb.* 496
Christendom *n.* 977, 985
Christian *n.* 977, 982
Christianity *n.* 974
chromatic *adj.* 805
chronicle *n.* 116, 483; *vb.* 483
chronicler *n.* 484
chronological *adj.* 116
chronometer *n.* 116
chronometry *n.* **116**
chuck *vb.* 290, 556
chuckle *n.* 783, 838; *vb.* 783, 789, 838
chum *n.* 882
chunky *adj.* 203, 204
church *n.* 977, 982, 985, 987, 990
church building *n.* **990**
churchdom *n.* **985**
church-goer *n.* 982
church member *n.* 977, 987
churchyard *n.* 372

churlish *adj.* 895
cigar *n.* 308
cigarette *n.* 308
cinema *n.* 529, 840
cipher *n.* 39, 466
circle *n.* 94, 247, 250, 323; *vb.* 229, 322, 323
circuit *n.* 140, 232, 250, 269, **322**, 323, **561**
circular *n.* 464, 523; *adj.* 250
circulate *vb.* 322, 323, 460
circulation *n.* **322**
circumambulate *vb.* 231, 322
circumference *n.* 232, 250
circumlocution *n.* 505
circumscription *n.* **231**
circumspect *adj.* 392, 434, 860
circumstance *n.* **8**, 153
circumstances *n.* 8, 229
circumstantial *adj.* 8
circumvent *vb.* 231, 555
circus *n.* 250, 559, 658
cistern *n.* 193
citadel *n.* 646
citation *n.* 663, 925
citizen *n.* 190, 871
city *n.* 183
city-dweller *n.* 190
civic *adj.* 379
civil *adj.* 379, 886, 987
civilian *n.* 871
civility *n.* 886
civilization *n.* 379
civilized *adj.* 379
clad *adj.* 227
claim *n.* 671, 737; *vb.* 549, 671, 917
claimant *n.* 697
clairvoyant *n.* 447, 984
clamber *vb.* 316
clammer *n.* 175
clamorous *adj.* 695, 780, 788
clamour *n.* 780, 788; *vb.* 695, 788
clamp *vb.* 47
clamp down on *vb.* 669
clan *n.* 11
clandestine *adj.* 461
clang *n.* 783; *vb.* 783, 784, 787
clanger *n.* 431
clanging *n.* 784; *adj.* 784, 787

clap *vb.* 282, 838, 878, 925
clarify *vb.* 456
clarity *n.* 452, 502, 823
clash *n.* 175, 282; *vb.* 14, 282, 642, 787, 791, 805, 883
clasp *n.* 49, 712; *vb.* 50, 712, 720, 758, 890
class *n.* 7, 55, **97**, 122, 206, 470, 472, 474; *vb.* 97
classified *adj.* 81, 466
classify *vb.* 81, 83, 97, 496
classroom *n.* 475
clatter *vb.* 783, 787
clause *n.* 498
clean *adj.* 46, **583**, 937, 951; *vb.* 341, **583**, 775, 807
cleaner *n.* 676
cleanliness *n.* 583, 585, 951
cleanness *n.* **583**, 951
cleanse *vb.* 583
cleanser *n.* 775
clear *adj.* 46, 413, 452, 458, 502, 512, 678, 797, 802, 823, 921; *vb.* 320, 583, 921, 961
clearance *n.* 182, 200, 690, 727
clear-cut *adj.* 452, 823
clear-headed *adj.* 949
clearmindedness *n.* 438
cleavage *n.* 48
cleave *vb.* 48, 50
cleft *n.* 200, 259
clemency *n.* 670, 907
clergyman *n.* **986**
cleric *n.* 986; *adj.* 985
clerical *adj.* 986
clerical dress *n.* 989
clerk *n.* 484
clever *adj.* 426, **434**, 627, 631
cliché *n.* 495, 498
click *vb.* 24, 452, 782
client *n.* 545, 716, 726
cliff *n.* 214
climate *n.* 8, 229, 348
climax *n.* 89, 212
climb *vb.* 273, 316
climb down *vb.* 538
clinch *n.* 712; *vb.* 47, 50, 408, 712
clincher *n.* 414
cling *vb.* 50, 712
clip *vb.* 203
clipper *n.* 277

clippings n. 44
clique n. 94, 641
cloak n. 461, 463, 549;
    vb. 461
clock n. 116
clog vb. 265
cloister n. 885
clonk n. 785; vb. 785
close n. 89, 184, 559;
    adj. 47, 50, 154, 199,
    419, 759, 882; vb.
    144, 263, 461
closed book n. 427, 453
closed shop n. 99, 681
close-fisted adj. 750
close friend n. 882
close in on vb. 292
close-lipped adj. 517
close shave n. 600
closure n. 89, 144, 263
clot vb. 332
cloth n. 989
clothe vb. 227
clothes n. 227
cloud n. 363, 803; vb.
    461, 799, 803
cloudburst n. 175, 358
cloudless adj. 664, 797
cloudy adj. 358, 363,
    503, 799, 803, 824
clout n. 963; vb. 282,
    963
clown n. 842
clowning n. 433
cloy vb. 56, 865
club n. 96, 191; vb. 282,
    639
cluck vb. 787, 789
clue n. 401, 447, 482
clumsy adj. 511, 628
cluster n. 94
clutch vb. 712, 758
clutter n. 80
coach n. 276, 473; vb.
    470
coagulate vb. 332, 334
coagulated adj. 362
coal n. 367, 765, 800
coalesce vb. 13, 52
coalition n. 641
coarse adj. 258, 511,
    849, 887, 952
coastline n. 352
coat n. 206, 225; vb.
    225, 342, 805
coating n. 206, 225
coat of arms n. 482
coax vb. 547, 695
cock n. 380
cocktail n. 309
cock-up n. 628
cocky adj. 875

coddle vb. 306
code n. 103, 466, 954
codification n. 954
coerce vb. 175, 674
coexist vb. 60, 122
coextensive adj. 28, 218
coffee n. 309; adj. 810
coffee-bar n. 191
coffee-break n. 616
coffer n. 193, 732
coffin n. 372
cog vb. 259
cogitation n. 384, 410
cognition n. 426
cognitive adj. 382
cognizability n. 452
cognizant adj. 426
cohabit vb. 889
cohabitant n. 889
cohere vb. 50
coherence n. 50, 337
cohesive adj. 50
coil n. 251; vb. 249
coin vb. 449, 731
coinage n. 495
coincide vb. 13, 24, 28,
    60, 122
coincidence n. 24, 60,
    105, 122, 553
coincidental adj. 60,
    158
coke n. 765
cold n. 760; adj. 754,
    760, 806, 863
cold-blooded adj. 754,
    908
cold feet n. 856, 858
cold shoulder n. 924;
    vb. 885
cold war n. 650
coliseum n. 658
collaborate vb. 180,
    639
collaborator n. 640
collage n. 488
collapse n. 164, 588,
    617, 662; vb. 254,
    588, 617
collate vb. 397
collateral n. 701; adj.
    11
colleague n. 640
collect vb. 94, 567, 705,
    716
collective n. 709; adj.
    24
collectively adv. 60
college n. 475
collide vb. 282
collision course n. 296
colloid n. 362; adj. 362
colloquial adj. 495

colloquialism n. 494,
    495
colonist n. 190
colonize vb. 191
colony n. 94
coloration n. 805
colossal adj. 32
colour n. 509, 805, 811;
    vb. 403, 509, 805
colour-blind adj. 819,
    820
colourful adj. 805
colourlessness n. 806,
    843
colours n. 482
column n. 91, 208, 217
coma n. 754
combat n. 651; vb. 637,
    649
combatant n. 655
combination n. 45, 52
combine vb. 45, 47, 52,
    639
combustible n. 765;
    adj. 761, 765
combustion n. 761
come vb. 298
come about vb. 153,
    430
come across vb. 186,
    419
come after vb. 85, 119,
    287
comeback n. 147, 395,
    589
come back to vb. 395
come before vb. 84, 118
come by vb. 716
come clean vb. 462
comedian n. 842
come down vb. 273,
    317
come-down n. 874
come down on vb. 669,
    963
comedy n. 529
come first vb. 286
come forward vb. 292,
    693
come home vb. 298,
    755
come in vb. 300, 716
come into vb. 705
come into conflict with
    vb. 25
come into sight vb. 292,
    823
come into view vb. 823,
    825
comely adj. 844
come near vb. 292
come next vb. 85

come of vb. 156
come of age vb. 133
come off vb. 153, 661
come on vb. 587
come out vb. 88, 144,
    301, 464
come out with vb. 462
come round again vb.
    140
come round to vb. 420
come short vb. 315,
    445, 571
comestible adj. 306
comet n. 329
come to vb. 743
come to a head vb. 659
come to an agreement
    vb. 699, 704
come to an end vb. 89
come to blows vb. 642
come together vb. 94,
    296
come to life vb. 368
come to light vb. 825
come to mind vb. 384,
    441
come to nothing vb. 2,
    315, 369, 576, 662
come to the point vb.
    504
come up vb. 153
come up against vb. 25
come up to vb. 28, 570
comfort n. 636, 834; vb.
    636, 834, 836, 899,
    907
comfortable adj. 634,
    664, 827, 834
comforting adj. 834,
    907
comic adj. 851
coming n. 292, 298; adj.
    123, 154
coming out n. 88
command n. 501, 622,
    626, 667, 671; vb.
    208, 622, 667, 671
commandeer vb. 720
commander n. 623, 675
commanding adj. 667,
    671
commandment n. 626
commemorate vb. 441,
    878
commemorative adj.
    441, 878
commence vb. 88, 605
commend vb. 925
commendable adj. 579,
    925
commensurate adj. 28

comment *n.* 456, 526; *vb.* 456, 526

commentary *n.* 456, 526

commentator *n.* 456, 526, 974

commerce *n.* 150, 725

commercial *adj.* 725

commercial traveller *n.* 727

commiserate *vb.* 907

commission *n.* 94, 557, 609, 685; *vb.* 557, 685

commissioner *n.* 688, 689

commissioner for oaths *n.* 959

commit *vb.* 609, 685, 698, 714

commit adultery *vb.* 952

commitment *n.* 605, 698, 737, 919, 980

commit oneself *vb.* 534, 540, 605, 919

commit suicide *vb.* 370

committed *adj.* 534, 698, 737, 980

committee *n.* 94, 625, 688

commodities *n.* 729

commodity *n.* 327

common *n.* 356; *adj.* 35, 138, 508, 666, 709, 843, 867

commoner *n.* 871

commonly *adv.* 138

common people *n.* **871**

commonplace *n.* 432; *adj.* 138, 666, 843

common sense *n.* 434

commotion *n.* 326, 611

communal *adj.* 379, 709

communicant *n.* 982

communicate *vb.* **460**, 464, 514, 519, 523

communication *n.* 460, 464, 492, 514, 523

communicative *adj.* 460

communion *n.* 979

communiqué *n.* 465

communism *n.* 709

community *n.* 183, 379, 641, 709

commutable *adj.* 150

commutation *n.* 149

commute *vb.* 142, 149, 150

commuter *n.* 190, 270

compact *adj.* 50, 203, 204, 332, 334, 504; *vb.* 332

companion *n.* 640, 882

company *n.* 94, 620, 641

comparable *adj.* 28

comparative *adj.* 27, 455

compare *vb.* 27, 218, 397

comparison *n.* 18, 27, **397**, 455, 499

compartment *n.* 55

compass *n.* 182, 322

compassion *n.* 670, 907

compassionate *adj.* 670, 899, 907

compatible *adj.* 24, 105, 882

compatriot *n.* 11

compel *vb.* 177, 531, 562, 674, 755

compelling *adj.* 674, 755

compendious *adj.* 54, 527

compendium *n.* **527**

compensation *n.* **31**, 721, 738, 917, 965

compensatory *adj.* 31, 721, 943, 965

compete *vb.* 649

competence *n.* 159, 627, 956

competent *adj.* 159, 579, 627, 956

competition *n.* 649

competitive *adj.* 649

competitor *n.* 638, 854

compile *vb.* 58

complacency *n.* 831

complain *vb.* 642, 788, 832, **926**, 930

complainer *n.* 832

complaint *n.* 586, 696, 926, 930

complement *n.* 28, 60

complete *adj.* 54, **56**, 581, 659; *vb.* 581, 609, **659**, 661

completely *adv.* 54, 56

completeness *n.* 54, **56**

completion *n.* 89, 581, **659**, 661

complex circularity *n.* **251**

complexion *n.* 805

complexity *n.* 503

compliance *n.* 532, 673, 692, 702

compliant *adj.* 532, 654, 919

complicate *vb.* 835

complicated *adj.* 453, 503, 633

compliment *n.* 886, 888, 925, 927; *vb.* 886, 888, 925

comply *vb.* 105, 570, 654, 673, 702

component *n.* 55, 192, 327

compose *vb.* 58, 81, 163, 521, 528, 792

composed *adj.* 757

composer *n.* 166, 491, 528, **793**

composite *adj.* 45

composition *n.* 45, **58**, 81, 339, 488, 521, 522, 526, 528, 792

compositor *n.* 522

composure *n.* 757

compound *n.* 45, 184; *vb.* 36, 52

comprehend *vb.* 58, 98, 452

comprehensible *adj.* 452

comprehension *n.* 410, 452

comprehensive *adj.* 54, 56, 98, 101

compress *vb.* 37, **197**, 205, 332, 504

compressed *adj.* 332, 504

compressor *n.* 197

comprise *vb.* 58, 98

compromise *n.* 30, 699, **704**; *vb.* 704

compulsion *n.* 439, 531, 562, **674**

compulsive *adj.* 674

compulsory *adj.* 531, 674, 919

compunction *n.* 833

compunctious *adj.* 941

compute *vb.* 38, 400

computer *n.* 38, 400, 565

comrade *n.* 640, 882

con *n.* 631, 684; *vb.* 631

concatenation *n.* 47, 85

concavity *n.* **254**

conceal *vb.* 225, **461**, 466

concealment *n.* **461**, 824

concede *vb.* 424, 462, 690, 692

conceited *adj.* 873, 875

conceivable *adj.* 404

conceive *vb.* 88, 163, 368, 382, 449

concentrate *vb.* 96, 296, 334, **384**, **390**

concentration *n.* 296, 332, **384**, **390**, 611

concept *n.* 386

conception *n.* 382, 386, 420

concern *n.* 387, 392, 557, 605, 620; *vb.* 9, 526, 609, 856

concerned *adj.* 388, 392

concerning *adv., prep.* 9

concert *n.* 180, 643, 790, 792, 840

concerto *n.* 792

concession *n.* 690, 704, 744

conciliation *n.* 650, 652

concise *adj.* 203, 432, **504**, 527

conciseness *n.* **504**

conclude *vb.* 56, 89, 410, 530

conclusion *n.* 89, 144, 235, 410, 659

conclusive *adj.* 408, 413, 430, 659

concoct *vb.* 163, 477, 558, 930

concomitant *n.* 60; *adj.* 60

concord *n.* 24, **643**, 790

concordance *n.* 494, 524

concordat *n.* 699

concrete *adj.* 3, 327, 332

concur *vb.* 24, **180**, 424, 692

concurrence *n.* 24, **180**, 296, 692

concurrent *adj.* 24, 60, 122, 180, 296

condemn *vb.* 892, 926, **962**

condemnation *n.* **962**

condemned *adj.* 938

condemned cell *n.* 964

condensation *n.* 346

condense *vb.* 203, 332, 345, 504, 527

condescend *vb.* 869, 874, 886

condiment *n.* **307**

condition *n.* 7, 562, 825; *vb.* 470, 545

conditional *adj.* 403, 700

conditioning n. 470, 545

conditions n. 8, **700**

condolence n. 907

conduce vb. 155

conducive adj. 178, 563

conduct n. 172, 606, **621**, 622; vb. 268, 606, 609, **621**, 622

conduit n. 360

confectionery n. 306

confederate n. 640; adj. 641; vb. 47

confederation n. 641

confer vb. 159, 519, 715, 965

conference n. 94, 519, 625

confess vb. 420, 462, 941, 982

confession n. 420, 941, 974, 982

confidant n. 624, 882

confide vb. 462, 624

confidence n. 408, 420, 443, 466, 854

confident adj. 420, 443, 854, 857

confidential adj. 466

confine vb. 205, 234, 681, 712

confirm vb. 401, 408, 413, **468**, 699, 929

confiscate vb. 720

conflict n. 649; vb. 637, 642, 805, 883

confluence n. 221, 296

conform vb. 16, 24, **105**, 702

conformist n. 20, 105

conformity n. 16, **105**, 244, 643

confound vb. 82, 399, 414, 869

confront vb. 239, 637, 644, 649

confrontation n. 637, 649

confuse vb. 82, 187, 399

confused adj. 80, 399, 439

confusedly adv. 80

confusion n. 80, 326

confuted adj. 414

congeal vb. 332, 334, 762

congelation n. 760

congenial adj. 827

congenital adj. 5

congestion n. 332, 572

conglomerate n. 332

conglomeration n. 45

congratulate vb. 838, 878, **888**

congratulate oneself vb. 879

congratulation n. 838, **888**

congregate vb. 50, 94

congregation n. 94, 982, 987

congress n. 94, 519, 625, 641

congressman n. 625

congruity n. 16, 24, 105

conjecture n. 386, 396, 447, **448**; vb. 448

conjugal adj. 896

conjugate vb. 499

conjunction n. 499

conjunctivitis n. 820

conjure vb. 449, 984

conjurer n. 984

con man n. 480, 631, 906

connect vb. 47, 81

connected adj. 9, 47, 52, 60, 81

connection n. 9, 47, 49, 201

connoisseur n. 304, 436, 848

connotation n. 450, 459

conquer vb. 316, 661, 679

conqueror n. 661

conscience n. 382, 919

conscience-stricken adj. 833, 941

conscientiousness n. 392, 864, 931

conscious adj. 382, 426, 753

conscript n. 655; vb. 651

conscription n. 674

consecrate vb. 980, 985

consecration n. 715, 980

consecutive adj. 85, 91

consensus n. 24, 424, 643

consent n. 424, 690, **692**, 698; vb. 690, 692, 698

consequence n. 60, 85, 87, 156, 573

consequent adj. 85, 156

consequential adj. 119, 156, 573

conservation n. 374, 392, 599

conservatism n. 143

conservative n. 105, 143; adj. 143, 977

conserve n. 306; vb. 599, 748

consider vb. 384, 390, 415, 420, 526, 982

considerable adj. 32, 75, 573

considerate adj. 390, 392, 434, 886

consideration n. 384, 390, 392, 415, 886

consign vb. 268, 714

consignee n. **688**

consignment n. 268

consist vb. 1, 58, 98

consistency n. 50, 105, 143

consistent adj. 16, 24, 105

consolation n. 176, 834, 907

consolation prize n. 663

console vb. 176, 834, 907

consolidate vb. 52, 334

consolidation n. 332

consonance n. 24, 643, 790

consonant n. 493, 512; adj. 24, 105

conspicuous adj. 253, 458, 462, **823**, 877

conspiracy n. 558

conspire vb. 558

conspirer n. 558

constable n. 956

constancy n. 16, 91, 114, 140, 143, 152, 535

constant n. 152; adj. 91, 140, 143, 145, 152, 535

constellation n. 329

consternation n. 856

constituency n. 183, 540

constituent n. 55, 192; adj. 55, 73

constitute vb. 58, 98

constitution n. 5, 58, 339, 954

constitutional n. 269; adj. 954

constrain vb. 531, 674

constraint n. 674, 681

constrict vb. 197

construct vb. 58, 163, 242, 477, 930

construction n. 163, 242, 494

constructor n. 166

consul n. 688

consult vb. 624

consultant n. 624

consultation n. 519

consultative adj. 624

consume vb. 304, 569, 575, 740, 761

consumer n. 304, 726

consummate adj. 89, 581; vb. 56, 581, 659, 896

consummation n. 89, 156, 212, 581, 896

consumption n. 569

contact n. 47, **201**, 758; vb. 201

contagious adj. 586

contain vb. 98, 234, 707, 712

container n. **193**, 275

contaminate vb. 584, 588, 952

contemplate vb. 384, 415, 552

contemplative adj. 384, 434

contemporaneous adj. 120, 122

contemporary n. 122; adj. 60, 120, 122, 125

contempt n. 853, 869, **924**

contemptible adj. 580, 869, 924

contemptuous adj. 853, 924

contend vb. 414, 615, **649**, 651

contender n. 655

content n. 450, **831**; adj. 831

contented adj. 827, 831

contentious adj. 409, 651

contents n. 192, 223

contest n. **649**; vb. 604, 649

contestant n. 638; adj. 649

context n. 8

contiguity n. 199, 201

continent n. 352; adj. 944, 951

contingencies n. 700

contingent adj. 8, 403, 679, 700

contingent duration n. **111**

continual adj. 114, 138, 143, **145**

continuance *n.* 91, 107, **145**, 535
continue *vb.* 91, 107, 112, 138, 145, 535
continuity *n.* 50, **91**, 143
continuous *adj.* 91, 257
contort *vb.* 245, 251
contour *n.* 232, 242
contraband *n.* 724; *adj.* 955
contraception *n.* 169
contract *n.* 24, 468, 698, **699**, 919; *vb.* **197**, 203, 205 557, 698, 699
contraction *n.* **197**, 205, 504
contractual *adj.* 699
contradict *vb.* 14, 25, 181, 402, 414, 425, 469, 637
contradiction *n.* 14, 181, 239, 412, 414, 469, 637
contraption *n.* 565
contrary *n.* 239; *adj.* 14, 15, 239, 402, 469, 883
contrast *n.* 106, 239, 397; *vb.* 14, 397, 805
contravene *vb.* 469, 703, 955
contribute *vb.* 40, 155, 639, 715, 738
contribution *n.* 41, 917
contributor *n.* 715, 905
contributory *adj.* 563
contrite *adj.* 833, 941
contrivance *n.* 565
contrive *vb.* 477, 631
control *n.* 159, 177, 235, 622, 667, 681, 707, 956; *vb.* 177, 622, 667, 681, 707, 956
controller *n.* 623
control oneself *vb.* 681, 757, 944
controversial *adj.* 409, 410
conurbation *n.* 183
convalescence *n.* 589, 618
convene *vb.* 94
convenience *n.* 575, 827
convenient *adj.* 136, 575, 577, 748
convent *n.* 990
convention *n.* 94, 103, 519, 545, 625, 699

conventional *adj.* 103, 143, 545, 699, 843
converge *vb.* 47, 94, 96, 224, 296
convergence *n.* 224, **296**
conversation *n.* 410, **519**
converse *n.* 239; *vb.* 410, 514, 519
conversely *adv.* 14
conversion *n.* 142, **146**, 606, 714
convert *n.* 146, 941, 980; *vb.* 142, 146, 606, 714
convexity *n.* **252**
convey *vb.* 268, 275, 450, 460, 714, 715
conveyance *n.* 268, 276
conveyancing *n.* 714
convict *n.* 684; *vb.* 681, 960, 962
convicted *adj.* 941
conviction *n.* 408, 420, 530, 534, 962
convince *vb.* 177, **420**, 470
convincing *adj.* 547
convivial *adj.* 827
conviviality *n.* 884
convocation *n.* 94, 625
convolution *n.* 251
convoy *n.* 268
convulsion *n.* 326, 586
coo *vb.* 789
cook *vb.* 306, 759
cooker *n.* 763
cookery *n.* 306
cook up *vb.* 163
cool *adj.* 391, 579, 754, 757, 760, 883; *vb.* 348, 762
cooling apparatus *n.* 764
cooling-off period *n.* 135
coolness *n.* 391, 757, 837, 883
cooperate *vb.* 52, 180, 636, **639**, 709
cooperation *n.* 60, 180, **639**, 709
cooperative *n.* 641, 709; *adj.* 180, 639, 641, 709
co-opt *vb.* 540
coordinate *vb.* 81, 81
coordinated *adj.* 81
co-ownership *n.* 709
cop *n.* 956
copious *adj.* 32, 168

copper *n.* 956; *adj.* 810, 816
copse *n.* 374
copulate *vb.* 889
copy *n.* 20, **22**, 62, 77, 486, 488, 521, 522, 524; *vb.* 20, 62, 77, 165, 488, 521
copyist *n.* 521
coral *n.* 816; *adj.* 811
cord *n.* 49, 207
cordial *adj.* 884
cordiality *n.* 747, 882, 884
core *n.* 5, 90, 224, 527
cork *n.* 265, 331; *vb.* 265
corn *n.* 252, 374
corner *n.* 184, 233, 246, 254; *vb.* 707
corner-stone *n.* 217
cornucopia *n.* 168, 572
corona *n.* 250, 800
coronation *n.* 685
corporality *n.* 3, 327
corporal punishment *n.* 963
corporation *n.* 956
corpse *n.* **371**
corpulent *adj.* 194
correct *adj.* 430, 499, 510, 915, 977; *vb.* 587, 589, 963
correction *n.* 587, 963
corrective *adj.* 585, 589, 591, 963
correlate *n.* 22; *vb.* 12
correlation *n.* 9, **12**, 18
correspond *vb.* 12, 24, 150, 218, 523
correspondence *n.* 9, 12, 18, 24, 105, 397, 521, **523**
correspondent *n.* 395, 460, 523
corroborate *vb.* 217, 401, 408
corroborative *adj.* 401
corrode *vb.* 588
corrosion *n.* 53
corrugate *vb.* 260, 261
corrupt *adj.* 431, 477, 869, 932, 936; *vb.* 547, 58ᵒ, 584, 588, 936
corruption *n.* 495, 551, 588, 932, 936
cosmetic *adj.* 211, 846
cosmetics *n.* 844
cosmic *adj.* 329
cosmology *n.* 329
cosmonaut *n.* 274

cosmopolitan *n.* 903; *adj.* 101
cosmos *n.* 329
cost *n.* 743; *vb.* 743
costly *adj.* 745
costs *n.* 31, 740, 963
costume *n.* 227
cosy *adj.* 827
cottage *n.* 191
cough *n.* 359; *vb.* 359
cough up *vb.* 738
council *n.* 94, 519, **625**, 641
councillor *n.* 625
counsel *n.* 597, 624, 959; *vb.* 470, 519, 597, 624
counsellor *n.* 473, 624
count *n.* 38, 870; *vb.* 38, 400
countable *adj.* 38
count against *vb.* 588
countdown *n.* 274
countenance *n.* 236, 825
counter *n.* 482; *adj.* 181; *vb.* 637, 647
counteract *vb.* 31, 181, 648, 686
counteraction *n.* **181**
counterattack *n.* 647
counterbalance *n.* 31, 152; *vb.* 31, 181, 330
counter-evidence *n.* **402**
counterfeit *n.* 20, 487; *adj.* 20, 431, 477; *vb.* 20, 477
counterfoil *n.* 482
countermand *n.* 686, 691; *vb.* 686
countermeasure *n.* 181
counterpart *n.* 18, 20, 22, 28
counterpoise *vb.* 330
counter-productive *adj.* 576
counterweight *n.* 152, 181, 330
countless *adj.* 75, 78
count on *vb.* 443
country *n.* 183
countryman *n.* 871
county *n.* 183
coup *n.* 148
coup de grâce *n.* 659
coupé *n.* 276
couple *n.* 61; *vb.* 47, 61
couplet *n.* 61
coupling *n.* 47, 49
courage *n.* **857**
courier *n.* 460, 467

course n. 269, 306, 358, 360, 470, 559
course of action n. 558
course of time n. **110**
court n. 234, 559, 658, 870, 957; vb. 882, 890
court danger vb. 859
courteous adj. 392, 886, 922
courtesy n. **886**, 899
courtship n. 890
cousin n. 11
cove n. 353
covenant n. 698, 699, 701; vb. 698, 699
cover n. 193, 225, 306, 463, 595; vb. 206, 225, 461, 646, 798, 801
cover for vb. 149
covering n. 211, 222, **225**, 461, 801
covert n. 254, 374, 463, 595
covet vb. 861, 914
covetous adj. 750, 861, 914
covetousness n. 750, 861, 914
cow n. 381
coward n. 162, 858
cowardice n. **858**
cowardly adj. 858
co-worker n. 640
coy adj. 876
crack n. 200; vb. 264, 456, 782
crack down on vb. 669, 963
cracker n. 306
crackle n. 782
crack up vb. 439, 856, 925
cradle n. 325
craft n. 277, 557, 631
craftsman n. 619
crafty adj. 478, 631, 932
cram vb. 56, 470, 472
crank n. 106, 440
cranky adj. 439
crash n. 282, 739, 782; vb. 282, 739, 780, 782, 787
crash-land vb. 273, 317, 321
crass adj. 849
crate n. 193
crater n. 254
crave vb. 695, 861, 914
craven adj. 858
craving n. 861

crawl vb. 281, 881
crawl with vb. 75
crayon vb. 488
craze n. 125, 439, 539, 850, 861
crazy adj. 433, 435, 439, 861, 889
creak vb. 781, 787
cream n. 306, 342, 365, 579, 813; adj. 807, 813; vb. 342
creamy adj. 362, 365
crease n. 260; vb. 260
create vb. 155, 163, 242, 449, 558
creation n. 21, 163, 329, 366
creative adj. 21, 163, 449
creator n. 155, 166, 491, 966
creature n. 366, 368, 373, 379
crèche n. 475
credence n. 420
credible adj. 404, 406, 420
credit n. 420, 718, 731, **736**, 868, 909, 925; vb. 736, 742
creditable adj. 925
credit card n. 718, 731, 736
creditor n. 718, 736
credulous adj. 422
creed n. 420, 974
creek n. 354, 358
creep vb. 316, 461
cremate vb. 372, 761
cremation n. 372
crematorium n. 372, 763
crescent n. 247, 559; adj. 36, 247
crest n. 212, 358, 482, 872
crestfallen adj. 837, 874
cretin n. 437, 440
crevasse n. 254
crew n. 94, 272
crib n. 22; vb. 20
crier n. 467
crime n. 938, 955
criminal n. 684, 906, 940; adj. 932
criminality n. 932, 938
crimp n. 260; vb. 251, 260
crimson adj. 811
cringe vb. 856
cringing adj. 881
cripple vb. 245, 588

crisis n. 80, 136, 665
crisp adj. 760; vb. 306
crispy adj. 338
criterion n. 23, 27, 103, 400
critic n. 456, 524, 526, 848, 928
critical adj. 136, 382, 398, 415, 573, 594, 926
criticism n. 456, 624, 926
criticize vb. 696, 832, 893, **926**, **962**
critique n. 398, 456, 526
croak vb. 787, 789
crocodile n. 91
crocus n. 813
croft n. 378
crook n. 247, 480, 723, 906, 940, 989; vb. 247
crooked adj. 29, 219, 245
crop n. 374, 567, 705; vb. 203
crop up vb. 153, 825
cross n. 221, 592, 830, 964; adj. 893, 895; vb. 45, 221, 313, 478
cross-examination n. 394, 960
cross-eyed adj. 820
crossing n. **221**, 313
cross purposes n. 642
crotchety adj. 539
crouch vb. 209, 319
crow vb. 789
crowd n. 75, 94, 821, 871; vb. 75, 94
crown n. 212, 250, 659, 663, 677; vb. 212, 685, 868, 878
crucial adj. 136, 573
crucifix n. 221
crucifixion n. 370, 828, 963
crucify vb. 830, 963
crude adj. 511, 887
cruel adj. 669, 900, 908
cruise n. 271; vb. 269, 271
crumb n. 33, 340
crumble vb. 162, 164, 338, 340, 588
crumple vb. 258
crunch vb. 340
crush n. 94, 889; vb. 164, 340, 364, 414, 661, 874
crushed adj. 837, 874
crushing n. 874

crustacean n. 373
crutch n. 217
crux n. 221
cry n. 597, 782, 788, 789, 839; vb. 788, 789, 833, 839
cry-baby n. 162, 858
cry out for vb. 531, 562
cry over vb. 833
cryptic adj. 466
crystal adj. 802
crystal-clear adj. 458
crystallize vb. 332, 334
cry wolf vb. 478, 598
cube n. 246
cuckoo vb. 789
cuddle vb. 890
cudgel vb. 282
cuff n. 963
cuisine n. 306
cul de sac n. 635
culinary adj. 306
cull vb. 540
culminate vb. 56, 212, 659
culmination n. 89, 581
culpable adj. 157, 938
culprit n. 684
cultivate vb. 378, 470
cultivated adj. 848, 886
cultivator n. 378
culture n. 426, 848, 886
cultured adj. 426, 848, 886
culvert n. 360
cumbersome adj. 330, 628
cumulative adj. 36
cuneiform n. 493; adj. 246
cunning n. **631**, 932; adj. 478, 631
cup n. 193, 663
curate n. 986
curative adj. 589, 591
curator n. 593, 683
curb n. 281, 635, 681; vb. 37, 235, 281, 681
curdle vb. 332, 773
cure n. 176, 181, 589, 591, 834; vb. 589, 591, 599
curfew n. 128, 681
curiosity n. **388**, 866
curious adj. 388, 394
curl n. 247, 251; vb. 247, 251, 260
currency n. 731
current n. 140, 358, 359; adj. 120, 125, 153, 464, 492, 545
current affairs n. 465

deduce *vb.* 410, 448
deduction *n.* 42, 43, 87, 410, 744
deed *n.* 609
deem *vb.* 420, 448
deep *n.* 351; *adj.* 148, 182, 210, 805
deepen *vb.* 36, 210, 835
deep-freeze *n.* 764; *vb.* 762
deep-seated *adj.* 210, 545
deface *vb.* 845, 847
defamation *n.* 869, 928
defamatory *adj.* 926, 928, 930
default *n.* 315, 739; *vb.* 739
defeat *n.* 445, 660, 662; *vb.* 414, 661
defeatist *adj.* 855
defecate *vb.* 310
defect *n.* 43, 57, 582, 660, 662, 847
defection *n.* 189, 538, 920, 932
defective *adj.* 55, 57, 580, 582, 847
defence *n.* 402, 593, 595, **646**, 648, 929, 960
defenceless *adj.* 160
defend *vb.* 410, 593, 646, 647, 648, 929, 959
defendant *n.* 684, 960
defer *vb.* 135, 424, 654, 920
deference *n.* 654, 922
defiance *n.* 637, **644**, 672, 880
deficiency *n.* 29, 35, 57, 189, 315, 571, 660
deficient *adj.* 29, 35, 57, 315, 582, 660
deficit *n.* 57, 315, 737
defile *vb.* 584, 588, 608, 928, 936
defilement *n.* 584, 588, 608, 928
define *vb.* 102, 235, 496, 525
defining *adj.* 456
definite *adj.* 408, 823
definite article *n.* 499
definite space *n.* **183**
definition *n.* 235, 450
deflate *vb.* 874
deflated *adj.* 874
deflation *n.* 197, 874
deflect *vb.* 285

deformed *adj.* 243, 245, 845
deformity *n.* 245, 582, 845, 847
defraud *vb.* 478, 722
defrost *vb.* 345, 761
deft *adj.* 280, 627
defunct *adj.* 369
defy *vb.* 25, 331, 637, 644, 672
degenerate *n.* 940; *adj.* 147, 936; *vb.* 53, 147, 588, 590, 936
degradation *n.* 608, 686, 869, 928
degrade *vb.* 588, 686, 869
degree *n.* 7, 27, 93, 400, 766
dehydrate *vb.* 350, 599
de-ice *vb.* 761
deification *n.* 983
deign *vb.* 874
deism *n.* 974
deity *n.* 966
déjà vu n. 441
dejection *n.* **837**
delay *n.* 135, 281; *vb.* 135, 281
delegate *n.* 149, 625, 688, 689; *vb.* 685, 714
delete *vb.* 42, 485
deliberate *adj.* 410, 530, 543, 552; *vb.* 384
deliberation *n.* 384, 410, 860
delicacy *n.* 162, 205, 306, 338, 770, 848
delicate *n.* 753; *adj.* 162, 205, 331, 338, 510, 594, 735, 848, 864
delicatessen *n.* 306
delicious *adj.* 306, 767, 770, 772, 829
delight *n.* 306, 770, 827, 829; *vb.* 755, 829, 840, 889
delighted *adj.* 756, 827
delightful *adj.* 755, 770, 827, 829
delineate *vb.* 232, 486, 525
delirious *adj.* 827
delirium *n.* 756
deliver *vb.* 268, 601, 680, 714
deliverance *n.* 600, **601**, 680
delivery *n.* 268, 512, 514, 621, 715

delude *vb.* 478
deluge *n.* 358, 572; *vb.* 349
delusion *n.* 412, 457, 478
demand *n.* 562, 671, 695; *vb.* 562, 671, 695, 727, 743
demarcation *n.* 48, 231, 235
dematerialize *vb.* 2, 328, 826, 984
demeanour *n.* 621
demented *adj.* 439
demise *n.* 89, 369
democracy *n.* 667, 678
demolish *vb.* 164, 319
demolition *n.* 164
demon *n.* 969
demonism *n.* 983
demonstrate *vb.* 401, **413**, 456, 458, 696
demonstration *n.* **413**, 458, 696, 825
demonstrator *n.* 106, 148
demoralize *vb.* 837, 936
demote *vb.* 686
demur *n.* 533; *vb.* 533, 696
demure *adj.* 876, 951
den *n.* 234, 463, 595
dendrochronology *n.* 116
denial *n.* 414, 469, 542, 694
denigrate *vb.* 928
denomination *n.* 496, 641, 979
denominational *adj.* 979
denominator *n.* 39
denote *vb.* 450, 482
dénouement n. 89
denounce *vb.* 892, 928, 930, 962
dense *adj.* 75, **332**, 334, 435
density *n.* 204, **332**, 400
dent *n.* 254, 847
denude *vb.* 228
denunciation *n.* 901, 926, 930, 962
deny *vb.* 402, 414, 469, 542, 637, 691, 694, 944
deodorant *n.* 775
depart *vb.* 151, 285, 293, **299**, 600, 687, 826
department *n.* 55, 97
departure *n.* 285, 293,

299, 369, 600, 687, 826
depend *vb.* 420, 679, 854
dependable *adj.* 392, 702, 868, 931
dependant *n.* 132, 287, 676
dependence *n.* 9, 420, 679
dependent *adj.* 420, 679, 700
depict *vb.* 20, 486, 488
deplete *vb.* 358, 569
depleted *adj.* 57, 569, 588
deplore *vb.* 941
deport *vb.* 99, 963
deposit *n.* 55, 367, 567, 701, 738; *vb.* 567
depository *n.* 193, 567, 732
depot *n.* 567
deprave *vb.* 588, 608
depreciate *vb.* 696, 744, 746, 928
depreciation *n.* 37, 43, 744, 928
depress *vb.* 209, 254, 319, 837, 841
depression *n.* 37, 169, 209, 210, 254, 259, **319**, 837
deprive *vb.* 706, 720
deprived *adj.* 435, 706
depth *n.* 26, 209, **210**, 400
deputation *n.* 685, 688
deputize *vb.* 685, 689
deputy *n.* 149, 688, **689**; *adj.* 689
derail *vb.* 187
deranged *adj.* 439
derelict *adj.* 607
dereliction *n.* 393, 920
deride *vb.* 838, 853, 924, 928
derivation *n.* 155, 410, 494
derivative *n.* 494; *adj.* 156
derive *vb.* 156, 157, 410, 716
derogatory *adj.* 928
descend *vb.* 317, 869
descendant *n.* 11, 171
descent *n.* 11, 171, **317**, 870
describe *vb.* 413, 460, 496, **525**
description *n.* 460, 465, 486, 496, **525**

descriptive *adj.* 456, 525

desecrate *vb.* 608, 981

desert *adj.* 350; *vb.* 556, 607, 898

deserter *n.* 538, 555, 672, 858

desertion *n.* 189, 556, 600, 672, 898, 920

deserts *n.* 917

deserve *vb.* 573, 917, 963

desiccate *vb.* 350

design *n.* 23, 58, 242, 482, 488, 552, 558; *vb.* 58, 488, 543, 552, 558

designate *adj.* 119, 123; *vb.* 102, 450, 482, 486, 496

designer *n.* 491, 558

desirable *adj.* 577, 579

desire *n.* 388, 530, 552, 854, **861**; *vb.* 530, 532, 854, 861, 914

desist *vb.* 89, 144

desolate *adj.* 169, 588, 837

desolation *n.* 164, 569

despair *n.* 828, 837, **855**, 856; *vb.* 828, 855

desperate *adj.* 706

desperation *n.* 855

despise *vb.* 542, 923, 924

despondency *n.* 445, 837, 855

despotism *n.* 669, 900

dessert *n.* 306

destination *n.* 235, 284, 298, 552

destined *adj.* 154, 531, 543

destiny *n.* 154

destitute *adj.* 708, 735

destroy *vb.* 82, **164**, 370, 569

destroyer *n.* **167**, 277

destruction *n.* 2, 53, **164**, 370

destructive *adj.* 164, 175, 370, 580

detach *vb.* 48, 51

detached *adj.* 48, 391, 757

detachment *n.* 48, 391, 757, 933

detail *n.* 8, 55, 460

detailed *adj.* 8, 525

detain *vb.* 681, 712

detect *vb.* 419, 774, 795

détente *n.* 643

detention *n.* 681

deter *vb.* 548, 635

deteriorate *vb.* 37, 164, 588, 590

deterioration *n.* 126, 142, 569, **588**, 590

determination *n.* 400, 415, 530, 534, 540, 857

determine *vb.* 89, 155, 177, 400, 413, 530, 534, 543, 552

determined *adj.* 534, 535, 857

determinism *n.* 531

deterrent *n.* 548

detest *vb.* 862, 892

detonate *vb.* 782

detonator *n.* 765

detour *n.* 285, 322, 561

detract *vb.* 42, 391

detriment *n.* 580, 588

detrimental *adj.* 164, 578, 580

devastate *vb.* 164

devastation *n.* 569

develop *vb.* 36, 196, 242, **288**, 324, 587

developing *adj.* 36, 129, 603

development *n.* 36, 153, 196, 288, 324, 587

deviate *vb.* 15, 219, 247, 285, 505

deviation *n.* 15, 29, 142, **285**, 431

device *n.* 565

devil *n.* 969, 984

devilish *adj.* 900, 969, 984

devious *adj.* 932

devise *vb.* 58, 163, 449, 558

devolution *n.* 667, 685, 714

devolve *vb.* 667, 685, 714, 919

devoted *adj.* 673, 702, 882, 889, 982

devotee *n.* 545

devote oneself to *vb.* 605

devotion *n.* 673, 702, 889, 980

devour *vb.* 304, 569, 948

devout *adj.* 974, 980, 982

dew *n.* 349

dexterity *n.* 240

dexterous *adj.* 627

diabolical *adj.* 900, 969, 984

diabolism *n.* 984

diagnosis *n.* 396, 398, 456

diagonal *n.* 219; *adj.* 219

diagram *n.* 486

dial *999 vb.* 591, 598

dialect *n.* 492

dialectical materialism *n.* 327

dialogue *n.* 394, 410, 519

diameter *n.* 204, 400

diametrical *adj.* 14

diamond *n.* 246

diarrhoea *n.* 310

diary *n.* 116, 441, 483

dice *vb.* 48, 306

dichotomy *n.* 63

dictate *n.* 671; *vb.* 531, 671, 674

dictator *n.* 623, 669

dictionary *n.* 83, 494, 524

didactic *adj.* 470

die *n.* 23; *vb.* 2, 89, 293, **369**, 588, 826

die-hard *n.* 143, 537

diet *n.* 625, 947; *vb.* 205, 947

differ *vb.* 14, 15, 19, 151, 425, 642

difference *n.* 10, 15, **19**, 104, 106, 425, 642

different *adj.* 14, 15, 19, 104, 106

differentiate *vb.* 15, 398

different time *n.* **121**

differing *adj.* 25, 425

difficult *adj.* 405, 615, **633**, 887

difficulty *n.* **633**, 665, 830

diffuse *adj.* 505; *vb.* 95, 297, 346, 464

diffuseness *n.* **505**

dig *n.* 254; *vb.* 210, 254, 378

digest *n.* 527; *vb.* 304, 472, 527

digestible *adj.* 306

digger *n.* 312

digit *n.* 39

dignified *adj.* 510, 848, 868, 870, 873, 982

dignity *n.* 510, 868, 870, 873

dig one's heels in *vb.* 537

digression *n.* 285, 505, 561

digs *n.* 191

dilapidated *adj.* 126

dilapidation *n.* 569, 588

dilated *adj.* 196

dilatory *adj.* 135

dilemma *n.* 136, 409, 633

diligent *adj.* 390, 392, 535, 611, 702

dilute *vb.* 37, 162

diluted *adj.* 162, 507

dim *adj.* 798, **799**, 806, 820, 895; *vb.* 799

dimension *n.* 26, 194, 400

diminish *vb.* 37, 76

diminutive *adj.* 33, 195

dimness *n.* 128, **799**, 806

dimple *n.* 254

din *n.* 780, 791

dine out *vb.* 304

dingy *adj.* 805, 809

dinner *n.* 306

diocese *n.* 183

dip *n.* 254, 319, 321; *vb.* 319, 321, 349

diplomat *n.* 688

diplomatic *adj.* 392, 886

dipsomania *n.* 950

direct *adj.* 248, 476, 502, 508; *vb.* **284**, 290, 470, 529, 622, 624, 667, 671, 956

direction *n.* 103, 178, 269, **284**, 392, 470, 559, 622, 626, 671, 956

directive *n.* 671; *adj.* 622

director *n.* 558, **623**, 675

directory *n.* 83

dirge *n.* 839

dirt *n.* 584, 952

dirty *adj.* 584, 952; *vb.* 584

disable *vb.* 160, 162

disabled *adj.* 160, 586

disadvantage *n.* 551, 578

disadvantageous *adj.* 137, 576, 578

disagree *vb.* **25**, 425, 586, 637, 642, 696, 771, 926

disagreeable *adj.* 771, 830, 862, 895

disagreeing *adj.* 25, 425, 642

disagreement *n.* 15, **25**, 106, 425, 642, 926

disallow *vb.* 691, 694

disappear *vb.* 2, 113, 826

disappearance *n.* 189, 600, **826**

disappeared *adj.* 189, 826

disappoint *vb.* 445, 832

disappointing *adj.* 445, 571

disappointment *n.* **445**, 662, 830

disapproval *n.* 425, 542, 696, **926**

disapprove *vb.* 425, 542, 637, 696, **926**

disarm *vb.* 160

disarrangement *n.* 80, **82**

disaster *n.* 551, 662, 665, 900

disastrous *adj.* 551, 662, 665, 855

disband *vb.* 53, 82, 95

disbelief *n.* 409, 421, 975

disbelieving *adj.* 421, 975

disc *n.* 250, 484, 794

discard *vb.* 542, 556, 607, 713

discarded *adj.* 126

discern *vb.* 398, 426, 434, 818

discerning *adj.* 384, 398, 426, 434

discharge *n.* 301, 303, 310, 680, 911, 961; *vb.* 290, 301, 303, 310, 601, 680, 738, 740, 911, 921, 961

disciple *n.* 146, 287, 428, 474

disciplinarian *n.* 669

discipline *n.* 79, 470, 681, 963; *vb.* 470, 669, 681, 963

disciplined *adj.* 81, 681, 944

disclaim *vb.* 469, 538, 542

disclosure *n.* 419, 458, **462**, 464, 976

discoloration *n.* 582, 806

discomfort *n.* 828; *vb.* 830

disconcert *vb.* 82, 391, 445, 832

disconnect *vb.* 48, 92

disconnected *adj.* 51, 80, 92

discontent *n.* 445, 828, **832**, 926

discontinue *vb.* 89, 92, 144, 546, 556

discontinuity *n.* **92**

discord *n.* 25, 425, **642**, 787, **791**

discount *n.* 42, 43, **744**

discourage *vb.* 548, 633, 832, 837

discourse *n.* 514, 518, 526

discourteous *adj.* **887**, 923

discourtesy *n.* **887**, 923

discover *vb.* 186, 419, 472

discoverer *n.* 155, 166

discovery *n.* **419**, 460

discredit *vb.* 414, 588, 869, 928

discreet *adj.* 392, 434

discrepancy *n.* 15, 25

discrete *adj.* 48

discretion *n.* 530, 860

discriminate *vb.* 15, 398, 540, 916

discriminating *adj.* 392, 398, 434, 540, 848, 864

discrimination *n.* 15, **398**, 848, 916

discuss *vb.* 410, 514, 519, 526, 624, 700

disdain *n.* 853, 924; *vb.* 924

disease *n.* 586

disembark *vb.* 298

disembodied *adj.* 4, 328

disentangle *vb.* 46, 48, 81, 248

disfigure *vb.* 245, 845, 847

disfigurement *n.* 582, 845, 847

disfranchise *vb.* 918

disgrace *n.* 869; *vb.* 588, 869

disgraceful *adj.* 869

disgruntle *vb.* 832

disgruntled *adj.* 832

disguise *n.* 18, 461, 463; *vb.* 20, 146, 461

disgust *n.* 892; *vb.* 771, 892

dish *n.* 306

dishearten *vb.* 832

dishevel *vb.* 82

dishevelled *adj.* 584

dishonest *adj.* 477, 478, 631, 932

dishonour *n.* 869, 923; *vb.* 588, 869, 923

dish out *vb.* 717

disillusion *vb.* 445

disinclination *n.* 389, 533, 862

disinfect *vb.* 583

disingenuous *adj.* 477

disinherit *vb.* 720

disintegrate *vb.* 48, 53, 164, 328

disintegration *n.* 48, 53, 164, 588

disinter *vb.* 372

disinterested *adj.* 541, 757, 915, 933

disinterestedness *n.* **933**

dislike *n.* 637, **862**, 883, 892; *vb.* 771, 862, 892

dislocate *vb.* 48, 82, 187

dislodge *vb.* 187, 312

disloyal *adj.* 431, 672, 920

disloyalty *n.* 703, 920, 932

dismal *adj.* 798, 837, 895

dismantle *vb.* 164

dismay *n.* 837, 856

dismembered *adj.* 48

dismiss *vb.* 99, 295, 303, 389, 542, 686, 920, 961

dismount *vb.* 298

disobedience *n.* 644, **672**, 703, 981

disobey *vb.* 644, 672, 703, 955

disorder *n.* **80**, 175, 584, 586, 668, 955; *vb.* 82

disorderly *adj.* 82, 887

disorganized *adj.* 80, 82

disorientate *vb.* 285

disown *vb.* 469, 538, 542

disparage *vb.* 418, 548, 926, 928

disparagement *n.* **928**

disparate *adj.* 15, 19, 29, 104

dispassionate *adj.* 757, 863, 915, 933

dispatch *n.* 268, 460, 465, 523; *vb.* 268, 523, 613

dispatch bearer *n.* 467

dispel *vb.* 95

dispensation *n.* 713, 921

dispense *vb.* 95, 715, 717

disperse *vb.* 48, 82, 95, 297

dispersion *n.* **95**

dispirited *adj.* 837

displace *vb.* 85, 187, 312, 706

displacement *n.* **187**, 686

display *n.* 413, 825; *vb.* 413, 458

displeasure *n.* 445, 893, 926

disposal *n.* 81, 713, 727

dispose *vb.* 81, 717

disposed *adj.* 81, 179, 532, 751

dispose of *vb.* 89, 303, 609, **713**, 717

disposition *n.* 5, 532, 545, 751

dispossession *n.* 706, 720, 918

disproof *n.* **414**

disproportion *n.* 10, 29, 245

disproportionate *adj.* 25, 29, 245

disprove *vb.* 414

dispute *n.* 25, 410, 642; *vb.* 25, 410, 414, 637, 642, 649

disqualify *vb.* 99, 160, 918

disquiet *n.* 828; *vb.* 856

disregard *n.* 391, 393, 672, 703, 920; *vb.* 99, 389, 391, 393, 555, 644, 672, 703, 887, 924

disreputable *adj.* 869, 932

disrepute *n.* **869**

disrespect *n.* 869, 887, **923**, 924

disrespectful *adj.* 880, 887, 923, 924

disrupt *vb.* 82

disruption *n.* 175

dissatisfaction *n.* 445, 828, **832**, 862, 926

dissect *vb.* 48, 53

dissemble *vb.* 461, 477

disseminate *vb.* 95, 378, 460, 464

dissension *n.* 25, 425, 637, 642

dissent *n.* **425**, 696; *vb.* 151, 425, 642

dissenter *n*. 106, 425, 975

dissertation *n*. **526**

dissident *n*. 979; *adj.* 106, 425, 672, 979

dissimilarity *n*. **19**, 25, 29, 106

dissimulation *n*. 19

dissipate *vb*. 95, 346, 569, 749

dissipation *n*. 95, 569, 945

dissociation *n*. 10, 48

dissolute *adj*. 936, 952

dissolution *n*. 48, 53, 164, 345, 369, 686, 898

dissolve *vb*. 2, 53, 164, 345, 686, 826

dissonance *n*. 25, 787, 791

dissuade *vb*. **548**, 624

dissuasion *n*. **548**, 624

distance *n*. 194, **198**, 400, 885; *vb*. 198

distant *adj*. **198**, 517, 781, 885

distaste *n*. 862

distemper *n*. 225

distend *vb*. 196

distil *vb*. 346

distinct *adj*. 48, 102, 452, 512, 778, 823

distinction *n*. 398, 868, 870

distinctive *adj*. 5

distinguish *vb*. 15, 398, 452

distinguished *adj*. 208, 573, 868, 870

distort *vb*. 245, 457, 471, 477, 487, 588, 845

distorted *adj*. 245, 477, 582

distortion *n*. 245, 416, 457, 477, 487, 845

distracted *adj*. 391, 442

distraught *adj*. 756

distress *n*. 445, 665, 828; *vb*. 830

distressed *adj*. 735

distressing *adj*. 551, 830

distress signal *n*. 598, 902

distribute *vb*. 95, 464, 715, 717

distribution *n*. 81, 717

district *n*. 183

distrust *n*. 421, 913; *vb*. 423

disturb *vb*. 82, 137, 187, 326, 856

disturbance *n*. 80, 137, 175, 326

disunite *vb*. 48, 51

disunity *n*. 17

disuse *n*. 546, 569, **607**; *vb*. 607

ditch *n*. 261, **360**, 646; *vb*. 556

dither *n*. 326, 756

ditto *adv*. 77

dive *n*. 321; *vb*. 271, 273, 321

diverge *vb*. 15, 48, 95, 151, 219, **297**

divergence *n*. 285, **297**

divergent *adj*. 15, 219, 285, 297, 978

diverse *adj*. 15, 104

diversified *adj*. 17, 104

diversify *vb*. 817

diversion *n*. 142, 285, 449, 840

diversity *n*. 15, 17, 19, **104**, 817 ·

divert *vb*. 391

diverting *adj*. 840

divest *vb*. 228, 720

divide *vb*. 38, 48, 55, **63**, 95, 97, 717

dividends *n*. 741

divination *n*. 447, 984

divine *adj*. 966, 974; *vb*. 447, 448, 984

divinity *n*. **966**

divisibility *n*. 51

division *n*. 25, 38, 48, 55, 97, 425, 655, 717

divisive *adj*. 642

divorce *n*. 48, 713, **898**; *vb*. 48, 898

divulge *vb*. 458, 462

do *n*. 878; *vb*. 570, 577, 605, **609**, 673, 702

do away with *vb*. 370

docile *adj*. 654, 673

dock *n*. 298, 957; *vb*. 298

docket *n*. 482; *vb*. 482

doctor *n*. 428, 436, 473; *vb*. 477

doctrine *n*. 420, 626, 974

document *n*. 401, 483, 521; *vb*. 401, 483, 521

dodge *n*. 478, 631; *vb*. 533, 555

dodger *n*. 480, 600

doe *n*. 381

doer *n*. 609, 619

dog *n*. 380; *vb*. 287, 554

doggedness *n*. 534, 535

dogma *n*. 420, 974

dogmatic *adj*. 468, 537

do-gooder *n*. 899, 903, 905

do in *vb*. 370

doing *n*. 609, 702; *adj.* 609

do-it-yourself *adj*. 628

doldrums *n*. 837

doleful *adj*. 837

dole out *vb*. 95, 715, 717

doll up *vb*. 844

doltish *adj*. 435

domain *n*. 956

dome *n*. 225, 252

domestic *n*. 676; *adj.* 190

domestic animal *n*. 373

domesticate *vb*. 377

domesticated *adj*. 190

domestic science *n*. 306

domicile *n*. 191

dominance *n*. 34, 159, 177

dominant *adj*. 159, 177, 667

dominate *vb*. 177, 208, 667, 669, 679

domineer *vb*. 667, 669

dominion *n*. 667

don *n*. 428, 473; *vb*. 227

donate *vb*. 715

donor *n*. 715, 905

doom *n*. 543; *vb*. 962

door *n*. 262

doorman *n*. 676

do over *vb*. 645

dormancy *n*. 459, 610, 612

dorsal *adj*. 237

dose *n*. 26, 591

dot *n*. 33

dotage *n*. 130

dote on *vb*. 889, 983

double *n*. 28, 149, 971; *adj.* 62; *vb*. 62, 149, 260

double-cross *vb*. 478, 932

double dealing *n*. 477, 631, 932; *adj.* 477, 932

double entendre n. 454, 842

double-sidedness *n*. 61

doubt *n*. 409, 421, 975; *vb*. 409, 421, 423

doubtful *adj*. 407, 409, 421

dough *n*. 364, 731

douse *vb*. 762

dove *n*. 656

dovetail *vb*. 24, 47

dowager *n*. 870, 898

dowdiness *n*. 849

down *adj*. 837; *adv*. 209

down-and-out *n*. 697; *adj.* 735

downcast *adj*. 837

downfall *n*. 164, 317, 662

downgrade *vb*. 686

down-hearted *adj*. 837

down-payment *n*. 55, 738

downpour *n*. 358

downward *adj*. 219, 317

doze *n*. 612, 617; *vb*. 612

dozen *n*. 70

drab *adj*. 805, 809, 843

draft *n*. 558, 602; *vb*. 521, 558

drag *n*. 181, 635; *vb*. 181, 291, 294

drag up *vb*. 441

drain *n*. 360; *vb*. 319, 358, 569, 806

drained *adj*. 617

drake *n*. 380

dram *n*. 309

drama *n*. **529**, 866

dramatic *adj*. 529, 752, 755, 866

dramatis personae n. 529

drape *n*. 801; *vb*. 216

draught *n*. 309, 359

draught animal *n*. 291

draughtsman *n*. 491

draughty *adj*. 348, 359

draw *n*. 28, 294, 553; *vb*. 28, 291, 294, 308, 312, 390, 486, 488, 525, 705, 889

drawback *n*. 582

drawer *n*. 491

drawing *n*. 291, 488

drawl *n*. 515; *vb*. 515

draw up *vb*. 558

dread *n*. 856; *vb*. 856

dreadful *adj*. 830, 856

dream *n*. 4, 449, 552, 854; *vb*. 391, 449, 552, 612, 854, 861

dream up *vb*. 558

dreamy *adj*. 384

dreary *adj*. 798, 841, 843

dredge *vb*. 312

dredge up *vb*. 441

dregs *n.* 44, 576, 871
drench *vb.* 349, 572
dress *n.* 227; *vb.* 227, 568, 844
dressage *n.* 269
dress down *vb.* 926, 963
dressing *n.* **227**
dribble *vb.* 319, 358
dried *adj.* 350
drift *n.* 178, 450; *vb.* 178, 257, 612
drill *n.* 264; *vb.* 264, 378, 470
drink *n.* **309**, 343; *vb.* 304, 950
drinker *n.* 304, 950
drink in *vb.* 390, 472
drinking *n.* **304**
drip *n.* 349, 841; *vb.* 319, 358
drip-dry *vb.* 350
drive *n.* 173, 269, 282, 290, 559, 645, 674; *vb.* 173, 269, 282, 290, 295, 377, 547, 674
drive at *vb.* 450
drivel *n.* 451
driver *n.* 270
driving *n.* 269; *adj.* 674
drizzle *n.* 358; *vb.* 358
droll *adj.* 851
drone *vb.* 783, 784, 789
droop *vb.* 216, 317, 319, 837, 841
drop *n.* 37, 210, 249, 254, 309, 317, 321; *vb.* 37, 317, 319, 358, 556, 617, 706
drop anchor *vb.* 271, 298
drop in *vb.* 300
drop out *vb.* 660
droppings *n.* 310
drought *n.* 350, 861
drown *vb.* 321, 349, 370, 963
drowsy *adj.* 612, 617, 841
drudge *n.* 615, 619, 676; *vb.* 615
drug *n.* 173, 591; *vb.* 754
drum *n.* 249
drumming *n.* 325
drunk *n.* 950; *adj.* 950
drunkard *n.* 304, 950
dry *adj.* **350**, 773, 787, 843, 949; *vb.* 306, 350
dryness *n.* **350**, 843
dualism *n.* 61

duality *n.* **61**
dub *vb.* 496, 497
dubious *adj.* 407, 421, 932
duchess *n.* 870
duchy *n.* 183
duck *n.* 74, 381; *vb.* 321, 349, 555
duct *n.* 360
dud *n.* 662
due *n.* 737, 917; *adj.* 737, 917
duel *n.* 649
dueness *n.* **917**
dues *n.* 716, 743, 917
dug-out *n.* 254
duke *n.* 870
dull *adj.* 174, 256, 435, 666, 754, 768, 771, 785, 798, 799, 806, 843; *vb.* 256, 754, 785, 799
dullness *n.* 174, 435, 768, 806, **843**
dumb *adj.* 435, 513, 517
dumbfound *vb.* 513, 866
dummy *n.* 22, 23, 149; *adj.* 149
dump *vb.* 727
dumpy *adj.* 195, 203, 204
dunce *n.* 429, 437, 630
dung *n.* 310
dungeon *n.* 234, 682
duo *n.* 792
dupe *n.* **479**, 853; *vb.* 478
duple *adj.* 61
duplicate *n.* 22; *adj.* 13, 62; *vb.* 62, 165
duplication *n.* **62**, 77, 165
duplicity *n.* 477, 932
durability *n.* 143, 337
durable *adj.* 112, 161, 337
duration *n.* 107, 145
duress *n.* 674
during *adv., prep.* 107
dusk *n.* 128, 799, 809
dust *n.* 340, 371, 576
duster *n.* 485
dusty *adj.* 340, 350, 584, 809
dutiful *adj.* 673, 919
duty *n.* 557, 685, 737, 743, **919**
dwarf *n.* 195, 970; *adj.* 203
dwell *vb.* 191

dwindle *vb.* 37, 197, 569
dye *n.* 805
dying *n.* 369; *adj.* 130, 861
dynamic *adj.* 159, 173, 611
dynamite *n.* 657
dysentery *n.* 310

E

eager *adj.* 443, 532, 756, 861
earl *n.* 870
earlier *adj.* 84, 118; *adv.* 121
earliness *n.* **134**
early *adj.* 117, 134
early warning *n.* 597
earmark *vb.* 482
earn *vb.* 705, 917
earner *n.* 716
earnest *n.* 701; *adj.* 532, 752, 837
earnings *n.* 705, 738, 741
earring *n.* 216
earshot *n.* 199, 795
earth *n.* 329, 352
earthquake *n.* 325
earthworks *n.* 646
earthy *adj.* 352
ease *n.* 616, **634**, 827, 831, 834; *vb.* 335, 634, 834
ease off *vb.* 281, 616
east *n.* 284
easy *adj.* 634, 952
easy-going *adj.* 670, 757
eat *vb.* **304**, 569, 767
eat away *vb.* 569, 588
eating *n.* **304**
eavesdropping *n.* 460, 795
ebb *vb.* 37, 358
eccentric *n.* 106, 440; *adj.* 106, 439
ecclesiastical *adj.* 985
echo *n.* 22, 283, 778, 784; *vb.* 77, 283, 784
eclipse *n.* 798; *vb.* 34, 314, 461, 798
ecology *n.* 366, 376
economical *adj.* 392, 748
economics *n.* 622
economize *vb.* 37, 748

economy *n.* 392, **748**; *adj.* 746
ecstasy *n.* 756, 827
eddy *n.* 323, 358; *vb.* 323, 358
edge *n.* **233**, 235, 255, 769; *vb.* 233, 255
edgy *adj.* 756, 856, 894
edible *adj.* 306
edict *n.* 626, 671, 954
edifice *n.* 163
edify *vb.* 470, 550, 579
edit *vb.* 456
edition *n.* 524
editor *n.* 456, 524
educate *vb.* 470
educated *adj.* 426
education *n.* 426, 470
educational *adj.* 460, 470
eerie *adj.* 971, 984
efface *vb.* 485
effect *n.* 87, **156**, 877; *vb.* 155, 163, 609, 659
effective *adj.* 159, 172, 563, 627
effeminate *adj.* 162, 381
effervesce *vb.* 363, 786
efficacy *n.* 159, 575
efficient *adj.* 159, 557
effluent *n.* 301, 358
effort *n.* 604, 615
effortless *adj.* 634
effrontery *n.* 880
egg *n.* 250, 306
egg-timer *n.* 116
ego *n.* 382
egoist *n.* 904, 934
egotism *n.* 875, 904
ego-trip *n.* 873
eight *n.* 70; *adj.* 70
eject *vb.* 301, 303
ejection *n.* 99, **303**, 310, 312
elaborate *adj.* 509; *vb.* 196
elapse *vb.* 107, 110
elasticity *n.* **336**
elated *adj.* 756, 827, 838
elbow *n.* 246
elder *n.* 34, **132**, 987; *adj.* 130
eldest *adj.* 130
elect *adj.* 119; *vb.* 540
election *n.* 540
electorate *n.* 540
electric chair *n.* 964
electricity *n.* 159, 765
electrify *vb.* 159, 755
electrocute *vb.* 370, 963
electronic *adj.* 125

elegance *n.* **510**, 844, 848

elegy *n.* 372, 839

element *n.* 5, 55, 155, 327

elementary *adj.* 88

elements *n.* 192, 348

elevated *adj.* 208, 318, 868, 873

elevation *n.* 208, **318**

elevator *n.* 316

eleven *n.* 70

elevenses *n.* 306

eleventh hour *n.* 136

elf *n.* 970

elicit *vb.* 155, 547

eligible *adj.* 896, 897

eliminate *vb.* 46, 99, 164, 303

elite *n.* 579, 870

elixir *n.* 591

ellipse *n.* 247, 250

ellipsis *n.* 504

elliptic *adj.* 504

elocution *n.* 518

elongated *adj.* 202

elope *vb.* 600, 896

eloquent *adj.* 514, 516

elsewhere *adj.* 189

elucidate *vb.* 413, 456

elude *vb.* 555, 600

emaciated *adj.* 205, 588

emanation *n.* 156, 301, 774

emancipation *n.* 601, 680

emasculate *vb.* 160, 169

embalm *vb.* 372, 599, 776

embankment *n.* 559, 646

embargo *n.* 99, 681, 691

embarkation *n.* 299

embark on *vb.* 605

embarrass *vb.* 578, 633, 869, 874

embarrassed *adj.* 811, 830, 874, 876

embassy *n.* 685, 688

embed *vb.* 311

embellish *vb.* 509, 844, 846

ember *n.* 800

embezzle *vb.* 722

embezzler *n.* 723, 739

embittered *adj.* 893

emblazon *vb.* 482

emblem *n.* 482, 677, 872

embody *vb.* 52, 98, 222, 486

emboss *vb.* 482, 489

embrace *n.* 886, 890; *vb.* 50, 98, 702, 886, 890

embrocation *n.* 365

embroider *vb.* 481, 509, 846

embryology *n.* 375, 376

embryonic *adj.* 88

emerald *adj.* 812

emerge *vb.* **301**, 313, 324, 600, 825

emergence *n.* 298, **301**

emergency *n.* 136, 153, 562

emigrant *n.* 100, 270

emigration *n.* 299

eminent *adj.* 34, 208, 573, 868, 870

emissary *n.* 460, 467, 688

emit *vb.* 301, 303, 774, 778

emollient *n.* 365

emolument *n.* 705, 738

emotion *n.* 326, 752, 756, 889

empathy *n.* 752

emperor *n.* 675

emphasize *vb.* 417, 456, 468, 481, 512, 573

employ *vb.* 107, 557, 575, 606, 685

employee *n.* 619, 676

emporium *n.* 730

empower *vb.* 159, 161, **667**, **685**, 954

emptiness *n.* 2, 189, 333, 875

empty *adj.* 189, 333, 451; *vb.* 301, 358, 569

empty-handed *adj.* 735

empty-headed *adj.* 383, 427, 435

emulate *vb.* 20

emulsion *n.* 362

enable *vb.* 159, 404

enact *vb.* 529

enactment *n.* 486, 954

enamel *n.* 225

enamoured *adj.* 889

encampment *n.* 186

enchant *vb.* 827, 829, 889, 984

encircle *vb.* 231, 250

enclose *vb.* 98, 225, 229, **234**

enclosure *n.* 184, **234**, 378

encompass *vb.* 182, 229, 231

encore *n.* 62, 77; *adv.* 77

encounter *n.* 296, 649; *vb.* 649, 857

encourage *vb.* 217, 547, 618, 624, 636, **836**, 857, 907

encroachment *n.* 314, 645, 918, 955

encrust *vb.* 226

encumbrance *n.* 635, 711

encyclopedia *n.* 426, 524

end *n.* **89**, 156, 235, 237, 369, 552, 659; *vb.* 89, 659

endanger *vb.* 594

endearment *n.* **890**

endeavour *n.* 604; *vb.* 604

endemic *adj.* 586

endless *adj.* 78, 91, 114

endless duration *n.* **114**

endorsement *n.* 408, 424, 468, 690, 963

endow *vb.* 568, 715

endowment *n.* 5, 627, 714

endurance *n.* 112, 114, 143, 152, 337, 535, 757

endure *vb.* 91, 112, 145, 535, 648, 752, 757, 828

enemy *n.* 638, 645, 883

energetic *adj.* 32, 159, 161, 173, 368, 585, 611

energize *vb.* 161, 173, 618, 755

energy *n.* 159, 161, 173, 368, 611

enfeeble *vb.* 130, 162, 507

enforce *vb.* 954

enfranchise *vb.* 678, 680

engage *vb.* 557, 605

engaged *adj.* 698

engage in battle *vb.* 649, 651

engagement *n.* 557, 605, 649, 698, 890

engine *n.* 276, 565

engineer *n.* 558

engrave *vb.* 490, 521, 522

engraver *n.* 491

engraving *n.* **490**

engrossed *adj.* 384

enhance *vb.* 36, 318, 509, 846

enigma *n.* 409, 453, 466

enjoy *vb.* **752**, 770, **827**, 861

enjoyable *adj.* 827, 829

enjoy immunity *vb.* 921

enjoy oneself *vb.* 827, 840

enlarge *vb.* 36, 40, 196, 202, 505

enlighten *vb.* 460, 470, 797

enlist *vb.* 83, 302, 557, 651

enliven *vb.* 173, 368, 618, 836, 840

enmity *n.* **883**

ennoble *vb.* 318, 868, 870

ennui *n.* 841

enormous *adj.* 32, 194

enough *adj.* 75, 570

enquire *vb.* 388, 394

enquiry *n.* **394**, 526

enrage *vb.* 893

enrapture *vb.* 547, 827, 829, 889

enrich *vb.* 509, 587

enrol *vb.* 83, 483, 641

ensconce *vb.* 461

ensemble *n.* 54, 793

enshrine *vb.* 372, 983

enshroud *vb.* 225

ensign *n.* 482

enslave *vb.* 679

ensnare *vb.* 463, 478

ensue *vb.* 85, 119, 153, 156, 287

ensure *vb.* 408

entail *vb.* 98, 459

entangle *vb.* 82, 221

entente *n.* 643, 699

enter *vb.* 298, **300**, 483, 742

enterprise *n.* 173, 288, 604, **605**, 611, 627, 857

entertain *vb.* 840, 884

enter upon *vb.* 88, 605

enthralling *adj.* 547, 829, 866

enthrone *vb.* 685, 868

enthusiasm *n.* 532, 611, 752

enthusiastic *adj.* 532, 611, 756, 827

entice *vb.* **547**, 770

entire *adj.* 54, 56, 581, 659

entirety *n.* 54, 56, 59

entitled *adj.* 917

entity *n.* 1, 3, 59
entomb *vb.* 372
entomology *n.* 375
entrance *n.* 262, 298, **300**, 559
entrant *n.* 638
entrap *vb.* 478
entreat *vb.* 695, 982
entrée *n.* 306
entrench *vb.* 152, 186
entrepreneur *n.* 728
entrust *vb.* 685, 714, 718
entry *n.* 298, 300
entwine *vb.* 251
enumerate *vb.* 38, 83, 102
enunciate *vb.* 512, 514
envelop *vb.* 225, 229, 234, 461
envelope *n.* 193, 234
envious *adj.* 914
environment *n.* 8, 183, 229
envisage *vb.* 449
envoy *n.* 460, **467**, 685, 688
envy *n.* **914**; *vb.* 914
ephemeral *adj.* 113
epic *n.* 525, 528
epicure *n.* 304, 945, 948
epigram *n.* 432, 842
epilogue *n.* 87, 89
episode *n.* 153
epistle *n.* 523
epitaph *n.* 372
epithet *n.* 496
epitome *n.* 527
epitomize *vb.* 203
epoch *n.* 109
equal *n.* 28; *adj.* 13, **28**, 159
equality *n.* 13, **28**, 244
equalize *vb.* 28, 31
equate *vb.* 13, 218, 397
equation *n.* 28, 397
equator *n.* 63, 250
equestrianism *n.* 269
equidistant *adj.* 90, 218
equilibrium *n.* 28, 152
equip *vb.* 227, 564, 568, **602**
equipment *n.* 568, 711
equity *n.* 711, 915
equivalence *n.* 12, 28, 450
equivalent *n.* 18, 28, 456; *adj.* 12, 13, 18, 28
equivocal *adj.* 409, 453, 454
equivocate *vb.* 454, 477

era *n.* 109
eradicate *vb.* 164, 303, 485
erase *vb.* 485
erect *adj.* 214, 248, 318; *vb.* 214, 318
erection *n.* 163, 318
erode *vb.* **37**, 53, 164, 341, 569, **588**
Eros *n.* 889, 967
erotic *adj.* 952
err *vb.* 285, 431, 936
errand *n.* 685
errand-boy *n.* 467
erratic *adj.* 151, 539
erring *adj.* 409
erroneous *adj.* 412, **431**, 916
error *n.* **431**, 457, 471
erudite *adj.* 426, 472
eruption *n.* 148, 175, 301, 782
escalate *vb.* 36, 196
escalator *n.* 316
escape *n.* 293, 301, 555, 595, **600**, 826; *vb.* 293, 555, **600**, 826
escapism *n.* 449
escarpment *n.* 208
escort *n.* 683; *vb.* 268
esoteric *adj.* 453, 984
especial *adj.* 34, 102
Esperanto *n.* 492
espouse *vb.* 896
essay *n.* 526, 604
essence *n.* 1, 5, 450
essential *n.* 5, 531, 562; *adj.* 1, 5, 531, 562, 573
establish *vb.* 81, 88, 152, 161, 413, 685, 929, 954
established *adj.* 126, 152, 413, 545
establishment *n.* 88, 152, 191, 413, 620, 641, 667, 730
estate *n.* 7, 378, 711
esteem *n.* 922, 925; *vb.* 384, 861, 868, 889, 925
estimate *n.* 447, 743; *vb.* 38, 400, 415, 448, 743
estrange *vb.* 883, 892
estuary *n.* 353
etcher *n.* 491
etching *n.* 490
eternal *adj.* 78, 114, 966
eternity *n.* 78, 108, 112, **114**
ethereal *adj.* 4, 328, 333

ethics *n.* 935
ethnic *adj.* 11, 379
etiquette *n.* 545
etymology *n.* 492, 494
Eucharist *n.* 988
eunuch *n.* 160
euphemism *n.* 455, 509
euphoria *n.* 827
euthanasia *n.* 370
evacuate *vb.* 293, 299, 310, 600
evacuee *n.* 885
evade *vb.* 393, 412, 533, **555**, 600, 920
evaluation *n.* 400, 415, 456, 743
evanescent *adj.* 113, 799, 826
evangelical *adj.* 976, 977
evangelist *n.* 974
evangelize *vb.* 146
evaporate *vb.* 2, 95, **346**, 350, 826
even *adj.* 16, 28, 39, 140, 244, 248, 257; *vb.* 215, 257
evening *n.* **128**; *adj.* 128
event *n.* 153, 465, 649
eventful *adj.* 611
eventuality *n.* 153
everlasting *adj.* 114, 966
every *adj.* 54
everybody *n.* 54, 101
everything *n.* 54
eviction *n.* 99, 303
evidence *n.* **401**, 458, 460, 482, 483; *vb.* 401
evident *adj.* 413, 458, 823
evil *n.* **551**, 592, 932, 936; *adj.* **551**, 592, 932, 936
evildoer *n.* **906**, 940
evil spirit *n.* **969**
evocative *adj.* 441, 450
evoke *vb.* 155, 547
evolution *n.* 142, 288, **324**, 366
ewe *n.* 381
ex- *adj.* 118, 124
exacerbate *vb.* 36, 588, 835
exact *adj.* 392, 430, 864; *vb.* 671, 743
exacting *adj.* 392, 398, 669, 864
exactness *n.* 392, 502
exaggeration *n.* 417, 477, **481**, 487, 879

exalt *vb.* 318, 868, 982
exalted *adj.* 32, 208, 318, 868
examination *n.* 394, 415, 526
examine *vb.* 384, 390, 394, 396, 415, 526
examinee *n.* 395
example *n.* 23, 597
exasperation *n.* 835, 893, 894
excavate *vb.* 210, 254, 312
exceed *vb.* 32, 34, 314
excel *vb.* 34, 314
excellence *n.* 34, 579, 581, 935
excellent *adj.* 34, 579, 844, 935
except *vb.* 99; *prep.* 99
excepting *adv.*, *prep.* 42
exception *n.* 403, 921
exceptional *adj.* 21, 32, 573, 579
excerpt *n.* 55
excess *n.* 44, 569, **572**, 945, 948
excessive *adj.* 481, 572, 691, 745, 945
exchange *n.* 142, 149, 150, 410, 714, 725, 730; *vb.* 142, 149, 150, 714, 725
exchequer *n.* 732
excise *n.* 743
excitability *n.* 753, **756**
excitation *n.* 326, **755**
excite *vb.* 752, 755, 829
excited *adj.* 756, 759, 827
exclaim *vb.* 788
exclude *vb.* 42, **99**, 542, 691, 694
exclusion *n.* 99, 542, 694
exclusive *adj.* 99, 641, 707, **979**
exclusively *adv.* 56
excommunicate *vb.* 99, 885
excrement *n.* 310
excrescent *adj.* 252
excrete *vb.* 303, 310
excretion *n.* **310**
excruciating *adj.* 828
excursion *n.* 269, 840
excuse *n.* 549, 929; *vb.* 549, 911, 929
execration *n.* 901
execution *n.* 172, 370, 609, 621, 963
executive *n.* 623, 675,

failure n. 315, 393, 431, 445, 571, 660, **662**
faint vb. 162, 617
faint-hearted adj. 162, 858
faintness n. 162, 507, 617, **781**, 799, 806
fair n. 840; adj. (average) 30, 666; (of weather) 759; (whitish) 807; (good-looking) 844; (just) 915, 931, 933
fairy n. 953, 970
fairy story n. 525
faith n. 420, 854, 974, 980
faithful adj. 430, 456, 673, 702, 882, 977
faithless adj. 409, 421
fake n. 20; adj. 20, 477, 478; vb. 20, 477, 852
fall n. 37, 317, 321, 358; vb. 37, 317, 321, 588, 936
fallacy n. 412, 431
fall apart vb. 51
fall away vb. 538, 588
fall back vb. 289, 293
fall back on vb. 606
fall down vb. 431, 662
fallen adj. 662
fallen angel n. 969
fallen woman n. 953
fall for vb. 422, 889
fallible adj. 431, 582
fall ill vb. 586
fall in vb. 254
falling star n. 329
fall in love vb. 889
fallow adj. 603, 612
fall on vb. 153, 179
fall short vb. 29, 35, 315, 571, 582, 662
fall through vb. 662
fall to vb. 716, 919
false adj. 2, 477, 478
falsehood n. 431, **477**
false reasoning n. **412**
falsification n. 457, 471, 477, **487**
falter vb. 325, 515, 536, 662
fame n. 868
familiar adj. 138, 426, 545, 882
familiarize vb. 470, 545
family n. 11, 55, 97, 171
famished adj. 861, 947
famous adj. 573, 868
fan n. 764; vb. 348
fanatic n. 148, 537, 611

fanciful adj. 449, 539
fancy n. 448, 449, 539, 861; adj. 509, 846; vb. 448, 449, 540, 861, 889
fan out vb. 297
fantastic adj. 433, 449, 851, 866
fantasy n. 449, 481
far adj. 198
farce n. 433, 529, 851
fare n. 306, 743
farewell n. 299
far-flung adj. 198
farm n. 377, 378; vb. 377
farm out vb. 717
far-reaching adj. 32, 182
far-sighted adj. 434
farthest adj. 198
fascinate vb. 294, 547, 755, 889
fascinating adj. 547, 755, 829
fascism n. 669
fashion n. 125, 242, 545, 559, **850**
fast n. 947; adj. 280, 613, 805; vb. 947; adv. 280
fasten vb. 47, 50, 152, 263
fastidiousness n. 392, 540, **864**
fasting n. **947**; adj. 947
fat n. 306; adj. 194
fatal adj. 164, 369, 370
fatalism n. 531
fate n. 123, 154, **158**, 531, 543, **553**
fat-head n. 437
father n. 11, 170
fathom vb. 452
fathomless adj. 210
fatigue n. **617**, 841
fatten vb. 204, 377
fatty adj. 365
fault n. 200, 315, 431, 582
faultless adj. 581, 937
faulty adj. 582
fauna n. 366, 373
faux pas n. 431
favour n. 636, 670, 715, 886, 899, 907, 922; vb. 540, 925
favourable adj. 854, 925
favourite n. **891**
favouritism n. 916
fawning n. 927; adj. 881

fear n. **856**, 858, 980; vb. 856
fearless adj. 857
feasible adj. 404, 406
feast n. 306; vb. 304
feat n. 605, 609
feathery adj. 331
feature n. 5, 8, 55, 825
fecundity n. 168
federal adj. 379, 641
federation n. 641
fed up with adj. 862
fee n. 738, 743, 917
feeble-minded adj. 435
feebleness n. 160, 162, **507**, 666, 781
feed vb. 304, 377
feedback n. 395
feeder n. 559
feel n. 339, 398, 758; vb. 411, **752**, 758
feel better vb. 834
feeler n. 394, 396
feel for vb. 758, 907
feeling n. 411, **752**, 758; adj. 752
feel like vb. 532
feel small vb. 874
fees n. 917
feign vb. 477, 852
felicitate vb. 888
felicitous adj. 510
fell n. 208; vb. 48
fellow n. 11, 122, 131, 380, 473
fellow-feeling n. 899, 907
fellowship n. 60, 639, 641, 988; vb. 988
fellow-worker n. 640
female n. **381**; adj. 381
femininity n. 162, 381
feminism n. 381
fen n. 355
fence n. 230, 234
fend for oneself vb. 678
fend off vb. 646
ferment n. 80, 175; vb. 331, 363, 773
ferry n. 277; vb. 271
fertile adj. 163, 168
fertilize vb. 378
fervour n. 506, 752, 759
festive adj. 878
festivity n. 838, 840
festoon vb. 846
fetch vb. 705, 718, 743
fete n. 840
fetid adj. 777
fetish n. 967, 983, 984
fetter n. 681; vb. 635, 681

feud n. 642, 649
fever n. 326, 439, 586
few adj. 33, 76, 139
fewness n. 33, **76**
fiancée n. 698, 889
fiasco n. 662
fib vb. 477
fibber n. 480
fibre n. 207, 339
fibrous adj. 337
fickle adj. 151, 536, 538, 539
fiction n. 525
fictitious adj. 2, 449
fiddle n. 478; vb. 722, 742
fidelity n. 673, 931
fidgety adj. 151, 611, 756, 856
field n. 184, 352, 356, 378, 557, 658
fiend n. 175, 969
fierce adj. 175, 900
fiery adj. 506, 759, 893
fiesta n. 840
fifth columnist n. 480
fight n. 642, 649, 651; vb. 25, 615, **637**, 642, 645, 649
fight back vb. 647
fighter n. 645, 655
figurative adj. 455
figure n. 39, 489; vb. 38
figure-head n. 253
figure of speech n. **455**, 498
figure out vb. 452
filament n. **207**
filch vb. 722
file n. 83, 202; vb. 83, 91, 255, 257, 341
filial adj. 171
filibuster n. 135; vb. 135
fill n. 865; vb. 56, 107, 265, 865
fill in vb. 149, 460, 483
fillip n. 173; vb. 613
fill up vb. 568
filly n. 381
film n. 225, 363, 483, 803; vb. 483
filter vb. 319
filth n. 584, 952
final adj. 89, 237, 408, 659
finality n. 543
finance n. 731; vb. 636, 718
financier n. 718, 728
find vb. 415, 419, 960

find fault with *vb.* 832, 926, 930, 962
fine *n.* 963; *adj.* 205, 255, 333, 340, 579, 844; *vb.* 963
finesse *n.* 631
finger *vb.* 758
fingerprint *n.* 482
finicky *adj.* 392, 864
finish *n.* 56, 89, 257, 510, 659; *vb.* 89, 144, 414, 581, 659
fiord *n.* 353
fire *n.* 506, 759, 763; *vb.* 645, 686, 755, 761, 765
firearm *n.* 657
fireproof *adj.* 762
fireside *n.* 191, 763
fireworks *n.* 800
firing squad *n.* 963
firm *n.* 620, 641; *adj.* 143, 152, 161, 334, 337, 534, 535, 669
first *adj.* 34, 88
first-class *adj.* 34, 579
first hand *adj.* 21
firth *n.* 353
fish *n.* 306, 373
fishy *adj.* 373, 932
fissure *n.* 254
fit *n.* 326, 439, 586, 893; *adj.* 585, 915; *vb.* 47, 105, 568, 602
fitful *adj.* 141, 539
fit in with *vb.* 24
fit out *vb.* 227, 602
fitting *adj.* 577, 915
fittings *n.* 568
five and over *n.* **70**
fix *n.* 633; *vb.* 47, 152, 311, 589
fixation *n.* 439
fixative *n.* 49
fixed *adj.* 47, 143, 152, 543
fixtures *n.* 152, 568, 711
fizz *n.* 363; *vb.* 363, 786
fizzle out *vb.* 144, 162, 662
flabbergasted *adj.* 866
flabby *adj.* 668
flaccid *adj.* 507
flag *n.* 467, 482, 677; *vb.* 617, 841
flagellant *n.* 946
flagon *n.* 193
flagrant *adj.* 458, 877
flail *vb.* 282
flake *n.* 33, 206, 340; *vb.* 206
flake out *vb.* 617

flamboyant *adj.* 877
flame *n.* 797, 800; *vb.* 759
flammable *adj.* 761, 765
flank *n.* 238; *vb.* 238
flap *n.* 225, 326; *vb.* 216, 326, 359, 756
flare *n.* 797, 800; *vb.* 756, 797
flash *n.* 115, 539, 797, 800; *vb.* 797
flashback *n.* 147, 441
flashlight *n.* 800
flashy *adj.* 509, 805, 849, 877
flask *n.* 193
flat *n.* 191, 356; *adj.* 215, 257, 768, 791, 843
flat out *adv.* 280
flattery *n.* 881, 886, **927**
flaunt *vb.* 877
flavour *n.* 767; *vb.* 307
flavourless *adj.* 768, 771
flaw *n.* 431, 582, 847
flawless *adj.* 54, 581
flay *vb.* 228, 963
fleck *n.* 33
fledgling *n.* 125
flee *vb.* 555, 600, 826
fleece *vb.* 377, 478, 722
fleeting *adj.* 113
flesh *n.* 306, 327, 379
flesh and blood *n.* 3, 327
fleshly *adj.* 945
fleshy *adj.* 194, 364
flex *vb.* 247
flexible *adj.* 151, 335, 336, 668
flexuous *adj.* 251
flicker *vb.* 326, 759, 797
flickering *adj.* 141
flick through *vb.* 472, 818
flight *n.* 273, 293, 299, 555, 600, 826
flighty *adj.* 151, 539
flimsy *adj.* 162, 205, 335, 338
flinch *vb.* 283, 555, 856
fling *vb.* 359
flint *n.* 765
flippancy *n.* 842
flirt *n.* 953; *vb.* 890
flirtation *n.* 889, 890
flit *vb.* 113
float *vb.* 216, 257, 331
flock *n.* 75, 94, 982, 987; *vb.* 75, 94
flog *vb.* 963

flood *n.* 358, 572; *vb.* 349, 358, 572
floodlight *n.* 800
floor *n.* 206, 209, 213
flop *n.* 662
flora *n.* 366
floral *adj.* 374
florid *adj.* 846, 849
flounder *vb.* 409, 633, 662
flourish *n.* 877; *vb.* 36, 168, 585, 661, 664, 877
flout *vb.* 644
flow *n.* 85, 91, 301, 313, 343, 358
flower *n.* 374; *vb.* 163
flowering *n.* 127; *adj.* 129
flowery *adj.* 509
fluctuate *vb.* 141, 142, 151, 325, 536
flue *n.* 361
fluency *n.* 501, 514, 516
fluffy *adj.* 331, 335
fluid *n.* 243, 309, 343; *adj.* 343, 347
fluidity *n.* 343, 345
fluke *n.* 158, 553
flurry *n.* 359, 611, 613
flush *adj.* 28, 215; *vb.* 811
fluster *n.* 756
fluted *adj.* 261
flutter *vb.* 325, 326, 359
flux *vb.* 345
fly *vb.* 110, 113, 273, 280
foam *n.* 363; *vb.* 363, 893
focal *adj.* 90, 96, 224
focalize *vb.* 296
focus *n.* 90, **96**, 224; *vb.* 96, 224, 390
fodder *n.* 305; *vb.* 377
foe *n.* 638, 883
fog *n.* 363, 409, 427, 799
foil *vb.* 445, 635, 648, 662
fold *n.* 206, **260**; *vb.* 251, 260, 739
foliage *n.* 374
folk *n.* 379
follow *vb.* 85, 105, 119, 237, **287**, 452, 673, 702
follower *n.* 119, 287, 424, 474, 554, 640, 821
following *n.* 85, **287**; *adj.* 85, 119, 156, 554
follow up *vb.* 392, 554

follow-up *n.* 87
folly *n.* 385, 433, **435**
fond *adj.* 861, 889
fondle *vb.* 758, 890
fondness *n.* 861, 889, 890
food *n.* 305, **306**
fool *n.* 429, **437**, 440, 479; *vb.* 478
fool around *vb.* 433, 435
foolhardy *adj.* 613, 859
foolish *adj.* 385, 433, 435, 451
foot *n.* 213, 528
footing *n.* 93
footpath *n.* 559
footprint *n.* 482, 483
fop *n.* 852
foray *n.* 645
forbearance *n.* 670, 757, 907, 911
forbears *n.* 11, 86
forbid *vb.* 99, 635, 691, 955
forbidding *adj.* 669, 691
force *n.* **159**, 161, 175, 177, 506, 674; *vb.* 175, 282, 531, 562, **674**
forced *adj.* 507, 511
force in *vb.* 300, 311
force oneself *vb.* 533
forces *n.* 655
ford *vb.* 313
fore *adj.* 236
foreboding *n.* 447, 597; *adj.* 447
forecast *n.* 154, 348, 447; *vb.* 154, 443, 446, 447, 558
foregoing *adj.* 84, 118
foreground *n.* 199, 236
foreign *adj.* 100, 222
foreknowledge *n.* 447
foreman *n.* 623, 958
foremost *adj.* 236, 573
foreordain *vb.* 531, 543
forerun *vb.* 84, 118
forerunner *n.* 86, 467
foresee *vb.* 443, 446, 447
foreshadow *vb.* 447, 976
foresight *n.* 134, 434, **446**, 447, 860
forest *n.* 374
forestall *vb.* 134
foretaste *n.* 55, 118
foretell *vb.* 447, 543
forethought *n.* 392, 446, 447, 860

forever *adv.* 114
forewarn *vb.* 447, 597
foreword *n.* 86, 88
forfeit *n.* 43, 701; *vb.* 706
forge *vb.* 477
forge ahead *vb.* 288
forgery *n.* 20, 22
forget *vb.* 385, 393, 442
forgiveness *n.* 601, 670, 907, **911**
forgo *vb.* 556
forgotten *adj.* 124, 126, 442
fork *n.* 246, 255, 297, 358; *vb.* 63, 297
fork out *vb.* 738
forlorn *adj.* 837
form *n.* **242**, 339, 474, 482, 825; *vb.* 58, 242
formal *adj.* 511, 988
formalism *n.* 981
formalize *vb.* 81
formation *n.* 242, 655
formative *adj.* 129, 242
former *adj.* 84, 118, 124, 126
formless *adj.* 243
formula *n.* 39, 103, 498, 626
formulate *vb.* 81, 468, 498
fornicate *vb.* 952
fornicator *n.* 953
forsake *vb.* 556
forswear *vb.* 477
forte *n.* 627
forthcoming *adj.* 154, 292
forthright *adj.* 476, 632
forthwith *adv.* 115
fortification *n.* 646
fortify *vb.* 161, 173, 646, 857
fortitude *n.* 534, 857
fortress *n.* 595, 646
fortuitous *adj.* 136, 158, 553
fortunate *adj.* 661
fortune *n.* 158, 447, 550, 553, 734
forum *n.* 96, 625, 658
forward *adj.* 236, 288, 880; *vb.* 268; *adv.* 288
forward-looking *adj.* 125, 288
fossilize *vb.* 334
foster *vb.* 470, 636
foul *adj.* 584, 777; *vb.* 584

foul play *n.* 551, 900, 916, 932
found *vb.* 88
foundation *n.* 88, 155, 213, 217, 401, 602
founder *n.* 155; *vb.* 588
foundry *n.* 620
fountain *n.* 358, 567
four *n.* 67; *adj.* 67
fourfold *adj.* 68
fowl *n.* 306, 373
fracas n. 80
fraction *n.* 39, **73**, 717
fracture *n.* 48; *vb.* 48
fragile *adj.* 162, 338
fragment *n.* 33, 55, 73, 717; *vb.* 48, 338
fragrance *n.* 774, **776**
frail *adj.* 162, 338, 507, 586
frame *n.* 5; *vb.* 558, 930
frame of mind *n.* 751
frame of reference *n.* 700
framework *n.* 5, 232
franchise *n.* 540; *vb.* 690
frangible *adj.* 338
frank *adj.* 476, 508, 632, 931
fraternity *n.* 11, 882
fraud *n.* 478, 631, 722
fraudulent *adj.* 477, 478, 631, 932
freak *n.* 440, 539, 866
freckled *adj.* 817
free *adj.* 10, 530, 600, **678**, 708, 715, 897, 911; *vb.* 48, 600, 601, 678, 680, 921
freedom *n.* 600, **678**, 690, 921
freedom from mixture *n.* **46**
free thinking *n.* 975
free time *n.* 614
free will *n.* 530, 678
freeze *vb.* 332, 334, 599, 760, 762
freight *n.* 192, 268
frenzied *adj.* 439, 859
frenzy *n.* 80, 175, 439, 861
frequency *n.* 27, **138**, 140, 400
frequent *adj.* 138, 545; *vb.* 188
fresh *adj.* 125, 359, 599, 760
freshen *vb.* 348, 583
fret *vb.* 837
fretting *n.* 828

friable *adj.* 338, 340
friar *n.* 986
friary *n.* 990
friction *n.* 181, **341**, 642
fridge *n.* 764
friend *n.* 640, 882
friendless *adj.* 885
friendly *adj.* 643, 882, 884, 886
friendship *n.* 643, 650, **882**
frighten *vb.* 856, 902
frightful *adj.* 845
frigid *adj.* 160, 169, 754, 760
frill *n.* 509, 846
fringe *n.* 233, 235
frisky *adj.* 320
fritter away *vb.* 749
frivolous *adj.* 539
front *n.* 222, **236**, 658, 852; *adj.* 236
frontier *n.* 233, 235
frost *n.* 760; *vb.* 762
frosted *adj.* 804, 807
froth *n.* 363
frown *n.* 895; *vb.* 895
frown on *vb.* 926
frozen *adj.* 332, 760, 762
frugal *adj.* 392, 748, 944
fruit *n.* 156, 163, 306
fruitful *adj.* 163, 168, 661
fruitless *adj.* 169, 576, 662
frustrate *vb.* 181, 445, 635, 648, 662
fry *vb.* 306, 759
fuel *n.* **765**; *vb.* 765
fugitive *n.* 555, 600
fulcrum *n.* 217
fulfil *vb.* 56, 659, 661, 673, 702
fulfilment *n.* 659, 827
full *adj.* 54, 56, 204, 570, 865
fullness *n.* 32, 56, 567
fulminate *vb.* 780
fulsome *adj.* 168
fumble *vb.* 409, 758
fumbler *n.* 630
fume *n.* 344, 777; *vb.* 175, 346, 756, 759, **893**
fumigate *vb.* 583, 775
fun *n.* 829, 836, 840, 842
function *n.* 39, 172, 557, 878; *vb.* 172, 609
functional *adj.* 172, 575

functionary *n.* 623
fundamental *adj.* 5, 88, 155, 213, 573
fundamentalist *adj.* 977
funds *n.* 731
funeral *n.* 372
fungus *n.* 167, 592
funk *n.* 858; *vb.* 856, 858
funny *adj.* 842, 851
furious *adj.* 175, 893
furlough *n.* 614
furnace *n.* **763**
furnish *vb.* 163, 568, 715
furniture *n.* 711
furrow *n.* 254, **261**
further *adj.* 40; *vb.* 217, 288, 587; *adv.* 40
furthest *adj.* 89, 198
furtive *adj.* 461, 478
fury *n.* 175, 756, 893
fuse *n.* 765; *vb.* 45, 47, 52, 345
fusion *n.* 45, 47, 52, 639
fuss *n.* 326, 756, 877; *vb.* 756, 864
fussy *adj.* 392, 864
futile *adj.* 576, 662, 855
future *n.* **123**; *adj.* 123
future events *n.* **154**
futuristic *adj.* 125
fuzzy *adj.* 243, 503, 824

G

gabble *vb.* 516
gad about *vb.* 269
gadget *n.* 565
gag *n.* 842; *vb.* 681
gaiety *n.* 836
gain *n.* 288, 550, 705; *vb.* 36, 116, **705**, 720
gala *n.* 840
galaxy *n.* 329
gale *n.* 175, 359
gallant *adj.* 857, 886
gallery *n.* 818
galley *n.* 522
gallivant about *vb.* 269
gallows *n.* 964
galore *adj.* 75
galvanize *vb.* 755
gamble *n.* 158, 553; *vb.* 158, 553
gambler *n.* 553
game *n.* 306, 373, 649, 840; *adj.* 532, 857
gamekeeper *n.* 683

gamut *n.* 182
gang *n.* 94
gangster *n.* 370, 906
gang up against *vb.* 639
gaol *n.* 682
gap *n.* 92, 200, 262
gape *vb.* 262, 818, 866
garb *n.* 227
garbage *n.* 44
garble *vb.* 487, 515
garden *n.* 234, 374, 378
gardener *n.* 378
garish *adj.* 805, 846, 877
garment *n.* 227
garnish *vb.* 846
garrison *n.* 646
garrulous *adj.* 516
gas *n.* 159, 344, 765; *vb.* 963
gaseity *n.* **344**
gash *n.* 588
gasify *vb.* 344, 346
gasp *n.* 359; *vb.* 359
gastronomy *n.* 304
gate *n.* 262
gatecrash *vb.* 300
gate-crasher *n.* 884
gather *n.* 260; *vb.* **94**, 196, 260, 296, 448, 567
gaudy *adj.* 805, 846, 877
gauge *n.* 400, 482; *vb.* 400, 482
gay *n.* 106, 953; *adj.* 836, 952
gaze *vb.* 818
gazette *n.* 483, 524
gear *n.* 227
geld *vb.* 160, 169
gem *n.* 579, 846
gene *n.* 5
genealogy *n.* 170
general *adj.* 101
generality *n.* **101**
generalize *vb.* 101
generally *adv.* 138, 545
generate *vb.* 11, 155, 163
generation *n.* 11, 109, 163, 171
generative *adj.* 163, 170
generic *adj.* 101
generosity *n.* 747, 886
generous *adj.* 715, **747**, 899, 965
genetics *n.* 366
genial *adj.* 827, 836, 884
genius *n.* 382, 428, 434, 627, 629
genocide *n.* 370, 963

gentle *adj.* 176, 670, 907
gentleman *n.* 380
gentlemanly *adj.* 380, 886
gentleman's agreement *n.* 698, 699
gentry *n.* 870
genuine *adj.* 1, **21**, 430, 632
geography *n.* 329
geology *n.* 367
geometry *n.* 38
gesticulate *vb.* 482
gesture *n.* 482, 549; *vb.* 482
get *vb.* 705, 716, 720, 726
get across *vb.* 460
get along with *vb.* 24, 643
get around *vb.* 464
get at *vb.* 460, 547, 893
get-at-able *adj.* 292
getaway *n.* 600
get away with *vb.* 600, 722, 921
get back *vb.* 647, 705, 721
get by *vb.* 661, 666
get down *vb.* 298, 837
get down to *vb.* 605
get dressed *vb.* 227
get even with *vb.* 647, 912, 963
get in with *vb.* 177, 882
get on *vb.* 661, 664
get one's own back *vb.* 647, 912
get on one's nerves *vb.* 787, 893
get on with *vb.* 24, 643
get over *vb.* 460, 659
get ready *vb.* 602
get rid of *vb.* 303, 607, 634, 680
get the hang of *vb.* 452, 472
get to *vb.* 298
get-together *n.* 884
get up *vb.* 318, 472, 477
get-up-and-go *n.* 173, 611
get used to *vb.* 545
get well *vb.* 589
ghastly *adj.* 856
ghost *n.* 328, **971**
ghostly *adj.* 4, 328, 971
ghost-writer *n.* 149, 524
giant *n.* 194; *adj.* 208
gibberish *n.* 453
gibe *vb.* 853

gift *n.* 627, 652, 715, 829
gifted *adj.* 627
gift of the gab *n.* 514, 516
giggle *vb.* 838
gild *vb.* 846
ginger *adj.* 816
gipsy *n.* 447
gird *vb.* 322
girder *n.* 217
girdle *n.* 49; *vb.* 229
girl *n.* 131, 381
girl-friend *n.* 882, 889
girth *n.* 204
gist *n.* 224
give *vb.* 335, 568, **715**, 965
give and take *n.* 150, 639, **704**
give away *vb.* 462, 717, 896
give in *vb.* 654
given *adj.* 1, 715
give off *vb.* 301, 774
give out *vb.* 301, 774, 778
giver *n.* 715, 905
give up *vb.* 556, 654, 855
give up office *vb.* 687
give way *vb.* 162
giving *n.* 636, **715**, 747
glaciate *vb.* 762
glacier *vb.* 760
glad *adj.* 827, 836
gladden *vb.* 829, 836
gladly *adv.* 532
glamorous *adj.* 829, 844
glamour *n.* 547, 829, 844
glance *n.* 818; *vb.* 818
glare *n.* 797; *vb.* 797, 818
glaring *adj.* 458, 805, 823
glass *n.* 193, 257, 822
glasses *n.* 822
glassy *adj.* 257, 802
glaze *n.* 225; *vb.* 225, 369, 257
gleam *n.* 797; *vb.* 797
glean *vb.* 378, 540, 705
glee *n.* 827, 836
glib *adj.* 516
glide *vb.* 257, 273
glider *n.* 278
glimmer *n.* 460, 797; *vb.* 326, 797
glimpse *n.* 818; *vb.* 818
glint *n.* 797
glisten *vb.* 797

glitter *n.* 797; *vb.* 797
global *adj.* 101
globe *n.* 249, 329
globe-trotter *n.* 270
globule *n.* 249, 363
gloom *n.* 798, 799, 837
gloomy *adj.* 798, 799, 837, 843, 895
glorification *n.* 925, 972
glorify *vb.* 318, 868, 982
glorious *adj.* 664, 972, 982
glory *n.* 868, 972; *vb.* 873
gloss *n.* 211, 225, 257, 456, 797; *vb.* 225, 257, 456
glossary *n.* 83, 494
gloss over *vb.* 393
glossy *adj.* 257, 797
glow *n.* 759, 797, 805; *vb.* 759, 797, 811
glue *n.* 49, 362; *vb.* 50
glum *adj.* 895
glut *n.* 572, 865
glutton *n.* 304, 948
gluttony *n.* 304, 750, 945, **948**
gnome *n.* 970
go *vb.* 172, **266**, **299**
goad *vb.* 547, 613
go after *vb.* 85, 119, 287, 554, 882
go-ahead *n.* 424, 690; *adj.* 605, 611
goal *n.* 89, 298, 552
go along with *vb.* 424, 639
go around *vb.* 322
go around with *vb.* 882
go away *vb.* 299, 826, 896
go back *vb.* 147, 289, 441
go back on *vb.* 556
go bad *vb.* 588
gobble *vb.* 304, 789, 948
go before *vb.* 84, 118, 286
go behind *vb.* 85
go-between *n.* 467, 653
go beyond *vb.* 314
goblin *n.* 970
God *n.* 966, **967**
goddess *n.* 967
God-forsaken *adj.* 198, 885
godhead *n.* 966
godless *adj.* 975, 981
godly *adj.* 966, 974, 980

go down vb. 317, 321, 586, 662
godsend n. 550
go for vb. 284, 540, 552, 743, 861
goggles n. 801, 822
go in vb. 300
go in for vb. 472, 605
go into vb. 394, 472
go it alone vb. 678
gold adj. 813, 816
golden adj. 664, 813
golden age n. 664, 827
golden calf n. 967, 983
golden handshake n. 687, 715
golden rule n. 899
gold-mine n. 567
go mad vb. 439
gondola n. 277
gone adj. 124, 706, 855
gone off adj. 771
gone on adj. 889
gong n. 784
good n. 550; adj. 550, 579, 585, 673, 899, 931
goodbye n. 518
good deed n. 899
good example n. 939
good-for-nothing n. 612, 940
good health n. 585
good humour n. 836
good-looking adj. 844
good luck n. 158
good manners n. 886
good memory n. 441
good name n. 868
good neighbour n. 899, 905
goodness n. 579, 907, 931, 935
good person n. 939
goods n. 163, 711, 729
good spirit n. 968
good taste n. 848
good time n. 840
good turn n. 550, 886, 899
goodwill n. 643
go off at a tangent vb. 285, 505
go off with vb. 722
go on vb. 1, 138, 145, 535
go on about vb. 516, 832
go on strike vb. 696
goose n. 381
go out vb. 144, 301

go out of control vb. 326
go out with vb. 882, 890
go over vb. 77
gorge n. 200, 210, 254; vb. 56, 304, 865
gorgeous adj. 844
go round vb. 250
go shopping vb. 726
go-slow n. 144, 281
gospel n. 430, 976
gossamer n. 207
gossip n. 388, 516, 869, 928; vb. 388, 516
go through vb. 313, 752, 828
go through the motions vb. 477, 852
go through with vb. 659
go together vb. 60, 882
go to law vb. 960
go to pieces vb. 588, 856
go to press vb. 522
go to the bottom vb. 321
gouge n. 259, 261, 312; vb. 254, 312
go under vb. 321, 662, 665, 739
go up vb. 316, 745
gourmand n. 304, 848, 948
gourmandise n. 304
gourmet n. 304
govern vb. 177, 622, 667, 681
governess n. 473, 675, 683
government n. 621, 622, 625, 667
governmental adj. 622, 667
governor n. 623, 675
go with vb. 24, 60, 882
go wrong vb. 431
grab vb. 705, 720, 758
grace n. 844, 848, 907, 911
graceful adj. 510, 844, 848
gracious adj. 510, 899, 907, 966
gradation n. 27
grade n. 27, 93, 400, 474; vb. 27, 97
gradual adj. 27
graduate n. 474; vb. 27, 400
graft vb. 378

grain n. 33, 306, 340, 374
grammar n. 492, 499
grammarian n. 492
grammatical adj. 492, 499
granary n. 193
grand adj. 509, 844, 868, 870
grandeur n. 870, 877
grandiloquent adj. 509
grandiose adj. 509, 877
grandstand n. 818
grange n. 191, 378
grant n. 636, 715; vb. 424, 690, 692, 715
grant permission vb. 424
granular adj. 339
granulate vb. 340
granule n. 340
grapevine n. 465
graphic adj. 488, 506, 521, 525
graphics n. 488
grapple vb. 758
grasp n. 410, 707, 712; vb. 50, 426, 452, 472, 707, 712, 720, 758
grasping adj. 705, 720, 750
grass n. 356, 374, 460
grassland n. 356, 378
grassy adj. 374, 812
grate n. 763; vb. 341, 787, 805
grateful adj. 909
gratify vb. 829, 831, 865
grating adj. 787, 791
gratitude n. 909
gratuity n. 715, 965
grave n. 372; adj. 573, 837
graven image n. 983
gravestone n. 372
gravitate towards vb. 178
gravity n. 294, 330, 573, 837
graze vb. 201, 341, 377, 758
grease n. 306, 342, 365, 584; vb. 342, 365
greasy adj. 365, 584
great adj. 32, 573, 579, 868, 870
greater adj. 34
greatness n. 26, 32, 194, 579, 868, 870
greedy adj. 720, 750, 861, 934, 948
greedy-guts n. 948

green n. 559, 812; adj. 129, 422, 427, 812, 913
greenhorn n. 429, 479, 630
greenhouse n. 378
greet vb. 886, 922
greeting n. 518, 886, 922
gregarious adj. 884
gremlin n. 970
grey n. 809; adj. 30, 130, 363, 799, 809
grey matter n. 434
grid n. 159, 221
grief n. 828, 837, 839
grievance n. 916
grieve vb. 830, 833, 837, 839
grill n. 221; vb. 306, 394, 759
grim adj. 669, 830
grimace n. 895; vb. 245, 895
grimy adj. 584
grin n. 838; vb. 838
grin and bear it vb. 757, 836
grind vb. 341, 615, 787
grip n. 193, 712; vb. 50, 712, 720, 758
gripping adj. 755
gristle n. 337
groan n. 788; vb. 696, 788
groceries n. 305
groggy adj. 586, 950
groom vb. 377, 470
groove n. 184, 261, 545; vb. 261
grope vb. 409, 758
gross n. 70; adj. 54, 56, 849, 936
grotesque adj. 245, 845
grotto n. 254
grouch n. 832; vb. 895
ground n. (reason) 155, 401, 547, 929; (land) 213, 352, 658; vb. 319, 470
groundwork n. 213, 602
group n. 55, 94, 97, 641, 793; vb. 52, 94, 97
grovel vb. 209, 881, 922
grow vb. 36, 168, 196, 242, 288, 316, 324
growl vb. 783, 789, 895
grown-up n. 133; adj. 133
growth n. 36, 196, 252, 288, 324
grow up vb. 133

grudge *n.* 832, 893; *vb.*
914
grudgingly *adv.* 533
gruelling *adj.* 615
gruff *adj.* 787, 887, 894
grumble *vb.* 783, 832
grumbler *n.* 832
grumpy *adj.* 894
grunt *vb.* 789
guarantee *n.* 424; *vb.*
408, 468, 698, 701
guard *n.* 593, 646, 683;
vb. 392, 593, 646
guardian *n.* 593, 683,
905
guardroom *n.* 682
guerdon *n.* 965
guerrilla *n.* 148
guess *n.* 386, 396, **447**,
448; *vb.* 396, 411,
448
guest *n.* 100, 884
guffaw *vb.* 838
guidance *n.* 470, 624
guide *n.* 103, 217, 473,
623; *vb.* 470, 621,
622, **624**
guidebook *n.* 460, 524
guile *n.* 477, 478, 631,
932
guileless *adj.* 422, 476,
632, 937, 951
guillotine *n.* 964; *vb.*
370, 963
guilt *n.* **938**
guilty *adj.* 938
guinea pig *n.* 396, 716,
828
guise *n.* 227, 463, 549
gulf *n.* 200, 254, **353**
gullibility *n.* **422**
gully *n.* 254, 360
gulp *n.* 309; *vb.* 304,
948
gum *n.* 365; *vb.* 50
gun *n.* 657; *vb.* 370
gunman *n.* 167, 370
gunpowder *n.* 657
gurgle *vb.* 358
guru *n.* 473
gush *vb.* 301, 358, 532
gust *n.* 359
gusto *n.* 827
gusty *adj.* 359
guts *n.* 535, 857
gutter *n.* 261, 360
guzzle *vb.* 304, 948, 950
gypsy *n.* 270
gyration *n.* 323

H

habit *n.* 79, 138, **545**
habitat *n.* 191, 229
habitation *n.* 188, **191**
hack *n.* 524, 619, 676
hackneyed *adj.* 426
haggard *adj.* 205, 617
hail *n.* 760; *vb.* 886, 925
hair *n.* 207
hair-dressing *n.* 844
hairless *adj.* 228
hairy *adj.* 207, 258
halcyon days *n.* 664,
827
hale *adj.* 585
half *n.* 63; *adj.* 63
half a dozen *n.* 70
half-and-half *adj.* 45
half-done *adj.* 55, 57,
660
half-hearted *adj.* 533,
863
half-price *adj.* 746
half-remembered *adj.*
441
halfway *n.* 30, 704; *adj.*
30, 90, 560; *adv.* 90
half-wit *n.* 437
half-witted *adj.* 435
hall *n.* 191, 529
hallmark *n.* 482
hallow *vb.* 980
hallucination *n.* 478
halo *n.* 250, 800
halt *n.* 144; *vb.* 144,
267, 691
halve *vb.* 63
hamlet *n.* 183
hammer *vb.* 282
hammer out *vb.* 659,
699
hamper *n.* 193; *vb.* 635,
681, 691
hand *n.* 238, 521
handbook *n.* 524
hand down *vb.* 714
handful *n.* 26, 76, 633
handicap *vb.* 162
hand in one's notice *vb.*
687
handiwork *n.* 163
handle *n.* 872; *vb.* 172,
606, 609, 622, 725
hand out *vb.* 715, 717
hand-out *n.* 464, 465,
715
hand over *vb.* 268

handshake *n.* 886
handsome *adj.* 844
handwriting *n.* 521
handy *adj.* 575, 627
handyman *n.* 629
hang *vb.* **216**, 370, 963
hang around *vb.* 188,
612
hanger-on *n.* 287, 640,
881
hanging *n.* **216**, 370,
963
hangman *n.* 370, 963
hangover *n.* 44, 950
hanker *vb.* 861, 914
haphazard *adj.* 158,
399, 409, 553
happen *vb.* 1, 107, 153,
825
happening *n.* 153
happiness *n.* 550, 661,
664, 831, **836**
happy *adj.* 827, 831,
836, 950
happy medium *n.* 30
happy returns *n.* 888
harangue *n.* 518
harass *vb.* 830, 893
harbour *n.* 298, 353,
595; *vb.* 461, 593,
712
hard *adj.* **334**, 337, 537,
633, 669, 942
harden *vb.* 332, 334,
337, 754
hardened *adj.* 537, 942
hard-hearted *adj.* 648,
754, 908
hard labour *n.* 963
hardly *adv.* 33, 139
hardness *n.* **334**, 537,
633, 669, 754
hardship *n.* 633, 665,
735
hard-working *adj.* 611,
615
hardy *adj.* 161
harlot *n.* 953
harm *n.* 551, 900; *vb.*
580, 608, 900, 916
harmful *adj.* 164, 580,
592, 916
harmonious *adj.* 24, 79,
105, 244, **643**, **790**
harmony *n.* 24, 244,
510, 643, 650, **790**
harness *n.* 49; *vb.* 47
harrow *vb.* 378, 830
harrowing *adj.* 828, 856
harsh *adj.* 258, 642,
669, 787, 900, 908
harsh sound *n.* **787**

harvest *n.* 128, 163,
567; *vb.* 378, 567
haste *n.* 280, **613**
hasty *adj.* 393, 544, 603,
613
hatch *n.* 262; *vb.* 449,
477, 558
hatchway *n.* 262
hate *n.* 862, **892**, 900;
vb. 862, **892**
hatred *n.* 862, 883, 892
haughty *adj.* 873, 875,
924
haul *n.* 291, 724; *vb.*
268, 291
haunt *vb.* 188, 441, 830,
971
have *vb.* 707
have a go *vb.* 604
have fun *vb.* 840
have in mind *vb.* 552
have it in for *vb.* 892,
900
haven *n.* 595
have nothing to do
with *vb.* 10, 542, 862
have no time for *vb.*
923
have-nots *n.* 871
have on *vb.* 227, 478
have one's own way *vb.*
530
have one's say *vb.* 468
have on one's mind *vb.*
384
havoc *n.* 164
hawk *vb.* 695, 727
hawker *n.* 697, 728
hazard *n.* 553, 594; *vb.*
553
hazel *adj.* 810
hazy *adj.* 363, 799, 824
H-bomb *n.* 657
head *n.* 89, 236, 675;
vb. 212, 236, 284,
286
headache *n.* 633, 950
headlines *n.* 465
headlong *adj.* 613, 859
headmaster *n.* 473
headquarters *n.* 96
head start *n.* 34
headstone *n.* 372
headstrong *adj.* 537,
859
headway *n.* 288
heal *vb.* 589, 591
health *n.* **585**
heap *n.* 567; *vb.* 567,
747
hear *vb.* 778, **795**, 960
hearing *n.* **795**, 960

hearsay n. 465
heart n. 223, 224, 368, 751, 857
heart-broken adj. 828, 837
heartening adj. 836, 857
hearth n. 191, 763
heartlessness n. 908
heart-to-heart n. 519
heartwarming adj. 836
hearty adj. 585
heat n. 759, 763; vb. 306, 761
heath n. 356
heathen n. 975, 983
heating n. 761
heatwave n. 759
heave vb. 291, 303, 318, 834
heaven n. 329, 972
heavenly adj. 770, 966, 972
heavy adj. 330, 332, 511, 573, 617, 841
heavy drinker n. 950
heavy-handed adj. 628, 669
heavy-laden adj. 828
heavyweight adj. 573
heckle vb. 425, 696
hedge n. 234; vb. 555
hedonistic adj. 827, 945
heed n. 390, 392, 860; vb. 390, 392, 673, 702
heedless adj. 391, 442, 859
hefty adj. 161
height n. 26, 208, 400, 581
heighten vb. 36, 318, 481, 835
heinous adj. 936
heir n. 171, 710, 716
helicopter n. 278
helix n. 251
hell n. 828, 973
helmsman n. 272
help n. 563, 636, 639, 834; vb. 563, 575, 577, 636, 639, 676
helper n. 624, 640, 905
helpful adj. 550, 575, 636
helping n. 305, 717
helpless adj. 160, 162, 855
hem n. 233; vb. 233
hem in vb. 234
hemisphere n. 63
hen n. 381

henpecked adj. 673
herald n. 86, 467; vb. 118, 286
herb n. 306, 307, 374
herbivore n. 373
herd n. 94, 373, 377, 871; vb. 377
hereafter n. 123; adv. 123
hereditary adj. 5
heresy n. 106, 975, 978
heretical adj. 106, 412, 975, 978
heritage n. 11
hermit n. 885, 946
hero n. 661, 857, 939
heroic adj. 857
hesitant adj. 515, 533, 536, 856
hesitate vb. 325, 409, 421, 515, 533, 536
heterodox adj. 978
heterogeneous adj. 15, 17, 45, 104
hew vb. 48, 489
hexagon n. 70, 246
heyday n. 664
hidden adj. 453, 459, 461, 466, 824
hide vb. 225, 461, 466, 593
hideous adj. 245, 845
hide-out n. 463
hiding n. 461, 463
hierarchy n. 97
hi-fi n. 794
high adj. 32, 208, 318, 777, 868
high birth n. 870
highest adj. 212, 579
high-flown adj. 509, 877
high-handed adj. 880, 887
high hopes n. 443, 854
highlight vb. 468, 481
high living n. 945
highly-strung adj. 756
high opinion n. 922
high-pitched adj. 787
high principles n. 931
high-rise adj. 208
high spirits n. 836
high tea n. 306
high time n. 135
highway n. 559
highway code n. 313
highwayman n. 723
hijack vb. 722
hijacker n. 723
hike n. 269; vb. 269
hiker n. 270

hilarious adj. 851
hill n. 208, 316, 559
hind n. 381; adj. 237
hinder vb. 181, 548, 635, 637, 681
hindmost adj. 198, 237
hindrance n. 548, 635, 681
hindsight n. 441
hinge n. 49, 217
hint n. 459, 460, 482; vb. 459, 460
hire vb. 557, 685, 719
hire out vb. 718
hire purchase n. 718, 731
hiss vb. 786, 788, 853, 926
hissing sound n. 786
historian n. 484
historical adj. 124, 430
history n. 124
histrionics n. 529, 877
hit n. 282, 661; vb. 282, 758, 963
hit and miss n. 396
hit back vb. 647
hitch n. 635
hitch-hiker n. 270
hit it off vb. 24, 643
hit-or-miss adj. 158
hit upon vb. 419
hive off vb. 48
hoard n. 567; vb. 567
hoarse adj. 787
hoary adj. 126, 807, 809
hoax n. 478, 598, 631; vb. 478, 631
hob n. 763, 970
hobble vb. 281
hobby n. 840
hoe vb. 378
hog n. 948; vb. 707
hoist vb. 318
hold n. 707, 712; vb. 50, 420, 707, 712
hold against vb. 588
hold back vb. 533, 681, 694, 876
hold dear vb. 441, 889, 922
holder n. 193, 710
hold forth vb. 470, 514
holding n. 378, 711, 712
hold off vb. 295, 648
hold one's breath vb. 443
hold out vb. 648, 693
hold out for vb. 535
hold up vb. 135, 217, 635
hold-up n. 635, 722

hold water vb. 410
hole n. 254, 262, 319; vb. 264
holiday n. 144, 612, 614, 840
holiday-maker n. 270
hollow n. 210, 254, 262; adj. 254, 852; vb. 210, 254
holocaust n. 370
holy adj. 935, 974, 980, 982
Holy Communion n. 988
holy orders n. 985
Holy Spirit n. 967
homage n. 982
home n. 11, 191, 595; adj. 190
homecoming n. 298
homeless adj. 59, 187
homely adj. 508, 827
home-made adj. 628
homesickness n. 861
homestead n. 191, 377, 378
homework n. 470, 472
homicide n. 370
homogeneity n. 13, 16, 46, 59
homo sapiens n. 379
homosexual n. 106, 953; adj. 952
honest adj. 430, 476, 915, 931
honey n. 772, 891
honeymoon n. 829, 896; vb. 896
honour n. 663, 868, 872, 909, 922, 982; vb. 868, 878, 922, 982
honourable adj. 868, 931
hood n. 225, 801, 989
hooded adj. 225
hoodwink vb. 478, 819
hook n. 49; vb. 47, 896
hooligan n. 906
hoop n. 250; vb. 788
hoot vb. 482, 788, 853
hooter n. 116, 482
hop n. 320; vb. 320
hope n. 406, 420, 443, 854; vb. 406, 443, 552, 854
hopeful adj. 443, 854
hopelessness n. 405, 576, 855
horizon n. 198
horizontal adj. 215, 248
horn n. 598

horn of plenty *n.* 168
horology *n.* 116
horoscope *n.* 329, 447
horrible *adj.* 580, 771
horrid *adj.* 580, 845
horrifying *adj.* 856
horror *n.* 845, 856
horse *n.* 275
horsemanship *n.* 269
horse-power *n.* 159
horse-racing *n.* 269
horse-rider *n.* 270
horticultural *adj.* 374, 376, 378
hospitable *adj.* 716, 884
hospitality *n.* 302, 747, 884
host *n.* 75, 968
hostage *n.* 701
hostel *n.* 191
hostile *adj.* 637, 665, 883, 892
hostilities *n.* 649, 651
hot *adj.* 759, 769
hotel *n.* 191
hour *n.* 109
hour-glass *n.* 116
hourly *adv.* 140
house *n.* 191, 620
household *n.* 11; *adj.* 426
householder *n.* 190
housekeeper *n.* 676, 683
housekeeping *n.* 622, 748
hover *vb.* 154, 216
hovercraft *n.* 278
howl *vb.* 359, 788, 789, 839
hub *n.* 96, 224
huddle *n.* 94; *vb.* 94
hue *n.* 805
hug *n.* 712, 886; *vb.* 50, 712, 886, 890
huge *adj.* 32, 194
hull *n.* 225
hum *n. vb.* 781, 783, **784**, 789
human *n.* 368; *adj.* 379
human being *n.* 379
humane *adj.* 903
humanitarian *adj.* 899, 903
humanity *n.* 379
human rights *n.* 917
human sound *n.* **788**
humble *adj.* 35, 654, 833, 871, **874**, 941, 980; *vb.* 869, 874, 922

humble oneself *vb.* 833, 874, 941, 982
humid *adj.* 349, 759
humiliate *vb.* 869, **874**, 923
humility *n.* 654, **874**, 980
humorous *adj.* 842
humour *n.* 5, 751, 842
hump *n.* 252
hunch *n.* 134, 411; *vb.* 319
hunchbacked *adj.* 245
hundred *n.* 70
hunger *n.* 861, 947; *vb.* 861
hunger strike *n.* 696
hungry *adj.* 735, 861, 947
hunt *n.* 554; *vb.* 394, 554
hurdle *n.* 230, 235, 320, 635
hurricane *n.* 175, 359
hurried *adj.* 613, 859
hurry *n.* 280, 611, 613; *vb.* 280, 613
hurt *n.* 828; *adj.* 893; *vb.* 580, 608, 830, 900, 916
hurtful *adj.* 164, 551, 580, 828, 830
husband *n.* 896; *vb.* 377, 748
husbandry *n.* 378, 622, 748
hush *n.* 779, 781; *vb.* 267, 779
hush-hush *adj.* 461, 466
hush up *vb.* 466
husk *n.* 225
husky *adj.* 787
hut *n.* 191
hybrid *n.* 45, 495
hydrated *adj.* 347
hydro- *adj.* 347
hydro-electricity *n.* 159, 765
hydrogen bomb *n.* 657
hygienic *adj.* 585
hymn *n.* 792, 982
hyperbole *n.* 481
hyper-critical *adj.* 832, 864
hyper-sensitive *adj.* 753
hypnosis *n.* 754
hypochondriac *n.* 440
hypocrisy *n.* 477, 981
hypocrite *n.* 480, 631
hypothesis *n.* 157, 386, 396, 448

hypothetical *adj.* 2, 396, 448
hysteria *n.* 439, 756
hysteric *n.* 440

I

ice *n.* 347, 760; *vb.* 762
iceberg *n.* 754, 760
icon *n.* 983
icy *adj.* 760, 762
idea *n.* **386**, 415, 420, 449, 552
ideal *n.* 581, 939; *adj.* 449, 581
idealist *n.* 449, 864, 903
identical *adj.* 13
identification *n.* 397, 419, 482, 496
identify *vb.* 482, 496
identity *n.* **13**
idiom *n.* 492, 498
idiosyncractic *adj.* 102
idiosyncrasy *n.* 5, 102, 501
idiot *n.* 437, **440**, 630
idiotic *adj.* 435
idle *adj.* 174, 610, **612**; *vb.* 107, 174, 281, 612
idler *n.* 281, 612, 940
idol *n.* 967, 983
idolatry *n.* 975, **983**
idolize *vb.* 982, 983
idyllic *adj.* 528
ignite *vb.* 761
ignited *adj.* 759
ignoble *adj.* 871
ignominious *adj.* 869
ignoramus *n.* **429**, 437, 630
ignorance *n.* 385, **427**
ignorant *adj.* 427
ignore *vb.* 385, 389, 393, 672, 694, 887, 911
ill *n.* 551, 900; *adj.* 586
illegal *adj.* 691, 916, **955**
illegality *n.* **955**
illegible *adj.* 453
illegitimate *adj.* 171, 916, **955**
ill feeling *n.* 642, 883
ill health *n.* **586**
ill-humoured *adj.* 895
illicit *adj.* 691, 916, 952, 955
illiterate *adj.* 427

illness *n.* 586, 828
illogical *adj.* 412, 451
illuminate *vb.* 456, 797
illusion *n.* 4, 449, 478
illustrate *vb.* 413, 456, 486, **488**, 525
illustration *n.* 23, 397, 413, 456, 486, **488**, 525
illustrative *adj.* 456, 486
illustrious *adj.* 573, 868
image *n.* 386, 486, 489, 525, 983
imagery *n.* 455
imaginable *adj.* 404
imaginary *adj.* 2, 449, 970
imagination *n.* **449**
imagine *vb.* 448, **449**
imbecile *n.* 437, 440; *adj.* 435
imbecility *n.* 383, 435, 439
imitate *vb.* 18, 20
imitation *n.* **20**, 486, 719; *adj.* 149
immaculate *adj.* 581, 583, 935
immanent *adj.* 5, 966
immateriality *n.* 4, **328**, 574
immaturity *n.* 129, 427, 582, 603
immeasurable *adj.* 78
immediate *adj.* 115, 134
immensity *n.* 194
immerse *vb.* 311, **321**, 349
immersed *adj.* 210
immigrant *n.* 100, 190, 270; *adj.* 100
immigration *n.* 300
imminent *adj.* 123, 134, 154, 902
immobile *adj.* 152, 174, 267
immoderate *adj.* 32, 393, **572**, 749, 918, 945
immoral *adj.* 932, 936, 952
immortal *adj.* 114, 966
immortalize *vb.* 114, 868
immovable *adj.* 143, 152, 267, 669, 757
immunity *n.* 593, 678, 921
immutability *n.* 152
imp *n.* 969, 970
impact *n.* 282

impair *vb.* 160, 588

impale *vb.* 264, 963

impart *vb.* 464, 470, 715

impartial *adj.* 476, 541, 915, **933**

impassioned *adj.* 506, 752

impassive *adj.* 863

impatient *adj.* 613, 756, 893

impeach *vb.* 686, 930

impeccable *adj.* 581, 935, 937

impede *vb.* 635, 681

impediment *n.* 515, 635, 681

impel *vb.* 266, 282, 290, 674

impend *vb.* 123, 154

impenetrable *adj.* 265, 332, 334, 453

impenitence *n.* **942**

imperative *n.* 562; *adj.* 531, 562

imperceptible *adj.* 33, 824

imperfect *adj.* 35, 57, 315, **582**, 847, 952

imperfection *n.* 35, 315, **582**, 952

imperfect speech *n.* **515**

imperfect vision *n.* **820**

imperialism *n.* 379

imperishable *adj.* 114

impermeable *adj.* 332, 334

impersonation *n.* 20

impertinent *adj.* 880, 923

imperturbable *adj.* 757

impervious *adj.* 265, 337, 803

impetuous *adj.* 613, 756, 859

impetus *n.* 282, 290, 547

impiety *n.* **981**

impinge *vb.* 282

implacable *adj.* 912

implant *vb.* 300, 311

implausible *adj.* 405, 407, 421

implement *n.* 192, 565; *vb.* 659

implicate *vb.* 930

implication *n.* 450, 459

implicit *adj.* 5

implore *vb.* 695, 982

imply *vb.* 401, 448, 450, 459, 482

impolite *adj.* 887, 923

imponderability *n.* 4, 331

import *n.* 450, 573; *vb.* 268, 450

importance *n.* 456, **573**

important *adj.* 177, **573**, 922

importer *n.* 728

importunity *n.* 695

impose *vb.* 700, 919

imposing *adj.* 573, 870

imposition *n.* 963

impossibility *n.* **405**

impostor *n.* 480, 852, 940

impotence *n.* **160**, 169

impoverish *vb.* 162, 735

impracticable *adj.* 407, 576, 628

impractical *adj.* 449

imprecatory *adj.* 695, 901

imprecise *adj.* 431, 503, 916

impregnable *adj.* 593

impregnate *vb.* 311

impress *vb.* 242, 441, **468**, 482, 490, **522**, 752, 755, 922

impression *n.* 22, 386, 411, 420, 482, 483, 522, 752

impressionable *adj.* 242, 753

impressive *adj.* 529, 573, 755, 844

imprint *n.* 482; *vb.* 522

imprison *vb.* 234, 681, 963

improbability *n.* **407**, 409

improbity *n.* **932**

improper *adj.* 137, 511, 916, 918

improve *vb.* 288, 472, **587**, 618

improvement *n.* 288, 550, **587**

improvise *vb.* 142, 544, 603

imprudent *adj.* 393, 435, 859

impudent *adj.* 880, 887

impulse *n.* **282**

impulsive *adj.* 411, 544, 613, 756, 859

impurity *n.* 582, 584, 847, **952**

impute *vb.* 157, 930

inability *n.* 160, 628

inaccessible *adj.* 198, 405

inaccurate *adj.* 431, 477, 916

inaction *n.* **610**, 616

inactive *adj.* 174, 281, 607, **612**

inactivity *n.* 174, **612**

inadequate *adj.* 315, **571**, 582, 662

in advance *adj.* 134; *adv.* 84, 236, 286

inadvisable *adj.* 578

inane *adj.* 433, 435

inanimate *adj.* 367

inanity *n.* 451

inapplicable *adj.* 10, 106

inappropriate *adj.* 10, 106, 137, 500, 511, 578

in arrears *adj.* 737, 917

inarticulate *adj.* 513, 515

inattention *n.* 385, **391**, 703

inattentive *adj.* 389, **391**, 393, 442, 863

inaudibility *n.* 453, 779, 781, 796

inaugural *adj.* 88

inaugurate *vb.* 88, 685

inauspicious *adj.* 137

inborn *adj.* 5, 223

incandescent *adj.* 761

incantation *n.* 984

incapable *adj.* 160

incapacitate *vb.* 160

incapacity *n.* 169

incense *vb.* 893

incentive *n.* 173, 547

incessant *adj.* 114, 138, 145

incest *n.* 952

inch *vb.* 281

incident *n.* 153

incidental *adj.* 8, 60, 139

incineration *n.* 372, 761

incinerator *n.* 763

incise *vb.* 490

incision *n.* 259

incisive *adj.* 255, 506

incite *vb.* 175, 755, 893

inclination *n.* 178, 219, 532, 861

incline *vb.* 178, 219, 319, 530, 861

include *vb.* 58, **98**

inclusion *n.* **98**

inclusive *adj.* 54, 5., 98

incoherence *n.* **51**, 453

incoherent *adj.* 80, 453

incombustibility *n.* **762**

income *n.* 705, **741**

incomparable *adj.* 21, 579

incompatibility *n.* 14, 106, 637

incompetent *adj.* 160, 576, 628

incomplete *adj.* 55, 57, 315, 582, 660

incompleteness *n.* 57

incomprehensible *adj.* 385, 453, 503

incomprehension *n.* 427

incompressibility *n.* 332

inconceivable *adj.* 405, 856

inconclusive *adj.* 409

incongruence *n.* 25

incongruent *adj.* 10, 19

incongruous *adj.* 15, 17, 25, 106

inconsequential *adj.* 10, 574

inconsiderable *adj.* 33, 574

inconsiderate *adj.* 391, 393, 887, 900

inconsistent *adj.* 14, 17, 25, 51, 106, 412

inconspicuous *adj.* 824

inconstant *adj.* 142, 151, 536, 538, 539

incontinence *n.* 952

incontrovertible *adj.* 408

inconvenience *n.* 578, 635; *vb.* 578, 633, 830

inconvenient *adj.* 137, 576, 578

incorporate *vb.* 52, 58, 98, 302

incorrect *adj.* 431, 500, 511

incorrigible *adj.* 942

incorruptible *adj.* 114

increase *n.* 36, 40, 196; *vb.* **36**, 40, 196, 664, 745

incredible *adj.* 579, 866

incredulity *n.* 409, 421, **423**, 866

increment *n.* 41

incriminate *vb.* 926, 930

incumbency *n.* 557

incumbent *n.* 190, 986; *adj.* 919

inopportune *adj.* 137, 578

in order *adv.* 79, 605

inordinate *adj.* 572, 945

inordinately *adv.* 32

inorganic matter *n.* 367

in part *adv.* 55

in progress *adj.* 57; *adv.* 288

inquire *vb.* 695

inquirer *n.* 697

inquiry *n.* 394, 695

inquisition *n.* 963

inquisitive *adj.* 388, 394

inroad *n.* 645

insalubrious *adj.* 586

insane *adj.* 435, 439

insanitary *adj.* 586

insanity *n.* **439**

inscription *n.* 483, 490, 521

inscrutable *adj.* 453

insect *n.* 373

insecure *adj.* 409, 594

insensible *adj.* 754

insensitive *adj.* 754, 942

insensitivity *n.* **754**, 863

inseparable *adj.* 47, 50, 54, 882

insert *n.* 230; *vb.* 40, 230, **311**, 483

insertion *n.* **311**

inside *n.* 223, 226; *adj.* 223, 681

insidious *adj.* 459, 932

insight *n.* 410, 411, 434

insignia *n.* 482, 677

insignificant *adj.* 451, 574

insincere *adj.* 477, 852, 927, 932, 981

insinuate *vb.* 311, 459, 460

insinuation *n.* 311, 928, 930

insipid *adj.* 162, 507, 666, 768, 843

insist *vb.* 547, 669, 700

insistent *adj.* 506

insobriety *n.* 950

insolence *n.* 644, 672, 873, **880**, 924

insoluble *adj.* 332, 405

insolvent *adj.* 706, 735, 739

inspect *vb.* 390, 394, 818

inspection *n.* 390, 392, 394, 396, 818

inspector *n.* 623

inspiration *n.* 411, 755, 976

inspire *vb.* 547, 755, 836, 854, 857

inspired *adj.* 411, 449, 506, 756, 976

instability *n.* 17, 151, 536, 756

install *vb.* 186, 302, 311, 685

installation *n.* 620, 685

instalment *n.* 55, 738

instance *n.* 23, 456

instant *n.* 115; *adj.* 602

instantaneous *adj.* 115

instantly *adv.* 115

instead *adv.* 149

instigate *vb.* 547

instigator *n.* 166, 547

instill *vb.* 470

instinct *n.* 382, 411, 531, 545

instinctive *adj.* 411, 531, 544

institute *n.* 475; *vb.* 88

institution *n.* 475, 620, 988

in store *adj.* 154; *adv.* 567

instruct *vb.* 470, 514

instructed *adj.* 426

instruction *n.* 103, 426, **470**, 624, 626

instructive *adj.* 460, 470, 597

instructor *n.* 473

instrument *n.* **565**, 609, 619

instrumental *adj.* 563, 565

instrumentalist *n.* 793

instrumentality *n.* 172, **563**

insubordinate *adj.* 644, 672

insubstantial *adj.* 4, 328, 331, 333, 451

insufficiency *n.* 315, **571**

insular *adj.* 183, 416

insulate *vb.* 226, 761

insult *n.* 869, 923; *vb.* 644, 887, 923

insulting *adj.* 880, 923

insuperable *adj.* 405

insurance *n.* 701

insurgence *n.* 672

insurgent *n.* 672; *adj.* 148, 672

insurmountable *adj.* 405

insurrection *n.* 148

insurrectionist *n.* 148, 672

insusceptible *adj.* 754

intact *adj.* 54, 599

intangible *adj.* 4, 328, 824

integer *n.* 39

integral *adj.* 5, 39, 54, 55, 56, 223

integrate *vb.* 52, 105

integration *n.* 24, 45, 52, 56, 59

integrity *n.* 56, 476, 931, 935, 937

intellect *n.* **382**, 434

intellectual *n.* 428; *adj.* 382, 384, 426

intelligence *n.* 382, 426, **434**, 460

intelligent *adj.* 382, 426, **434**

intelligibility *n.* **452**, 502

intemperance *n.* **945**, 948, 950

intend *vb.* 552

intended *n.* 698; *adj.* 552

intense *adj.* 173, 752, 759, 805

intensification *n.* 196, 835

intensify *vb.* 36, 173, 196, 481, 835

intensity *n.* 27, 32, 506, 759, 805

intention *n.* 284, 530, **552**

intentional *adj.* 530

interact *vb.* 12, 150

intercession *n.* 230, 653, 695, 982

intercessor *n.* 653, 982

interchange *n.* 12, **150**, 519, 714; *vb.* 150

interdiction *n.* 691

interest *n.* 41, 388, 755; *vb.* 294, 547, 755, 829

interested *adj.* 388

interesting *adj.* 755

interfere *vb.* 181, 635, 653

interior *n.* 223, 352; *adj.* 223, 352

interjection *n.* 230, 499

interlude *n.* 144

intermediary *n.* 653; *adj.* 230

intermediate *adj.* 30, 90, 230, 560, 563

interminable *adj.* 78, 114, 202

intermingle *vb.* 45

intermission *n.* 92, 144

intermittent *adj.* 92, 139

internal *adj.* 5, 223

international *adj.* 101

internationalism *n.* 903

internecine *adj.* 164, 370

internee *n.* 684

internment camp *n.* 682

interplay *n.* 12; *vb.* 12

interpose *vb.* 230, 653

interpret *vb.* 456

interpretation *n.* 450, **456**

interpreter *n.* 456, 974

interrogate *vb.* 394

interrupt *vb.* 92, 137, 144, 230, 887, 923

interruption *n.* 92, 230

intersect *vb.* 221, 246

intersperse *vb.* 230

interval *n.* 92, 109, 144, **200**, 267

intervention *n.* 92, 230, 563, 635, 653

interview *n.* 394, 410, 519, 884; *vb.* 394

interviewer *n.* 394

intimacy *n.* 882

intimate *vb.* 882; *adj.* 199, 882; *vb.* 450, 459, 460, 482

intimation *n.* 448, 460, 482, 597

intimidate *vb.* 856, 902

intolerance *n.* 537, 900

intonation *n.* 501, 512, 778

intoxicate *vb.* 950

intractable *adj.* 537, 672

intransigent *adj.* 537

intrepid *adj.* 857

intricate *adj.* 251, 453, 503, 633

intrigue *n.* 558, 631; *vb.* 755

intrinsic *adj.* 1, 5, 223

introduce *vb.* 84, 88, 300, 302, 311

introductory *adj.* 86, 88, 602

introspective *adj.* 384

intrude *vb.* 137, 300, 388, 645

intruder *n.* 388, 645

intrusive *adj.* 137, 388

intuition *n.* **411**, 531, 753

keep one's temper *vb.* 757

keep order *vb.* 593, 956

keepsake *n.* 441

keep up *vb.* 217, 460

kernel *n.* 90, 224, 306

key *n.* 357; *adj.* 136

keyed up *adj.* 756

kick *n.* 769, 827; *vb.* 282

kick against *vb.* 644

kid *n.* 131; *vb.* 478, 842

kidnap *vb.* 720, 722

kidnapper *n.* 720, 723

kill *vb.* 370, 963

killing *n.* **370**; *adj.* 370, 851

killjoy *n.* 548

kill time *vb.* 612

kiln *n.* 763

kind *n.* 97; *adj.* 882, 886, 899, 903, 935

kindergarten *n.* 475

kindhearted *adj.* 899

kindle *vb.* 755, 761

kindness *n.* 670, 747, 886, 899, 935

kindred relations *n.* **11**

king *n.* 675

kingdom *n.* 183

kingdom of heaven *n.* 972

kink *n.* 251

kinship *n.* 11

kiosk *n.* 730

kip down *vb.* 612

kiss *n.* 886, 890; *vb.* 758, 886, 890

kitty *n.* 709

kleptomaniac *n.* 440

knack *n.* 627

knead *vb.* 335

kneel *vb.* 319, 922

knell *n.* 372

knife *n.* 255; *vb.* 370

knight *n.* 870; *vb.* 868

knit *vb.* 47, 221

knock *n.* 282, 782; *vb.* 282, 782, 926, 928

knock down *vb.* 164

knock off *vb.* 144, 370, 659, 722, 744

knot *n.* 49

know *vb.* **426**, 452, 882

know-all *n.* **428**, 436, 875

know-how *n.* 426, 627

knowing *n.* 410, 426; *adj.* 426, 434

knowledge *n.* **426**, 460, 472

knowledgeable *adj.* 426, 434, 472

knuckle down *vb.* 615

Koran *n.* 976

L

label *n.* 482, 496, 743; *vb.* 482, 496

laboratory *n.* 620

laborious *adj.* 615, 633

labour *n.* 615, 619; *vb.* 615

laboured *adj.* 511

labourer *n.* 378, 619

lace *n.* 49, 846

lack *n.* **57**, 76, 189, 315, 571, 582, 706, 708; *vb.* 35, 57, 76, 189, 562, 571

lacklustre *adj.* 806

laconic *adj.* 504, 517

lacquer *n.* 225, 365

lactescent *adj.* 807

lad *n.* 131

ladder *n.* 316

laden *adj.* 56

lady *n.* 381, 870

lady-like *adj.* 381, 886

lag behind *vb.* 287, 315

lagoon *n.* 353, 354

laid up *adj.* 586

lair *n.* 595

laissez-faire *n.* 610

laity *n.* **987**

lake *n.* **354**, 805

lame *vb.* 588

lamellar *adj.* 206

lament *n.* 839; *vb.* 839

lamentation *n.* **839**

lamina *n.* 206

laminate *n.* 206; *adj.* 206; *vb.* 206

lamp *n.* 800

lance *vb.* 264

lancet *n.* 264

land *n.* **352**, 378, 711, 711; *vb.* 273, 298, 317

landed gentry *n.* 870

landlady *n.* 710

landlord *n.* 710

landscape *n.* 488

landscape gardener *n.* 378

landslide *n.* 317, 662

land travel *n.* **269**

lane *n.* 559

language *n.* **492**, 512, 514

languish *vb.* 162, 174, 586, **612**, 617, 837

lanky *adj.* 205, 208

lantern *n.* 800

lap *n.* 322; *vb.* 260, 322

lapel *n.* 260

lapidary *n.* 491

lapse *n.* 110, 144, 147, 315, 431, 938; *vb.* 110, 147, 869, 936

lap up *vb.* 390

larceny *n.* 722

lard *vb.* 306

larder *n.* 305

large *adj.* 26, **32**, 194, 204

largesse *n.* 715, 747

lark about *vb.* 435

larynx *n.* 512

lascivious *adj.* 952

laser *n.* 797

lash *n.* 964; *vb.* 175

lass *n.* 131

lassitude *n.* 617, 841

last *adj.* 89, 659; *vb.* 107, 112, 143, **145**

last-minute *adj.* 135

last resort *n.* 595

last rites *n.* 372

last straw *n.* 659

last word *n.* 89, 667, 939

late *adj.* 117, 124, 135, 369

lately *adv.* 125

latency *n.* **459**, 824

lateness *n.* **135**

later *adj.* 85, 119, 123; *adv.* 121

lateral *adj.* 238

latest *adj.* 120, 850

lather *n.* 363; *vb.* 583

latitude *n.* 182, 204, 678

lattice *n.* 221

laud *vb.* 982

laudable *adj.* 925

laugh *n.* 838; *vb.* 644, 827, 838, 851, 853, 924

laugh off *vb.* 393, 477

launch *n.* 277; *vb.* 271, 290

launch into *vb.* 605

launder *vb.* 583

laurel *n.* 663

lavender *n.* 814; *adj.* 814

lavish *adj.* 509, 745, 747, **749**; *vb.* 569, 740, 747

law *n.* 103, 626, 671, 954, 976

lawful *adj.* 667, 915, 954

lawless *adj.* 80, 644, 668, 672, **955**

lawn *n.* 374, 812

lawsuit *n.* **960**

lawyer *n.* **959**

laxity *n.* 51, 335, 393, **668**

lay *adj.* 628, **987**

layabout *n.* 906

lay at *vb.* 157, 693

lay bare *vb.* 419, 456, 458, 462

lay claim to *vb.* 917

lay down *vb.* 671

layer *n.* **206**; *vb.* 206

lay hold of *vb.* 705, 720

lay in wait *vb.* 463

lay it on *vb.* 481, 509, 927

layman *n.* 630, 987

lay-off *n.* 686

lay on *vb.* 805

lay out *vb.* 372, 740

lay-preacher *n.* 974, 987

lay siege to *vb.* 645

lay waste *vb.* 164, 645

lazy *adj.* 393, 612

lead *n.* 286, 529; *vb.* 34, 84, 236, 284, **286**, 573, 622

lead astray *vb.* 431, 936

leader *n.* 125, 253, **623**, 675

leading *n.* (printing) 522

lead to *vb.* 155

leaf *n.* 374, 812

leaflet *n.* 464

league *n.* 641, 699

leak *n.* 600; *vb.* (escape) 301, 358; (disclosure) 462

lean *adj.* 205; *vb.* (tend) 178; (incline) 219

lean on *vb.* 679, 854

leap *n.* 200, **320**, 321; *vb.* 320

leapfrog *n.* 320; *vb.* 320

leap year *n.* 109

learn *vb.* 441, 472

learner *n.* 428, **474**

learning *n.* 426, **472**

lease *n.* 708, 714; *vb.* 718, 719

leave *n.* 614, 690, 921;

vb. **299**, 556, 600, 660, 687
leave alone *vb.* 555, 610
leaven *n.* 142, 331; *vb.* 318
leave of absence *n.* 614
leave out *vb.* 99
leave-taking *n.* 299
leave undone *vb.* 393, 660
leavings *n.* 44
lechery *n.* 952, 953
lecture *n.* 470, 518, 926; *vb.* 470, 514, 926
lecturer *n.* 473, 514
lecture theatre *n.* 475
ledge *n.* 217
ledger *n.* 742
leer *n.* 818; *vb.* 818
leeway *n.* 182, 200, 678
left *n.* 241; *adj.* 44, 241
legacy *n.* 714, 715
legal adviser *n.* 959
legality *n.* 915, **954**
legalize *vb.* 424, 690, 954
legal proceedings *n.* 960
legal tender *n.* 731
legation *n.* 685
legend *n.* 525
legerdemain *n.* 478
legible *adj.* 452
legion *n.* 75; *adj.* 75
legislation *n.* 622, 954
legislative *adj.* 103, 622
legislator *n.* 623
legist *n.* 959
legitimacy *n.* 915, 954
leisure *n.* **614**, 840
leisurely *adj.* 281, 614
leitmotif n. 387
lemon *n.* 813
lend *vb.* 568, **718**, 736
lending *n.* **718**
length *n.* 26, 198, **202**, 400
lengthen *vb.* 36, 202
lengthy *adj.* 202, 505
lenience *n.* **670**
lenient *adj.* **670**, 690, 907
lens *n.* 247, 822
Lent *n.* 947
leper *n.* 885
leprechaun *n.* 970
lesbian *n.* 106, 953; *adj.* 952
lesion *n.* 588
lessee *n.* 710
lessen *vb.* 37, 76, 197, 333, 403

lesser *adj.* 35, 209
lesson *n.* 470, 472, 597
let *vb.* 690, 718
let down *vb.* 445, 874
let fall *vb.* 319
let go *vb.* 556, 713
lethal *adj.* 164, 370
lethargy *n.* 174, 281, **612**, 754
let off *vb.* 601, 911, 961
let on *vb.* 462
let out *vb.* 196, 462, 680, 718
let pass *vb.* 911
let slip *vb.* 680, 706, 920
letter *n.* **493**, 522, 523; *vb.* 482, 493
lettering *n.* 521, 846
letter of the law *n.* 669, 908
let up *vb.* 144, 176, 281, 616
level *n.* 27, 93, 206, 215; *adj.* 28, **215**, 248, 257; *vb.* 16, 257, 400
level-headed *adj.* 757
lever *n.* 217
leviathan *n.* 194
levitation *n.* 331, 984
levity *n.* 331, 836, 859
levy *n.* 743, 917; *vb.* 716, 743
lewdness *n.* 952
lexical *adj.* 494
lexicography *n.* 492, 494
lexicology *n.* 494
lexicon *n.* 83, 494
liability *n.* **179**, 701, 737, 919, 938
liaison *n.* 889, 952
liar *n.* 480, 940
libel *n.* 928; *vb.* 928, 930
liberal *adj.* 570, 715, **747**, 965
liberated *adj.* 678, 680, 961
liberation *n.* 601, **680**, 921
liberator *n.* 905
libertine *n.* **953**
liberty *n.* 678, 690
library *n.* 475, 524, 567
librate *vb.* 325
licence *n.* 690
license *vb.* 690, 954
licentiousness *n.* 952
lick *vb.* 758, 963
lick into shape *vb.* 470, 570
lid *n.* 225

lie *n.* 431; *vb.* 185, 477, 932
lie down *vb.* 215
lie low *vb.* 209, 459, 461, 593
lieutenant *n.* 675
life *n.* 107, 159, **368**, 557, 611
life-blood *n.* 368
life-giving *adj.* 170
life-guard *n.* 593
lifeless *adj.* 174, **369**, 507, 612, 843
lifelike *adj.* 18, 525
life-line *n.* 600
life peer *n.* 870
life science *n.* 375
lifetime *n.* 112
life-work *n.* 557
lift *n.* 316, 318; *vb.* 318
lift restrictions *vb.* 713, 921
ligature *n.* 49
light *n.* **797**, 800; *adj.* (not heavy) **331**, 333, 344; (of colour) 797, 807
lighted *adj.* 797
lighten *vb.* 634, 797, 834
lighter *n.* 277, 765
light-hearted *adj.* 836
lighthouse *n.* 800
lighting *n.* 797
light music *n.* 792
lightness *n.* **331**, 797, 807
lightning *n.* 800
light up *vb.* 755, 797
like *adj.* 13, 18; *vb.* 540, 770, 827, 861, **889**
like clockwork *adv.* 140
likely *adj.* 123, 404, **406**, 447; *adv.* 406
likely to *adj.* 179
like-minded *adj.* 24, 424
liken *vb.* 18, 397
likeness *n.* **18**, 20, 22, 486, 488
like to *vb.* 532
liking *n.* 178, 861, 922
lilac *adj.* 814
lily-livered *adj.* 858
limb *n.* 374
limber *adj.* 335
lime *adj.* 812
limerick *n.* 528
limit *n.* 89, 233, **235**, 400, 659; *vb.* 231, **235**, 403, 681

limitation *n.* 231, 235, 403, 681
limitations *n.* 700
limited *adj.* 195, 205, 235
limited space *n.* **184**
limitless *adj.* 78, 202
limp *adj.* 335, 507; *vb.* 281
limpid *adj.* 502, 802
line *n.* 11, 170, 202, 655, 729; *vb.* 81, 226
lineage *n.* 11, 170, 171
lineal *adj.* 171
linearity *n.* 202
liner *n.* 277
linger *vb.* 112, 135, 281
lingua franca n. 492
linguist *n.* 456, 492
linguistic *adj.* 450, 492
lining *n.* **226**
link *n.* 9, 49; *vb.* 9, 47, 52, 157, 397
lip reading *n.* 796
lip service *n.* 981
liquefaction *n.* **345**
liquefied *adj.* 343, 345
liquefy *vb.* 343, 345, 761
liquescent *adj.* 343
liquid *n.* 309, **343**, 347; *adj.* 343, 347
liquidate *vb.* 164, 370, 739
liquidize *vb.* 164
liquor *n.* 343
lisp *n.* 515; *vb.* 515
list *n.* **83**, 97; *vb.* 38, 83, 483
listen *vb.* 390, 778, 792, 795
listless *adj.* 174, 281, **612**, 863
lit *adj.* 759, 797
litany *n.* 988
literal *n.* 431; *adj.* 456, 493, 494, 977
literature *n.* 528
lithe *adj.* 335
lithographer *n.* 491
lithography *n.* 490
litigation *n.* 960
litter *n.* 576
little *adj.* 33, 195, 203; *adv.* 33
little by little *adv.* 27
liturgical *adj.* 988
live *adj.* 172; *vb.* 1, 188, 191, 368
live apart *vb.* 898
live comfortably *vb.* 734

maiden *n.* 897; *adj.* 88

mail *n.* 467, 523, 657; *vb.* 268, 523

main *n.* 360; *adj.* 34, 573

mainland *n.* 352

maintain *vb.* 91, 143, 145, 217, 304, 468, 568, 599, 636, 712, 929

majesty *n.* 868, 870, 877

major *adj.* 34, 130

majority *n.* 72, 75, 133

make *n.* 97; *vb.* 155, 163, 242, 705

make advances *vb.* 882, 890

make a face *vb.* 895

make a fortune *vb.* 664, 734

make a go of *vb.* 661

make amends *vb.* 31, 589, 721, 943

make a mess of *vb.* 628

make a mistake *vb.* 431, 500

make an example of *vb.* 963

make a noise *vb.* 778

make a speech *vb.* 514

make-believe *n.* 477; *adj.* 449, 477

make certain *vb.* 408

make clear *vb.* 452, 456

make do *vb.* 149, 606, 666

make exceptions *vb.* 403

make excuses *vb.* 549

make eyes at *vb.* 890

make for *vb.* 271, 284

make friends with *vb.* 882

make fun of *vb.* 842, 853

make headway *vb.* 288

make it *vb.* 661

make it up *vb.* 652, 911

make known *vb.* 460, 462, 464

make light of *vb.* 393, 418, 574

make love to *vb.* 889

make nothing of *vb.* 574

make off with *vb.* 722

make one jump *vb.* 444, 856

make one think of *vb.* 441

make out *vb.* 288, 441, 452

make over *vb.* 714

make passes *vb.* 890

make peace *vb.* 652

make plain *vb.* 456, 458, 462

make possible *vb.* 404

make preparations *vb.* 602

make progress *vb.* 288, 587

maker *n.* 166, 967

make sense *vb.* 410, 452, 456

makeshift *adj.* 149, 162, 603

make the best of *vb.* 757

make too much of *vb.* 417, 481

make up *vb.* 58, 163, 449, 477

make-up *n.* 5, 58, 339, 751, 844

make up for *vb.* 31

make up one's mind *vb.* 530, 540

malady *n.* 586

malapropism *n.* 433, 497, 500

male *n.* 380; *adj.* 380

malevolence *n.* 900, 936

malformed *adj.* 245, 582

malice *n.* 893, 900

malign *vb.* 608, 900, 928, 936

malleable *adj.* 151

maltreat *vb.* 588, 608, 900, 916

mammal *n.* 373

man *n.* 133, 368, 373, 379, 380

manage *vb.* 392, 605, 606, 621, 622, 661, 666, 748

manageable *adj.* 634

management *n.* 392, 606, 609, 621, **622**, 675

management of animals *n.* 377

manager *n.* 623, 675, 728

manage to *vb.* 661

mandate *n.* 626, 671, 685

mangled *adj.* 245

manhood *n.* 133, 380

mania *n.* 439

maniac *n.* 175, 440

manifest *adj.* 458, 825;

vb. 401, 413, 458, 482, 823, 825

manifestation *n.* 419, **458**, 462

manipulate *vb.* 477, 758

mankind *n.* **379**

manliness *n.* 380, 857

manner *n.* 501, 559, 621, 825

mannerism *n.* 501

manners *n.* 886

man of learning *n.* 428, 436, 524

man of many talents *n.* 629

man of means *n.* 734

man of the world *n.* 629

manor *n.* 191

manpower *n.* 619

mansion *n.* 191

manslaughter *n.* 370

manual *n.* 460, 524

manufacture *n.* 163; *vb.* 163

manufacturer *n.* 166

manure *n.* 310; *vb.* 378

manuscript *n.* 483, 521, 524

many *adj.* 72, 75

many-coloured *adj.* 817

many-sided *adj.* 151

map *n.* 269, 460, 486; *vb.* 400

mar *vb.* 847

march *vb.* 91, 269, 696

mare *n.* 381

margarine *n.* 306

margin *n.* 44, 182, 200, 233; *vb.* 233

marine *n.* 272; *adj.* 271, 277, 351

mariner *n.* **272**

marital *adj.* 896

maritime *adj.* 271, 277, 351

mark *n.* 97, 202, 235, 400, 441, **483**, 521, 522; *vb.* 382, 390, 482, 483

mark down *vb.* 743, 746

marker *n.* 482

market *n.* 96, 559, 726, **730**; *vb.* 377, 725, 727

mark up *vb.* 743

maroon *adj.* 810, 811

marooned *adj.* 713

marquee *n.* 225

marquis *n.* 870

marred *adj.* 588

marriage *n.* 47, **896**

marrow *n.* 224

marry *vb.* 47, 896

marsh *n.* 355

marshal *n.* 958; *vb.* 81

marsupial *n.* 373

martial *adj.* 651

martyr *n.* 980; *vb.* 830, 963

martyrdom *n.* 828

marvel *n.* 866; *vb.* 866

marvellous *adj.* 32, 579, 844, 866

Marxism *n.* 327

mascot *n.* 984

masculine *adj.* 380

mash *vb.* 335, 364

mask *n.* 225, 461, 463, 549; *vb.* 146, 225, 819

mass *n.* 26, 75, 94, 194, 327, 330, 332, 567, 988; *vb.* 75, 192

massacre *n.* 370, 963

massage *vb.* 341, 758

masses *n.* 26, 32, 871

massive *adj.* 32, 204

mast *n.* 208

master *n.* 34, 131, 436, 629, **675**; *vb.* 441, 472, 679

masterly *adj.* 579

masterpiece *n.* 488, 581, 844

master-plan *n.* 558

mastery *n.* 501, 707

masticate *vb.* 304

mat *n.* 225

match *n.* 397, 649, 765, 800, 896; *vb.* 24, 28, 61, 218, 397, 896

matchless *adj.* 34

mate *n.* 882, 896; *vb.* 61, 889

material *n.* 192, 327; *adj.* 3, 327

material existence *n.* 3

materialist *n.* 981

materialistic *adj.* 327, 975

materiality *n.* 3, **327**

materialize *vb.* 242, 327, 825, 984

materials *n.* **566**

maternal *adj.* 11, 170

mathematics *n.* 38

matriculate *vb.* 83, 483

matt *adj.* 805

matter *n.* 3, 153, 327, 387, 573; *vb.* 573

matter in hand *n.* 605

matter-of-fact *adj.* 508

mirage n. 4
mire n. 355
mirror n. 822; vb. 20, 486
mirth n. 836, 838
misadventure n. 153, 662, 665
misanthropy n. **904**
misapprehend vb. 416
misappropriation n. 608, 722
misbehaviour n. 672, 887, 938
miscalculation n. 412, 416
miscarriage n. 445
miscarriage of justice n. 955
miscarry vb. 662
miscellany n. 45, 104, 527
mischief n. 900
mischief-maker n. 906
misconception n. 416, 431, 457
misconduct n. 938
misconstrue vb. 416, 457
misdate vb. 117
misdemeanour n. 938
misdirection n. 285, **471**
misemployment n. 608
miser n. 750
miserable adj. 828, 837
miserly adj. 571, 750, 934
misery n. 828, 837, 841
misfire vb. 628
misfit n. 10
misfortune n. 153, 551, 665, 900
misgiving n. 409, 421, 833
misgovern vb. 668
misguidance n. 471
misguided adj. 285
mishandle vb. 608, 628
mishap n. 153
mishmash n. 45
misinform vb. 471
misinstruction n. 471
misinterpretation n. 412, 416, 451, **457**, 487
misjudgment n. **416**, 431, 481
mislay vb. 187, 706
mislead vb. 431, 471, 477, 478
mismanagement n. 431, 608, 628

misnomer n. **497**
misogynist n. 904
misplace vb. 187, 706
misprint n. 431
mispronunciation n. 500, 515
misquote vb. 457
misrepresentation n. 471, 477, 478, 481, **487**
miss n. 131, 381; vb. 137, 315, 391, 393, 660, 662, 706
misshapen adj. 243, 245, 845
missile n. 290
missing adj. 189, 315, 571, 600, 706, 826
missing link n. 92, 324
mission n. 557, 651, 685, 688, 990
missionary n. 903, 974
mist n. 4, 346, 358, 363, 803
mistake n. 431, 457, 471, 500, 582, 608; vb. 497
mistaken adj. 285, 431
mistiming n. 117, 137
mistranslation n. 457
mistreat vb. 608
mistress n. 675, 889, 953
mistrust n. 421; vb. 421
misty adj. 349, 363, 799, 803
misunderstanding n. 25, 416, 431, 457, 642
misusage n. 500
misuse n. 569, **608**; vb. ⁓588, 608
mite n. 131
mitigate vb. 176, 403, 591, 834
mitigation n. 636, 834
mitre n. 989
mix vb. 45, 52, 58, 82, 399
mixed up adj. 80, 453
mixer n. 884
mixture n. 45, 52, 104, 591
mix-up n. 80
mnemonic n. 441
moan vb. 788, 832
moat n. 234, 261, 360, 646
mob n. 75, 94; vb. 175, 888
mobile adj. 142, 151, 266
mobilization n. 94, 651

mob rule n. 668, 955
mock adj. 18, 20, 149; vb. 853, 869, 924, 928
mocker n. 928, 981
mockery n. 477, 853
mock-up n. 23
modal adj. 8
mode n. 7, 545, 850
model n. 22, 486, 581, 939; vb. 23, 242, 489
modeller n. 491
moderate adj. **176**, 560, 746, 757, 944; vb. 142, **176**, 403, 652
moderation n. **176**, 944
modern adj. 120, 125, 850
modernization n. 125, 587, 589
modest adj. 33, 176, 418, 508, 517, 874, **876**
modesty n. 508, 517, 874, **876**
modify vb. 15, 142, 335, 403
modulation n. 142
module n. 279
moist adj. 347, 349, 358
moisten vb. 349
moisture n. 346, **349**
molecule n. 327
mollify vb. 176, 335, 652
molten adj. 343, 345, 759
moment n. 115, 573
momentary adj. 113
momentous adj. 136, 177, 573
momentum n. 282
monarchic adj. 870
monastery n. 990
money n. **731**, 734
money-lender n. 718
mongol n. 440
mongrel n. 45; adj. 45
monitor vb. 394
monk n. 885, 986
monocle n. 822
monograph n. 526
monologue n. **520**
monopolize vb. 707
monopoly n. 681
monotony n. 16, 91, 841
monsoon n. 358
monster n. 175, 194, 906
monstrous adj. 845, 936
month n. 109

monthly adv. 140
monument n. 372, 441, 483
moo vb. 789
mooch about vb. 612
mood n. 5, 751
moody adj. 756, 894, 895
moon n. 329, 800
moor n. 208, 355, 356; vb. 186, 271, 298
moot adj. 409
moot point n. 387
mop vb. 583
mope vb. 837, 895
moral n. 432; adj. 931, 935
moralize vb. 470
moral obligation n. 919
moratorium n. 135
more adj. 72
moreish adj. 770
moreover adv. 40
more than enough n. 572
morgue n. 372
moribund adj. 130, 369
morning n. **127**; adj. 127
moron n. 437, 440
moroseness n. 895
morphology n. 242, 499
morsel n. 33, 306
mortal n. 368, 379; adj. 369, 370, 379
mortgage n. 701, 718
mortgagee n. 736
mortgagor n. 737
mortification n. 874, 946
mortuary n. 372
mosaic n. 817
mosque n. 990
motel n. 191
moth n. 167
mothball vb. 135
moth-eaten adj. 126
mother n. 11, 170; vb. 676
motion n. **266**; vb. 482
motionless adj. 174, 267
motivate vb. 155, 547
motivator n. 547
motive n. 8, 155, **547**
motley adj. 17, 45, 104, 817
motor n. 276; vb. 269
motorcycle n. 276
motoring n. 269
motorist n. 270
motorway n. 559

newness n. 21, **125**
news n. 460, **465**
newspaper n. 464, 483
next adj. 85, 119, 199
nibble n. 304, 306
nice adj. 770, 829, 864
niche n. 184, 254
nick n. 259, 682; vb. 259, 722
nickname n. 496, 497; vb. 497
nicotine n. 308
niece n. 11
niggardly adj. 750
nigh adv. 199
night n. 128, 798; adj. 128
nightfall n. 128, 798
nightmare n. 449, 830
nihilist n. 167
nil n. 74
nimble adj. 280, 611, 842
nimbus n. 800
nine n. 70
nip n. 760; vb. 197, 203
no n. 425
nobility n. 34, **870**
noble adj. 32, 318, 868, 870
nobody n. 74
nocturnal adj. 128
nod n. 424, 482, 612, 690; vb. 325, 482
node n. 49
nod off vb. 612
noise n. 778, 780, 788, 791
noiseless adj. 779
noisome adj. 777
nomad n. 270
nomadic adj. 266
nom de plume n. 497
nomenclature n. **496**
nominal adj. 496
nominate vb. 496, 540, 685, 985
nominee n. 688
non-acceptance n. 425, 926
non-adhesive adj. 51
nonaggressive adj. 650
nonce adj. 495
nonchalant adj. 757
non-combatant n. **656**
non-completion n. **660**
nonconformist n. 106, 425, 979; adj. 25, 106, 979
none n. 74
nonentity n. 2, 574
non-existence n. **2**

non-expectation n. **444**
non-flammable adj. 762
non-imitation n. **21**
non-material existence n. **4**
non-observance n. 672, **703**, 920
non-payment n. **739**
non-possession n. **708**
non-preparation n. **603**
non-resonance n. **785**
non-retention n. **713**
nonsense n. 433, 451, 516
non sequitur n. 412
non-starter n. 662
non-stop adj. 138
non-uniformity n. **17**, 29
noon n. 127
no one n. 74
noose n. 463, 964
norm n. 30, 103
normal adj. 438, 545
normalize vb. 16
normative adj. 103
north n. 284
nostalgia n. 861
nosy adj. 388, 394
notable adj. 32, 573, 868
notary n. 959
notation n. 39
notch n. **259**; vb. 258, 259
note n. 41, 441, 456, 460, 482, 483, 523, 778; vb. 382, 390, **483**
nothing n. 74
notice n. 390, 460, 464, 482, 597, 624, 818; vb. 390, 818
noticeable adj. 458, 823
notify vb. 460, 464, 597, 624
notion n. 386, 420, 448, 449
notorious adj. 426, 869
nought n. 74
noun n. 499
nourish vb. 304
nourishing adj. 585
novel n. 525; adj. 125
novelist n. 521, 524, 525
novelty n. 21, 125, 142
novice n. 474, 630
now adv. 120
nowadays adv. 120
no way adv. 405

noxious adj. 777
nuance n. 27
nucleus n. 224
nude n. 228; adj. 228
nudge n. 482; vb. 482
nuisance n. 551, 830
null adj. 74
nullify vb. 2, 164, 469, 686
numb adj. 754; vb. 754
number n. 26, **39**, 72, 499; vb. 38, 482
numbering n. 38
numbing adj. 760
numeral n. 39
numeration n. **38**
numerous adj. 32, 72, 75
nun n. 986
nunnery n. 990
nuptial adj. 896
nurse n. 676, 683; vb. 304, 589, 676
nursery n. 378, 475
nurture vb. 304, 470, 712
nut n. 49, 306, 440
nutrition n. 304, 306
nutritious adj. 306, 585
nymph n. 970

O

oaf n. 437
oafish adj. 435
oath n. 468, 901
obdurate adj. 537, 942
obedience n. 654, **673**, 702, 874
obedient adj. 654, **673**, 702, 919
obesity n. 194
obey vb. 105, 654, 673, 874
obituary n. 369, 372
object n. 327, 552, 716; vb. 25, 425, 637, 642, 696, 892, 926
objection n. 425, 696, 926
objectionable adj. 862, 926
objective n. 298, 552; adj. 3, 6, 327, 430, 933
obligation n. 531, 562, 605, 674, 737, 919
oblige vb. 674, 919
obliged adj. 909, 919

obliging adj. 886, 899
oblique adj. 219; vb. 531
obliteration n. 164, **485**
oblivion n. **442**
oblivious adj. 393, 442, 754
oblong n. 246
obscene adj. 901, 952
obscure adj. 453, **503**, 798, 799, 824; vb. 461, 798, 799
obscurity n. 453, **503**, 799, 803, 824
obsequious adj. 881, 886
observable adj. 458, 823
observance n. **702**, 878, 977, 988
observant adj. 390, 702, 818
observation n. 101, 384, 386, 390, 396, 818
observatory n. 329
observe vb. 105, 390, 392, 673, 702, 818, 878, 988
observer n. 460, 821
obsess vb. 830, 984
obsessed adj. 439
obsolete adj. 2, 126
obstacle n. 635, 681
obstinacy n. **537**, 644
obstinate adj. 143, 535, 537
obstruct vb. 265, 635, 637, 648, 691
obtain vb. 1, 661, 705, 716, 720, 726
obtainable adj. 292, 404, 464, 705
obtrusive adj. 253, 877
obtuse adj. 256
obtuse angle n. 246
obvious adj. 452, 458, 502, 634, 823
occasion n. 136, 155, 878; vb. 155
occasionally adv. 138, 139
occult adj. 984
occupancy n. 188, 707
occupation n. 557, 605
occupier n. 190, 710
occupy vb. 107, 188, 191, 557, 707
occur vb. 1, 107, 153, 384, 430, 825
ocean n. **351**
octagon n. 70, 246
octave n. 70

octet n. 70
odd adj. 29, 39, 439
oddity n. 439, 866
odds n. 158
ode n. 528
odious adj. 892
odorous adj. 774, 776
odour n. 774
of course adv. 408
off adj. 53, 240; adv. 614
offal n. 310
offence n. 923, 938, 955
offend vb. 892, 923
offender n. 906
offensive n. 645; adj. 295, 777, 845, 869, 880, 887, 892, 923, 936
offer n. 693, 695; vb. 532, 693, 715
offering n. 715, 943
offertory n. 715
offhand adj. 544, 887
office n. 557, 620, 985
office-boy n. 467
officer n. 625, 675, 956
official n. 623, 675, 683; adj. 430, 557, 622, 667
officious adj. 880
offset n. 31; vb. 31
off-shoot n. 979
offside adj. 240
offspring n. 11, 171
often adv. 138
ogle vb. 818, 890
oil n. 306, 342, 365, 765; vb. 342, 365, 547
oiliness n. 365, 886
oily adj. 257, 365, 477
ointment n. 342, 365, 591
O.K. adj. 579; adv. 79
old adj. 124, 126, 130, 606
old-fashioned adj. 126
old maid n. 897, 951
old master n. 488
oldness n. 126, 130
olive adj. 812
olive branch n. 652
omen n. 447, 597
ominous adj. 154, 447, 594, 902
omission n. 57, 99, 393, 431, 662, 703, 920
omitted adj. 189
omnibus n. 524; adj. 54
omnipotent adj. 159, 966

on adv. 288; adv., prep. 9
on and on adv. 114
once adj. 124
one n. 59; adj. 13, 59
on edge adj. 443, 856
on end adj. 214
oneness n. 13, 59
onerous adj. 615
one-sided adj. 416
one-time adj. 118, 124, 687
ongoing adj. 288
onlooker n. 821
only adj. 46, 59
onomatopoeia n. 455
onset n. 88, 298
onslaught n. 175, 645, 649
on time adj. 134, 136
ontological adj. 1
onus n. 919
onward adv. 288
ooze vb. 301, 319
opacity n. 803
opal glass n. 804
opaque adj. 799, 803
open adj. 262, 348, 409, 458, 462, 476, 508, 632, 753, 823; vb. 88, 182, 262, 348
open-handed adj. 747, 965
opening n. 88, 254, 262, 462, 518; adj. 88
openness n. 476, 594
open up vb. 462
opera n. 529, 792
opera glasses n. 822
operate vb. 159, 172, 575, 591, 609
operation n. 172, 396, 591, 605, 609, 651
operative n. 619; adj. 172, 609
ophthalmic adj. 818
opinion n. 386, 415, 420, 624
opponent n. 638, 655, 883
opportune adj. 136
opportunity n. 136, 406, 678
oppose vb. 14, 25, 181, 239, 414, 425, 637, 644, 648, 649, 696, 926
opposed adj. 533, 883
opposite n. 239; adj. 14, 220, 239, 883; adv., prep. 239

opposition n. 181, 239, 397, 637, 926
oppress vb. 669, 837, 900
oppressive adj. 330, 669, 759, 900
opt vb. 540
optical adj. 818
optical illusion n. 4
optical instrument n. 822
optimism n. 417, 854
optimum adj. 579
option n. 540
opulence n. 734
opus n. 163, 792
oracle n. 436, 447
oral adj. 512, 514
orange n. 816; adj. 816
oration n. 518
orator n. 514
orb n. 249, 329
orbit n. 250, 322, 323; vb. 274
orchard n. 378
orchestra n. 793
ordain vb. 671, 685, 985
ordeal n. 828
order n. 79, 81, 85, 93, 103, 622, 663, 872; vb. 79, 248, 622, 671, 902
orderliness n. 79, 583
orderly n. 676; adj. 79; adv. 79
ordinance n. 103, 671, 954, 988
ordinary adj. 508, 574, 580, 666, 867, 871
ordure n. 310
ore n. 367
organ n. 563
organic adj. 366
organism n. 366, 368
organization n. 58, 79, 81, 564, 622, 641
organize vb. 58, 79, 81, 558, 622
organizer n. 558, 623
orgy n. 306, 950
orientate vb. 284, 545
orifice n. 262
origin n. 88, 155, 170
original n. 23; adj. 21, 88, 102, 125, 155, 430
originality n. 21, 102, 449
ornament n. 509, 844; vb. 844
ornamentation n. 509, 846
ornate adj. 509, 846

ornithology n. 375
orphan n. 885
orthodox adj. 545, 977
orthodoxy n. 977
orthography n. 493
oscillation n. 140, 325
ostentation n. 875, 877
ostracize vb. 99
other adj. 40
otherworldly adj. 328, 980
ought vb. 919
oust vb. 686
out adj. 189, 600
outbreak n. 88, 175, 645
outburst n. 175, 645, 756, 893
outcast n. 885; adj. 44
outclass vb. 29
outcome n. 87, 156
outcry n. 780, 788
outdated adj. 126
outdistance vb. 280, 314
outdo vb. 314
outer adj. 222
outer space n. 329
outfit n. 227, 568
outflow n. 301, 301
outgoing adj. 687
outgoings n. 740
outgrowth n. 252
outing n. 269, 840
outlast vb. 112
outlaw n. 885; vb. 963
outlay n. 740
outlet n. 262
outline n. 232, 242, 498, 558, 602, 825; vb. 232, 525, 558
outlive vb. 112
outlook n. 154, 284, 420, 443
outlying adj. 222
outmanoeuvre vb. 478
outmatch vb. 34
outmoded adj. 126
outnumber vb. 75
out of date adj. 126
outpace vb. 198, 280
outpost n. 198
outpour n. 301
output n. 163, 705
outrage n. 608, 900; vb. 830, 887
outrageous adj. 175, 433, 851, 869, 880, 936
outright adj. 54
outrun vb. 198
outset n. 88

outside *n.* 222, 232; *adj.* 6, 100, 222, 921
outskirts *n.* 198
outspeed *vb.* 198
outspoken *adj.* 887
outstanding *adj.* 44, 573, 737, 917
outstay *vb.* 112
outstretched *adj.* 202
outstrip *vb.* 29, 198, 280, 314
outward *adj.* 6, 100, 222, 825
outwit *vb.* 478, 631
oval *n.* 250; *adj.* 250
ovation *n.* 878, 925
oven *n.* 763
over *adj.* 44
over again *adv.* 77
over against *adv., prep.* 239
overall *adj.* 98, 101
over and above *adv.* 40
overawe *vb.* 922
overbalance *vb.* 317
overbearing *adj.* 669
overcast *adj.* 363, 798
overcharge *vb.* 745
overcome *vb.* 661
overcompensate *vb.* 31
overdo *vb.* 481, 572, 611, 615, 617
overdraft *n.* 739
overdrawn *adj.* 706, 737
overdue *adj.* 117, 135, 737, 917
overeat *vb.* 945, 948
overestimation *n.* 416, 417
overfeed *vb.* 865
overfill *vb.* 865
overflow *n.* 600; *vb.* 56, 358
overflowing *adj.* 75, 865
over-generous *adj.* 749
overgrown *adj.* 194
overhanging *adj.* 216
overhaul *vb.* 280
overhear *vb.* 795
overjoyed *adj.* 827
overlap *n.* 206, 260; *vb.* 206, 260
overlay *n.* 206; *vb.* 206, 226
overload *vb.* 330
overlook *vb.* 208, 391, 393
overlord *n.* 34
overplay *vb.* 481
overrate *vb.* 416, 417

overrun *vb.* 314
overseer *n.* 623, 675
oversensitive *adj.* 753, 894
overshadow *vb.* 34, 154, 208, 798
overshoot *vb.* 314
oversight *n.* 392, 621, 622
overstatement *n.* 417, 481
overstepping *n.* **314**, 918
overtake *vb.* 280
overthrow *n.* 148, 164, 662; *vb.* 148, 164, 220, 414, 686
overture *n.* 693, 792
overturn *vb.* 82, 164, 220, 414
overvalue *vb.* 416, 417
overwhelm *vb.* 414, 572, 661, 866, 922
overwhelming *adj.* 32
overwork *vb.* 611
owe *vb.* 737
owing *adj.* 737, 917
own *vb.* 707
owner *n.* 710
ownership *n.* 707
own up *vb.* 462, 833, 941
ox *n.* 380
oxygen *n.* 348
ozone *n.* 348

P

pace *n.* 269; *vb.* 269
pacesetter *n.* 125
pacification *n.* 176, 650, **652**
pacifist *n.* 656; *adj.* 650
pack *n.* 94; *vb.* 56, 75, 192
package *n.* 193; *vb.* 234
packet *n.* 193, 277
pact *n.* 698, 699
pad *vb.* 226
padding *n.* 226, 505
paddle *vb.* 271
paddock *n.* 184
padre *n.* 986
pagan *n.* 975, 983
page *n.* 467, 522
pageant *n.* 458, 529, 825
pageantry *n.* 877
pail *n.* 193

pain *n.* 551, 586, **828**, 830; *vb.* 830
painful *adj.* 551, 753, 805, 828
painfulness *n.* **830**
pain in the neck *n.* 592, 841
pains *n.* 392
painstaking *adj.* 392, 615
paint *n.* 225, 805; *vb.* 225, 488, 525, 805
painter *n.* 491
painting *n.* 486, **488**
pair *n.* 61; *vb.* 61
pal *n.* 882
palatable *adj.* 306, 767, 770
palatalize *vb.* 512
palate *n.* 767
palatial *adj.* 827
palaver *n.* 516
pale *adj.* 371, 806, 807, 812
palindrome *n.* 220
paling *n.* 234
pall *n.* 372
palliate *vb.* 591
pallid *adj.* 806
pally *adj.* 882
palm *n.* 663
palmist *n.* 447
palpable *adj.* 758
palpitate *vb.* 326, 756, 783
palpitation *n.* 325
palsy *n.* 326
paltry *adj.* 574, 580
pampa *n.* 356
pamphlet *n.* 464
panacea *n.* 591
pandemonium *n.* 780, 973
panel *n.* 206, 625, 688, 958
pang *n.* 828, 833
panic *n.* 615, 856; *vb.* 856
pannier *n.* 193
panoply *n.* 657
panorama *n.* 54, 818
pansy *n.* 162, 814, 953
pant *n.* 359; *vb.* 359, 756
pantheism *n.* 974
pantheon *n.* 967
pantomime *n.* 529
pantry *n.* 305
pap *n.* 364
paper *n.* 460, 518, 521, 526; *vb.* 225
paperback *n.* 524

par *n.* 30
parable *n.* 455, 525
parabola *n.* 247
parabolic *adj.* 455, 525
parachute *vb.* 273, 317
parade *n.* 458, 825, 877; *vb.* 91, 458, 877
paradise *n.* 449, 827, 972
paragon *n.* 581, 939
parallel *n.* 397; *adj.* 28, 218; *vb.* 218, 397
parallelism *n.* **218**, 397
parallelogram *n.* 218, 246
paralysis *n.* 754
paralyze *vb.* 160, 754
paramount *adj.* 34, 573
paranoid *n.* 440
paranormal *adj.* 447
paraphernalia *n.* 568, 711
paraphrase *vb.* 20, 456
parapsychology *n.* 447
parasite *n.* 373, 612, 881
parasol *n.* 225, 801
parcel *n.* 193, 717; *vb.* 234, 717
parch *vb.* 350, 759
parchment *n.* 521
pardon *vb.* 601, 670, 680, 907, 911, 961
pare *vb.* 203, 228
parent *n.* 11, 86, 170
parenthood *n.* **170**
parish *n.* 183, 987
parishioner *n.* 987
parity *n.* 28
park *n.* 234, 559; *vb.* 186
parliament *n.* 625
parochial *adj.* 183
parody *n.* 20, 487, 853
parrot *n.* 20; *vb.* 20
parse *vb.* 499
parsimony *n.* 748, **750**
parson *n.* 986
part *n.* 55, 73, 327, 529, 717; *vb.* 48, 55, 637, 642, 898
partake *vb.* 304, 709
partial *adj.* 55, 73, 660, 861, 916
participant *n.* 619, 709
participate *vb.* 605, 639, 709
participation *n.* 188, 639, 709
participle *n.* 499
particle *n.* 33, 195, 340, 499

particular adj. 5, 8, 102, 392, 398, 864
particularize vb. 102
particularly adv. 34
parting n. 48, 299, 369, 642
partisan adj. 641, 916, 979
partition n. 230; vb. 48
partly adv. 55
partner n. 640, 709, 710, 896
partnership n. 60, 180, 639, 709
part of speech n. 499
part with vb. 556, 713
party n. 94, **641**, 655, 840, 884, 896, 950, 960
party-minded adj. 979
pass n. 200, 690, 890; vb. 107, 110, 310, **313**, 424, 427, 954
passable adj. 579, 666
passage n. 200, 262, 266, **313**, 360, 559, 792
pass away vb. 369
passé adj. 126
passenger n. 270
passer-by n. 821
pass for vb. 18
passing n. 369
passion n. 752, 889, 893
passionate adj. 506, 752, 759, 889
passive n. 499; adj. 174
pass on vb. 714
pass out vb. 617
pass over vb. 393, 670, 920
passport n. 690
pass sentence vb. 960
password n. 690
past n. **124**; adj. 118, 124
paste n. 49, 362, 364; vb. 50
pastel adj. 805
pasteurize vb. 583
pastime n. 840
pastor n. 986
pastry n. 306
pasturage n. 305
pasture n. 305, 352, 356, 374
pasty adj. 806
pat vb. 758, 890
patch n. 183, 378; vb. 589
patched adj. 126, 817
patent adj. 458, 823

paternal adj. 11, 170
path n. 559
patience n. 757, 911
patient adj. 654, 757
patio n. 184
patisserie n. 306
patriarch n. 11, 132, 986
patrimony n. 11
patriotic adj. 903
patrol n. 593, 655, 683; vb. 593
patron n. 217, 545, 640, 726, 905
patronage n. 636, 726
patronize vb. 636, 726
patronizing adj. 873, 886
patter vb. 358, 783
pattern n. 23, 58, 79, 339, 488; vb. 81
pauper n. 735
pause n. 92, 144, 267, 612, 614, 616; vb. 92, 144, 267, 610, 612
pave vb. 225
paw vb. 758
pawn n. 701; vb. 701, 719
pawnbroker n. 718
pay n. 731, 738, 965; vb. 726, **738**, 740, 965
payable adj. 737, 917
pay attention vb. 390
pay back vb. 647
payee n. 716
paymaster n. 733
payment n. 726, **738**, 740, 965
payroll n. 619, 738
peace n. 267, **650**, 779, 831
peaceful adj. 267, 616, 643, **650**, 831
peace-maker n. 653, 656
peace-offering n. 652
peace of mind n. 757, 831
peach n. 816, 844
peak n. 89, 212
peal vb. 780, 783
pearly adj. 804, 807
peasant n. 378, 871; adj. 378
pebble n. 352
peculiar adj. 102, 106, 439
pedagogics n. 470
pedagogy n. 470
pedant n. 537, 864

pedantic adj. 392, 702, 864
peddle vb. 727
pedestal n. 213
pedestrian n. 270
pedlar n. 270, 697, 728
peek n. 818
peel n. 225; vb. 228
peel off vb. 51
peep n. 818; vb. 818
Peeping Tom n. 795, 821
peer n. 28, 122, 870
peg out vb. 617
pejorative adj. 923, 928
pellucid adj. 502, 802
pelt vb. 280
pen n. 184, 234; vb. 521
penalty n. 963
penance n. 943
penchant n. 178, 545
pencil n. 797; vb. 488
pendant n. 216, 482
pendulum n. 216, 325
penetrability n. 335
penetrate vb. 300, 313, 441, 452
penetrating adj. 384, 434, 769, 787
penetration n. 300, 434
pen-friend n. 523
peninsula n. 352
penitence n. 833, **941**
pennant n. 482
penniless adj. 708, 735
penny-pinching n. 750; adj. 750
pen-pal n. 523
pension n. 191, 687
pension off vb. 686
pensive adj. 384, 837
pentagon n. 70, 246
pent-up adj. 681
penumbra n. 798
people n. 379, 871; vb. 191
pep n. 173
pepper n. 307; vb. 307
perceive vb. 382, 419, 426, 452, 795, 818
perceptible adj. 458, 823
perception n. 382, 384, 752, 818
perceptive adj. 398, 426, 434
perch vb. 319
percolate vb. 300, 319
percussion n. 794
perennial adj. 114, 138
perfect adj. **581**, 659,

937, 951; vb. 56, 581, 659
perfection n. **581**, 659, 937, 951
perfectionist n. 864
perforation n. 262, 264
perforator n. **264**
perform vb. 163, 172, 529, 609, 659, 702, 792, 919, 988
performance n. 163, 172, 529, 609, 659, 702
performer n. 529, 609, 619, 793
perfume n. 776; vb. 776
peril n. 594
perimeter n. 232, 250
period n. **109**
periodic adj. 109, 138, 140
periodical n. 464, 524; adj. 140
peripatetic adj. 269
periphery n. 232, 250
periphrastic adj. 505
perish vb. 164, 369, 826
perishable adj. 113
perjury n. 477
perk up vb. 618, 836
permanence n. 112, **143**, 152
permeable adj. 264
permeate vb. 45, 319
permissible adj. 954
permission n. 424, **690**, 692, 921, 925
permissive society n. 952
permit n. 690; vb. 690, 954
permutation n. 142
pernickety adj. 864
perpendicular adj. 214, 248
perpetual adj. 78, 91, 114
perpetuate vb. 114
perpetuation n. 91, 145
perpetuity n. 78, 91, 114
perplex vb. 409, 633
perplexing adj. 409, 633
persecute vb. 900
perseverance n. 534, **535**, 611, 980
persevere vb. 145, **535**, 611, 648, 980
persist vb. 112, 143, 145, 535, 695

persistence *n.* 145, 534, 535

person *n.* 368, 379, 499

personal *adj.* 379, 966

personal effects *n.* 711

personality *n.* 5, 58, 382, 751

personification *n.* 455, 486

personnel *n.* 619, 676

perspective *n.* 488, 818

perspicacity *n.* 434

perspicuity *n.* 502

perspiration *n.* 310

persuade *vb.* 177, 420, 547, 624

persuasion *n.* 420, 547

perturb *vb.* 82

peruse *vb.* 394

perverse *adj.* 936

perversion *n.* 412, 457, 471, 477, 487, 608, 978

perversity *n.* 936

pervert *n.* 953; *vb.* 431, 457, 487, 588, 608

perverted *adj.* 936

pessimism *n.* 418, 443, 855

pest *n.* 892

pester *vb.* 695, 830

pestilence *n.* 167

pestilent *adj.* 592

pet *n.* 373, 891; *vb.* 890

petal *n.* 374

peter out *vb.* 37

petition *n.* 394, 695, 982; *vb.* 394, 695, 982

petitioner *n.* **697**, 982

petrify *vb.* 332, 334, 856

petrol *n.* 342, 765

petty *adj.* 416, 574

phantom *n.* 971; *adj.* 971

Pharisee *n.* 981

pharmaceutical *n.* 591

phase *n.* 109; *vb.* 558

phasing *n.* 140

phenomenal *adj.* 866

phenomenon *n.* 153, 825, 866

philanthropy *n.* 899, **903**

philosopher *n.* 428

philosophic *adj.* 757

philosophize *vb.* 384, 410

phlegmatic *adj.* 757

phobia *n.* 439

phoneme *n.* 512

phonetics *n.* 492, 512, 778

phoney *n.* 480; *adj.* 20

phosphorescence *n.* 797

photograph *n.* 483, 486; *vb.* 483

photographer *n.* 491

photography *n.* 486

phrase *n.* 494, **498**, 792; *vb.* 498

phraseology *n.* 501

physical *adj.* 3, 327, 827

physiognomy *n.* 236

physiology *n.* 366, 375

piazza *n.* 559

pick *vb.* 378, 398, 540

picket *vb.* 144, 696

pickle *n.* 307, 633; *vb.* 599

pick-me-up *n.* 173, 591

pick on *vb.* 830

pick-pocket *n.* 723; *vb.* 722

pick up *vb.* 318, 472, 587, 589, 618

picnic *n.* 269, 306, 840

pictogram *n.* 493

pictorial *adj.* 488, 525

picture *n.* 397, 486, 488, 525; *vb.* 449, 486, 525

picturesque *adj.* 488, 829

piece *n.* 55, 59, 306, 717, 792

pièce de résistance n. 581

piecemeal *adv.* 55

pier *n.* 213, 217

pierce *vb.* 264

piercing *adj.* 255, 760, 780, 787

piety *n.* **980**

pig *n.* 948

pigment *n.* 805

pigmy *n.* 195

pile *n.* 217, 567; *vb.* 192

pile-up *n.* 282

pile up *vb.* 94, 567

pilfer *vb.* 722

pilferer *n.* 723

pilgrim *n.* 270, 980

pilgrimage *n.* 269

pill *n.* 591

pillage *n.* 722; *vb.* 164, 722

pillar *n.* 152, 208, 217, 939

pillow *n.* 217

pilot *n.* 272, 273, 277, 396; *vb.* 271, 273

pilot scheme *n.* 396, 558

pimple *n.* 252

pin *n.* 255, 264

pinch *vb.* 197, 722

pine *vb.* 861

pink *adj.* 811

pin-up *n.* 844

pinnacle *n.* 212

pioneer *n.* 86, 125, 190; *vb.* 84

pious *adj.* 980

pip *n.* 306

pipe *n.* 308, 360; *vb.* 789

pipe-dreaming *n.* 449, 854

pipeline *n.* 360

piquancy *n.* 506, 769

pirate *n.* 723

pirouette *n.* 323; *vb.* 323

pit *n.* 210, 254, 658

pitch *n.* 234, 321, 365, 400, 512; *vb.* 290

pitfall *n.* 463, **596**

pith *n.* 224

pithy *adj.* 432, 450, 504

pitiable *adj.* 907

pitiful *adj.* 33, 580, 907

pitilessness *n.* **908**

pity *n.* **907**; *vb.* 907, 924

pivot *n.* 90, 217; *vb.* 323

pivotal *adj.* 224

pixie *n.* 970

placard *n.* 464

placate *vb.* 176, 652

place *n.* 184, 185, 186, 559; *vb.* 186

placement *n.* 85, 186

place of business *n.* 730

place of learning *n.* **475**

placid *adj.* 267, 757

plagiarize *vb.* 20

plague *n.* 167, 592, 665; *vb.* 314, 830

plain *n.* **356**; *adj.* 46, 452, 476, 502, **508**, 823

plain living *n.* 946

plainness *n.* 46, 452, **508**, 823

plain speech *n.* 452, 502, 508

plaintiff *n.* 930, 960

plait *n.* 49, 221, 251; *vb.* 221, 251

plan *n.* 23, 81, 386, 552, **558**, 602, 605; *vb.* 58, 81, 552, **558**, 602

plane *n.* 215, 278; *vb.* 215, 257

planet *n.* 329, 800

planetarium *n.* 329

planned *adj.* 543, 552, 558

plant *n.* 307, **374**, 620; *vb.* 378

plantation *n.* 374, 378

planter *n.* 378

plants *n.* 366

plaque *n.* 489

plastic *adj.* 142, 151, 242, 335, 768

plastic surgery *n.* 844

plate *n.* 193, 206, 490; *vb.* 225

plateau *n.* 356

platitude *n.* 432, 451

platonic *adj.* 951

plausible *adj.* **404**, 406, 420, 825, 929

play *n.* 529, 678, 840; *vb.* 477, 529, 792, 797

play-acting *n.* 852

play down *vb.* 418, 574, 928

player *n.* 529, 793

playful *adj.* 836

play games *vb.* 840

playground *n.* 658

playhouse *n.* 529

play on words *n.* 454, 842

plea *n.* 401, 549, 695, 929, 960

plead *vb.* 410, 514, 695, 959

plead guilty *vb.* 462, 941

pleadings *n.* 960

pleasant *adj.* 827, 829, 840

please *vb.* 829

pleased *adj.* 756, 827, 831, 909

pleased with oneself *adj.* 873

please onself *vb.* 678

pleasing *adj.* 790, 792, 829, 844

pleasurableness *n.* **829**

pleasure *n.* **827**, 840

pleasure trip *n.* 840

pleat *n.* 260; *vb.* 260

plebeian *n.* 871; *adj.* 849, 871

plebiscite *n.* 540

pledge *n.* 468, **698, 699**, 701, 919; *vb.* 468, **698, 699**, 701

preceding *adj.* 84, 118, 134
precept *n.* 103, **626**
precinct *n.* 184
precious *adj.* 139
precious stone *n.* 846
precipice *n.* 214
precipitate *adj.* 544, 613
precipitation *n.* 349, 358, 613
precipitous *adj.* 859
precis *n.* 527
precise *adj.* 392, 504, 864
preclude *vb.* 99, 691
precocious *adj.* 134
preconception *n.* 412, 416, 446
precursor *n.* **86**, 467
predate *vb.* 117
predecessor *n.* 86
predestination *n.* 531, 543
predetermination *n.* **543**
predicament *n.* 153, 633
predict *vb.* 443, 447, 543
predictable *adj.* 447
prediction *n.* 154, **447**, 543
predilection *n.* 178, 861
predisposed *adj.* 178, 751
predisposition *n.* 178, 545
predominate *vb.* 34, 101
pre-eminent *adj.* 34
pre-empt *vb.* 134
pre-existence *n.* 118
prefabricated *adj.* 602
preface *n.* 86, 88; *vb.* 84
prefer *vb.* 540, 916
preference *n.* 84, 178, 540
prefix *n.* 41, 86, 499; *vb.* 40
pregnant *adj.* 163, 450
prehistoric *adj.* 124, 126
prejudge *vb.* 416
prejudice *n.* 412, 416, 578, 916
preliminary *n.* 86, 88; *adj.* 86, 396
prelude *n.* 86, 88, 792; *vb.* 84
premature *adj.* 134, 137, 859

premeditated *adj.* 530, 543
première *n.* 88
premise *n.* 410, 448
premises *n.* 730
premium *n.* 663, 724, 965; *adj.* 579
premonition *n.* 411, 597
preoccupation *n.* 384, 390
preoccupied *adj.* 442
prep *n.* 470, 472
preparation *n.* 81, 86, 470, 591, **602**
preparatory *adj.* 86, 396, 602
prepare *vb.* 81, 306, 470, 521, 568, **602**
prepared *adj.* 443, 532, 602
preposition *n.* 499
preposterous *adj.* 481, 851
prerequisite *n.* 531
prerogative *n.* 34, 667, 917
prescribe *vb.* 671
prescribed *adj.* 954
prescription *n.* 591, 626
prescriptive *adj.* 103
presence *n.* **188**, 971
presence of mind *n.* 860
present *n.* 120, 715; *adj.* 1, 120, 153, 188; *vb.* 460, 529, 693, 715, 825, 965
presentation *n.* 413, 458, 460, 501, 529, 693, 715, 825
present-day *adj.* 120, 125
present events *n.* **153**
present time *n.* **120**
preservation *n.* **599**
preserve *vb.* **599**, 712
preside *vb.* 956
president *n.* 675
press *vb.* 257, 282, 290, 319, 695, 712, 758
pressed man *n.* 655
pressing *adj.* 674
pressure *n.* 159, 177, 282, 290, 330, 665, 674
pressure group *n.* 547, 697
prestige *n.* 177, 667, 829, 868
prestigious *adj.* 829, 868
presumable *adj.* 406

presume *vb.* 416, 420, 448, 867, 880, 910, 918
presuppose *vb.* 448
pretend *vb.* 20, 449, 477, 549, 852
pretender *n.* 852
pretentious *adj.* 509, 849, 852, 875, 877, 879
pretext *n.* **549**
pretty *adj.* 844
prevail *vb.* 1, 34, 101, 112, 661
prevail on *vb.* 547
prevalent *adj.* 32, 75, 545
prevaricate *vb.* 454, 477
prevent *vb.* 99, 181, 548, 635, 648, 691
preview *n.* 118
previous *adj.* 84, 118, 134, 687
prey *n.* 724, 828
price *n.* 579, **743**; *vb.* 743
priceless *adj.* 579, 851
prick *vb.* 255, 264, 758
prickly *adj.* 255, 258, 894
pride *n.* **873**
pride oneself on *vb.* 873
priest *n.* 986
prig *n.* 951
prim *adj.* 951
primary *adj.* 21, 155, 573
primate *n.* 986
prime *n.* 129; *adj.* 39, 579; *vb.* 470
prime mover *n.* 155, 966
primer *n.* 88, 524
primitive *n.* 190; *adj.* 88, 124, 126, 134
prince *n.* 675
princely *adj.* 870
princess *n.* 675
principal *n.* 473, 675; *adj.* 34, 573
principality *n.* 183
principle *n.* 5, 23, 103, 155, 420, 626
principles *n.* 558, 931
print *n.* 490, 522; *vb.* 464, 482, 490, 521, **522**
printer *n.* 491, 522
printing *n.* 490, 521, **522**

prior *n.* 986; *adj.* 84, 118, 134
priority *n.* 84, **118**, 286, 573
priory *n.* 990
prism *n.* 246, 805
prison *n.* 234, **682**
prisoner *n.* **684**, 701
privacy *n.* 461, 885
private *adj.* 466
privilege *n.* 34, 678, 872, 917, 921
prize *n.* 663, 715, 724, 965; *vb.* 573, 861, 889
pro *n.* 953; *adj.* 689
probability *n.* 158, **406**
probable *adj.* 404, 406
probationary *adj.* 396, 604
probationer *n.* 474
probe *n.* 394, 396; *vb.* 394
probity *n.* **931**, 937
problem *n.* 387, 409, 410, 633, 828, 830
problematical *adj.* 409
procedure *n.* 103, 545, 558, 559
proceed *vb.* 110, 266, 288, 313, 558, 661
proceedings *n.* 483
proceeds *n.* 705, 716, 741
process *n.* 172, 559
processed *adj.* 602
processing *n.* 146, 163
procession *n.* 91, 458
proclaim *vb.* 458, 460, 464, 671
procrastinate *vb.* 135, 920
procreation *n.* 163
procuration *n.* 705
procure *vb.* 705
prod *n.* 547; *vb.* 547
prodigal *n.* 749, 940; *adj.* 569, 749
prodigality *n.* 569, 749
prodigal son *n.* 941
prodigy *n.* 866
produce *n.* 163, 705; *vb.* 155, **163**, 172, 458, 529
producer *n.* 155, **166**
product *n.* 38, 156, 163, 729
production *n.* 163, 529
productive *adj.* 163, 168, 705
productiveness *n.* **168**
profanation *n.* 608, 901

pull down *vb.* 164, 319, 588

pulling *n.* **291**, 312

pull off *vb.* 659, 661

pull oneself together *vb.* 681, 757

pull one's socks up *vb.* 587

pull out *vb.* 312

pull through *vb.* 589

pull together *vb.* 639

pull up *vb.* 318

pull-up *n.* 191

pulp *n.* 364; *vb.* 364

pulpiness *n.* **364**

pulsar *n.* 329

pulsate *vb.* 140

pulsation *n.* 140, 325

pulse *n.* 140, 325; *vb.* 325

pulverize *vb.* 164, 340

pummel *vb.* 282

pump *vb.* 359

pun *n.* 454, 842

punch *n.* 264, 506, 769; *vb.* 282, 482

punctiliousness *n.* 392, 864

punctual *adj.* 115, 134, 136

puncture *n.* 48; *vb.* 48, 255, 264

pungency *n.* **769**

pungent *adj.* 769, 773, 774

punish *vb.* 647, 926, 962, **963**

punishment *n.* 647, 917, **963**

punk *n.* 792

puny *adj.* 162, 195

pup *n.* 880

pupil *n.* 131, 474

purchase *n.* 707, **726**; *vb.* 705, 726

purchaser *n.* 710, 726, 737

purdah *n.* 461

pure *adj.* 46, 581, 583, 935, 937, **951**, 977

purgatory *n.* 943

purge *vb.* 583, 911

purify *vb.* 46, 333, 348, 583, 775, 807

purist *n.* 864

puritanical *adj.* 669, 946, 951

purity *n.* 46, 876, 935, 937, **951**

purloin *vb.* 722

purple *n.* **814**; *adj.* 814

purport *n.* 450; *vb.* 450

purpose *n.* 547, 552; *vb.* 530, 552

purposeful *adj.* 552

purposeless *adj.* 451, 576

purr *vb.* 781, 783, 784, 789

purse *n.* 193, 732

purser *n.* 733

pursue *vb.* 287, 552, 554, 890

pursuer *n.* 554

pursuit *n.* **554**, 557, 605

push *n.* 303, 645; *vb.* 282, **290**, 547, 645

push ahead *vb.* 288

push along *vb.* 299

push around *vb.* 902

push back *vb.* 295

push down *vb.* 319

push off *vb.* 299

push-over *n.* 634, 661

pushy *adj.* 173, 611

put *vb.* 186

put about *vb.* 464

put across *vb.* 460

put aside *vb.* 567, 607

put a stop to *vb.* 144

put asunder *vb.* 898

putative *adj.* 448

put away *vb.* 304, 370, 567, 681

put back *vb.* 589

put by *vb.* 567

put down *vb.* 370

put forward *vb.* 693

put in *vb.* 300, 311

put into *vb.* 456

put into action *vb.* 609

put it to *vb.* 394

put off *vb.* 135

put on *vb.* 225, 227, 477, 529 805, 852

put-on *n.* 852; *adj.* 477, 852

put on a brave face *vb.* 477

put oneself out *vb.* 604, 615

put out *vb.* 578, 762, 830, 893

put over *vb.* 460

putrefaction *n.* 53, 777

putrid *adj.* 584, 588, 777

put right *vb.* 589

put together *vb.* 47, 52, 163

put up *vb.* 191

put-up job *n.* 930

put up with *vb.* 424, 757, 828

puzzle *n.* 409, 453, 466; *vb.* 409

pylon *n.* 159

pyramid *n.* 246

pyre *n.* 372

Q

quack *vb.* 787, 789

quadrangle *n.* 67, 184

quadratic *adj.* 67

quadrilateral *n.* 67, 246

quadrisection *n.* **69**

quadruped *n.* 373

quadruple *adj.* 68; *vb.* 68

quadruplet *n.* 67

quadruplication *n.* **68**

quagmire *n.* 355

quail *vb.* 858

quake *n.* 326; *vb.* 325, 326, 856

qualification *n.* 41, 142, **403**

qualifications *n.* 627

qualified *adj.* 130, 602, 627

qualify *vb.* 142, 403, 570

quality *n.* 5, 58, 579, 935

qualm *n.* 421, 533, 833

quandary *n.* 409, 633

quantify *vb.* 26, 400

quantitative *adj.* 26

quantity *n.* **26**, 32, 75, 400

quarrel *n.* 25, 642, 893; *vb.* 25, 642

quarrelsome *adj.* 642, 883

quarry *vb.* 312

quart *n.* 69

quarter *n.* 69, 183; *vb.* 69

quartet *n.* 67, 792

quasar *n.* 329

quash *vb.* 681, 686

quasi- *adj.* 497

quaternity *n.* **67**

queen *n.* 675

Queen's English *n.* 492

queer *n.* 106, 953; *adj.* 952

quell *vb.* 37, 89, 652, 681

quench *vb.* 762

query *n.* 394

quest *n.* 269, 388, 394, 554; *vb.* 554

question *n.* 387, **394**, 695; *vb.* 388, **394**, 421

questionable *adj.* 407, 409, 421, 869, 932

questioner *n.* 388, 394

questionnaire *n.* 394

queue *n.* 91; *vb.* 91

quibble *vb.* 454

quick *adj.* **280**, 434, **613**, 842

quicken *vb.* **280**, 368, 613, 752, 755

quicksand *n.* 355, 596

quick-tempered *adj.* 756

quick-witted *adj.* 842

quiescent *adj.* 267, 459

quiet *n.* 267, 616, 779; *adj.* 517, 616, 650, 779, 781, 876; *vb.* 652, 779

quieten *vb.* 176

quiet time *n.* 982

quilt *vb.* 226

quintessence *n.* 5

quintet *n.* 70

quintuple *adj.* 70

quintuplet *n.* 70

quip *n.* 842

quirk *n.* 539

quisling *n.* 480

quit *vb.* 299, **556**, 687

quite *adv.* 56

quiver *n.* 325; *vb.* 325, 326, 756, 760, 856

Quixote *n.* 449

quiz *n.* 394; *vb.* 394

quoit *n.* 250

quota *n.* 305, 717

quotation *n.* 743

quote *vb.* 20

quotient *n.* 38

R

rabbi *n.* 986

rabble *n.* 871

rabid *adj.* 148, 439

race *n.* 11, 554, 613, 649; *vb.* 280, 649

racialist *adj.* 379

rack *n.* 217, 964

racket *n.* 780, 791

raconteur *n.* 525

racy *adj.* 506, 769

radiate *vb.* 297

601, 721, 726, 911, 943
redeemer n. 905, 967
rediscover vb. 165
red-letter day n. 878
redress n. 943, 965; vb. 589, 943, 965
reduce vb. 37, 76, 197, 203, 588, 743, 744
reduction n. 37, 42, 195, 197, 527, 744
redundancy n. 505, 686
redundant adj. 505, 572
reduplication n. 62, 165
re-echo vb. 784
reef n. 357, 596
reek n. 777; vb. 759, 777
re-entry n. 274
re-establish vb. 589
refer vb. 9, 157, 450
referee n. 415, 653
reference n. 157, 401, 450
reference book n. 524
referendum n. 450, 540
refill n. 56
refine vb. 142, 333, 587
refined adj. 398, 510, 805, 844, 848, 886
reflect vb. 384, 486, 797, 982
reflection n. 22, 384, 441, 797
reflector n. 822
reflex adj. 411, 531, 544
reform n. 587; vb. 142, 146, 587, 589
reforming n. 165; adj. 903
refractory adj. 537, 672
refrain n. 528, 792; vb. 89, 144, 555, 610, 944
refresh vb. 161, 348, 472, 589, 618
refresher n. 591
refreshment n. 147, 306, **618**, 829
refresh one's memory vb. 441
refrigeration n. 599, **762**
refrigerator n. 305, **764**
refuge n. 463, **595**, 885
refugee n. 270, 600, 885
refund n. 31, 721, 738; vb. 31, 589, 721, 738
refurbish vb. 125, 587, 589
refusal n. 469, 542, 691, **694**
refuse n. 576; vb. 425,

469, 533, 542, 691, **694**
refutation n. 414
refute vb. 402, 686
regain vb. 705, 721
regal adj. 870
regalia n. 482, 677
regard n. 388, 390, 392, 868, 922; vb. 390, 420, 868, 889
regarding adv., prep. 9
regenerate adj. 146, 974; vb. 165, 589
regent n. 675
reggae n. 792
region n. 183
register n. 83, 116, 302, 483; vb. 83, 483
registrar n. 484
regress n. 147, 289; vb. 147, 289, 590
regression n. 37, 147, **289**, 590
regret n. 445, 828, 832, **833**; vb. 828, 833, 837, 941
regular n. 545; adj. 16, 79, 81, 91, 138, **140**, 244, 545
regularity n. 16, 79, 138, **140**, 244, 257, 545
regulate vb. 81, 140, 621, 622
regulation n. 81, 103, 622, 954
rehabilitate vb. 589, 721
rehearse vb. 77, 525, 602
reign vb. 667
reigning adj. 870
reimburse vb. 31, 721, 738, 965
reinforce vb. 161, 173, 226, 468, 646
reinforcement n. 196, 217
reinstate vb. 147, 589, 721
reissue n. 77; vb. 77, 125, 464
reiterate vb. 77, 140
reject vb. 25, 99, 393, 425, 469, **542**, 694
rejection n. 99, 421, **542**, 694, 926
rejects n. 44
rejoice vb. 829, 838
rejoicing n. **838**
rejoin vb. 395

rejuvenation n. 147, 589
rekindle vb. 589
relapse n. 147, 586, **590**; vb. 147, 590
relate vb. 9, 397, 460, 525
related adj. 9, 11, 60
relation n. **9**, 11, 12, 397
relationship n. 9, 889, 952
relative n. 11; adj. 9, 12, 27
relative quantity n. **27**
relax vb. 144, 176, 267, 335, 612, 614, 840, 907
relaxation n. 614, 616, 834, 840
relay n. 268; vb. 268
release n. 460, 465, 600, 601, 680, 713, 911, 921, 961; vb. 601, 634, 680, 713, 921, 961
relegate vb. 303
relent vb. 335, 907
relentless adj. 900, 908
relevant adj. 9, 573
reliable adj. 152, 408, 868, 931
reliance n. 408, 420, 854
relic n. 44, 371, 441, 483
relief n. 149, 176, 181, 253, 489, 591, 601, 618, 636, **834**, 899
relieve vb. 149, 176, 591, 601, 618, 634, 636, 686, **834**, 899
religion n. **974**
religious adj. 392, 974, 982
religious service n. **988**
relinquishment n. 546, **556**, 607, 687, 713
relish n. 307, 767, 827, 861; vb. 767, 770, 827, 861
relocate vb. 268
reluctant adj. 281, 533, 694, 876
rely vb. 420, 443, 854
remain vb. 91, 112, 143, 145, 535
remainder n. 44
remains n. 44, 371, 483
remake vb. 77, 165, 589
remark vb. 395, 456
remarkable adj. 32, 866

remedy n. 365, **591**, 834; vb. 591
remember vb. 441, 878
remembrance n. 483
remind vb. 441
reminiscences n. 441
reminiscent adj. 441
remiss adj. 393, 668
remission n. 43, 144, 601, 744, 911, 961
remit vb. 268, 601, 715, 911
remittance n. 268, 738
remnant n. 44, 76
remodel vb. 77, 146, 589
remonstrate vb. 696
remorse n. 833, 941
remote adj. 198, 885
remould vb. 165
removal n. 42, 48, 142, 268, 293, 299, 303, 312
remove vb. 42, 99, 187, 228, 268, 293, 303, 312, 485, 680, 720, 722, 826
remuneration n. 31, 721, 738, 965
remunerative adj. 705, 738, 965
renaissance n. 165, 589
rend vb. 48
render vb. 456, 486, 715, 792
rendezvous n. 96, 884; vb. 94
renegade n. 538
renew vb. 77, 125, 142, 165, 589
renounce vb. 469, 542, 556, 713
renovate vb. 125, 142, 165, 589
renown n. 868
rent n. 743; adj. 48, 262; vb. 191, 719
renunciation n. 469, 538, 542, 556, 713
reoccurrence n. 77, 138
reorganization n. 81, 142
reorganize vb. 142, 587, 589
repair n. 589; vb. 589, 721
reparation n. 31, 589, 721, 943, 965
repartee n. 395, 519, 842
repatriation n. 721

repay *vb.* 647, 721, 738, 943

repeal *n.* 686; *vb.* 686

repeat *n.* 77; *vb.* 20, 62, 77, 138, 140, 165

repeated and prolonged sound *n.* **783**

repel *vb.* 295, 648, 885, 892

repent *vb.* 833, 907, 941

repercussion *n.* 156, 283

repetition *n.* 62, 77, 140, 505

repetitive *adj.* 77, 841

replace *vb.* 147, 149, 187, 686

replay *n.* 77

replenish *vb.* 56, 568

replete *adj.* 56, 570, 865

replica *n.* 20, 22

reply *n.* 283, 395, 402, 523; *vb.* 395

report *n.* 415, 460, 465, 468, 483, 523, 525, 778, 782; *vb.* 460, 465, 483, 521, 525

reporter *n.* 460, 524

repose *n.* 612, **616**; *vb.* 215

repository *n.* 732

reprehensible *adj.* 926

represent *vb.* 20, **486**, 488, 525, 685, 689

representation *n.* 20, 22, **486**, 488, 489, 525, 558, 685

representative *n.* 625, 688, 689; *adj.* 18, 101, 482, 486

repress *vb.* 679, 681, 691, 779

reprieve *n.* 135, 601, 911, 961; *vb.* 907, 911, 961

reprimand *n.* 926, 963; *vb.* 926, 963

reprint *n.* 20, 22, 77, 524; *vb.* 165, 464

reprisal *n.* 647, 912

reproach *n.* 869, 926; *vb.* 926

reproduce *vb.* 20, 163, 165, 486

reproduction *n.* 22, 77, 163, **165**, 486

reprove *vb.* 926, 930, 963

reptile *n.* 373

repudiate *vb.* 414, 469, 542, 686, 694

repugnance *n.* 637, 862, 883, 892

repugnant *adj.* 862, 892, 936

repulse *vb.* 295, 694

repulsion *n.* **295**, 892

repulsive *adj.* 295, 777, 892

reputable *adj.* 177, 868, 931

reputation *n.* 177, 868

repute *n.* **868**

request *n.* 394, 671, **695**, 982; *vb.* 394, 671, 695

requiem *n.* 372, 839

require *vb.* 531, 562, 571, 671, 674

requirement *n.* 8, 315, **562**, 671

requital *n.* 31, 647, 912, 943

rescue *n.* 589, 600, 601, 680; *vb.* 589, 601, 636, 680

research *n.* 396; *vb.* 396

researcher *n.* 394, 396, 428

resemblance *n.* 18, 105, 397

resentful *adj.* 883, 893, 900, 913

resentment *n.* 832, **893**, 913, 914

reservation *n.* 403, 421, 425, 700

reserve *n.* 149, 198, 517, 568, 681, 876; *adj.* 149; *vb.* 712

reserves *n.* 564, 567, 731

reservoir *n.* 193, 354, 567

reside *vb.* 188, 191

residence *n.* 188, 191, 707

resident *n.* 190, 710; *adj.* 188

residual *adj.* 44

residue *n.* 44

resign *vb.* 654, 687

resignation *n.* 654, **687**, 757

resilience *n.* 336

resin *n.* 365; *vb.* 365

resist *vb.* 295, 537, 637, 644, **648**, 694

resistance *n.* 181, **648**

resistant *adj.* 337

resolute *adj.* 152, 534, 857

resolution *n.* 415, 530, **534**, 611, 857

resolve *n.* 534; *vb.* 53, 530, 534, 552

resonance *n.* 778, **784**

resort to *vb.* 606

resounding *n.* 784; *adj.* 780

resourceful *adj.* 449

resources *n.* 564, 566, 711, 734

respect *n.* 868, 886, **922**; *vb.* 868, 922

respectful *adj.* 673, 922

respiration *n.* 359

respite *n.* 135, 144, 614

respond *vb.* 283, 395, 752, 909

responsibility *n.* 179, 557, 701, 917, 919, 956

responsible *adj.* 133, 179, 702, 919, 956

responsive *adj.* 395, 909

rest *n.* 44, 92, 144, 213, 217, **267**, 610, 612, 614, 616; *vb.* 144, 267, 612, 614, 616

restate *vb.* 77, 456

restaurant *n.* 191

restitution *n.* 31, 147, 589, **721**, 738, 943

restless *adj.* 266, 611, 756, 832

restoration *n.* 147, **589**, 618, 721

restorative *n.* 591; *adj.* 585, 589, 591

restore *vb.* 147, 589, 591, 618, 680, 721, 911

restrain *vb.* 37, 144, 176, 403, 635, **681**, 691

restrained *adj.* 176, 508, 517, 681, 876, 944

restraint *n.* 37, 176, 281, 548, 635, **681**, 876, 944

restrict *vb.* 99, 231, 235, 403, 635, 681, 691

restrictions *n.* 700

result *n.* 44, 87, 156, 163, 460; *vb.* 85, 119, 156

resumé *n.* 527; *vb.* 589

resumption *n.* 77, 589

resurgence *n.* 589

resurrection *n.* 147, 165, 589, 972

resuscitate *vb.* 589, 618

retail *vb.* 727

retailer *n.* 727, 728

retain *vb.* 441, 707, 712

retaliate *vb.* 647, 912, 963

retaliation *n.* 395, **647**, 912

retard *vb.* 135, 281, 635

retarded *adj.* 435

retch *vb.* 303

retention *n.* 441, **712**

reticent *adj.* 466, 517, 681, 876

retinue *n.* 91

retire *vb.* 289, 293, 299, 687

retired *adj.* 118, 124, 687

retirement *n.* 89, 293, 687, 826

retiring *adj.* 517, 876, 885

retort *n.* 395, 647; *vb.* 395, 647

retrace *vb.* 441

retraction *n.* 538, 686

retreat *n.* 289, **293**, 299, 463, 595, 600, 885; *vb.* 289, 293, 556

retribution *n.* 647, 943, 963

retrieve *vb.* 589, 601, 705, 720, 721

retrograde *adj.* 289

return *n.* 147, 289, 298, 721; *vb.* 147, 163, 298, 589, 647, 721

reunion *n.* 47, 884

revalue *vb.* 745

reveal *vb.* 228, 262, 419, 456, 458, 462

revealed *adj.* 976

revealing *adj.* 228, 802

revel *vb.* 827, 838, 840

revelation *n.* 419, 420, 458, 462, 464, 974, **976**

revenge *n.* 647, **912**; *vb.* 647

revengeful *adj.* 908, 912

revenue *n.* 741

reverberate *vb.* 283, 784

reverberation *n.* 283, 778

revere *vb.* 868, 922, 982

reverence *n.* 922, 980, 982

reverend *n.* 986

reversal *n.* 147, 220, 289, 538, 686

reverse *n.* 237, 239; *adj.*

14, 289; *vb.* 147, 220, 686

reversion *n.* **147**, 220, 590

review *n.* 394, 415, 456, 524, 526; *vb.* 394, 415, 441, 472, 526

reviewer *n.* 456, 524, 526

revile *vb.* 853, 901, 928

revise *vb.* 142, 472, 587

revitalize *vb.* 589

revival *n.* 147, 165, 589

revive *vb.* 77, 165, 368, 441, 589, 618

revoke *vb.* 538, 686

revolt *n.* 148, 644, 672; *vb.* 148, 644, 672

revolting *adj.* 148, 771, 892

revolution *n.* **148**, 323, 644, 672

revolve *vb.* 140, 323

revolver *n.* 657

revue *n.* 529

reward *n.* 663, 705, 909, 917, **965**; *vb.* 738, 909, 965

reword *vb.* 77, 456, 498

rhetorical *adj.* 455, 509

rhetorician *n.* 514

rhombus *n.* 246

rhyme *n.* 528; *vb.* 528

rhythm *n.* 140, 510, 512, 528

rhythmical *adj.* 790

rib *vb.* 842

ribbon *n.* 49, 207, 663, 846, 872

rich *adj.* 163, 168, 509, 664, **734**, 770, 772, 790, 805

riches *n.* 664, 711, 734

rickshaw *n.* 276

rid *vb.* 634

riddle *n.* 466; *vb.* 264

ride *n.* 269; *vb.* 269

rider *n.* 41, 270

ridge *n.* 252, 357

ridicule *n.* **853**, 924; *vb.* 788, 842, 853, 869, 924, 928

ridiculousness *n.* 433, **851**

riding *n.* 269

rifle *n.* 657; *vb.* 722

rift *n.* 200, 642

rig *vb.* 568

right *n.* **240**, 667, **915**, 917, 929, 954, 956; *adj.* 240, 430, 915, 931, 954, 977

right angle *n.* 246

righteous *adj.* 915, 935

right-hand man *n.* 624, 640, 676, 689

right side *n.* **240**

rigid *adj.* 334, 669, 946

rigorous *adj.* 392, 669, 864, 946

rigour *n.* 669

riled *adj.* 893, 894

rim *n.* 233, 250; *vb.* 233

rind *n.* 225

ring *n.* 250; *vb.* 231, 322, 460, 482, 784

ringing *n.* 778, 784; *adj.* 780, 784

riot *n.* 80, 672

ripe *adj.* 364

ripen *vb.* 659

ripple *n.* 325, 358, 781; *vb.* 251, 358, 783

rise *n.* 36, 41, 208, 316, 320; *vb.* 32, 34, 36, 88, 214, 252, 273, 316, 320

risk *n.* 553, 594; *vb.* 158, 553, 594, 604, 718, 857

risqué *adj.* 952

rite *n.* 988

ritual *n.* 16, 545, 988; *adj.* 988

rival *n.* 638, 883; *vb.* 28

rivalry *n.* 642, 913

river *n.* 358

riverside *adj.* 352

road *n.* 559

roamer *n.* 270

roaming *n.* 269

roar *n.* 780, 838; *vb.* 175, 359, 780, 789, 838, 893

roast *vb.* 306, 759

rob *vb.* 645, 722

robber *n.* 723

robbery *n.* 722

robe *n.* 225

robes *n.* 989

robot *n.* 565

robust *adj.* 143, 161, 337, 585

rock *n.* 152, 330, 352, 367, 792; *vb.* 325, 326

rocket *n.* 279; *vb.* 316

rod *n.* 677, 677, 964

rodent *n.* 373

rogue *n.* 480, 723, 906, 940

roguish *adj.* 477

role *n.* 529, 557

roll *n.* 83, 249, 306, 323,

325, 783; *vb.* 249, 323, 325, 358, 783

roller *n.* 197, 358

roman *adj.* 521

romance *n.* 449, 889

romantic *adj.* 752

roof *n.* 225; *vb.* 225

room *n.* 182, 678

roomy *adj.* 182, 204

roost *vb.* 319

root *n.* 39, 88, 155, 213, 306, 374, 494

rooted *adj.* 47

rope *n.* 49, 207, 964

roster *n.* 83

rosy *adj.* 585, 811

rot *n.* 53, 451, 592; *vb.* 53, 584, 588

rota *n.* 83, 140

rotary *adj.* 323

rotate *vb.* 323

rotation *n.* 140, **323**

rotten *adj.* 53, 162, 580, 584, 588

rotund *adj.* 249

rough *adj.* 57, 175, 258, 887, 908

roughage *n.* 305

roughness *n.* **258**

round *n.* 249, 649, 792; *adj.* 249, 250; *vb.* 249, 256

roundabout *adj.* 505, 561

rounded *adj.* 247, 249

round form *n.* **249**

rouse *vb.* 611, 889

rousing *adj.* 547

rout *n.* 662

route *n.* 269, 559

routine *n.* 16, 79, 91, 140, 545; *adj.* 16, 140, 545

rove *vb.* 269

row *n.* 85, 202, 206, 642

rowdy *adj.* 780, 887

rowing *n.* 271

royal *adj.* 870

rub *vb.* 341, 342, 758

rubber *n.* 485

rubbish *n.* 451, 576

rub in *vb.* 468

ruby *adj.* 811

rude *adj.* 511, 849, 880, 887, 910, 923

rudiment *n.* 155

rudimentary *adj.* 88

rue *vb.* 833

ruffian *n.* 175, 906

ruffle *vb.* 82, 258, 260, 893

rug *n.* 225

rugged *adj.* 258

ruin *n.* 164, 551, 569, 588, 662, 739; *vb.* 164, 588, 628, 735

rule *n.* **103**, 400, 522, 626, 667, 671, 954; *vb.* 415, 653, 667, 671

ruler *n.* 400, 675

rumble *vb.* 783

ruminate *vb.* 384

rumour *n.* 465

run *n.* 613; *vb.* 110, 172, 266, 280, 343, 345, 358, 622

run away *vb.* 293, 299, 896

runaway *n.* 555, 600

run down *vb.* 160, 853, 926, 928

run-down *n.* 460; *adj.* 586, 612, 617

rung *n.* 93

run in *vb.* 681

run into *vb.* 282

runner *n.* 270, 275, 467

running *n.* 172; *adj.* 91, 172, 343

runny *adj.* 51, 345, 358

run off with *vb.* 722, 896

run out *vb.* 89, 301

rupture *n.* 48; *vb.* 48

rural *adj.* 183, 378

ruse *n.* 478, 631

rush *n.* 280, 282, 358, 611, 613; *adj.* 603; *vb.* 280, 358, 359, 613, 645

russet *adj.* 810, 811

rust *n.* 167, 588, 592, 847; *adj.* 810, 811; *vb.* 53, 584

rustic *n.* 871; *adj.* 378, 871, 885

rustle *n.* 781, 783, 786; *vb.* 781, 783, 786

rusty *adj.* 126, 810, 811

rut *n.* 261, 545

ruthless *adj.* 900

S

Sabbath *n.* 616

sabbatical *n.* 614; *adj.* 616

sable *adj.* 808

sabotage *n.* 164

saboteur *n.* 480

shuffle *vb.* 82, 149, 281, 756

shun *vb.* 555, 694, 924

shut *vb.* 263

shut down *vb.* 144

shut-eye *n.* 612

shut in *vb.* 234

shut oneself up *vb.* 885

shut out *vb.* 691

shutter *n.* 801

shuttle *n.* 278, 325; *vb.* 268

shut up *vb.* 144, 234, 681

shy *adj.* 856, 858, **876**, 885

shy away *vb.* 533

shyness *n.* 858, **876**, 885

sibilant *adj.* 786

sick *adj.* 369, 586

sicken *vb.* 162, 586

sickly *adj.* 812

sickness *n.* 303, 586, 828

side *n.* 11, 233, 238

side by side *adv.* 238

sidedness *n.* **238**

side-splitting *adj.* 851

sideways *adj.* 219, 238; *adv.* 238

side with *vb.* 641

sidle up to *vb.* 292

siege *n.* 645

siesta *n.* 612

sieve *n.* 264

sift *vb.* 46, 415, 540

sigh *vb.* 359, 781

sight *n.* 753, 818

sightly *adj.* 844

sightseeing *n.* 269

sightseer *n.* 270, 821

sign *n.* 401, 447, 458, **482**, 597; *vb.* 424, 482, 699, 701, 714, 726

signal *n.* 482; *vb.* 482

signatory *n.* 424

signature *n.* 482, 496

significance *n.* 450, 456, 573

significant *adj.* 136, 450, 573

signify *vb.* **450**, 482

sign of authority *n.* **677**

signpost *vb.* 284

silence *n.* 267, 513, 517, **779**; *vb.* 414, 513, 779

silent *adj.* 513, 517, 779, 895

silhouette *n.* 232, 488; *vb.* 488

silky *adj.* 257

silly *adj.* 433, 435

silver-haired *adj.* 809

silvery *adj.* 807

similarity *n.* **18**, 105, 218, 397

simile *n.* 397, 455

simmer *vb.* 306

simmer down *vb.* 757

simple *adj.* (not mixed) 46; (gullible) 422, 632, 937, 951; (foolish) 427, 435; (easy to understand) 452, 502, 508; (easy) 634

simple circularity *n.* **250**

simple-minded *adj.* 435, 632

simpleton *n.* 429, 437, 479

simplify *vb.* 46, 53, 456

simulate *vb.* 20, 477, 852

simultaneous *adj.* 60, 122

sin *n.* 431, 672, 703, 938; *vb.* 672, 981

sincere *adj.* 430, 476, 931

sine qua non n. 60, 700

sinew *n.* 207

sinful *adj.* 916, 936, 938, 952, 975, 981

sing *vb.* 528, 789, 792, 982

singer *n.* 793

single *adj.* 54, 59, 139, 897

single-minded *adj.* 534, 980

single out *vb.* 102

singular *adj.* 59

sinister *adj.* 665

sinistral *n.* 241

sink *vb.* 209, 210, 317, 319, **321**, 588

sink back *vb.* 590

sinker *n.* 330

sinless *adj.* 951

sinner *n.* 906, 940, 981

sinuate *vb.* 251

sip *n.* 309; *vb.* 767

siphon *n.* 360

sir *n.* 380

siren *n.* 116, 482, 598, 970

sirupy *adj.* 772

sister *n.* 11, 986

sit *vb.* 23, 185

sit down *vb.* 319

site *n.* 185, 186

sit-in *n.* 144, 696

sit on *vb.* 466, 679

sit on the fence *vb.* 409, 541

sit pretty *vb.* 831

sitting *n.* 984

sitting duck *n.* 479

situation *n.* 8, 93, 153, **185**, 229, 557

six *n.* 70; *adj.* 70

sixth sense *n.* 411, 753

size *n.* 26, 27, 32, **194**, 362, 400

size up *vb.* 415

sizzle *vb.* 306, 759, 786

skeleton *n.* 232, 371, 527

sketch *n.* 232, 486, 488, 525, 558; *vb.* 232, 488, 525, 558

sketchy *adj.* 57

skew *adj.* 219

skewer *vb.* 264

skilful *adj.* 627

skill *n.* 159, 426, 501, **627**

skilled *adj.* 579, 602

skilled worker *n.* 619, 629

skim *vb.* 211, 257

skimp *vb.* 393, 750

skimpy *adj.* 57

skin *n.* 225; *vb.* 228

skinny *adj.* 205

skip *vb.* 320, 393

skirmish *n.* 645, 649

skirt *n.* 233; *vb.* 233, 238

skunk *n.* 777

sky *n.* 329, 348, 815

skyjacking *n.* 722

skyline *n.* 198

skyscraper *n.* 191, 208

slab *n.* 206

slack *adj.* 391, 612, 668, 920, 952

slacken *vb.* 281

slacker *n.* 858

slag *n.* 44

slam *vb.* 782, 926

slander *n.* 869, 928; *vb.* 928, 930

slanderer *n.* 928

slang *n.* 494, 495; *adj.* 495

slant *vb.* 219

slap *n.* 782, 963; *vb.* 282, 782, 963

slap in the face *n.* 694, 923

slapstick *n.* 529

slash *vb.* 203

slate *n.* 206

slaughter *n.* 164, 370, 963; *vb.* 370, 963

slave *n.* 35, 619, 676

slavery *n.* 679

slavish *adj.* 881

slay *vb.* 370

sleek *adj.* 257

sleep *n.* 612; *vb.* 612

sleep around *vb.* 952

sleep together *vb.* 889

sleep with *vb.* 889

sleepy *adj.* 612, 617

sleet *n.* 760

sleight of hand *n.* 478

slender *adj.* 33, 205

slice *n.* 55, 305, 717

slide *n.* 219, 486; *vb.* 257, 588

slide-rule *n.* 400

slight *n.* 869, 923, 924; *adj.* 33, 195, 203, 571; *vb.* 418, 923, 928

slim *adj.* 33, 205; *vb.* 205, 947

slime *n.* 584

slimy *adj.* 362

slink *vb.* 461

slip *n.* 431, 500, 522, 741, 938

slip back *vb.* 590

slippery *adj.* 51, 257, 594, 631

slipshod *adj.* 393, 500

slip-up *n.* 431

slit *n.* 261, 262; *vb.* 48, 264

sliver *n.* 55

slogan *n.* 432, 494, 498

slog away *vb.* 535, 615

slope *n.* 208, 219; *vb.* 219

sloppy *adj.* 584

slot *n.* 261, 262; *vb.* 261

slothful *adj.* 612

slough *n.* 355

slovenly *adj.* 500, 584, 920

slow *adj.* 174, **281**, 435; *vb.* 281, 616

slowcoach *n.* 281

slowness *n.* 135, **281**, 843

sluggard *n.* 612

sluggish *adj.* 174, 281, 612, 843

slum *n.* 845

slumber *vb.* 174, 612

slump *n.* 169, 317; *vb.* 317, 588

slur n. 869, 928, 930;
   vb. 515, 928, 930
slush n. 760
slushy adj. 355, 362
slut n. 953
sly adj. 461, 631, 932
smack vb. 282, 782
smack one's lips vb.
   767
small adj. 33, 195, 203,
   331
small arms n. 657
small change n. 731
smallholding n. 378
smallness n. 33, 195
small talk n. 516
smarmy adj. 927
smart adj. 125, 631; vb.
   828
smart aleck n. 875
smash vb. 164, 282, 645
smash-and-grab-raid n.
   722
smash hit n. 661
smash-up n. 282
smattering n. 76, 427
smear n. 584, 928, 930;
   vb. 342, 847, 869,
   928
smell n. 753, 774, 777;
   vb. 774, 776, 777
smell out vb. 394, 554,
   774
smelly adj. 777
smelt vb. 761
smile n. 838, 886; vb.
   838, 886
smirch n. 847; vb. 847
smirk n. 838; vb. 838
smite vb. 282
smitten adj. 889
smog n. 363
smoke n. 344, 346, 803;
   vb. 308, 346, 599,
   759, 803
smoke-signal n. 467
smoking adj. 759
smoky adj. 803, 809
smooth adj. 228, 257,
   335, 364, 477, 631,
   927; vb. 16, 215, 257,
   341, 758
smoothness n. 257
smother vb. 513, 759,
   762
smoulder vb. 759
smudge vb. 584, 847
smuggle vb. 722
smuggled adj. 955
smuggler n. 723
smut n. 952
snack n. 306

snack bar n. 191
snag n. 582, 635
snail n. 281
snake in the grass n.
   459, 596
snake-like adj. 251
snap vb. 338, 782, 789,
   893
snap out of it vb. 836
snapshot n. 486
snare n. 463, 596
snarl vb. 789
snatch vb. 720
sneak n. 858; vb. 461
sneer n. 895, 924, 926;
   vb. 696, 853, 895,
   924, 926
sneeze vb. 359, 786
sniff vb. 774
sniff out vb. 394, 554
snigger n. 838; vb. 838
snip n. 48
sniper n. 645
snivel vb. 839
snobbish adj. 875, 924
snoop n. 388, 460, 821;
   vb. 388, 394
snooty adj. 875, 924
snooze n. 612; vb. 612
snort vb. 789
snow n. 760; vb. 807
snowball n. 36; vb. 36
snowdrift n. 760
snowflake n. 760
snowstorm n. 760
snub n. 295, 694, 923;
   vb. 887, 923, 926
snuff n. 308; vb. 762
snug adj. 827
snuggle vb. 890
soak vb. 56, 349
soak up vb. 350
so-and-so n. 497
soapy adj. 363
soar vb. 32, 208, 273,
   316
sob n. 839; vb. 788, 839
sober adj. 837, 848, 944,
   949
soberness n. 848, 949
so-called adj. 497
sociability n. 882, 884
social n. 884; adj. 379
social conscience n.
   903
socialism n. 709
social services n. 903
society n. 379, 641, 850,
   870
sociology n. 379
socket n. 184
sod n. 374

sodden adj. 349
sodomy n. 952
soft adj. 257, 331, 335,
   670, 781, 805, 889
soft drink n. 309
soften vb. 267, 335,
   513, 652, 834
soft-hearted adj. 670,
   907
softness n. 335, 364,
   670, 778, 781
soft nothings n. 890
soft soap n. 927
sog vb. 349
soggy adj. 364
soi-disant adj. 497
soil n. 352, 378; vb.
   584, 847
soirée n. 884
sojourn n. 269; vb. 191
solace n. 831, 907
solar adj. 329
solar energy n. 159, 765
solder vb. 50
soldier n. 655
soldier on vb. 535
sole adj. 59
solecism n. 412, 500
solemn adj. 468, 573,
   837, 982
solicit vb. 695
solicitor n. 959
solicitous adj. 392
solid n. 3, 332; adj. 3,
   50, 161, 332, 334, 337
solidarity n. 50, 639
solidify vb. 332, 334
solidity n. 3, 152, 204,
   332, 334
soliloquize vb. 520
soliloquy n. 520
solitary adj. 885
solitude n. 59, 461
solo n. 792
soloist n. 793
soluble adj. 345
solution n. 343
solve vb. 157, 456
solvent n. 343, 345
sombre adj. 798, 809,
   895
some adj. 26, 72
somebody n. 868
somersault n. 220; vb.
   220
something n. 327
sometime adj. 124, 687;
   adv. 121
sometimes adv. 138
somnolence n. 612, 617
son n. 171
sonata n. 792

sodden adj. 349

song n. 528, 792, 982
sonnet n. 528
sonorous adj. 778
soothe vb. 176, 591, 834
soothing adj. 589, 790,
   834
soothsayer n. 447, 984
sooty adj. 584, 808
sophism n. 412
sophisticated n. 848;
   adj. 423, 848
sophistry n. 412
soporific adj. 841
sorcery n. 984
sore n. 588; adj. 753,
   828, 893
sore point n. 893
sorrow n. 828, 830, 833,
   837, 839, 941; vb.
   837, 839
sorry adj. 833, 907, 941
sort n. 97; vb. 97, 540
sortie n. 645; vb. 645
SOS n. 598
soul n. 223, 368, 382,
   751
sound n. 353, 512, 778,
   795; adj. 410, 438,
   581, 585, 977; vb.
   512, 778
sounding board n. 396
sound out vb. 396
soundproof adj. 779
soup n. 306
soupçon n. 33
sour adj. 769, 773, 895
source n. 88, 155
source of light n. 800
sourness n. 773, 895
souvenir n. 441, 483
sovereign n. 675; adj.
   667
sow n. 381; vb. 95, 378
space n. 182, 198, 200,
   202, 329
space-age adj. 125
spaceman n. 274
spaceship n. 279
space travel n. 274
space traveller n. 274
spacious adj. 32, 182,
   204
spade vb. 254
spadework n. 602
span n. 109, 182, 202;
   vb. 47, 182, 313
spank vb. 963
spanner in the works n.
   580, 635
spare adj. 44, 607; vb.
   670, 907
spare time n. 614

straight face *n.* 837
straight form *n.* **248**
straightforward *adj.*
452, 476, 508, 632,
915, 931
strain *n.* 11, 97, 615,
792, 832; *vb.* 481,
617
strainer *n.* 264
strait *n.* 205, 353, 633
straiten *vb.* 205
straitjacket *n.* 712
strait-laced *adj.* 951
strand *n.* 207, 352
strange *adj.* 100, 466
stranger *n.* 100
strangle *vb.* 370, 963
stranglehold *n.* 712
strap *n.* 207; *vb.* 963
strapping *adj.* 161
stratagem *n.* 478, 631
strategy *n.* 558, 621
stratify *vb.* 206
stratosphere *n.* 348
stratum *n.* 206
stray *vb.* 285, 936
strayed *adj.* 706
streak *n.* 797, 797; *vb.*
817
stream *n.* 358, 474, 797;
vb. 257, 343, 349,
358, 359
streamer *n.* 482
streamlined *adj.* 125
street *n.* 559
street-walking *n.* 952
strength *n.* 32, 159, **161**,
173, 337, 400, 506,
585, 857
strengthen *vb.* 36, 159,
161, 173, 217, 304,
334, 337, 646, 857
strengthener *n.* 217
strenuous *adj.* 615, 633
stress *n.* 512, 528; *vb.*
468, 512, 573
stretch *n.* 109, 182, 336;
vb. 182, 196, 202,
336
stretch a point *vb.* 481,
668
stretch one's legs *vb.*
616
strew *vb.* 95
stricken *adj.* 665
strict *adj.* 669, 681, 837,
951, 977
stride *n.* 269
strife *n.* 25, 615, 649
strike *n.* 144, 696; *vb.*
144, **282**, 384, 696,
758, 963

strike a bad patch *vb.*
633
strike back *vb.* 647
strike out *vb.* 485, 686
striking *adj.* 458
string *n.* 49, 85, 202,
207; *vb.* 47
stringed instruments *n.*
794
stringent *adj.* 669
strings *n.* 700, 794
stringy *adj.* 207
strip *n.* 49, 202, 207; *vb.*
203, 228, 720, 817
stripe *n.* 677
striped *adj.* 817
stripling *n.* 131
striptease *n.* 228
strive *vb.* 604, 615, 642,
649, 651
stroke *n.* 341, 586, 609;
vb. 758, 890
stroll *n.* 269; *vb.* 269,
281
strong *adj.* 32, 159, **161**,
173, 337, 506, 534,
585, 769, 774
stronghold *n.* 595, 646
strong point *n.* 627
strongroom *n.* 732
strong-smelling *adj.*
777
strong-willed *adj.* 534
structure *n.* 5, 47, 163,
242, 339
struggle *n.* 649; *vb.* 615,
642, 649
strum *n.* 783; *vb.* 783
strut *n.* 217
stub *n.* 482
stubborn *adj.* 143, 537,
672, 942
stubby *adj.* 203, 204
stuck up *adj.* 875
stud *vb.* 817
student *n.* 131, **428**, 474
studious *adj.* 384, 390,
472, 611
study *n.* 390, 394, 472,
475, 488, 526; *vb.*
384, 390, 394, 472,
602
stuff *n.* 3, 327, 566, 729;
vb. 56, 75, 226, 265,
304, 865, 948
stuffing *n.* 192, 226, 265
stuffy *adj.* 843
stumble *vb.* 317, 515
stumble on *vb.* 158
stumbling-block *n.* 635
stun *vb.* 754, 796, 922
stunner *n.* 844

stunted *adj.* 195, 203
stupefy *vb.* 754, 866
stupendous *adj.* 32, 866
stupid *adj.* 427, 433,
435
stupidity *n.* 383, 427,
433, 435
stupor *n.* 754
stutter *n.* 515; *vb.* 515
sty *n.* 184
style *n.* 242, 492, **501**,
510, 850; *vb.* 496
stylish *adj.* 125, 850
subconscious *adj.* 382
subdivide *vb.* 48
subdue *vb.* 335, 679,
681, 779
subdued *adj.* 654, 781,
805
subject *n.* 387, 499,
525; *vb.* 679
subjection *n.* 35, 179,
679, 874
subject to *adj.* 35, 179,
679, 700, 919
subjugate *vb.* 679
sublimation *n.* 318, 346
sublime *adj.* 32, 208,
318, 868, 966, 982
subliminal *adj.* 382
sublimity *n.* 34
submarine *n.* 277
submerge *vb.* 321, 349
submerged *adj.* 210
submission *n.* **654**, 673,
757, 874
submissive *adj.* **654**,
673, 679, 757, 874
submit *vb.* 468, 654,
673, 693, 757, 874
subnormal *adj.* 435
subordinate *n.* 35, 676;
adj. 35, 679; *vb.* 679
subpoena *n.* 671, 960
subscribe *vb.* 424, 641
subscriber *n.* 424
subsequent *adj.* 85, 119,
156
subservient *adj.* 563,
673, 679, 874, 881
subside *vb.* 37, 197, 317
subsidiary *adj.* 563, 679
subsidize *vb.* 636, 715,
738
subsidy *n.* 636, 715,
738, 744
subsist *vb.* 1, 368
subsistence *n.* 1, 305
substance *n.* 3, 5, 223,
332, 450, 573
substandard *adj.* 35

substantial *adj.* 1, 3,
327, 450
substantiate *vb.* 161,
401, 413
substitute *n.* **149**, 540,
688, 689, 943; *vb.*
142, **149**, 689
substitution *n.* 142, **149**
substratum *n.* 206, 213
subsume *vb.* 98
subterfuge *n.* 478
subterranean *adj.* 210
subtle *adj.* 333, 459, 631
subtraction *n.* 38, **42**,
744
suburb *n.* 183
suburban *adj.* 183
subversion *n.* 148, 164
subversive *adj.* 148, 580
subvert *vb.* 148, 580
succeed *vb.* 85, 119,
287, 659, **661**
success *n.* 550, **661**
successful *adj.* 661, 664
succession *n.* 85, 91,
119, 287
successor *n.* 119
succinct *adj.* 203, 504,
527
succour *n.* 636
succulence *n.* 364
succulent *adj.* 306, 364
succumb *vb.* 179, 369
suck *vb.* 308
sucker *n.* 479
suckle *vb.* 304
suckling *n.* 131
suck up to *vb.* 881, 927
sudden *adj.* 115, 444,
544, 859
sudden and violent
sound *n.* **782**
suds *n.* 363
sue *vb.* 960
suffer *vb.* 586, 590, 648,
752, **828**, 963
suffer defeat *vb.* 662
sufferer *n.* 828
suffice *vb.* 28, 570, 831
sufficiency *n.* **570**
sufficient *adj.* 75, 570
suffix *n.* 41, 87, 499; *vb.*
40
suffocate *vb.* 370, 759
suffrage *n.* 540
sugar *n.* 772, 891; *vb.*
772
sugary *adj.* 772
suggest *vb.* 155, 401,
441, 450, 459, 460,
597, 624, 693

suggestion n. 441, 459, 460, 482, 624, 693
suggestive adj. 401, 450, 459, 482
suicide n. 370
sui generis adj. 59, 102
suit n. 227, 960; vb. 105, 577
suitable adj. 136, 302, 575, 577, 896, 915
suitcase n. 193
suite n. 91, 191, 792
suitor n. 889, 960
sulk vb. 895
sullenness n. 895
sullied adj. 584, 952
sully vb. 584, 847, 869, 928, 952
sultry adj. 759
sum n. 26, 54, 731; vb. 40
summarize vb. 203, 504, 525, 527
summary n. 441, 525, 527; adj. 504
summer n. 127, 664, 759; adj. 127
summer time n. 116, 127
summery adj. 127, 759
summing up n. 527, 960
summit n. 89, 208, 212, 519, 581
summon vb. 94, 671, 695, 857, 901
summons n. 671, 960
sum up vb. 527, 960
sun n. 329, 800
Sunday School n. 988
sunder vb. 63
sundown n. 128
sunglasses n. 801, 804
sunken adj. 209, 210, 254
sunny adj. 664, 759
sunrise n. 127, 797
sunset n. 128
sunshine n. 797
sup vb. 304
super adj. 579
superabundance n. 32, 572
superannuated adj. 130
superannuation n. 687
superb adj. 579
supercilious adj. 875, 924
superficial adj. 211, 435, 574, 825, 852
superfluity n. 32, 572
superimpose vb. 225

superintend vb. 392, 622
superintendent n. 623
superior n. 34, 675; adj. 34, 579, 868
superiority n. 34, 84, 579, 868
superlative n. 499; adj. 34, 481, 579
supermarket n. 730
supernatural adj. 447, 971, 984
superpose vb. 225
supersede vb. 85
superstition n. 984
supervision n. 392, 593, 621, 622, 956
supervisor n. 623, 675
supper n. 306
supplant vb. 85
supple adj. 335
supplement n. 40, 41, 87; vb. 40, 196, 568
supplementary adj. 40
supplicant n. 697, 982; adj. 982
supplication n. 695, 982
supplies n. 564, 566, 729
supply n. 568; vb. 564, 568, 602, 715
support n. 213, 217, 401, 424, 636, 929; vb. 152, 217, 392, 401, 410, 424, 636, 907
supporter n. 217, 287, 424, 640, 821, 905
suppose vb. 416, 420, 448, 449
supposed adj. 448, 459, 825
supposition n. 448
suppress vb. 164, 461, 466, 513, 679, 681, 691
supreme adj. 34, 579, 581, 667, 966
sure adj. 152, 408, 531
surety n. 420, 593, 701
surf n. 363; vb. 271
surface n. 182, 211, 222; adj. 211; vb. 225, 331
surfeit n. 572, 865; vb. 865
surge vb. 316, 320, 325, 358
surgery n. 591
surly adj. 887, 895
surmise n. 448; vb. 420, 448

surmount vb. 316
surname n. 496
surpass vb. 6, 34, 314
surpassing adj. 32, 34, 579
surplice n. 989
surplus n. 44, 572
surprise n. 444, 829, 866; vb. 444, 866
surrender n. 556, 687, 708; vb. 556, 654
surround vb. 229, 231, 231
surroundings n. 8, 183, 229
surveillance n. 392, 622
survey n. 456, 526, 527, 818; vb. 400, 415, 526, 527, 818
surveyor n. 415
survive vb. 112, 145, 368, 661, 898
surviving adj. 44, 112, 368
survivor n. 898
susceptibility n. 179, 753
susceptible adj. 753, 894
suspect vb. 409, 421, 448
suspend vb. 89, 99, 135, 216, 607, 686, 920
suspended sentence n. 961
suspense n. 144, 409, 443
suspension n. 99, 135, 216, 607, 610
suspicion n. 409, 421, 423, 460, 860, 913
sustain vb. 91, 143, 145, 152, 217, 304, 636
sustenance n. 217, 305
swab vb. 583
swag n. 724
swallow vb. 302, 304, 757
swamp n. 355; vb. 56, 349
swampy adj. 355
swank n. 873, 879
swan song n. 89, 369
swap vb. 150, 725
swarm n. 94; vb. 75, 94, 168, 314, 572
swarthy adj. 808
swastika n. 221
sway n. 159, 177, 667; vb. 177, 216, 325, 326, 547, 667
swear vb. 468, 698, 901

swearword n. 901
sweat n. 310, 615 vb. 615
sweep n. 182, 247; vb. 182, 358, 359, 583
sweeping adj. 32, 54, 56, 98
sweet n. 306, 772, 891; adj. 772, 776, 790, 889
sweeten vb. 772
sweetener n. 772
sweetheart n. 891
sweetmeat n. 306
sweetness n. 772
swell n. 358, 780; adj. 844; vb. 36, 196, 252, 343, 358, 359
swelter vb. 759
swerve vb. 247, 285
swift adj. 280, 613
swim vb. 271, 331
swindle n. 478; vb. 478, 722, 932
swindler n. 480, 723
swing n. 140, 325; vb. 140, 216, 323, 325, 326
swirl vb. 323, 358
swish vb. 783, 786
switch n. 149, 964; vb. 149
switched off adj. 385
switch off vb. 89, 754, 798
switch on vb. 755, 797, 829
swivel vb. 323
swollen adj. 196, 252
swollen-headed adj. 875
swoop n. 317, 321; vb. 317
sword n. 677
swot n. 474
sycophancy n. 881
syllable n. 493, 494
syllabus n. 83, 527
syllogism n. 410
symbol n. 482, 493, 677
symbolic adj. 455, 482
symbolism n. 455
symbolize vb. 450, 482, 486
symmetry n. 16, 28, 244
sympathetic adj. 24, 302, 670, 882, 899, 907
sympathize vb. 907
sympathy n. 24, 752, 907
symphony n. 792

symphony orchestra *n.* 793

symposium *n.* 94, 410, 519

symptom *n.* 447, 482, 597

symptomatic *adj.* 60, 401, 482

synagogue *n.* 990

synchronism *n.* **122**

synchronize *vb.* 24, 52, 122

syndicate *n.* 641

synod *n.* 625

synonym *n.* 28, 450, 494

synopsis *n.* 83, 527

syntactic *adj.* 499

syntax *n.* 492, 499

synthesis *n.* 52

syrup *n.* 362, 772

system *n.* 59, 79, 81, 103, 221

systematic *adj.* 79, 81, 140

systematize *vb.* 58, 81, 97

T

tab *n.* 482; *vb.* 482

table *n.* 83, 217, 306

tablet *n.* 591

taboo *n.* 691; *adj.* 691

tacit *adj.* 459

taciturnity *n.* **517**

tackle *vb.* 88, 605

tack on *vb.* 40

tacky *adj.* 362

tactful *adj.* 398

tactical *adj.* 621

tactics *n.* 559, 621

tactless *adj.* 887

tag *n.* 482, 496; *vb.* 482, 496

tail *n.* 87, 89, 91, 237; *adj.* 237; *vb.* 37, 287, 554

taint *n.* 847; *vb.* 584, 952

take *vb.* 268, **720**, 722

take action *vb.* 609

take advantage of *vb.* 136, 478, 575, 606, 952

take after *vb.* 18, 20

take away *vb.* 42, 720

take back *vb.* 31, 538

take care *vb.* 860

take care of *vb.* 392

take charge of *vb.* 593

take exception *vb.* 425, 893

take for granted *vb.* 443, 867, 880, 910

take from *vb.* 720

take heart *vb.* 836, 857

take in *vb.* 98, 302, 304, 452, 716, 795

take into account *vb.* 390

take it out of *vb.* 617

take it out on *vb.* 149, 900

take liberties *vb.* 918

take life *vb.* 370

take measures *vb.* 602

take notice *vb.* 390

take off *vb.* 20, 228, 273, 744

take on *vb.* 557, 605, 649

take out *vb.* 882

take over *vb.* 667

take pains *vb.* 615

take part in *vb.* 605, 639, 709

take place *vb.* 1, 153

take precautions *vb.* 860

take sides *vb.* 408, 639

take steps *vb.* 602, 609

take to *vb.* 545, 861

take umbrage *vb.* 893

take up *vb.* 540, 575, 716

take upon oneself *vb.* 605

taking *n.* **720**

takings *n.* 724, 741

tale *n.* 460, 465, 525

talent *n.* 434, 627

talisman *n.* 984

talk *n.* 470, 492, 514, 518, 519; *vb.* 514

talkativeness *n.* **516**

talk down *vb.* 273

talker *n.* 514

talk into *vb.* 547

talk out of *vb.* 548

talk over *vb.* 624

tall *adj.* 32, 202, **208**, 318

tally *vb.* 24, 38

tame *adj.* 507, 654; *vb.* 377, 679

tan *n.* 810, 813; *adj.* 813; *vb.* 963

tandem *n.* 61, 276

tang *n.* 767, 769

tangency *n.* 201

tangent *n.* 285

tangerine *n.* 816

tangible *adj.* 3, 327, 758

tangle *n.* 45, 82; *vb.* 221

tangy *adj.* 769

tanker *n.* 277

tantalize *vb.* 547, 755

tantamount *adj.* 28; *adv.* 199

tantrum *n.* 893

tap *n.* 265, 360, 782; *vb.* 282, 358, 758, 782

tape *n.* 207; *vb.* 483

tape-measure *n.* 400

taper *n.* 800; *vb.* 37, 205, 255

tape-recorder *n.* 484, 794

tape-recording *n.* 483

tardy *adj.* 135

target *n.* 552, 716, 853

tariff *n.* 743

tarnish *n.* 847; *vb.* 584, 847, 869, 928

tarpaulin *n.* 225

tarry *vb.* 135, 281

tart *adj.* 769, 773

tartan *n.* 817

tart up *vb.* 844

task *n.* 557, 605

tassel *n.* 846

taste *n.* 339, 398, 753, **767**; *vb.* 767

tasteful *adj.* 398, 510, 848, 876

taste good *vb.* 770

tasteless *adj.* 511, 768, 771, 849

tastelessness *n.* 399, 511, **768**, 771, 849

tasty *adj.* 767, 770, 829

taunt *n.* 926; *vb.* 644, 853, 926

taut *adj.* 334

tautological *adj.* 451

tautology *n.* 505

tavern *n.* 191

tawdry *adj.* 849

tax *n.* 743

taxi *n.* 276; *vb.* 273

taxonomy *n.* 97, 375

tea *n.* 306, 309

tea-break *n.* 616

teach *vb.* 420, **470**

teacher *n.* 428, **473**, 624, 974, 986

teaching *n.* **470**

team *n.* 94

team-mate *n.* 640

team up with *vb.* 639

teamwork *n.* 639

tear *vb.* 48, 280, 613

tea-room *n.* 191

tears *n.* 839

tease *vb.* 755, 830, 842

technique *n.* 488, 606

tedious *adj.* 841, 843

teem *vb.* 75, 572

teenager *n.* 131

teens *n.* 70, 129

teeter *vb.* 325

teeth *n.* 159

teetotalism *n.* 944, 949

telecommunications *n.* 467

telegram *n.* 460, 467

telegraphic *adj.* 504

telepathy *n.* 447

telephone *n.* 467; *vb.* 460

telescope *n.* 329, 822; *vb.* 203

television *n.* 467, 840

tell *vb.* 38, 460, 465, 514, 525, 624

tell apart *vb.* 398

teller *n.* 733

tell fortunes *vb.* 447

telling *adj.* 525

tell off *vb.* 926

tell on *vb.* 460

tell-tale *n.* 460; *adj.* 462

tell tales *vb.* 516

tell the future *vb.* 447

temerity *n.* 859

temper *n.* 5, 751; *vb.* 142, 176, 334, 335, 403

temperament *n.* 5, 751

temperamental *adj.* 756, 894

temperance *n.* 935, **944**, 949

temperate *adj.* 176, 759, 944, 949

temperature *n.* 400, 759

tempest *n.* 175, 359

tempestuous *adj.* 359

temple *n.* 990

temporal *adj.* 107, 116, 987

temporary *adj.* 113, 149, 396

tempt *vb.* 547

temptation *n.* 547

tempting *adj.* 306, 770

tempt providence *vb.* 594, 859

ten *n.* 70; *adj.* 70

tenable *adj.* 420

tenacious *adj.* 50, 337, 534, 535, 537

tenancy *n.* 707

tenant *n.* 190, 710

tend *vb.* **178**, 284, 377, 392

tendency *n.* **178**, 284, 545, 751

tender *n.* 693; *adj.* 129, 335, 670, 752, 753, 889; *vb.* 693

tenderize *vb.* 335

tendril *n.* 207, 251

tenement *n.* 191

tenet *n.* 420, 974

tenor *n.* 178, 284, 450, 778

tense *n.* 499; *adj.* 756, 856

tension *n.* 25, 615, 642, 832

tent *n.* 225

tentative *adj.* 396, 448, 604

tenuous *adj.* 333

tenure *n.* 707

tepid *adj.* 759

tergiversation *n.* 538

term *n.* 93, 109, 494; *vb.* 496

terminal *n.* 89; *adj.* 89, 237

terminate *vb.* 89, 144, 164, 659

terminology *n.* 494, 496

terminus *n.* 89, 235, 298

terms *n.* 700

terms of reference *n.* 557

terrace *n.* 559

terra firma n. 352

terrain *n.* 352

terrestrial *adj.* 329, 352

terrible *adj.* 580, 856

terrific *adj.* 579

terrify *vb.* 856

territory *n.* 183, 956

terror *n.* 856

terrorism *n.* 955

terrorist *n.* 167, 175, 370

terse *adj.* 203, 432, 504

test *n.* 394, 396; *vb.* 408, 413

testify *vb.* 401, 413, 468

testimonial *n.* 441, 483

testimony *n.* 401, 468, 483

tether *vb.* 47

text *n.* 432, 524

textbook *n.* 524

textile *n.* 221

textural *adj.* 339

texture *n.* **339**

thank *vb.* 909, 965

thankful *adj.* 909

thankless *adj.* 576, 910

thanks *n.* 909

thanksgiving *n.* 838, 982

thaw *vb.* 345, 761

theatre *n.* 529, 840

theatrical *adj.* 529, 852, 877

theft *n.* 722

theism *n.* 974

theme *n.* 387

theology *n.* 974

theorem *n.* 410

theoretical *adj.* 448

theorist *n.* 448

theorize *vb.* 448

theory *n.* 157, 386, 448

therapeutic *adj.* 585, 589, 591

thermal *adj.* 759

thermometer *n.* 759, **766**

thermostat *n.* 766

thesaurus *n.* 83, 494

thesis *n.* 387, 410, 448, 526

thick *adj.* **204**, 332, 364, 435

thicken *vb.* 204, 332

thicket *n.* 374

thickness *n.* **204**, 206, 332

thickset *adj.* 203, 204

thick-skinned *adj.* 754

thief *n.* **723**, 906

thin *adj.* 33, 76, **205**, 333, 507, 571; *vb.* 27, 333

thing *n.* 3, 163, 327, 609

thing added *n.* **41**

thing subtracted *n.* **43**

think *vb.* **384**, 420, 448

thinkable *adj.* 404

think about *vb.* 552

think ahead *vb.* 558

thinker *n.* 448

think-tank *n.* 624

thinness *n.* 76, **205**, 333

third *n.* 66; *adj.* 65

third party *n.* 653

thirst *n.* 350, 388, 861; *vb.* 861

thirst-quencher *n.* 309

thirsty *adj.* 350

thorn *n.* 255, 255

thorn in the flesh *n.* 592

thorny *adj.* 255, 633

thorough *adj.* 56, 148, 392

thoroughfare *n.* 313

thought *n.* **384**, 386, 392, 420, 441

thoughtful *adj.* 384, 392, 410, 434, 837, 886

thoughtless *adj.* 385, 391, 393, 603, 859, 887, 900, 910

thousand *n.* 70

thrall *n.* 679

thrash *vb.* 282, 963

thread *n.* 49, 207; *vb.* 313

threadbare *adj.* 228

threadlike *adj.* 205, 207

threat *n.* 154, 594, **902**

threatening *adj.* 154, 594, 651, 902

three *n.* 64; *adj.* 64

thresh *vb.* 378

threshold *n.* 233, 235

thrifty *adj.* 392, 748

thrill *n.* 756, 827; *vb.* 752, 755, 756, 829

thrive *vb.* 36, 168, 661, 664

throat *n.* 262

throaty *adj.* 515, 787

throb *n.* 325, 783; *vb.* 140, 325, 783, 828

throne *n.* 957

throng *n.* 75, 94; *vb.* 75, 94

throughout *adv., prep.* 107

throw *vb.* 290

throw away *vb.* 556, 713, 749

throwaway *adj.* 544

throw in *vb.* 311

throw in the towel *vb.* 556, 654

throw light on *vb.* 456

throw off *vb.* 295, 546

throw out *vb.* 607

throw up *vb.* 303

thrust *n.* 173, 178, 282, 290, 645; *vb.* 290, 645

thud *vb.* 782, 785

thug *n.* 723, 906

thumb through *vb.* 472, 818

thump *vb.* 282, 783, 785

thunder *n.* 325, 784; *vb.* 780, 782

thunderbolt *n.* 444

thunderstorm *n.* 175, 358

thunderstruck *adj.* 444, 866

thundery *adj.* 358

thwart *vb.* 445, 635, 637, 648, 662

tick *vb.* 783

ticket *n.* 482, 483, 743

tickle *vb.* 758, 829

tick off *vb.* 926

tide *n.* 358

tidy *adj.* 79, 392, 583; *vb.* 583

tie *n.* 28, 49; *vb.* 28, 47, 681

tier *n.* 93, 206

tie-up *n.* 47

tight *adj.* 47, 334, 950

tight-fisted *adj.* 750

tight-lipped *adj.* 517

till *n.* 732; *vb.* 378

tilt *vb.* 219, 220, 317

timber *n.* 217

timbre *n.* 512, 778

time *n.* **107**, 109, 116, 400; *vb.* 116

time-honoured *adj.* 126, 922

timekeeping *n.* 116

timelessness *n.* 108, 114

timeliness *n.* **136**

timepiece *n.* 116

time-saving *adj.* 748

time-server *n.* 538, 934

timetable *n.* 116, 460

timid *adj.* 856, 858, 876

timing *n.* 116, 140

timorous *adj.* 856

tin *n.* 193; *vb.* 599

tincture *n.* 45, 805

tinder *n.* 765

tinge *n.* 805; *vb.* 805

tingle *vb.* 752, 756

tininess *n.* 33, 195

tinker *n.* 728

tinkle *n.* 784

tinny *adj.* 787

tinsel *n.* 846

tint *n.* 27, 805; *vb.* 488

tinted *adj.* 805

tiny *adj.* 33, 195, 203

tip *n.* 212, 233, 255, 715, 965; *vb.* 212, 220, 909

tip-off *n.* 460, 597

tipple *vb.* 304, 950

tipsy *adj.* 950

tirade *n.* 518

tire *vb.* 617, 841

tired *adj.* 612, 617, 841

tiresome *adj.* 830, 841

tissue *n.* 339

titbit *n.* 770, 829

tit for tat *n.* 150, 647

titillate *vb.* 758, 829

title *n.* 496, **872**

titled *adj.* 870

title-holder *n.* 661

unbiased *adj.* 415, 541, 915, **933**
unbind *vb.* 48, 601, 680
unblemished *adj.* 54, 581, 583, 935
unbolt *vb.* 262
unbosom *vb.* 462
unbound *adj.* 708, 921
unbreakable *adj.* 334, 337
unbroken *adj.* 54, 91, 145
unburden oneself *vb.* 462
uncanny *adj.* 971, 984
unceasing *adj.* 114, 145
uncertainty *n.* 325, **409**, 421, 454, 553
uncertified *adj.* 409
unchangeable *adj.* 13, 143, 152
unchanging *adj.* 16, 143, 669
uncharitable *adj.* 900
uncharted *adj.* 427
unchaste *adj.* 952
unclassified *adj.* 35
uncle *n.* 11
uncleanness *n.* **584**, 586, 777, 952
unclear *adj.* 409, 453, 503, 633, 803
uncoil *vb.* 81, 248
uncomfortable *adj.* 187
uncommon *adj.* 139
uncommunicative *adj.* 517, 863, 885
uncomplaining *adj.* 757, 831
uncompleted *adj.* 660
uncomplicated *adj.* 46, 632, 634
uncomplimentary *adj.* 926
uncompromising *adj.* 537, 669
unconcerned *adj.* 389, 391, 393, **863**, 933
unconditional *adj.* 56, 408
unconfirmed *adj.* 409
unconformity *n.* **106**
unconnected *adj.* 10, 48, 92
unconscious *n.* 382; *adj.* 427, 531, 754
unconsecrated *adj.* 987
unconsidered *adj.* 544
unconstitutionality *n.* 955
uncontrolled *adj.* 668, 672, 921

unconventional *adj.* 106
unconverted *adj.* 975
uncooperative *adj.* 642
uncouple *vb.* 48
uncouth *adj.* 511, 849
uncover *vb.* 419, 462
uncritical *adj.* 399, 416
unctuousness *n.* **365**, 927
uncultured *adj.* 427, 887
uncurl *vb.* 248, 324
undamaged *adj.* 54
undated *adj.* 117
undaunted *adj.* 535, 857
undecided *adj.* 325, 409, 536
undefiled *adj.* 937, 951
undependable *adj.* 932
under *adv.* 209
undercarriage *n.* 217
undercover *adj.* 459
undercurrent *n.* 358, 459, 596
underdeveloped *adj.* 459
underdog *n.* 35, 662, 871
underdone *adj.* 771
underestimation *n.* 416, **418**
underfoot *adv.* 209
underframe *n.* 217
undergo *vb.* 153, 752, 828
undergraduate *n.* 474
underground *n.* 276, 480, 559; *adj.* 148, 210; *adv.* 209
undergrowth *n.* 374
underhand *adj.* 461, 478, 631, 932
underline *vb.* 468, 573
underlying *adj.* 209, 213, 459
underneath *adv.* 209
underplay *vb.* 418
under-privileged *adj.* 735
underrate *vb.* 418, 923
understanding *n.* (knowledge) 382, 410, 426, 434; (agreement) 24, 643, 699, 704; (pity) 907
understate *vb.* 418, 477, 487
understood *adj.* 459
understudy *n.* 149, 529
undertaker *n.* 372

undertaking *n.* 557, 604, **605**, 609, 698, 699
undertone *n.* 781
undervalue *vb.* 416, 418
underwater *adj.* 210
underworld *n.* 973
underwrite *vb.* 701
undeserved *adj.* 918
undesirable *adj.* 578
undeveloped *adj.* 603
undiscerning *adj.* 399, 435
undiscovered *adj.* 427
undiscriminating *adj.* 399
undisputed *adj.* 24, 408, 430
undistinguished *adj.* 869
undivided *adj.* 54, 56
undo *vb.* 48, 164, 262, 680
undress *n.* 228; *vb.* 228
undressing *n.* **228**
undueness *n.* **918**
undulate *vb.* 140, 251, **325**, 358
unearth *vb.* 186, 372, 419
uneasy *adj.* 828, 832, 856
uneducated *adj.* 427, 628
unemotional *adj.* 754
unemployed *adj.* 607, 610, 612
unending *adj.* 202
unenterprising *adj.* 612
unenthusiastic *adj.* 533, 754
unequal *adj.* 29, 59
unequipped *adj.* 603
unequivocal *adj.* 408, 452
unerring *adj.* 408
uneven *adj.* 17, 29, 92, 141, 245, 258
unexpected *adj.* 158, 407, 444
unexplored *adj.* 885
unexpurgated *adj.* 952
unfailing *adj.* 408, 420
unfair *adj.* 416, 916, 918
unfaithful *adj.* 431, 538, 703, 920
unfamiliar *adj.* 106
unfashionableness *n.* 849
unfasten *vb.* 262
unfavourable *adj.* 137, 578, 665, 926

unfeeling *adj.* 669, 754, 908
unfinished *adj.* 57, 582
unfitting *adj.* 578, 916
unflinching *adj.* 534, 857
unfold *vb.* 262, 324, 458, 462
unforeseen *adj.* 444
unforgettable *adj.* 441
unforgivable *adj.* 916, 936
unforgiving *adj.* 908
unfortunate *adj.* 662, 665, 828
unfounded *adj.* 2
unfreeze *vb.* 761
unfriendly *adj.* 883, **885**, 887, 900
unfrock *vb.* 686, 869
unfruitful *adj.* 169
unfurl *vb.* 324, 462
ungodly *adj.* 936, 975, 981
ungracious *adj.* 887
ungrammatical *adj.* 500
ungrateful *adj.* 910
unguarded *adj.* 393, 603
unguent *n.* 342, 365; *adj.* 365
unhallowed *adj.* 981
unhappy *adj.* 665, 828, **832**, 837
unharmed *adj.* 593
unhealthy *adj.* 586
unheard of *adj.* 407, 444, 869
unheeding *adj.* 393
unhelpful *adj.* 576
unhesitating *adj.* 534
unhindered *adj.* 678
unhitch *vb.* 48
unholy *adj.* 975, 981
unhurt *adj.* 593
unhygienic *adj.* 586
unidentified *adj.* 497
uniform *n.* 227, 677; *adj.* 16, 46, 140, 152, 257
uniformity *n.* 13, **16**, 24, 28, 79
unify *vb.* 47, 52, 59
unilateral *adj.* 10
unimaginative *adj.* 508
unimpaired *adj.* 54
unimpeded *adj.* 678
unimportance *n.* 451, 574
unimpressed *adj.* 867
uninhabited *adj.* 189, 885

unwed *adj.* 897
unwell *adj.* 586
unwholesome *adj.* 580
unwieldy *adj.* 628
unwillingness *n.* 533
unwind *vb.* 324
unwise *adj.* 393, 416, 435, 578
unworthy *adj.* 918
unwrap *vb.* 324
unyielding *adj.* 112, 161, 334, 337, 534, 537
up *adv.* 208
update *vb.* 125, 587
upgrade *vb.* 587
upheaval *n.* 80, 148
uphill *adj.* 615, 633
uphold *vb.* 143, 145, 217, 929
upland *n.* 356
uplands *n.* 208
uplift *vb.* 318, 836
upper *adj.* 34
upper classes *n.* 870
uppermost *adj.* 212
upraised *adj.* 318
upright *adj.* 214, 248, 430, 915, 931, 935
uprising *n.* 358
uproar *n.* 80, 175, 780
uproot *vb.* 187, 312
upset *n.* 220, 414; *adj.* 837; *vb.* 82, 148, 830, 893
upshot *n.* 87, 156
upside-down *adj.* 220; *adv.* 80
upstanding *adj.* 214, 318
upstart *n.* 125, 880
upsurge *vb.* 36
uptight *adj.* 756, 894
up-to-date *adj.* 125
upward *adj.* 219, 316
urban *adj.* 183
urchin *n.* 970
urge *n.* 547, 861; *vb.* 468, 547, 613, 624, 674, 695
urgency *n.* 506, 562, 573, 613, 674, 695
urinate *vb.* 303, 310
urn *n.* 193, 372
usage *n.* 499, 501, 545, 606
use *n.* 606; *vb.* 575, 606, 707, 719
used *adj.* 126, 606
used to *adj.* 545
useful *adj.* 550, 575, 577
useless *adj.* 576, 662

usher in *vb.* 84
usual *adj.* 138, 545, 867
usurer *n.* 718
usurp *vb.* 918
utensil *n.* 565
utilitarian *adj.* 575
utilitarianism *n.* 903
utility *n.* 575, 606
utilize *vb.* 575, 606
utmost *n.* 235
utopia *n.* 449
utter *adj.* 56; *vb.* 512, 514, 788
utterance *n.* 492, 494, **498**, 512, 514, 788

V

vacant *adj.* 189, 385, 435, 451
vacate *vb.* 187
vacation *n.* 144, 612, 614
vaccine *n.* 591
vacillate *vb.* 151, 325, 536
vacuity *n.* 2, 189
vacuum *n.* 2, 189, 333
vagabond *n.* 270, 697
vagrant *n.* 270
vague *adj.* 4, 243, 409, 454, 503, 799, 824
vain *adj.* 576, 662, 855, 875
valentine *n.* 523, 890
valiant *adj.* 857
valid *adj.* 413, 430, 915, 954
validate *vb.* 413, 954
validity *n.* 430, 954
valley *n.* 200, 209, 254
valour *n.* 857
valuable *adj.* 573, 575, 579
valuables *n.* 711
value *n.* 575, 579, 743: *vb.* 573, 743, 889, 922
valuer *n.* 415
valve *n.* 265
vampire *n.* 906, 969
van *n.* 276
vandal *n.* 167
vandalism *n.* 722
vanished *adj.* 2, 189, 706, **826**
vanity *n.* 576, 873, **875**, 934
vaporization *n.* **346**

vaporous *adj.* 4, 344, 346
vapour *n.* 4, 343, 344, 346
variable *n.* 39; *adj.* 15, 17, 104, 142, **151**
variance *n.* 15, 425, 642
variant *n.* 15; *adj.* 15
variation *n.* 15, 19, 104, 142
variegation *n.* **817**
variety *n.* 19, 72, 104, 529
various *adj.* 104
varnish *vb.* 225, 257, 365
vary *vb.* 15, 142, 151
vase *n.* 193
vast *adj.* 32, 78, 182, 194
vastly *adv.* 32
vat *n.* 193
vault *n.* 252, 320, 329, 372, 732; *vb.* 320
vaulted *adj.* 247
vaunt *vb.* 879
veer *vb.* 142, 247, 285
vegetability *n.* **374**
vegetable *n.* 306
vegetate *vb.* 169, 174, 612, 666
vegetation *n.* 374
vehement *adj.* 173, 175, 506, 759
vehicle *n.* **276**, 563
veil *n.* 461, 463, 549, 801; *vb.* 225, 461, 801
veiled *adj.* 225, 459
velocity *n.* 266, **280**
vendetta *n.* 425, 642
vendor *n.* 697, 727
veneer *n.* 211, 225; *vb.* 206, 225
venerable *adj.* 126, 130
venerate *vb.* 922, 982
vengeance *n.* 647, 912
venomous *adj.* 164, 580, 592
vent *n.* 262, 361, 600
ventilate *vb.* 348, 583
ventilation *n.* 348, 775
ventilator *n.* 361, 764
venture *n.* 269, 553, 604, **605**; *vb.* 158, 553, 604, 918
veracity *n.* 476
verb *n.* 499
verbal *adj.* 450, 494, 514
verbalize *vb.* 498
verbose *adj.* 505, 516

verdict *n.* 415, 960
verge *n.* 233; *vb.* 233
verge on *vb.* 292
verify *vb.* 396, 401, 408, 413
veritable *adj.* 430
vermin *n.* 373
vernacular *n.* 492; *adj.* 190, 492
versatile *adj.* 151, 627
verse *n.* 528
versed *adj.* 602
version *n.* 456
vertebrate *n.* 373
vertical *adj.* 214, 248
verve *n.* 173, 368, 506, 611
very *adj.* 13; *adv.* 32
vespers *n.* 128, 988
vessel *n.* 193, 277
vestige *n.* 44
vestment *n.* 227, **989**
vet *n.* 377
veteran *n.* **132**, 629, 655; *adj.* 627
veterinary science *n.* 377
veto *n.* 681, 691, 694; *vb.* 691
vexed *adj.* 828, 893
via *adv.* 284
viable *adj.* 404
vibration *n.* 325, 326, 778, 784
vicar *n.* 689, 986
vicarious *adj.* 149, 685, 943
vicarious authority *n.* **685**
vice *n.* **936**; *adj.* 689
vicinity *n.* 199, 229
vicious circle *n.* 412
vicissitude *n.* 142
victim *n.* 479, 716, 828, 853
victimize *vb.* 478, 900
victor *n.* 661
Victorian *adj.* 126, 951
victorious *adj.* 661
victory *n.* 661
video-recorder *n.* 484
videotape *n.* 483
view *n.* 415, 420, 624, 818; *vb.* 818
viewer *n.* 821
vie with *vb.* 649
viewpoint *n.* 818
vigilant *adj.* 390, 392, 818, 860
vigilante *n.* 593
vigour *n.* 159, 161, 173, 368, **506**, 585, 611

vile *adj.* 580, 777, 892
vilify *vb.* 901, 928
villa *n.* 191
village *n.* 183
villain *n.* 906, 940
vindicate *vb.* 647, 912, 929, 961
vindication *n.* **929**
vindictive *adj.* 908, 912
vinegar *n.* 773
vineyard *n.* 378
violate *vb.* 314, 608, 672, 703, 920, 952, 955, 981
violence *n.* **175**, 674
violent *adj.* 175, 642
violet *n.* 814; *adj.* 814
VIP *n.* 868
viper *n.* 906
virgin *n.* 897; *adj.* 125, 427, 603, 897, 951
virgin territory *n.* 427
virile *adj.* 161, 380
virtual *adj.* 404
virtually *adv.* 199
virtue *n.* 876, 931, **935**, 951
virtuoso *n.* 793
virtuous *adj.* 931, 935, 951
virus *n.* 167, 586, 592
visa *n.* 690
viscosity *n.* 362, 400
viscount *n.* 870
visibility *n.* **823**
visible *adj.* 3, 458, 823, 825
vision *n.* 449, 458, **818**, 854, 971, 976
visionary *n.* 449, 903; *adj.* 4, 449
visit *n.* 269, 884; *vb.* 188, 269, 300, 971
visitor *n.* 100, 270, 884
visual *adj.* 488, 818
visualize *vb.* 449
vital *adj.* 368, 562
vitality *n.* 161, 173, 368, 506, 585, 836
vitalize *vb.* 173, 368
vitreous *adj.* 802
vivacious *adj.* 368, 836
vivacity *n.* 514
vivid *adj.* 441, 506, 509, 525
vivisection *n.* 370
vocabulary *n.* 494, 501
vocal *adj.* 512, 792
vocalist *n.* 793
vocalize *vb.* 512, 514
vocation *n.* 557, 985
vociferous *adj.* 780, 788

vogue *n.* 125; *adj.* 495
voice *n.* 492, **512**; *vb.* 512, 514
void *n.* 2, 74, 189; *adj.* 2, 333, 451; *vb.* 955
volatile *adj.* 151, 344, 346
volition *n.* 530
volte-face *n.* 147, 220, 289, 538
voluble *adj.* 509, 514, 516
volume *n.* 26, 194, 400, 524
voluntary *adj.* 530, 532
volunteer *vb.* 532, 693
voluptuous *adj.* 827, 945
vomit *vb.* 303
voodoo *n.* 984
voracity *n.* 750, 861, 948
vortex *n.* 323, 358
vote *n.* 540, 909; *vb.* 424, 540
voted *adj.* 424
voter *n.* 190, 540
vouch *vb.* 468
voucher *n.* 482, 741
vow *n.* 468, 698; *vb.* 468, 698
vowel *n.* 493, 512
voyage *n.* 271, 313; *vb.* 271
voyager *n.* 270
vulgar *adj.* 511, 849, 887, 952
vulnerable *adj.* 594, 753

W

wadding *n.* 226
wade *vb.* 271
wafer *n.* 306
waffle *vb.* 516
waft *vb.* 359
wag *n.* 842; *vb.* 325
wager *n.* 553
wages *n.* 731, 738, 741
wagon *n.* 276
wail *n.* 788, 839; *vb.* 788, 839
wait *vb.* 443, 610
wait and see *vb.* 135, 610
waiter *n.* 676
wait on *vb.* 287, 676
waive *vb.* 556, 713
wake *n.* 237

walk *n.* 269, 559; *vb.* 269
walk away with *vb.* 661
walker *n.* 270
walkie-talkie *n.* 467
walk out *vb.* 144, 556, 687
walkout *n.* 144
walk-over *n.* 634, 661
wall *n.* 217, 230, 234
wallet *n.* 193, 732
wallop *vb.* 282, 963
wan *adj.* 807
wand *n.* 677
wander *vb.* 269, 285, 505
wanderer *n.* 270
wandering *n.* 391
wane *n.* 37; *vb.* 37, 799
want *n.* 57, 562, 706, 861; *vb.* 57, 189, 530, 532, 562, 571, **861**
wanted *adj.* 562, 600
wanton *adj.* 936, 952
war *n.* 649, **651**
warble *vb.* 789
ward *n.* 183, 540
warden *n.* 593, 683
warder *n.* 683
ward off *vb.* 646
wardrobe *n.* 227
wardship *n.* 129
warehouse *n.* 567
wares *n.* 729
warfare *n.* 649, 651
warlike *adj.* 651
warm *adj.* 419, **759**, 805; *vb.* 306, 761, 836
warm-hearted *adj.* 882, 899
warmth *n.* 506, 752, 759, 805, 882
warm up *vb.* 306
warning *n.* 447, 460, **597**, 902; *adj.* 597
warp *vb.* 219, 247, 416, 487
warrant *n.* 424, 671, 685; *vb.* 690, 698, 917
warranty *n.* 701
warren *n.* 234, 254
warrior *n.* 655
wart *n.* 252
wary *adj.* 390, 860
wash *n.* 358, 805; *vb.* 583, 805
washed out *adj.* 612, 617, 806
wash-out *n.* 662
waste *n.* 44, 164, **569**,

576; *vb.* 569, 608, 749
waste away *vb.* 53, 586, 588
wasted *adj.* 205, 569
wasteful *adj.* 393, 569, 749
waste-pipe *n.* 600
waste time *vb.* 612
wastrel *n.* 612, 749, 940
watch *n.* 116, 646; *vb.* 392, 818
watchdog *n.* 593
watcher *n.* 821
watchful *adj.* 392, 443, 818, 860
watchman *n.* 683
watchword *n.* 432
water *n.* 309, **347**; *vb.* 378
water channel *n.* **360**
water down *vb.* 45, 162
waterfall *n.* 358
water in motion *n.* **358**
waterlogged *adj.* 349, 355
waterproof *adj.* 350, 593
watershed *n.* 230
water sports *n.* 271
watertight *adj.* 265, 350
water travel *n.* **271**
waterway *n.* 358
watery *adj.* 343, 347
wave *n.* 325, 358, 482; *vb.* 325, 482, 886
wavering *n.* 142, 151, 325, 409, 536; *adj.* 141, 151, 326, 536
wavy *adj.* 251
wax *n.* 342, 800; *vb.* 36, 225
way *n.* 198, 313, **559**
wayfarer *n.* 270
way out *n.* 301, 600
wayward *adj.* 151, 672
weak *adj.* **162**, 507, 586, 617, 628, 781, 858
weak-minded *adj.* 162, 435
weakness *n.* **162**, 178, 315, 507, 586, 617, 858, 936
weak spot *n.* 582, 594
wealth *n.* 168, 664, 711, 731, **734**
wean from *vb.* 546, 548
weapons *n.* 657
wear *vb.* 227
wear and tear *n.* 569
wear away *vb.* 341
wear down *vb.* 160, 547

weariness *n.* 612, 617,
841
wearisome *adj.* 633,
841
wear out *vb.* 569, 617
weather *n.* 348
weave *n.* 339; *vb.* 221,
313
web *n.* 221, 339
wed *adj.* 47; *vb.* 896
wedding *n.* 896
wedge *n.* 230, 246, 265
weed *n.* 374; *vb.* 378
weedy *adj.* 205
week *n.* 109
weep *vb.* 301, 833, 839,
907
weigh *vb.* 330, 397, 415
weight *n.* 26, 177, 194,
330, 400, 573; *vb.*
330
weighting *n.* 31
weightless *adj.* 331
weigh up *vb.* 384
weird *adj.* 971, 984
welcome *n.* 302; *adj.*
827; *vb.* 302, 884,
886
welcoming *adj.* 716
weld *n.* 49; *vb.* 50
welfare *n.* 550, 664
well *n.* 254, 567; *adj.*
585; *vb.* 301, 358
well-behaved *adj.* 673
well-being *n.* 550, 585,
664
well-dressed *adj.* 227
well-formed *adj.* 499,
844
well grounded *adj.* 426
well-meaning *adj.* 899
well-off *adj.* 664, 734
well-proportioned *adj.*
244, 510, 844
well-read *adj.* 426, 472
well thought of *adj.*
868, 922
well-turned *adj.* 510
well-versed *adj.* 426,
627
weltschmerz *n.* 837
west *n.* 284
wet *n.* 347, 349; *adj.*
347, 349; *vb.* 349
wet blanket *n.* 548, 841
whack *n.* 782; *vb.* 282,
782, 963
whacked *adj.* 617
whale *n.* 194
what's-its-name *n.* 497
wheedle *vb.* 547, 927
wheel *n.* 250

wheeled *adj.* 276
wheeze *vb.* 359, 786
when *adv., prep.* 107
whereabouts *n.* 185
wherewithal *n.* 564,
566
whet *vb.* 255, 755
while *adv., prep.* 107
while away *vb.* 107,
612
whim *n.* 449, 539
whimper *vb.* 788, 839
whimsical *adj.* 449,
539, 842, 851
whine *vb.* 784, 788,
789, 839
whip *n.* 964; *vb.* 282,
963
whip up *vb.* 175, 755
whirl *n.* 323; *vb.* 323,
358, 359
whirlpool *n.* 323, 358
whirlwind *n.* 323, 359
whirr *n.* 783, 786; *vb.*
783, 784, 786
whisk *n.* 359; *vb.* 359
whisper *n.* 460, 781; *vb.*
781
whistle *n.* 482, 786,
787; *vb.* 482, 786,
787, 789
white *n.* **807**, 951; *adj.*
583, 806, 807
white flag *n.* 652
whittle *vb.* 203
whiz *vb.* 280, 786
whizz-kid *n.* 629
whole *n.* 26, **54**, 59; *adj.*
39, 54, 56, 581, 585
wholehearted *adj.* 534
wholesale *adj.* 54, 56,
98
wholesome *adj.* 438,
585
whoop *vb.* 788, 840
whore *n.* 953
wicked *adj.* **551**, 580,
900, 916, 932, 936,
981
wickerwork *n.* 221
wide *adj.* 101, 182, 204
widen *vb.* 36, 182, 204
widespread *adj.* 32, 54,
101, 182
widow *n.* 898; *vb.* 898
widowhood *n.* **898**
width *n.* 26, **204**, 400
wife *n.* 896
wiggle *vb.* 251
wild *adj.* 175, 433, 439,
859, 889
wilful *adj.* 530

will *n.* **530**; *vb.* 530, 714
willies *n.* 856
willingness *n.* **532**, 692
willpower *n.* 530, 534
wilt *vb.* 837
wily *adj.* 478, 631
win *vb.* 661, 705, 720
wince *vb.* 283
wind *n.* 359; *vb.* 251,
322
windfall *n.* 550, 715
window *n.* 262
wind up *vb.* 89, 116,
739
windy *adj.* 344, 348,
359
wine *n.* 309
wink *n.* 482, 818; *vb.*
482, 818
winner *n.* 661
winnings *n.* 724
winnow *vb.* 46, 48, 378
win over *vb.* 547
winsome *adj.* 829, 889
winter *n.* **128**; *adj.* 128
wintry *adj.* 128, 760
wipe *vb.* 341
wipe out *vb.* 164, 485,
911
wire *n.* 207, 460, 467;
adj. 611; *vb.* 460
wireless *n.* 467
wiry *adj.* 207
wisdom *n.* 382, 392,
426, **434**
wisecrack *n.* 842
wish *n.* 530, 854, 861;
vb. 530, 854, 861
wishful thinking *n.* 449,
478, 854
wishy-washy *adj.* 162,
507, 666, 768
wisp *n.* 4, 207
wit *n.* 434, **842**
witchcraft *n.* 984
withdraw *vb.* 42, 289,
293, 299, **312**, 538,
556, 600, 687, 731,
826
withdrawn *adj.* 681,
885
wither *vb.* 350, 588
withhold *vb.* 461, 694,
712
within hearing *adv.* 199
within reach *adj.* 404
without *adv., prep.* 42;
prep. 571
with reference to *adv.,
prep.* 9
withstand *vb.* 646, 648

with strings attached
adj. 700
with the exception of
adv., prep. 42
with young *adj.* 163
witness *n.* 401, 483; *vb.*
401, 413
witty *adj.* 840, 842
wizard *n.* 447, 984
wizened *adj.* 197, 205
wobble *n.* 326; *vb.* 325,
326
woe *n.* 580
wold *n.* 356
woman *n.* 133, 381
woman-hater *n.* 904
womanizer *n.* 953
women's rights *n.* 917
wonder *n.* **866**; *vb.* 866
wonderful *adj.* 32, 579,
844
wont *n.* 545
woo *vb.* 882, 889, 890
wood *n.* 374, 765
woodwind *n.* 794
word *n.* **494**, 698; *vb.*
498
word for word *adj.* 450,
456
wording *n.* 501
Word of God *n.* 976
word order *n.* 499
wordy *adj.* 505
work *n.* 163, 488, 521,
524, **557**, 605, 615,
792; *vb.* 172, 557,
615, 676
workable *adj.* 406
work against *vb.* 181
worked up *adj.* 893
worker *n.* 609, 619, 676
work off *vb.* 149
work oneself up *vb.*
756
work one's way up *vb.*
316
work out *vb.* 38, 452,
552, 558, 659
workshop *n.* **620**
work together *vb.* 52,
180
work up *vb.* 755
world *n.* 329, 379
worldliness *n.* 327, 329,
981
world-weariness *n.* 837,
841
worldwide *adj.* 32, 101
worm in *vb.* 300
worn *adj.* 162, 588
worn out *adj.* 612, 617,
841

LIST OF CATEGORIES

I Abstract Relations

A Existence

1 existence
2 non-existence
3 material existence
4 non-material existence
5 being according to internal form
6 being according to external form
7 absolute state
8 circumstance

B Relation

9 relation
10 absence of relation
11 kindred relations
12 correlation
13 identity
14 absolute difference
15 variance
16 uniformity
17 non-uniformity
18 similarity
19 dissimilarity
20 imitation
21 non-imitation
22 copy
23 prototype
24 agreement
25 disagreement

C Quantity

26 quantity
27 relative quantity
28 equality
29 inequality
30 mean
31 compensation
32 greatness
33 smallness
34 superiority
35 inferiority
36 increase
37 decrease
38 numeration
39 number
40 addition
41 thing added
42 subtraction
43 thing subtracted
44 remainder
45 mixture
46 freedom from mixture
47 junction
48 separation
49 bond
50 coherence

51 incoherence
52 combination
53 decomposition
54 whole
55 part
56 completeness
57 incompleteness
58 composition
59 unity
60 accompaniment
61 duality
62 duplication
63 bisection
64 triality
65 triplication
66 trisection
67 quaternity
68 quadruplication
69 quadrisection
70 five and over
71 multisection
72 plurality
73 fraction
74 zero
75 multitude
76 fewness
77 repetition
78 infinity

D Order

79 order
80 disorder
81 arrangement
82 disarrangement
83 list
84 precedence
85 sequence
86 precursor
87 sequel
88 beginning
89 end
90 middle
91 continuity
92 discontinuity
93 position in a series
94 assemblage
95 dispersion
96 focus
97 class
98 inclusion
99 exclusion
100 extraneousness
101 generality
102 speciality
103 rule
104 diversity
105 conformity
106 uncomformity

E Time

107 time

108 absence of time
109 period
110 course of time
111 contingent duration
112 long duration
113 short duration
114 endless duration
115 point of time
116 chronometry
117 anachronism
118 priority
119 posteriority
120 present time
121 different time
122 synchronism
123 future
124 past
125 newness
126 oldness
127 morning; spring; summer
128 evening; autumn; winter
129 youth
130 age
131 infant
132 veteran
133 adulthood
134 earliness
135 lateness
136 timeliness
137 untimeliness
138 frequency
139 infrequency
140 regularity
141 irregularity

F Change

142 change
143 permanence
144 cessation
145 continuance
146 conversion
147 reversion
148 revolution
149 substitution
150 interchange
151 changeableness
152 stablity
153 present events
154 future events

G Causation

155 cause
156 effect
157 assignment of cause
158 chance
159 power
160 impotence
161 strength
162 weakness

List of Categories

List of Categories

481 exaggeration

C Means of communicating ideas

482 indication
483 record
484 recorder
485 obliteration
486 representation
487 misrepresentation
488 painting
489 sculpture
490 engraving
491 artist
492 language
493 letter
494 word
495 neologism
496 nomenclature
497 misnomer
498 phrase
499 grammar
500 solecism
501 style
502 lucidity
503 obscurity
504 conciseness
505 diffuseness
506 vigour
507 feebleness
508 plainness
509 ornament
510 elegance
511 inelegance
512 voice
513 muteness
514 speech
515 imperfect speech
516 talkativeness
517 taciturnity
518 address
519 conversation
520 monologue
521 writing
522 printing
523 correspondence
524 book
525 description
526 dissertation
527 compendium
528 poetry; prose
529 drama

V Volition

1 Individual volition

A Volition in general

530 will
531 necessity
532 willingness
533 unwillingness
534 resolution
535 perseverance
536 irresolution
537 obstinacy
538 change of mind
539 caprice
540 choice
541 absence of choice
542 rejection
543 predetermination
544 spontaneity
545 habit
546 absence of habit
547 motive
548 dissuasion
549 pretext
550 good
551 evil

B Prospective volition

552 intention
553 chance
554 pursuit
555 avoidance
556 relinquishment
557 business
558 plan
559 way
560 mid-course
561 circuit
562 requirement
563 instrumentality
564 means
565 instrument
566 materials
567 store
568 provision
569 waste
570 sufficiency
571 insufficiency
572 excess
573 importance
574 unimportance
575 utility
576 inutility
577 expedience
578 inexpedience
579 goodness
580 badness
581 perfection
582 imperfection
583 cleanness
584 uncleanness
585 health
586 ill health
587 improvement
588 deterioration
589 restoration
590 relapse
591 remedy
592 bane
593 safety
594 danger
595 refuge
596 pitfall
597 warning
598 indication of danger
599 preservation
600 escape
601 deliverance
602 preparation
603 non-preparation
604 attempt
605 undertaking
606 use
607 disuse
608 misuse

C Voluntary action

609 action
610 inaction
611 activity
612 inactivity
613 haste
614 leisure
615 exertion
616 repose
617 fatigue
618 refreshment
619 agent
620 workshop
621 conduct
622 management
623 director
624 advice
625 council
626 precept
627 skill
628 unskilfulness
629 expert
630 bungler
631 cunning
632 artlessness

D Antagonism

633 difficulty
634 ease
635 hindrance
636 aid
637 opposition
638 opponent
639 cooperation
640 auxiliary
641 party
642 discord
643 concord
644 defiance
645 attack
646 defence
647 retaliation
648 resistance
649 contest
650 peace

651	war	701	security	756	excitability
652	pacification	702	observance	757	inexcitability
653	mediation	703	non-observance		
654	submission	704	compromise		
655	combatant				**B Sensation**
656	non-combatant		**D Possessive relations**	758	touch
657	arms	705	acquisition	759	heat
658	arena	706	loss	760	cold
		707	possession	761	heating
	E Results of action	708	non-possession	762	refrigeration;
659	completion	709	joint possession		incombustibility
660	non-completion	710	possessor	763	furnace
661	success	711	property	764	refrigerator
662	failure	712	retention	765	fuel
663	trophy	713	non-retention	766	thermometer
664	prosperity	714	transfer	767	taste
665	adversity	715	giving	768	tastelessness
666	mediocrity	716	receiving	769	pungency
		717	apportionment	770	savouriness
	2 Intersocial volition	718	lending	771	unsavouriness
		719	borrowing	772	sweetness
	A General	720	taking	773	sourness
667	authority	721	restitution	774	odour
668	laxity	722	stealing	775	inodorousness
669	severity	723	thief	776	fragrance
670	lenience	724	booty	777	stench
671	command	725	business	778	sound
672	disobedience	726	purchase	779	silence
673	obedience	727	sale	780	loudness
674	compulsion	728	trader	781	faintness
675	master	729	merchandise	782	sudden and violent sound
676	servant	730	market	783	repeated and prolonged
677	sign of authority	731	money		sound
678	freedom	732	treasury	784	resonance
679	subjection	733	treasurer	785	non-resonance
680	liberation	734	wealth	786	hissing sound
681	restraint	735	poverty	787	harsh sound
682	prison	736	credit	788	human sound
683	keeper	737	debt	789	animal sound
684	prisoner	738	payment	790	melody
685	vicarious authority	739	non-payment	791	discord
686	annulment	740	expenditure	792	music
687	resignation	741	income	793	musician
688	consignee	742	accounts	794	musical instrument
689	deputy	743	price	795	hearing
		744	discount	796	deafness
	B Special	745	dearness	797	light
690	permission	746	cheapness	798	darkness
691	prohibition	747	liberality	799	dimness
692	consent	748	economy	800	source of light
693	offer	749	extravagance	801	shade
694	refusal	750	parsimony	802	transparency
695	request			803	opacity
696	protest			804	semitransparency
697	petitioner		**VI Affections**	805	colour
				806	absence of colour
	C Conditional		**A Affections in general**	807	white
698	promise	751	affections	808	black
699	contract	752	feeling	809	grey
700	conditions	753	sensitivity	810	brown
		754	insensitivity	811	red
		755	excitation	812	green
				813	yellow

List of Categories

814 purple
815 blue
816 orange
817 variegation
818 vision
819 blindness
820 imperfect vision
821 spectator
822 optical instrument
823 visibility
824 invisibility
825 appearance
826 disappearance

C   Personal

827 pleasure
828 pain
829 pleasurableness
830 painfulness
831 content
832 discontent
833 regret
834 relief
835 aggravation
836 cheerfulness
837 dejection; seriousness
838 rejoicing
839 lamentation
840 amusement
841 weariness
842 wit
843 dullness
844 beauty
845 ugliness
846 ornamentation
847 blemish
848 good taste
849 bad taste
850 fashion
851 ridiculousness
852 affectation
853 ridicule
854 hope
855 hopelessness
856 fear
857 courage
858 cowardice
859 rashness
860 caution
861 desire
862 dislike
863 indifference
864 fastidiousness
865 satiety
866 wonder
867 absence of wonder
868 repute
869 disrepute
870 nobility
871 common people
872 title
873 pride

874 humility
875 vanity
876 modesty; shyness
877 ostentation
878 celebration
879 boasting
880 insolence
881 servility

D   Sympathetic

882 friendship
883 enmity
884 sociability
885 unsociability
886 courtesy
887 discourtesy
888 congratulation
889 love
890 endearment
891 darling; favourite
892 hate
893 resentment; anger
894 irritability
895 sullenness
896 marriage
897 celibacy
898 divorce; widowhood
899 benevolence
900 malevolence
901 curse
902 threat
903 philanthropy
904 misanthropy
905 benefactor
906 evildoer
907 pity
908 pitilessness
909 gratitude
910 ingratitude
911 forgiveness
912 revenge
913 jealousy
914 envy

E   Moral

915 right
916 wrong
917 dueness
918 undueness
919 duty
920 neglect of duty
921 exemption
922 respect
923 disrespect
924 contempt
925 approval
926 disapproval
927 flattery
928 disparagement
929 vindication
930 accusation

931 probity
932 improbity
933 disinterestedness
934 selfishness
935 virtue
936 vice
937 innocence
938 guilt
939 good person
940 bad person
941 penitence
942 impenitence
943 atonement
944 temperance
945 intemperance
946 ascetism
947 fasting
948 gluttony
949 soberness
950 drunkenness
951 purity
952 impurity
953 libertine
954 legality
955 illegality
956 jurisdiction
957 tribunal
958 judge
959 lawyer
960 lawsuit
961 acquittal
962 condemnation
963 punishment
964 means of punishment
965 reward

F   Religious

966 divinity
967 God
968 good spirit
969 evil spirit
970 mythical being
971 ghost
972 heaven
973 hell
974 religion
975 irreligion
976 revelation
977 orthodoxy
978 heresy
979 sectarianism
980 piety
981 impiety
982 worship
983 idolatry
984 sorcery
985 churchdom
986 clergyman
987 laity
988 religious service
989 vestment
990 church building